Big Choices:
The Future of Social Security

Proceedings of a Conference Held on April 21, 2005

Edited by Kenneth S. Apfel and Betty Sue Flowers

Third in a Series
Big Choices in American Social Policy

Center for Health and Social Policy
Big Choices Series No. 3
Lyndon B. Johnson School of Public Affairs
The University of Texas at Austin

Lyndon Baines Johnson Library

2007

Library of Congress Control No.: 2006907097
ISBN–10: 0-89940-122-8
ISBN–13: 978-0-89940-122-5

Printed in the U.S.A.

Cover design by Doug Marshall
LBJ School Information Technology and Media Services

Contact information:
Lyndon B. Johnson School of Public Affairs,
The University of Texas at Austin,
Box Y, Austin, TX 78713-8925.
www.utexas.edu/lbj/pubs/

Supported in part by AARP.
The views presented here are those of the authors
and not necessarily those of AARP,
its directors, officers, or staff.

Contents

Tables

Additional tables appear in the reprinted articles in Chapters 8, 9, and 10.

Figures

Additional figures appear in the reprinted articles in Chapters 8, 9, and 10.

Preface

This book offers proposals for approaching one of the most significant choices now facing Americans—how to meet the challenges to the Social Security program. Our objective in sponsoring this book and the symposium on which it is based is to create a clear picture of the policy choices on all sides of the Social Security debate in order to help Americans create informed opinions about issues that deeply affect their lives. To accomplish this objective, we've organized the book in a way that we hope will offer the reader as much—or as little—as he or she might want to know about a particular approach. We also offer practical suggestions on citizen discussions about the issue, including a template for framing the issue for public discussion in the fairest possible way.

We begin with an overview ("Part I. Social Security and Future Challenges") that offers a broad summary of the key choices that we face in relation to this important social program and a discussion of the issues from an international perspective. This overview is followed by brief presentations that analyze the challenges from a number of different vantage points ("Part II: The Social Security Debate").

Part III ("Civic Dialogue and Deliberation: What the Public Has to Say") focuses on civic dialogue and deliberation, first explaining what we mean by those terms, then offering a two-page template that compares three approaches to the Social Security challenge in a form that can be used for citizen dialogues, and, finally, reporting on a citizens dialogue using this template.

The organization of this book is intended to be helpful to those who want to understand the issue in greater depth than is possible through simply listening to news reports. We also hope that by offering a non-partisan template for discussion, we can encourage classroom and citizen deliberation as an alternative to debate and partisan argument. This hope reflects our conviction that the best public policy is created when grassroots engagement meets informed expertise. For this meeting to be possible, a common language must be available so that an informed public can express its opinion in a nation-wide "conversation." Such expressions can offer a counterweight to the capture of public policy decisions by private interests.

The LBJ School is committed to fostering the *professional* expertise necessary to create effective public policy. The LBJ Library is committed to fostering the necessary level of *public* expertise—by sponsoring symposia, lectures, public issues forums, and books like this one—to help ensure that public policy is not only effective but also in the public interest. We hope that this partnership between a public policy school and a presidential library will illuminate the "Big Choices" that Americans face.

Kenneth S. Apfel
Sid Richardson Chair in Public Affairs
Director of the Center for Health and Social Policy
LBJ School of Public Affairs

Betty Sue Flowers
Director
Lyndon Baines Johnson Library and Museum

Acknowledgments

A number of people dedicated a great deal of time and effort to ensure the success of this endeavor. First and foremost, we want to thank Kristine Niemeyer, Senior Program Coordinator for the Center on Health and Social Policy at the LBJ School of Public Affairs, for her patience, perseverance, and professionalism, which helped to move this project to fruition.

We also want to thank Lindsay Littlefield, an LBJ School graduate student, who worked as a research assistant for this project and helped write and conduct research for this book.

We also want to thank Lauren Jahnke for her work in editing and formatting the book, and Taylor Willingham for organizing the Social Security dialogue that provided citizen feedback. We also want to thank Sharon Tutchings at the LBJ School and Marge Morton, Judy Allen, and Tina Houston at the LBJ Library for coordinating the logistics of the conference and ensuring that all participants and attendees had a worthwhile experience.

Lastly, we want to thank AARP, the Commonwealth Fund, the Sid Richardson Chair at the LBJ School, and the LBJ Library and Museum. Without all of their support we could not have been successful.

Kenneth S. Apfel
Sid Richardson Chair in Public Affairs
Director of the Center for Health and Social Policy
LBJ School of Public Affairs

Betty Sue Flowers
Director
Lyndon Baines Johnson Library and Museum

Part I

Social Security and Future Challenges

Chapter 1
Introducing the Issues

Bob Inman: Hello, I am Bob Inman. I am the Interim Dean of the LBJ School of Public Affairs. I am pleased to welcome you all here. I spent 31 years of my life, as some of you may know, in public service looking at the outside world. I was not permitted to look at my own country and its issues for a whole array of reasons, so I was focused on the rest of the world, and therefore I bring no expertise to the topic that draws you here today. I am 74 years old and so I am not one of those worried who is going to be paying into the system many years from now, although my children and future grandchildren probably would worry about that.

But I do worry about the country's overall record for savings. I look at many other countries in the world, particularly the Japanese, who have a much stronger system of saving, and thereby financing many things that take place in the society. I had the privilege of serving for 20 years on the board of a very successful employee-owned firm, and as we looked for ways to excite employees about the company in the future, we offered stock down at the lowest levels and we offered a savings plan, a 401(k), that for every dollar they put in we would add a dollar to match. They were not very interested in stock, because they did not know when that might show up, but the idea of a savings plan that they got somebody to match what they contributed had some appeal.

We are privileged that you all have agreed to come and participate. My compliments to Ken Apfel for making sure that all sides are here and represented in this process. I hope that you will all give us your wisdom and out of it will come ideas. I particularly want to acknowledge the wonderful support that we at the LBJ School get from the LBJ Library. This is now the third of these conferences that the library has shared sponsorship of where we look at very large issues, and it is that collaboration with the library that makes this a special place to convene these issues. So, welcome from me, from the LBJ School, and if I may, Dr. Flowers, you are welcome from the LBJ Library. Thank you all very much.

Betty Sue Flowers: Welcome. We are delighted to have you here. As Bob said, this is the third in a series of "Big Choices." When Ken and I first began talking about this we thought, "what could the LBJ Library and LBJ School do together that would be of use, not just intellectually interesting, but of use to Americans concerning some of the big issues that face us?" So we chose five topics, three of which we have done or we are currently doing: this one, Social Security, in 2005; the future of health insurance for America's families in 2003; and Medicare in 2004.

There is a certain kind of design to these conferences. The first part of the design is an overview that attempts to summarize all the sides of an issue and to look at the history, just to put it all on the table. Then we want scholars and practitioners and policymakers from both sides, those who have very strong points of view, to offer those points of view—people from think tanks and sometimes in former cases, people from Congress and other places. Today we also have an international perspective, which is really wonderful—I am delighted about that. Then tonight, after dinner, we have a session moderated by Texas Forums, which is an initiative the LBJ Library has undertaken under the National Issues Forum rubric. This event helps answer the question, "How do we get informed citizens to come together, not just to hammer at each other the way that you see on TV, not just to shout past each other? How do you get citizens (a) informed and (b) deliberating?"

We have trained over 179 moderators, mostly from Central Texas, but others have come from Colorado, California, and Chicago, in these technologies of deliberative discussion. And that is what we will be doing tonight in the atrium of the library. So I want to invite all of you after this afternoon's session to go to the Thompson Center for a light supper and conversation, and then to the LBJ Library from 7 to 9 for roundtable discussions. These will consist of about 8 to 10 people, and will be moderated to look at issues as we have framed them in three ways in relation to Social Security. This is a design that we are experimenting with. A publication will be produced from these sessions as well. So with no further adieu, here is Ken Apfel. Of all the topics, this is the one that must be closest to Ken's heart since he was Commissioner of Social Security under President Clinton.

Ken Apfel: Thank you all for coming today. Our annual "Big Choices" forums try to deal with some of the large social policy issues facing our country in the 21st century. We are joined today by a superb panel of experts with very wide-ranging views on this subject.

One of the most memorable moments of my years as Social Security Commissioner occurred five years ago in Hyde Park when we celebrated the 65th anniversary of the signing of the Social Security Act. I read aloud FDR's words about how important that particular moment in time was for this country and our democracy. At that time, our democratic system of government, our collective values, and our growing understanding of the real needs facing older Americans all came together to forge the beginning of the Social Security system, a system that has evolved over the past 70 years and it is going to continue to evolve in the future.

Nothing is static in America. It is our democratic institutions, our changing needs, and our values and beliefs that forge the evolving social policies in this country. But of all our social policies, perhaps the single most important program in our nation's history is Social Security. It is hard to overstate the importance of Social Security, which provides a foundation of financial support for about one in six Americans, with benefit protections available over a lifetime. Our social insurance system is critically important not only for older Americans, but also for the disabled, for survivors of deceased workers, and for families.

What does the future hold for Social Security? The future, in some ways, is in our hands. But to put the future in context, we need to start off with a discussion of the past. Why did we establish such a system and how has it evolved? What is the importance of the system today, and how does Social Security fit in with other components of retirement security? What are our future challenges? Lastly, what are the key options we face for the future?

We will begin with a little bit of history, going back nearly three-quarters of a century, to the middle 1930s and the Great Depression. There were crushing levels of poverty and dire financial conditions for many, including older workers and retirees. There was no real financial security in old age.

What Franklin Roosevelt helped to create, to use his words, was "some measure of security" in old age. The signing of the Social Security Act in 1935 represented a dramatic departure in the role of government in providing a foundation of economic support for older Americans. After its initial adoption, for the next half century the Social Security system was expanded to the point that it now provides a solid but modest foundation of support for most Americans over their lifetimes. The key elements of the social security system that were adopted in the 1930s and 1940s have remained largely intact ever since—intergenerational financing through payroll taxes paid by workers, a relatively modest and progressive benefit structure paid to workers and their dependents, with any excess tax revenues placed in a trust fund to pay future benefits.

While the main framework has remained the same, we have seen considerable expansion in three areas: the proportion of the workforce covered by Social Security, the overall scope of benefit protections, and the dollar amount of benefits that people receive from the system. These expansions over the first 50 years of Social Security's history represented the first real phase of Social Security's evolution. In the 1940s a little over half of the workforce paid into Social Security, but in the decades ahead, several laws were enacted that expanded coverage. Now nearly all workers pay into social security and become eligible for benefits.

In terms of the scope of benefit protections, the original act provided only retirement coverage for workers. By 1939 survivor benefits were added, and in the 1950s during the Eisenhower Administration and under the congressional leadership of Lyndon Johnson, disability benefits were added. During the Nixon Administration cost of living adjustments were added so that benefit payments would grow with inflation, so that people could count on the purchasing power of their benefits staying constant over a lifetime. During the Eisenhower and Kennedy Administrations, early retirement was permitted, so that workers could start receiving benefits at age 62 rather than 65. In addition, over the years, actual benefit levels for new generations of retirees were increased significantly. This period of expansion culminated in many respects during Lyndon Johnson's presidency, with significant benefit level increases as well as the adoption of Medicare to provide health insurance for older Americans.

The second real phase in Social Security's history started in the late 1970s and in many respects continues to this day—the growing understanding that demographic and economic changes taking place in the U.S. place real limits on the system. In 1977, benefit growth was slowed and in 1983, a series of changes were enacted to stabilize the system. Taxes were raised, the retirement age was increased, cost of living adjustments were delayed and benefits were modestly curtailed. Even with the limits and restraints adopted over the past quarter century, the system's main framework is still the same, with the results being that Social Security remains remarkably successful in addressing FDR's goal of providing "some measure of security" in retirement.

The impact of Social Security on the 20th century has been profound. I have said that Social Security was perhaps the single most important domestic accomplishment of the 20th century. That becomes obvious when we look at Social Security's impact on poverty: as recently as 1959, about 35 percent of all older Americans were living in poverty. That number is down to about 10 percent now and is projected to slowly decline in the decades ahead. I think this is one of the biggest accomplishments of the 20th century, and it is due in no small part to the Social Security system. If Social Security were gone tomorrow—and nobody in their right minds would consider such a thing—about half of all seniors would be living in poverty the day after tomorrow. It is now the foundation of support in retirement for almost all Americans. The liberalizations that took place during the latter half of the 20th century enabled a number of people to escape poverty and to have a solid but modest foundation of support in retirement.

A second big trend that took place during the second half of the 20th century relates to the age when workers left the labor force and entered retirement. In the beginning of the 20th century, workers often stayed in the labor force until they died or became very disabled, with an average retirement age of about 74 years old. The average retirement age has gone down considerably over the past century. People have been able to leave the work force at earlier ages based upon the income support systems that have been established over time, such as Social Security, pensions, and savings. Starting about 20 years ago the age that workers entered retirement leveled off. For some time now, the majority of workers have been leaving the labor force to enter retirement at about age 62. People are able to spend more of their lives in retirement. This is a sizeable change for our society.

So two of the biggest trends in the 20th century are (1) the near eradication of poverty for older Americans, and (2) the ability to be able to leave the labor market and to retire earlier in life, and Social Security played a major role in both.

Those two trends don't come cheap. Higher benefits, greater coverage, and earlier retirement all have costs. The Social Security system—as I said, an intergenerational system—has been financed through a payroll tax. Starting at just two percentage points back in the 1930s—that is, 1 percent on the employee and 1 percent on the employer—it is now 12.4 percent, shared equally. About 5 percent of our economy now goes to payroll taxes to finance the Social Security system. To me, that is part of the price of a civil society. There is a very real price for the benefits that we share as a society.

As Figure 1.1 shows, Social Security benefits, which are based on lifetime earnings, go up at higher incomes and are somewhat progressive. By and large, low wage earners receive higher replacement rates because Social Security replaces a higher share of pre-retirement earnings for lower wage workers. The system overall is moderately progressive and provides higher relative benefits for lower income persons in order to provide the foundation of support in retirement. High earners receive higher benefits overall but a lower replacement rate. However, because low wage earners often live shorter lives, the progressive nature that is built into the formula is undercut to some extent.

Social Security is a very sizeable source of income for older Americans. Figure 1.2

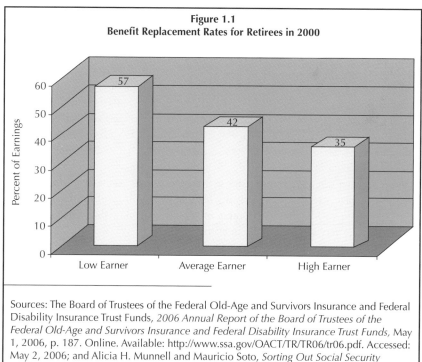

Figure 1.1
Benefit Replacement Rates for Retirees in 2000

Sources: The Board of Trustees of the Federal Old-Age and Survivors Insurance and Federal Disability Insurance Trust Funds, *2006 Annual Report of the Board of Trustees of the Federal Old-Age and Survivors Insurance and Federal Disability Insurance Trust Funds,* May 1, 2006, p. 187. Online. Available: http://www.ssa.gov/OACT/TR/TR06/tr06.pdf. Accessed: May 2, 2006; and Alicia H. Munnell and Mauricio Soto, *Sorting Out Social Security Replacement Rates,* Center for Retirement Research, November 2005, Number 19. Online. Available: http://www.bc.edu/centers/crr/facts/jtf_19.pdf, p. 1. Accessed: May 2, 2006

shows all income for all individuals over age 65 in America, with about 40 percent coming from Social Security, about 20 percent coming from pensions, 25 percent from earnings, and about 14 percent from assets. Social Security is clearly part of a multi-legged income "stool" for older persons, complemented by pensions and savings to support people in retirement. In addition, income from continued work is another source of income for many older Americans.

One of the questions that we will come back to over the course of today is how should that graph look 25 or 50 years from now for future generations? How much from Social Security? How much from savings? How much from work? How much from pensions?

Before doing that, let's pull this graph apart by dividing it into three groups based on elderly income. Figure 1.3 looks at older Americans at the bottom fifth of income—those with incomes below about $10,000. There is not a three or a four-

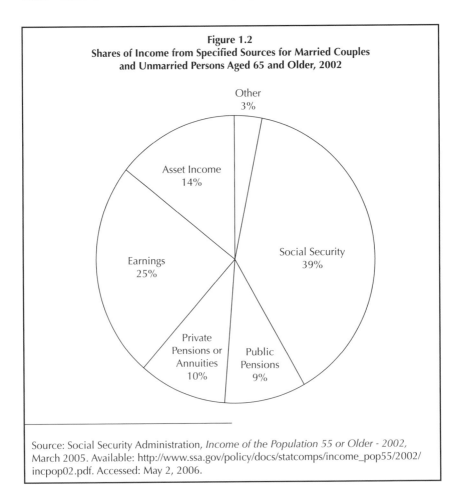

Figure 1.2
Shares of Income from Specified Sources for Married Couples and Unmarried Persons Aged 65 and Older, 2002

Other 3%

Asset Income 14%

Social Security 39%

Earnings 25%

Private Pensions or Annuities 10%

Public Pensions 9%

Source: Social Security Administration, *Income of the Population 55 or Older - 2002,* March 2005. Available: http://www.ssa.gov/policy/docs/statcomps/income_pop55/2002/ incpop02.pdf. Accessed: May 2, 2006.

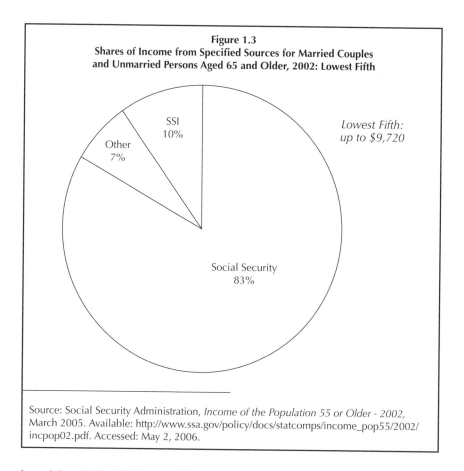

Figure 1.3
Shares of Income from Specified Sources for Married Couples
and Unmarried Persons Aged 65 and Older, 2002: Lowest Fifth

SSI
10%

Other
7%

Lowest Fifth:
up to $9,720

Social Security
83%

Source: Social Security Administration, *Income of the Population 55 or Older - 2002,* March 2005. Available: http://www.ssa.gov/policy/docs/statcomps/income_pop55/2002/ incpop02.pdf. Accessed: May 2, 2006.

legged "stool" for the bottom fifth—and actually, this is also true for the bottom two-fifths. There is really a one-legged "stool," which is Social Security, and a little bit of SSI welfare assistance for those who are very poor.

The chart raises questions. Should future Social Security benefits be cut for this group? Another question is can Social Security provide all this support for people at the bottom in the future? Can we continue with a system with so little savings and pension support for individuals near the bottom? Should we adopt policies to encourage more savings for this group?

If we look to the middle-income group in Figure 1.4, you will see that Social Security still represents almost two-thirds of all income for the middle fifth of older Americans (the fifths below and above this middle group are not shown). Now, though, we see pensions, earnings and savings all starting to emerge as pieces of the overall framework for individuals for economic security.

Figure 1.5 looks at the elderly with the top fifth of income, those with incomes

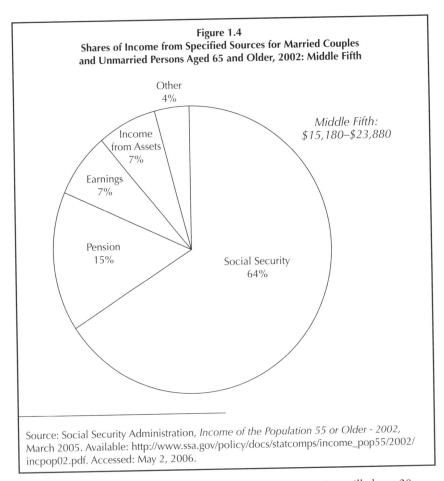

Figure 1.4
Shares of Income from Specified Sources for Married Couples
and Unmarried Persons Aged 65 and Older, 2002: Middle Fifth

Other
4%

Middle Fifth:
$15,180–$23,880

Income
from Assets
7%

Earnings
7%

Pension
15%

Social Security
64%

Source: Social Security Administration, *Income of the Population 55 or Older - 2002,* March 2005. Available: http://www.ssa.gov/policy/docs/statcomps/income_pop55/2002/ incpop02.pdf. Accessed: May 2, 2006.

above about $40,000 a year. We see Social Security representing still about 20 percent of income for those in the top fifth group. Now pensions amount to about 20 percent, earnings are a considerably larger share, and a very large amount in the asset and savings area as well. We now see a very strong four-legged stool. Earnings make up a significant share. It should be pointed out that many of these individuals are primarily younger individuals because there are clearly very few people at 70 years old who are still in the labor force.

Other questions emerge here. Should Social Security still be available for those with the highest incomes? Should we do more means testing in Social Security? Should we adopt policies to encourage this group to save more? These are big questions for the lower income, middle income, and for upper income elderly, particularly as we look to the future. The biggest question for today is what role do we want our Social Security system to play in the future?

Questions about the future are increasingly complicated, as everyone in the room knows, because we have a large and growing aging population. As Figure 1.5 shows, in 1946 there were about 11 million older Americans. Currently there are about 35 million older Americans, going up to about 70 million older Americans as my generation moves towards retirement. It should be pointed out that this aging trend is not likely to go away after the baby boomers have all died. We hope and expect that each generation will live longer lives and healthier lives, and when the baby boom generation had died, most likely, their children and grandchildren will be living even longer lives. This means that we do have a major demographic change taking place all over the world with a growing aging population. So we have a major increase of the senior population in the next 25 years or so, going from about 13 percent to about 20 percent of our population. It is not likely that these numbers are wrong to any significant extent, because they represent estimates of people who are alive today.

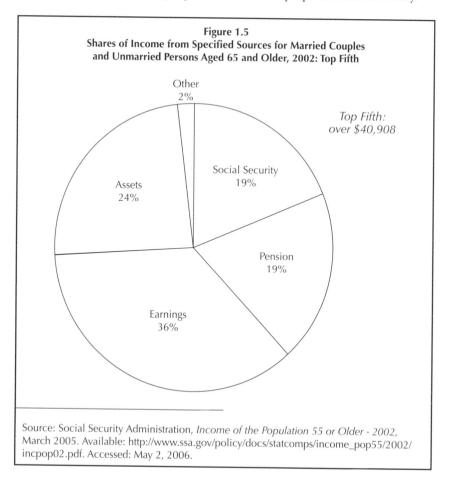

Figure 1.5
Shares of Income from Specified Sources for Married Couples and Unmarried Persons Aged 65 and Older, 2002: Top Fifth

Other
2%

Top Fifth: over $40,908

Social Security
19%

Assets
24%

Pension
19%

Earnings
36%

Source: Social Security Administration, *Income of the Population 55 or Older - 2002,* March 2005. Available: http://www.ssa.gov/policy/docs/statcomps/income_pop55/2002/incpop02.pdf. Accessed: May 2, 2006.

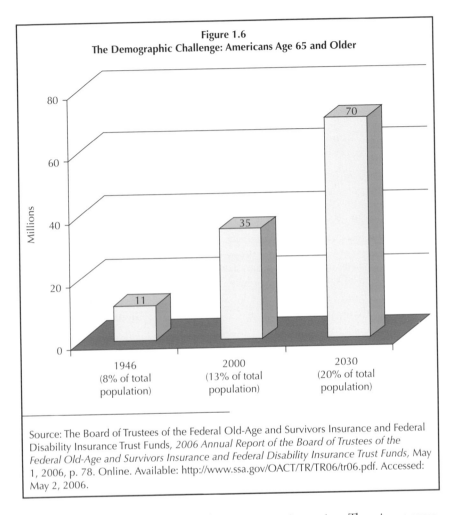

Figure 1.6
The Demographic Challenge: Americans Age 65 and Older

Source: The Board of Trustees of the Federal Old-Age and Survivors Insurance and Federal Disability Insurance Trust Funds, *2006 Annual Report of the Board of Trustees of the Federal Old-Age and Survivors Insurance and Federal Disability Insurance Trust Funds,* May 1, 2006, p. 78. Online. Available: http://www.ssa.gov/OACT/TR/TR06/tr06.pdf. Accessed: May 2, 2006.

Demographers all basically agree that we are an aging society. There is not agreement, however, on how we are going to deal with the aging society. There is also disagreement on how big a challenge this represents in the future.

I would like to raise another question: what is going to happen to the different pieces of the "stool"—Social Security, pensions, and savings—in the future? Frankly, it is very, very hard to know for sure. That depends upon future retirement behavior and future law changes. Let's start by looking at what we know about current trends, given current laws.

Social Security now replaces about 40 percent of earnings in total. Social Security under current law will likely only be replacing about a third of income in the years ahead, so it is going down in terms of its replacement rates. Replacement rates are one important measure, and a key question is how much of pre-retirement income should Social Security replace? Another way to look at measurements is that while replacement rates are going down, Social Security benefit levels for future generations are actually going up in real dollar terms. Every generation's Social Security benefits are roughly tied to increases in wages, so my parents' generation's benefits were lower than mine. My kids' generation's benefits, by current law, would be larger than mine. Since benefit levels are projected to go up, some argue that slowing the rate of benefit growth is acceptable.

This is a very controversial subject. Another controversial issue relates to the rate of return. Clearly, individuals who are now retired receive from Social Security what they put in very quickly. In the future it is going to take a lot longer, because we now have a fully developed social insurance system. Do lower returns create problems? Are the lower replacement rates sustainable? Does that put retirees at risk? These are examples of different lenses that one can look through to determine the dimensions of the adequacy of Social Security benefits in the future.

What do we know about pensions? Only about 60 percent of retirees are connected to a pension system and clearly there is greater pension coverage at top incomes than at the bottom. We know what is going on in the defined pension world and there has clearly been an erosion in coverage in this area, coupled with greater reliance on retirement savings such as 401(k)s and IRAs. Given the erosion of the employer-provided defined benefits system and the employer-provided retiree health system, the defined benefit pension will clearly be a shrinking source of support in the next 20 to 40 years.

What about savings? We know that overall savings rates have gone down dramatically in this country. Personal savings have declined from roughly 10 percent levels back in the 1970s to nearly zero today. What do we know about retirement savings? Clearly we have seen a sizable increase in 401(k)s and IRAs. Most of that increase, however, is held by people with higher incomes. About 60 percent of individuals are holding retirement accounts, but the average values are only about $50,000—very small amounts to sustain a family in retirement.

Some will argue that these trends call for significant efforts to strengthen retirement savings for the whole population. Others will say this is why it is centrally important to have the Social Security foundation stay strong so that is it there to complement the fact that lots of individuals do not have retirement savings. Those are big questions. They are big issues in Social Security and our entire retirement security system.

Work is a wild card. What happens to work in the 21st century? We saw that throughout the 20th century up until about 20 years ago people were entering retirement at earlier ages. We don't know what is going to happen in the future. Are we going to start seeing increasing numbers of people who are working later in life? Two or three years of extra time in the labor force can make a profound difference in terms of economic security in retirement. But it is an easier choice for me to work longer as a professor than it is for a roofer or a waitress.

So the future is cloudy in all these areas: Social Security, pensions, savings, and work. The U.S. has one of the strongest retirement systems in the world, but we clearly face challenges on all the legs of the stool.

The next question I want to ask is how big a Social Security problem do we really face? There is agreement that an aging society will place greater pressures on our society, but different people look at the facts and come to very different conclusions.

It is a fact that in about 12 years, Social Security payroll taxes are going to start falling behind spending. Since 1983, payroll taxes have been coming in at a faster rate, and that money has been deposited in the trust fund. By 2017, the money will be going out faster than it is coming in. There is going be a draw-down at that point in bonds to pay benefits. Some might say that 2017 is a gigantic date and that we need to be alarmed because it is right around the corner.

By 2041, the trust funds are projected to be exhausted. That means that all that money that has been "building up" in the last 20 years and will continue to do so for a little while longer will be depleted. By law, Social Security benefits continue without any changes until 2041. But what is the fiscal state of the country if no changes are made in 2025, 2030, or 2040? After 2042, new tax income will pay about three-quarters of all the benefit promises. Does that mean that the glass is one-quarter empty or three-quarters full? Or does it set the stage for some dramatic changes? It depends on how big a problem one believes that we face and how soon we must face it. We have differing perspectives based on the same facts, and there will be differing perspectives presented today. Is 2017—when money going out for benefits is more than money coming in—the main focus? Or should 2041—another 35 years from now—be the focus because the trust funds will be there until 2041 to pay benefits?

This date confusion goes right to the core issue about the importance of trust funds. Are they worthless IOUs? Or are they rock solid, backed up by the full faith and credit of the United States government? Clearly one of the hardest issues to confront in Social Security is dealing with the notion of the trust funds. I think it is fair to say that if the trust funds are depleted very rapidly in the decades ahead, that would not be good. That is one of the reasons that most observers believe that it would be better to take action on Social Security sooner rather than later.

Another source of confusion is how big the shortfall is. Is it $4 trillion or $11 trillion? Over the next 75 years, the shortfall is considered to be about $4 trillion. However, if we look over the infinite horizon, it is considerably larger, about $11 trillion dollars. I think that trillions are very hard to get your arms around. I found it hard getting my arms around millions. Then I worked in the United States Congress and I finally got used to billions. I can't comprehend trillions.

One way to make these gigantic numbers more understandable is to look at them as a share of our economy. But there are still different ways to frame the size of the problem in these terms as well. Is the shortfall about 0.5 percent of GDP, a fairly modest number? Over the next 75 years, the funds needed to finance the system is somewhere around 0.5 percent of GDP. But in 30 or 40 years and over the infinite horizon, the shortfall may be closer to 1.5 percent of GDP, clearly a bigger challenge.

So we have differing views about the size of the problem, depending on where one sits and how one views the data. Is there a crisis now? Is there a crisis right around the corner? Is there no real crisis, just a long-term manageable problem?

Beyond differences about the size of the problem, there is also differing language on possible solutions. Some people talk about the need for "individual choice" and "individual accounts." Some talk about the dangers of "private accounts" and Social Security "privatization." There is nothing wrong with any of these terms, but people who have a different vision of the problem tend to use a different language.

And that leads to a final difference—the fact that there are widely differing solutions to the problem. There are three main policy options for Social Security. The first option is to keep Social Security in its current form with increases in the payroll tax rate as well as moderate reductions in future Social Security benefit commitments. A second option would be to create individual and private savings accounts as a replacement for part of Social Security. This option would represent a significant departure from the current program—in effect, a third stage in the evolution of the Social Security system. The third option would be to significantly revamp future benefits by increasing the retirement age and means-testing the program. None of these options is entirely mutually exclusive. Our purpose in framing the options along these lines is to help focus the discussion.

To summarize: Should we be retaining Social Security generally in its current form, which is more of a tax-based solution? Should we have individual and private accounts—should that be the way that we move to the future, a substantial revision to the system? Should we significantly change benefits? That can be done from a number of perspectives in a number of different ways, possibly by increasing the retirement age or moving to more means-testing. Will these options strengthen or weaken the Social Security system? Some believe that any one option will strengthen our system and others believe the same option will weaken our system. If the fundamental goal of government policy in the area of retirement security is to assure adequate income in retirement, what should we do?

Big choices. Big differences. There are different perceptions and beliefs about the size of the problem, different language, and different conclusions on where the various choices will lead us. That is hard; it is why we haven't gotten this thing solved yet, frankly. What our country does on these big issues is spend time to talk through the issues and get people involved to think about the choices, and then try and come together through our democratic system to figure out what needs to be done for the long term. It is clear that something will have to happen, but there are still significant differences of opinion as to what we should do.

Table 1.1 summarizes a series of key options. The first column of numbers shows the traditional actuaries' projections and the share of the problem solved over the next 75 years. The second column goes all the way out to that 75th year and you will notice that savings projections for that year are lower. This series of changes are both on the tax side and the spending side.

There is plenty of controversy on all of these options. For example, the option including taking some of the trust funds and investing them in equities is a highly controversial proposal. This would resolve somewhere around half of the shortfall, potentially, over the next 75 years, but if the trust funds are fully depleted they won't resolve anything over the long term. There is some debate whether such a change would have any effect economically, and clearly this will be one of the issues that will be debated today—whether collective investment is the appropriate thing to do and whether such a thing will have any effect on the long-term solvency of Social Security.

Public conversation on these options is important. It was our democratic institutions that came together 70 years ago and forged something called the Social Security system. Those laws, based upon a shared set of values and beliefs, became the foundation of our retirement system. That system has changed a lot since 1935 and will continue to change in the years ahead. It is not a static system because we are not a static society, with static needs and values. The question is how should that system change to meet emerging challenges? It is up to us as a people to try to help find common ground.

This sounds a little bit like Norman Rockwell, but I believe that in the United States we need to get involved in the big issues, and this is a very big issue. It is important for us, for our parents and grandparents, and our kids and grandkids. America is at its best when we listen to each other, discuss, and then we try to use our democratic institutions to decide a future based on our collective values. It is "us" that we are talking about here; what we want our country to look like in the future.

We have time for a few questions, and then I am going to turn it over to Dalmer Hoskins to provide an international perspective.

Audience Member: On one of the charts where you were talking about possible choices, I was interested in the wage tax cap, where you said over 75 years it would solve 115 percent of the problem—is that what the 115 percent means? And is that the raising of the cap from $90,000 to $140,000?

Ken Apfel: No, that is eliminating the cap so that people like Bill Gates pay the full Social Security tax on every dollar of earned income. That is eliminating the cap entirely.

Audience Member: I have no problem with that. I am just wondering because I have heard in AARP publications that increasing it from $90,000 to $140,000 would take care of 47 percent of the problem, and you are saying that if you did it across the board for everyone it would be 115 percent?

Ken Apfel: Yes, over the 75-year period. But as you will hear over the course of the

Table 1.1
Effects of Policy Changes on Solvency

General Policy Options	Specific Initiatives	Actuarial Balance over 75 Years	Actuarial Balance in 75th Year
Approach 1: Reaffirming Social Security	Raise the Payroll Tax 2% (for employers and employees combined)	102%	35%
	Eliminate the Wage Tax Cap and Cap Benefits	115%	51%
	Benefit Reductions for newly eligible (5%)	32%	16%
	Invest 40% of the Trust Fund in Equities (with 6.5% rate of return)	46%	0%
Approach 2: Revising Social Security	Raise the Normal Retirement Age to 70	36%	28%
	Means-Testing Benefits[1]	50%	50%
	Major Benefit Reductions: Price Indexing	124%	138%
Approach 3: Reconstructing Social Security	Personal/Private Accounts with Offsets[2]	-26%	37%
	Combination of Personal/Private Accounts with Offsets Couple with Sliding-Scale Benefit Reductions[3]	100%	100%

Source: Social Security Administration, Chris Chaplain and Alice H. Wade, *Estimated OASDI Long-Range Financial Effects of Several Provisions Requested by the Social Security Advisory Board,* August 10, 2005, pp. 3-5. Online. Available: http://www.ssab.gov/documents/advisoryboardmemo—2005tr—08102005.pdf. Accessed: March 8, 2006.

Note: Table assumes an actuarial balance of -1.92 percent of taxable payroll over 75 years and -5.7 percent of taxable payroll in the 75th year.

1. Source for means-testing estimate is the authors.

2. Source for these two numbers is Stephen C. Goss and Alice H. Wade, *Estimates of Financial Effect for Three Models Developed by the President's Commission to Strengthen Social Security,* January 21, 2002, Memo to Daniel Patrick Moynihan and Richard D. Parsons. Online. Available: http://www.ssa.gov/OACT/solvency/index.html. Accessed: July 20, 2006.

3. Source for these two numbers is Stephen C. Goss, *Estimated Financial Effects of a Comprehensive Social Security Reform Proposal Including Progressive Price Indexing,* February 10, 2005, Memo to Bob Pozen. Online. Available: http://www.ssa.gov/OACT/solvency/RPozen_20050210.pdf. Accessed: July 20, 2006.

day, there are tradeoffs to every option. One of the big issues in this area is this would mean a dramatic increase in taxes for upper-income individuals—those making over $80,000 a year. Another issue is whether such a tax increase—with individuals not really getting much back for that increase—would that cause an erosion of the public support for the Social Security system. One of the things about all the options that you confront, and I don't have time to go through all of the pros and cons, is that there are tradeoffs to every one of the options that are out there. There are tradeoffs to individual accounts, tradeoffs to raising the wage cap, tradeoffs to changing the retirement age, benefit reductions, tax increases—they all inherently have tradeoffs.

Audience Member: If Bill Gates were to pay that, he would get a lot more, wouldn't he?

Ken Apfel: Yes, I believe with those numbers, he would.

Audience Member: He would. So would it not do means testing? Means testing is not part of this 115 percent?

Ken Apfel: No. If you did means testing as well, and have a large group of upper-income individuals paying much higher taxes and receiving no benefits at all, savings would be more, but so would the possible trade-offs.

Audience Member: In your comment on poverty, has the government's definition of poverty changed over time?

Ken Apfel: No, the U.S. poverty level definition goes back about 50 years. A long time ago, a woman working in the Social Security Administration developed a model to try to measure poverty based on a percentage of what it to takes to eat multiplied by three. That level of expense was considered the poverty level, increased for price inflation over the years. That same model has been used ever since. It is an absolute measure of poverty. In other words, if inflation goes up at 3 percent for a year, then the poverty level will go up at 3 percent. Europe has a different definition of poverty, a more relative measure, having to do with overall increases in wages. But we have an absolute level of poverty with increases based on price increases.

Audience Member: Because it does not include housing, for example?

Ken Apfel: Well, it includes all costs, in terms of overall levels of inflation for the person's whole market basket of goods and services. I would point out again that the 10 percent poverty figure is a dramatic improvement over the course of the last 40 to 50 years. But we still have about 20 percent of elderly widows in this country living in poverty and we still have some sizable poverty problems for elderly African Americans and Hispanics. In addition, millions of older Americans have incomes just slightly above the poverty level. Poverty still exists for many seniors, but nowhere near the extent to which it existed 40 or 50 years ago.

Audience Member: In the discussion of the trust fund, I am confused over what is in the trust fund. You are talking about it as if the full faith and credit of the U.S. is in the trust fund and President Bush apparently said it wasn't.

Ken Apfel: I am sure this will be one of the issues that our panel will discuss. Some view the trust funds as being worthless. I am not here today to take a position, but I am going to give you the two different sides of the arguments on the trust funds. Some people argue that the trust funds that have been building for the past 20 years have basically been borrowed, so when it is time to liquidate the trust funds to pay benefits that we are going to have to borrow more money and therefore it is going to have a tremendous impact on the economy. Some would say that could be the same as a worthless IOU. On the other hand, others say that the fund and all Treasury securities are backed by the full faith and credit of the United States government. We always redeem our bonds; we have had a 100 percent success rate doing that in the past, and we will in the future.

I know the trust fund is an enormously complicated issue, but I'm hoping we can keep our focus on what Social Security should be in the future. What are our choices and what should we do? I know that is colored to some extent by our perception of the trust funds, but I hope what we can do in the course of our discussions here is to talk about what choices we should make for the future.

Chapter 2
International Perspectives

Ken Apfel: I would like to introduce our next speaker, Dalmer Hoskins, the secretary general of the International Social Security Association headquartered in Geneva. The International Social Security Association was founded before the creation of our Social Security Act. It has been around since the 1920s. It represents the Social Security systems, the retirement systems, and the health care systems for about 150 nations throughout the world. Prior to his service as Secretary General, Dalmer held appointments at the Social Security Administration, the Health and Human Services Department, and the Employee Benefit Research Association. He will provide a view of all of these issues from a global perspective. He will give us a sense of what is going on in the world in terms of the aging challenge and the different ways various nations are trying to deal with these issues.

There are two noteworthy educational accomplishments that I want to tell you about. First, Dalmer did his doctoral work in Political Science at the University of Michigan, so he knows a lot about this subject. Also, his daughter got her master's here at the LBJ School of Public Affairs. Welcome, Dalmer Hoskins.

Dalmer Hoskins: Thank you very much, Ken. It is a very great pleasure to be able to accept an invitation from Ken, who I have known for a long time. Ken was a great help to me at my job at the International Social Security Association when he was Commissioner of Social Security. These jobs are political of course, in a sense that there are 150 countries, all with different objectives and different agendas, and counting on your own country to help you is very important. I received that help in good measure when Ken was the head of Social Security. It is true that my daughter graduated from the LBJ School, and that she met her husband here, who also graduated from the LBJ School, so there is a real family connection to this institution. I also have a Texas connection, with most of my family in Kerrville.

What I would like to do today is to give you a "motorcycle tour." We are going to rip through the whole world in 15 minutes, so obviously I am going to speak in a lot of generalities, and I hope you won't mind that. We can talk about that later during the question-and-answer period if you have questions and also during the forums this evening. I am looking forward to taking part in these discussions, because the world is indeed a very complicated place and it is one of the most incredible things about my job is that I am always learning something new about how Social Security has been implemented around the world. It is amazing how many different approaches and different solutions have been conceived and put in place not only to handle pension questions but also social insurance approaches to health, unemployment, and other social protection questions.

In the international parlance, Social Security covers sickness insurance, unemployment insurance, and disability insurance, as well as family allowances, rehabilitation, and occupational safety and health. Thus, the term "Social Security" has a much bigger definition in general than it does in the United States. When people talk about Social Security in other countries, they think first and foremost about health. The first thing they think about is health, then they think about pensions, and after that some of the other programs. There is in this regard a critical difference between the United States and some other countries.

I would like to point out how different the discussion in the United States is from many other places in the world, and my comments are going to be primarily confined to the OECD (Organization for Economic Cooperation and Development) countries, in other words, the industrialized countries in the world. The debate that is occurring in the European countries as well as in Japan, Australia, and New Zealand is at a very different place than it is in the United States. I don't know quite why that is, but the discussion that is now happening in the United States about public and private accounts as opposed to social insurance happened about a decade ago in these countries, and was more or less resolved and finished. So they find it odd when they look at the United States today and see that this debate is so intensely occurring here when it is something that they already did in the past.

One of the principle explanations is that the big financing problems in many of these countries happened before they occurred in the United States. In other words, they have had a more rapidly aging population, they have had older systems, and they have had more generous systems, and therefore some of the crises that occurred in Social Security occurred in other places several years before the United States. These few numbers will help me to explain why.

The contribution rates, for example, of a country like Germany have now been capped by law and they are going to increase up to 22 percent by the year 2020. Now this is in sharp contrast to the United States because here we are talking about figures in the range of 6 percent for workers and employers. The Japanese cap has been legislated at 18 percent, so these are countries that already have much higher contribution rates for pensions than the United States. They do have ceilings on their contributions, but generally speaking these countries have gotten accustomed to paying much higher contributions to their pension system than we do in the United States.

Another big issue is demography. These countries have much lower birth rates than the United States, and some countries like Germany, France, and Italy are facing shrinking populations in the near future as their birth rates fall well below the replacement rate. The numbers of workers who will be able to contribute to the system in the future are really decreasing much more dramatically than in the United States. The most outstanding example is Japan, where 35 percent of the population is going to be over 60 by 2020. So obviously there is a very critical imbalance of contributors to the Social Security system and people who are going to be getting a benefit. The Europeans, the Japanese, and other industrialized countries look at the debate in the United States and say, what is your problem? If we only had your problem, we would be among the happiest people in the world.

The problem in these countries is how to sustain systems that are much more expensive in an environment where the population is aging much more rapidly than in the United States. There has, of course, been an influx of immigration in these European countries, as there has in the United States. That immigration will help solve some of these problems in the European situation, but interestingly enough immigrants cannot completely fill the fall in birth rates.

One of the obvious reasons for that is that the immigrants earn Social Security credits and they get old and retire, too. They don't disappear, they tend to stay in the country where they have emigrated. So, leaving aside all of the other social issues associated with immigration, you can't just solve the European problems through immigration.

If we look at this time lag in the United States, we haven't had a major Social Security reform in the United States since 1983. This is quite astonishing to anyone from the OECD countries, who would say, "How is that possible, we have had many successive reforms and legislation during this period. How could you have gone on since 1983 without doing a big fix?" Well, the U.S. is a unique situation. But if we look at these other countries and what has happened I would say that there have been four lessons that have been learned.

These lessons are that there are two big paths that have been experienced in these countries. The first one that is that you can do a piecemeal reform or you can do a big-bang structural reform. The second lesson is that most of the countries that we are talking about decided many years ago that they were going to have a multi-pillared system, and that is over, the debate is finished. There will not be only three legs but in some cases four or five legs. A third lesson that these countries are now struggling with is individual choice, which is related to what Ken mentioned earlier about individual accounts. Individual choice is really complicated and they are struggling with how to get it right.

There is a fourth lesson that I will not spend much time on but need to mention and that is that Social Security reform in other parts of the world, in non-industrialized countries of the world, is taking place in a very different way. This is a very direct interest to the United States and Texas because Mexico, which is right next door, is having its own pension reform, and it is going in opposite directions from both the OECD countries and the United States.

So what about this first lesson, about whether it is a big-bang fix or a small fix? You would have to say that most other countries in the world have not gone for a big-bang fix, and in fact, what is very impressive, if you look at countries like Germany, France, or Sweden, is that they have a Social Security pension legislation reform almost every year. They are frequently making adjustments to benefits and contribution rates as well as eligibility conditions. They are very used to these laws being modified frequently and there are certain advantages to that, if you look at it from the outside, because doing what we do in the United States with these long periods of nothing followed by a big-bang fix is not only challenging but is also risky in some ways. You can make some very big mistakes when you have a big-bang fix.

If you look back to the history of the changes in 1983, we did make some mistakes and we had to go back and fix them. There are, however, a few countries that have had big-bang fixes. One of them is Sweden, and of course there are a whole group of countries in Eastern Europe after the fall of communism that have had big structural changes in their retirement systems. And of course we wouldn't want to leave out Chile, a country that is often used now as a model for Social Security reform, not only in Latin America but elsewhere in the world. If I had only known 15 years ago that Chile was going to be so important I would have gone there and done a Ph.D. on the Chilean Social Security system. But we thought it was small country, and how much influence could it have? Well, it turns out they have had a tremendous influence as one of the few countries that virtually privatized their Social Security system.

In those countries that did the big-bang fix, what is the reason why? One reason is because in a country like Chile or the countries of Eastern Europe, there was widespread lack of public support for the systems that were in place. The systems were unfair and even corrupt. We have to be honest about it—the Latin American countries in particular have had terrible problems with the misuse of the Social Security system. There was misuse of the money, where some people were retiring as early as age 40 or 45 while others had to wait until age 65, depending on whether you were lucky enough to belong to one of the privileged categories. Obviously, a system that creates new forms of social inequality cannot long enjoy public confidence. It was not difficult therefore for countries such as Chile to wipe away a system that had no public credibility.

Another reason of course is long-term financial sustainability, and the Swedish case is a prime example of that. The projected contribution rate for the Swedish program by 2050 was 36 percent of payroll, and that is not including the additional cost of health care, unemployment, and other social insurance costs. The Swedish consensus was that this was an impossible prospect and so they were willing to accept a big fix to the system.

I guess one would like to know for these other countries that do the more modest and ongoing fixes, what makes them different? I think one of the reasons is because the widespread support for the existing Social Security systems is quite extraordinary in the European countries as well as in Japan, Australia, and New Zealand. The public does believe in the need for such programs, and they are willing to support them for current and future generations. You don't hear very often a debate around such questions as "Am I getting a sufficient return in benefits for my contributions?"

The value for money on your contributions would be a subject that would hardly be mentioned in the public arena. The reason is that people have a very clear idea about the intergenerational shifting of resources and that people who are working today are paying for the people who are retired, and that they expect it to be the case when they retire. And so they wouldn't have very much faith in the 75-year projections and infinity projections that we sometimes engage in Washington. You are talking about countries that have experienced two world wars within the past century, and in many instances, total collapse in the value of their currencies. They have experienced what it means to start from zero all over again and so they have an understanding that the Social Security system is there to provide support against the risks and terrible things that can happen in the lives of citizens of the country.

Experience has shown that there is surprisingly widespread public support for these programs, which I think explains why big-bang fixes and revolutionary reforms don't happen that often. Another reason is that in most countries with existing Social Security systems, putting in place a transition from a public system to a privately based system is after all very expensive. Every member country of the European Union has a treaty obligation to observe the 3 percent deficit maximum. The Italians are already maxed out this year and they are going to be obliged to negotiate with their EU counterparts. Big-bang fixes involving big transition costs to the public purse are very hard to do under EU legislation, particularly if those countries participate in the common currency.

The idea that you must have several legs or pillars in your retirement system has become widely accepted now, but why is that? People think that the best system is one that is composed of a good public system, an employer-provided system, voluntary savings, and other ways to encourage people to save for their retirement. The big challenge for most countries is how to make that multi-pillared system work in a coordinated, coherent, and dependable fashion to guarantee that people will have adequate retirement income. That is where the debate is centered in those countries—how to get it together and to make it work to ensure a reliable stream of retirement revenue.

This means that most of these countries have something that we do not have in the United States, and that is an obligatory second pillar that means when you are employed, you as well as your employer have to contribute to an occupational pension plan. You can, of course, also have a 401(k), and you can also have IRAs and whatever else you want on a voluntary basis. But most people in these countries now have two compulsory, legally obligatory, layers of pension protection. There is the first one, the public one, and the second one, the employer-provided one.

When you talk about the savings rates in these countries, the largest savings of most people in the OECD countries would be in the second tier. There are tremendous amounts of money in the Netherlands, France, and Germany in that second tier protection level. Not everybody did it—the U.K. is an example of a country that didn't do it—and now the U.K. is struggling with the next stage of their pension reform, how to figure out what to do about a situation where less than 50 percent of the population, as in the United States, is participating in the second pillar system of pension protection. They have the same problem that we have, including the steady deterioration of defined benefit plans in favor or defined contribution plans.

When Margaret Thatcher and successive governments put in place the big policy shift, they embarked on downgrading the public pillar and upgrading the voluntary second pillar. They did not make it compulsory but rather counted on market forces. They of course did not anticipate that the stock market would go through several years of poor returns and that many traditional British industries would fold or move due to the global competition and other economic factors. The U.K. is therefore one of the prime examples of an advanced industrialized country that faces a severe retirement income savings gap and the prospect of increased poverty among the elderly in the future. The issue has developed into a burning political debate and the government is fully aware that they will have to find solutions for the future.

Tony Blair is now campaigning for re-election, and he is saying that he will fix this problem: "We will ensure that poverty among the elderly will not haunt the U.K. citizens as it did in the past." It is interesting to note that about one-third of the U.K. pensioners are already getting a supplementary welfare benefit, and it is going to rise in the future. It is going to rise primarily because they didn't fix this second pillar, and now they are going to have to go back and do it. They have the same problem that we have in the States, and that is that imposing or mandating employers to contribute to the second pillar looks like a new tax and nobody likes a new tax.

That is not to say there aren't problems elsewhere with the second pillar, and that is the third lesson that I would like to talk about. European countries have discovered that it's difficult to get people to do the right thing. How much sophistication can you expect in relation to an individual retirement plan? The Swedes have a new system where a carve-out of the pension contribution goes into a private, individual account. The contribution to the first-pillar public system was reduced by 2 percent in order to allow this individual account to be established.

This system has been in place about six years. In the first year, the Swedish government sent out a big book with about 600 options to choose from. Swedes could invest their money in Czech bonds or Australian gold or U.S. Disneyland stocks, for example. This was very popular, and the response was quite good. Something like 60 percent of the population actually opted for something. Six years down the road the active involvement, the active opting for some investment, is now down to 10 percent, and they are in a quandary. The suspicion among the experts is that too many choices just befuddle people. You give somebody a book with 600 options, and most people are just paralyzed.

Something fortunate happened in Sweden, and that is that if you don't choose anything, your money goes into a default fund that is run by the government, and the default fund has had better performance and lower administrative costs than the private sector options. That wasn't in the cards and so I think another reason why people are not doing anything is that the best deal has been the government fund.

That raises another issue about these private accounts and the experience of Chile and Poland and all the other countries in the world that have instituted these accounts, and that is that the administrative costs are generally too high. All the governments that have legislated privately-managed individual accounts are struggling with the issue that 25 to 35 percent of people's contributions go to administrative commissions, marketing, salesmen, TV ads, and everything else that goes on when you sell private retirement investment vehicles. There are ways of addressing this problem and Sweden is an interesting example of the government stepping in to mitigate the problem, but administrative costs remain a very big issue in Chile and elsewhere.

The Turner Commission in the U.K. caused big front-page news because one in every three pounds that is contributed to personal retirement accounts goes for administrative costs. If you work for a pension or a bank, you probably think that is okay. But if you are on the receiving end, you might not think it is okay. Beyond that there are big questions about how much you can expect people to plan for their future. How can they decide what investment vehicles are appropriate? When are you actually going to draw on your private account? And if you want to turn that into an annuity, there are some very sophisticated and complicated issues that are left to the consumer. If any of you are annuity specialists in this room, it is time to stand up and defend yourselves, because 99 percent of the world does not understand what an annuity is nor how to cope with it.

The case of Chile and other countries has shown that many people do the wrong thing. They are ill-advised, and they often make the wrong decisions for their retirement future. So it raises questions about how do you educate the public and whose job it is. Would you ask, for example, the Social Security Administration of the United States to provide advisor services for people on how to plan for their retirement? How would they do that in a neutral way without getting into political difficulty? These are the questions that most of the countries are struggling with regarding these multi-pillared systems.

Now the fourth lesson has to do with what is happening in most places in the world, not the industrialized countries of Europe and Asia, but what is happening in Latin America, your neighbor Mexico, and Africa and Southeast Asia. What has happened in the past decade in these countries is that we have realized that the U.S. and the European models, what we called the Bismarckian models or the Beveridge models, really are not appropriate for these countries. The old line that we used to give as advice, "Do like us and you will be lucky enough to have a Social Security system like the United States some day" is not appropriate.

This is increasingly the case because in most of these countries the number of people who are working in the formal sector of the economy has been declining.

Most new jobs in, for example, Poland, Brazil, and Mexico, are in the informal sector. People are not counted, they are not declared, they don't pay taxes, and they are invisible to the government. So this really creates a system where only a minority of the people is contributing to the Social Security system. Coverage is not growing, it is stagnating or diminishing in many of the countries in the world. So given this situation, there has been a very fundamental rethinking about what pensions will look like in the future in most of these developing and transition countries.

It is quite extraordinary for someone who has been in this business as long as I have that we have come back again to the old idea of universal pension payments paid out of state coffers and paid for by taxpayers. The basic idea behind such thinking is that it will not be possible in these developing societies to fund a public social insurance system in the way that we have done in the United States. Would it be better in these circumstances that when people turn 75, they would go to the post office and say "I am 75," and they would be eligible to receive a very small amount of money to keep them from being destitute. In certain countries there may be the administrative capacity to use means or asset testing to establish eligibility, but it may be far more efficient and less vulnerable to corruption in many countries simply to provide a very modest subsistence pension at a certain age. In the few countries that have introduced such pension benefits (such as Brazil, South Africa, and some of the Caribbean islands) the cost to the public purse has been very modest and research has demonstrated that a very small amount of money paid to older persons has a tremendous impact not only for the recipients but also for the younger generations that they help to support.

The better-off middle and upper-income classes will take care of themselves. They will have access to private insurance companies and banks to manage their retirement savings. Citibank and Prudential are already very active in India, for example.

So, in conclusion, what does the U.S. debate look like from an international perspective? First, it looks as if reform or change is not going to happen overnight in the U.S. The Social Security debate will go on for a number of years and it should therefore be an opportunity to ask the hard questions about what the Social Security program is for. Is it about income distribution? Is it about poverty alleviation? Is it about providing adequate retirement income for the future? Much of the talk to date has been about ensuring long-term financial sustainability, but you also need to ask, are people going to get enough, will they have enough in their old age to pay for living expenses, health care costs, and perhaps long-term care? These are the tough questions that need to be discussed now. Why was Social Security put there in the first place, and what purposes does it really serve?

The last question that I will raise has to do with a discussion that is already taking place in many other countries, and I think will gain in importance in the United States as well, and that is, what do we want in addition to providing old-age income protection? What are the other social and economic objectives that we want to achieve in the future? What about encouraging more flexible work in the future?

What about making a system where people can choose when they want to retire rather than being stuck with a given chronological age, such as 62, 65, or even 70? What about gender issues—what about women and the fact that many take time out to have children and to care for older family members? Not surprisingly, they have lower retirement earnings and old-age poverty, even in the richest countries, tends to increase significantly among the very old widows.

In most of the OECD countries there is growing anxiety about the fact that many people are not having children, and so the question is, what can you do to encourage a better combination of work and family life? Pension policy has a lot to do with that. There are many things that you can do in a pension system to address some of these bigger socio-economic questions. In addition, there is great concern in these countries about the fact that too many people are out of the labor force at relatively early ages because they have been kicked out for premature retirement, even if they don't necessarily want to quit working. Moreover, too many people are exiting the labor force by securing a disability pension, a problem that is high on the political agenda of such countries as the Netherlands, Sweden, Finland, and Switzerland. It is also an issue in the United States in spite of the fact that unemployment is generally lower than in Europe and elsewhere in the industrialized world.

The pension debate must therefore be placed within a larger discussion about what kind of society do you want to live in. And, since pension policies are all about promises made to future generations, we are discussing at the same time what kind of society we want our children and grandchildren to be living in.

Part II

The Social Security Debate

Chapter 3
The Social Security Debate

Pamela Herd: We have quite an amazing panel of speakers here today to talk to you about Social Security and Social Security reform.

Thomas Saving is the Jeff Montgomery Professor in Economics and Director of the Private Enterprise Research Center at Texas A&M University in College Station. He holds a Ph.D. in economics from the University of Chicago. His areas of expertise are anti-trust economics, monetary economics, and health economics. He has served in a variety of public capacities including as a public trustee for Social Security and Medicare as well as serving on the President's Commission to Strengthen Social Security.

Our second panelist is Peter Orszag, who is at the Brookings Institution. He received his Ph.D. in economics from the London School of Economics. He currently holds several positions: he is the co-director of the Tax Policy Center, which is a joint venture with the Urban Institute, as well as the director of the retirement security project, and a research professor at Georgetown. He served as a special assistant to President Clinton for economic policy, as well as being a senior adviser on the Council of Economic Advisers, one of the most prestigious appointments for an economist in the U.S. His areas of expertise include pensions, budget, tax policy, Social Security, higher education, and homeland security.

Our third panelist is Stuart Butler, who is the vice-president for domestic and economic policy at the Heritage Foundation. He holds a Ph.D. in American economic history from St. Andrews University in Scotland. His areas of expertise are in health, welfare, and Social Security policy. He also serves as an adjunct professor at Georgetown University. He has published a number of books including *Enterprise Zones: Greenlining the Inner Cities* in 1981, a book on privatizing in the federal government, and *Out of the Poverty Trap*. He frequently testifies before Congress and writes on topics of social policy.

Our fourth panelist is Barbara Kennelly, who served as a Congresswoman from the first district in Connecticut for 17 years. She had a lot of firsts in Congress, including serving at the first woman vice-chair of the House Democratic Caucus and the first woman chief majority whip. She was also a member of the subcommittee on

Social Security, which is obviously quite relevant to our discussions today. Following her congressional career, Kennelly was counselor to the Commission on Social Security when Ken Apfel was Commissioner. She is currently the CEO of the National Committee to Preserve Social Security and Medicare.

Our next panelist is Maya MacGuineas, who is currently the president of the Committee for a Responsible Federal Budget, as well as the director of the fiscal policy program at the New America Foundation. Her areas of expertise include the budget, entitlements, and tax policy. Her work has appeared in a variety of publications including *The Washington Post, The Financial Times, The Chicago Tribune,* as well as *Atlantic Monthly.* Prior to her current position she worked on the McCain campaign as an adviser on Social Security issues. She earned a master's in public policy from the JFK School of Government at Harvard.

Our final panelist today is John Rother, who is the director of policy and strategy at AARP. He is quite an authority on the issues of Medicare, managed care, long-term care, Social Security, pensions, and the challenges facing the boomer generation. In fact he has been talking on the challenges facing the boomer generation since the early 1980s. As well as policy and strategy at AARP, he oversees the AARP's research institute, which does a lot of research on policy issues related to the elderly. Prior to serving as the director of policy and strategy at AARP, he was the legislative director at AARP, and before that he spent a long time in the U.S. Senate serving in a variety of capacities.

Thomas Saving: Thank you, Pamela. I have a unique role here, not my usual role. Since no one from the administration is here, I am the one who is going to present the President's reform. When I say "Social Security reforms," I am only discussing those reforms that have something to do with personal accounts.

I want to briefly give you an idea of a way to talk about this problem. In a generation transfer system, the debt we owe the current generation, that is, everybody who is currently working and retired, has to be paid for by the new generations. In a system that is perfectly sustainable, the debt that we owe the current generation will equal what the next generation will pay. That's the way a system that is sustainable would work.

But the current system, for a number of reasons, does not always work like that. One obvious reason is demographics—the baby boom population. According to the 2005 trustee report just out, we will owe the current generation something like 13.7 trillion. Since the next generation will contribute a little less than a trillion dollars for that, somehow we'll have to find the rest. If we were to give the benefits to the current generation that are scheduled, and if we charge only the taxes that are scheduled, the next generation will have to pick up the slack.

One of the reform issue questions is, "Who participates in the reform system?" For the 1978 reform and the 1983 reform you could say that everyone participated, although not in everything, of course. But everyone participated in the acceleration of scheduled payroll tax increases that were moved forward to 1983. We changed the retirement age—but that reform did not start for a while. It is now at 66, and then we are going to have a 10-year hiatus before it starts moving again—two months a year, until it reaches 67 in 2022. In 1983, reformers said no one older than a certain age would participate in the retirement age change.

The second question is, "Is there any voluntarism to the reform?" Everyone participates in the taxation of benefits, so even though these funds are called "contributions," you could say that Social Security is not voluntary.

The third question is, "If you are going to change the system in some fundamental way—for example, moving to personal accounts—how do you compensate people for something we might refer to as 'accrued benefits?'" As you know, in Chile, they gave something called "recognition bonds," which served to make the debt real, in effect. Whatever the method, the question is, how you would do that?

In a reformed system, the next question would be, what does the benefit structure look like compared to the current one? That is an interesting question. Then, are there any guarantees, and what do they cost? And finally, how much of that current generation debt that I talked about does any reform actually pay off—or does it pay off any of it? Let's look at the President's commission as we try to answer each of those questions.

First, all individuals 55 and older stay in the old system. So the question, who participates?—only people younger than 55. Secondly, participation is voluntary, even for those who aren't eligible to be in the new system. To participate, people would be allowed to invest four percentage points, roughly a little less than a third of their Social Security taxes, in private accounts, up to a $1,000 a year. Then the defined benefits would be fixed at a constant purchasing power rate rather than at a constant replacement rate.

Senator Lindsay Graham has a proposal in Congress that is very similar to what the commission recommended. At retirement, the annuity value of the private accounts would offset the defined benefit payments, so you would have price indexing instead of wage indexing of benefits. Individual accounts would add to the reduced defined benefit only to the extent that they earned more than 2 percent. This provision is usually referred to as a "claw back." The total benefit consists of a Social Security system provided benefit equal to the real 2009 benefit plus the annuitized value of the excess over the base 2 percent earnings in your private account. Thus, the total retirement benefit is not guaranteed—but even so, this particular reform pays off about 34 percent of the current generation debt. So this is what the commission's actual path looks like for income. And you can see that the income falls because you are using up some of the income of the system to provide the private account deposits. You can see that the cost rate rises so that you have a deficit at the beginning, and ultimately the cost rate falls significantly compared to the status quo cost rate. This is right out of the commission's final report.

The President's plan, as best as I can tell you, allows all individuals 55 years and older to stay in the old system. As the President talks about it, the system would begin in 2009. At that point, these people over 55 would be at least 59 years old—but at this point, participation for anyone 55 or older is voluntary in the President's system. You don't get more than one chance to opt in, and once you opt in, you can't opt out. Then you get the same four percentage points of Social Security in a private account, again up to $1,000 a year. The cap grows at $100 a year, plus it is wage-indexed, so when both of these reforms take effect, private accounts will represent a much greater share of the current system's retirement benefit. Then those that stay in the existing system will draw benefits from a reformed and sustainable Social Security system, whatever you decide that means.

When Social Security's Chief Actuary Steve Goss provided the analysis for this plan (called scoring), I believe he assumed 100 percent participation. So, in his plan, no one would stay in the old system. But you could argue that the old system would continue to pay the current system's benefits, but those in it would have to pay the payroll tax rate that would cover the full cost of providing these benefits (referred to as the cost rate). So retirees would be stuck with that system, meaning that their taxes would rise over the next 30 years to upwards of 17 or 18 percent.

Then at retirement, in the President's system, the annuity value of private accounts will offset the defined benefit payments by the government taking back some of your account up to the 3 percent rate of return (again, commonly referred to as a "claw back"). Essentially, you keep all of the value of your account in excess of the base 3 percent rate of return. The commission plan also had a so-called claw-back but only at a 2 percent rate of return, meaning you keep all of the excess rate of return above the base 2 percent rate of return. Once again, the total retirement benefit is not guaranteed. It is important to see what's going on here—for example, the 3 percent rate of return is an idea that comes from the notion of the government's balance sheet

In valuing its future retirement costs, a firm has got to put on its balance sheet a liability that reflects the cost for paying promised benefits for future retirees. In this case, that future pension liability for the government, the way we as trustees are generating it, is calculated using a 3 percent discount rate for projected benefit payments. So if you borrow to fund a private account reform then claw back that part of the account at maturity assuming a 3 percent rate of return, you perfectly offset of revenue used to fund the private accounts. That is, the current borrowing at the 3 percent government borrowing rate required to fund the private accounts is completely repaid when individuals retire and the government takes back its contribution including interest earnings. Thus, you really aren't affecting the balance sheet of the government in any way. You aren't helping it. If you look at what the commission did, the commission actually improves the balance sheet of the government. Even if you fund the early deficits with borrowing, because of price indexing and the claw-back, you are improving the balance sheet of the government because you are reducing its future costs of retirement. If you look at the President's system, at least as I have seen it laid out, and compare it to Lindsay Graham's proposal, this is very different.

Lindsay Graham claws back at the realized government bond rate, which is then, in a sense, fiscally neutral.

I have structured a reform that duplicates exactly the redistribution that is inherent in the current system and pays for it entirely. But you can't do that with carve-outs only (a carve-out refers to the use of current Social Security system revenue to fund private accounts). You have to have what people refer to as "add-ons." And these add-ons must also pay for what has been carved out up front. Now as long as you pay for the transfer to private accounts in the end, you are all right. But if you try to borrow all of the funds for the reform for the transition from the current system to a reformed system, you accomplish absolutely nothing.

The real issue here is how to pay off the debt we owe the current generation. If we don't pay off any of that, we haven't really accomplished anything.

What I have tried to do is to lay out what the commission did and what the President did, and to point out that that there are alternatives to these kinds of reforms— and questions that you should ask of any reform. The commission's goal was to have the cost rate and the revenue rate be equal at the end of the 75-year period so that the system was permanently sustainable. Now while there are a lot of other reforms that do that, it is not necessarily clear, from the little bit we know about the President's reform, whether it does that. But certainly the proposal I mentioned does make social security perfectly sustainable with a long-run tax rate of 5.2 percent. In other words, the tax rate would go from the current 10.6 percent for pensions to 5.2 percent.

Peter Orszag: In thinking about Social Security reforms, we really need to step back for a second and think about retirement income. Financial planners tell you that you need about 70 percent of what you had been earning before retirement in order to live comfortably in retirement. It is not 100 percent because you can save on work-related expenses and spend a little more time shopping for bargains and what have you, but average earners do need about 70 percent. Social Security provides about half of that 70 percent, which means that you need to come up with the other 35 percent yourself. Both of those tiers of our retirement income system are under pressure, and both of them need reform. I think that there are ways forward on both, but for that core layer of protection, the current Social Security system actually delivers its benefits in a very desirable way. In particular, benefits are protected against financial market fluctuations.

There is a place for taking on risk and that is in the upper tier, not in the bottom tier, where benefits are protected against inflation. Again, this is very desirable for a bottom layer of income and it lasts as long as you are alive—you are not going to run out of that bottom tier, which is very important. Furthermore, Social Security provides something that you just can't buy in private markets. For the students in the room, you all have great futures because you are at a good school like UT Austin, but the fact of the matter is, I hate to break it to you, life might not turn out as great as you think. If it doesn't, Social Security is going to partially make up the difference.

Social Security basically provides a form of lifetime earnings insurance that you can't buy anywhere else, and again for that core tier of retirement income, that is very valuable. So in thinking about how we reform the system, you need to be thinking in terms of tiers of income and where it is appropriate to take risk and where the kinds of features that Social Security already has should be perpetuated.

I have put forward a plan with Peter Diamond, a professor at MIT, which has a variety of features. The first feature is that it restores long-term sustainable solvency to Social Security. That is presumably desirable, given the deficit; we want to actually fix the problem. Second, it retains the basic structure of the existing program for the reasons that I just delineated, for that bottom layer of financial income. For retirement income, we think the system is designed about right. Third, it doesn't have any account gimmicks or magic asterisks, which have unfortunately become quite common in Washington, D.C., with lots of accounting games left and right. That probably means that it is completely politically unviable, at least for now. But if we ever got serious about reform, it would be a very good plan to consider.

We combine benefit reductions and revenue increases rather than relying solely on one or the other, and that is partially because we want to attenuate downward pressure on that first tier. If you do all of the adjustment on the benefit side, you are really digging into that first tier way too much. We also protect the most vulnerable beneficiaries. As Ken mentioned earlier, there still are problems with widow poverty and some other isolated areas, so we have a variety of protections for disabled workers, children whose parents die in the middle of a career, workers who have lifetime low wages, and widows. The President's Commission also included many of these protections.

We do ask for some modest sacrifices from average earners, and we ask higher earners to play a larger role in re-establishing solvency, and this is for two reasons. The first is that life expectancy is going up, as you know. Many people know that better-educated workers have longer life expectancies than the less educated. Fewer people know that the gap between high-income and low-income workers in life expectancy is literally exploding, with very significant increases in life expectancy differentials across the income distribution occurring over the past 20 to 30 years in the United States. It is also occurring in the United Kingdom and in continental European countries. If you look at the concentration of obesity, the concentration of smoking, and the fact that fancy genetic-based technologies are not going to filter all the way down the income distribution immediately, many demographers believe that this trend towards an increasing discrepancy is going to continue. This trend means higher earners are getting their monthly benefits over an increasingly longer number of months compared to everyone else. We think it makes sense for them to therefore play a larger role in re-establishing solvency.

One way to do that is to revisit the tax cap. This year there are more than $800 billion in wages that are above the maximum taxable earnings level under Social Security of $90,000. That cap represents 15 percent of total wages. At the time of the last reform in 1983, the wages that were above the cap and therefore untaxed only represented 10 percent of the total. What has happened over the last 20 years is that wage gains at the top have been disproportionately rapid. We think it makes sense to take at least some of that back.

Because of time constraints, I am not going to go into all of the details of the plan. But I do want to talk about individual accounts as part of Social Security. I think it is very import to understand what is going on in the President's proposal. If you elect an account today under the administration's proposal, you get a dollar in your individual account today, and then you owe that dollar back plus interest at the 3 percent real (that is, after inflation) interest rate per year when you retire, with the collection done through a reduction in your traditional Social Security benefit. So this is really more like a loan or like investing on margin—that is, you are going to wind up better off if the rate of return you are going to get on your dollar exceeds the 3 percent real interest rate at which you are effectively borrowing. But you are going to wind up worse off if that doesn't happen.

There is a variety of estimates out there about the likelihood of your exceeding that 3 percent threshold. Bob Schiller at Yale, one of the nation's leading financial economists, suggests a 70 percent probability that you would fall below that threshold. Other people are saying it is much lower than that, but that is the right way to think about it from an individual perspective.

The other thing that is important to realize is that because the interest rate on the loan from the government to you is the projected government interest rate, this is a net neutral deal, assuming all the loans are fully repaid. So the government lends you money today, you pay it back at the same rate the government is borrowing the money, and after you pay it back, it is a wash. But that is the point—it is just a wash and not a net improvement. In fact, I think it is likely that the net effect will be negative, in other words, harmful to solvency, even over an infinite horizon, because not all the loans will be fully repaid.

Workers who die before retirement will be able to pass their accounts on to heirs, but the debt will not be passed on to heirs. Some workers will have insufficient traditional benefits to repay the debt back to Social Security, and it is unlikely that the government will reach into your pocket to collect the additional debt repayment. So, in reality, the President's plan is likely to have a negative effect on solvency. Even if it were just neutral, even if it were just a wash over the long term, there is still a very substantial adverse cash flow effect that occurs because the government is lending younger workers the money today. These workers won't pay the money back for 40 or 50 years, and in the meanwhile, the government is out the money. So the plan creates a cash flow problem in exchange for no net improvement in long-term solvency.

Even if you combine that plan with something that does restore long-term solvency, albeit entirely on the benefit side, you still have a very extended period in which public debt is higher than it would be without the plan. This conclusion is based on the administration's own economic report. In other words, the President's own analysis shows that the debt does not fall beneath the baseline until 2064. That is about 60 years. That would be like saying that we put the plan in place at the end of World War II, that we actually stuck with it the whole time, that policy-makers and politicians did not backslide and forgive some of the debts after 30, 40, or 50 years, and that only today would we actually be experiencing any net reduction in public debt as a result from that plan.

In fiscal policy, 60 years in an eternity. I find it extremely unlikely that policy-makers will actually stick with the plan throughout the whole 60-year period and that we would actually realize the net reduction in debt that is required to make the whole thing look good on paper. Some people say that this argument is all totally misleading because I was focusing on public debt. You know, issue a public debt today, and the government will, in exchange, again through those loans, be reducing your future Social Security benefits. So, in effect, we are trading implicit debt, promised future Social Security benefits, for explicit debt today, and really they are no different, so it shouldn't matter at all. And that is right in very simplified terms, such as those you might find in an introductory economics course, where everything is frictionless, and everyone is perfectly rational. But it is completely wrong in the real world.

I don't know of any country in the world that has gotten in trouble because it has large implicit debt. The thing about implicit debt is you don't need to roll it over in financial markets. But lots of countries have gotten in trouble because they have large explicit debt that you have to roll over in financial markets, and you are subjecting yourself to a greater risk of a financial market crisis when you have a large explicit public debt. So they are not equivalent, and the elevated levels of debt that occur on many of these plans for a very extended period of time is a serious concern.

Another consequence of the proposal is that if it were combined with something that actually restored solvency—the so-called price indexing proposal—it would have a serious effect on the two tiers of the retirement income replacement rate. The foundation provided by a defined benefit falls from about 35 percent of previous wages down to well under 10 percent—and that is just too small for a core tier of retirement income. Now some people would say that the personal account would offset it. But the fact of the matter is that for that core tier, accounts don't make a lot of sense.

Accounts are being sold on the basis of ownership and control, and the administration has officially said that you are not allowed access to them before retirement. I think it is completely unrealistic that we would sustain those kinds of restrictions. You have got $30,000 sitting in your account, your kid is sick, you need a new car, or your kid just got into UT Austin but without enough financial aid, and the legislature just increased tuition—you are telling me, Mr. President, that I can't pull my money out when you told me it was my money, and so I can't pay for my kid's tuition?

We have seen in a variety of other situations that with accounts, there is liberalized access, pre-retirement, over time. This might make sense in the upper tier, but it doesn't make sense in the bottom tier because it means the money is not there for retirement. There are many other concerns with accounts in the bottom tier where they just don't make sense. However, they do make sense on top of Social Security. But the funny thing about that is that we already do have individual accounts in the United States—they are called 401(k)s and IRAs. And frankly, we are not doing a very good job with them. We could be making the 401(k)s and IRAs work a lot better than they are. So let's take those accounts and make them work better rather than introducing a new system of accounts into Social Security where they don't belong. We also have this problem for the top 35 percent of the 70 percent needed for retirement—the tier in which you must save on top of Social Security. No Social Security reform plan in the world is going to change that fact.

So what can we do to make accounts work better? I think the key is to make it easier for families to navigate. We currently are loading all the decision-making responsibility on families who are busy, have kids, have jobs, have lots of things going on, and they walk into an employer and get this big book of their 401(k) options, like the 600 options in Sweden. People freeze in the face of that kind of complexity. We need to make the system sensible for people who are too busy to make decisions on their own while allowing people who have Ph.D.s in financial economics to spend their weekends figuring it out and doing what is optimal. You should not need a Ph.D. in financial economics to navigate the pension system. The evidence very strongly suggests that we know what works. For example, instead of asking people to sign up for a 401(k) when they go to work, which is complicated and makes them want to put off that decision, you simply put them in a 401(k) unless they opt out.

Your introductory economics course would tell you that makes no difference in the world because people are perfectly rational, they will decide what is right, and they will sign the paper one way or the other, so it won't matter. Again, in the real world, that is not what happens. With an opt-out system, you go from 13 percent participation rates to 80 percent.

So you should be in a 401(k) plan unless you opt out, your contribution rate should be increasing over time unless you opt out, you should be in a diversified index fund unless you opt out, and your funds should roll over when you switch jobs unless you opt out. And if you want to get fancy and opt out of any of those things, great—but the rest of us, who are busy with other things, just want sensible things happening to our savings decisions without even having to think about it. If we used opt-out systems on a much broader basis, we would get IRAs and 401(k)s working a lot better than they are today.

So, in conclusion, individual accounts don't make any sense within the core tier of retirement income provided by Social Security. Social security has problems that we do need to fix, and that grow larger over time, and that are better to address sooner rather than later—and there are a variety of ways of addressing them. But we do need to be careful not to be tricked by the charlatans who are putting forward plans that have massive account gimmicks contained in them because those plans really won't accomplish much. There are lots of new, exciting ways to boost saving in individual accounts, where they belong, in a tier above and beyond Social Security. Frankly, both sides of the Social Security debate should agree on that because whether you support individual accounts as part of Social Security or you don't, we should both agree that the accounts we have on top of Social Security could be made to work better and that we should just go do that.

Stuart Butler: I think it is extremely important that we have these kinds of discussions, like this one and the one I attended here last year on Medicare. It is essential that we have a real conversation, and that we address these major programs that affect retirement.

Part of the debate, of course, is about the public finances of the program. And that raises a lot of very fundamental issues about our obligations from one generation to the next, from young to old, and also from old to young. It also raises questions about whether finances and money going to these programs should pre-empt other programs and other commitments we have as a society and as a government.

Certainly, if you look at the long-term, the proportion of our gross national product devoted to these major programs, including Social Security, Medicare, and Medicaid, is going up relentlessly. Because these rising costs will have effects on other parts of the economy and other things we are trying to do, it is very important that we debate the implications of whatever we do to address the big picture and the numbers.

In addition, focusing on the more personal side of this issue, we should ask how Social Security in the future will affect our personal finances. Peter has already talked a little bit about that, and I agree a lot with what he said in terms of our need to address ideas to improve the existing savings for retirement, such as using automatic enrollment. But if we focus on the Social Security part of preparing for retirement and personal savings, we do need to ask what Social Security is for and what it should look like in the future.

It has been said already that when Social Security was developed, it was seen as part of a three-legged stool of savings, insurance, and pensions. And it was also seen as a "social security" that would assure you of a monthly check. The concern of many of us who want to look at structural reforms is not just the issue of the long-term viability, or solvency, but also the fact that Social Security, a key part of this multi-pillared system, has changed over time to such a degree that it needs to be revisited, reexamined, and altered. I would argue for these reforms and restructuring even if we could see a Social Security that would be in surplus forever.

Why? Although there are many reasons, I want to focus on three. The first reason is that as the program has matured over time—and this is true of all the social insurance programs around the world—payroll taxes have risen steadily as the population ages. The system has matured to such a degree that we now have a significant impact of those payroll taxes on personal savings—another leg of the stool. And that is of particular importance to people who are lower-income and modest-income, rather than upper-income people.

When the system was first put into place, the combined taxes on Social Security from the employer and employee, which still comes out of compensation, was

2 percent. Now it is 12.4 percent. It has risen very significantly, and meanwhile, particularly among lower-income people, savings, especially long-term savings, has essentially collapsed. Somebody earning $20,000 a year, which is not exactly a high income, is paying something like $2,500 in Social Security taxes, so there is not much left for personal savings after that. So one leg of preparing for retirement—personal savings—which President Roosevelt thought of as being critical to thinking about retirement, has essentially disappeared since that era for modest-income Americans.

That also has implications beyond just the personal, because when you look back to previous generations to see what happened in lower-income communities to build capital over time, you saw savings. You saw people reinvesting in each other's businesses—loan funds were very common in immigrant communities. This is how capital was saved and regenerated and how businesses formed, and how people got more and more affluent over time. That does not happen in lower-income communities today, in part because so much of people's income goes in the form of taxes to retirement.

It is very important, therefore, to look at ways to build up within the Social Security system a mechanism that basically puts back into place that third leg—to establish some kind of personal individualized system that allows wealth to be created, particularly within the lower-income community.

Some say, as Peter did, that there are ways of encouraging saving beyond the Social Security system. I am not against those at all, but I think we have to be realistic that even with automatic enrollment, which I think will make a difference, we are still going to see millions of people living from paycheck to paycheck, from rent payment to rent payment, feeling unable to add any additional funds into a personal account outside of Social Security, in addition to the payroll tax, because they just don't have any money to save.

Now we can subsidize people to save and some people argue for that. But that raises lots of questions about how you design it, how fair it's seen to be, what the politics of it would be, and so on. We could certainly do that, but first we should understand a very central feature of the way the Social Security system has evolved over time. It has grown, and the taxes have grown, and that growth in taxes has had a crowding-out effect on another critical part of preparing for your retirement. Everybody who talks about encouraging savings recognizes this is a problem that needs to be fixed within the system. So looking at personal accounts in some form is an approach to trying to deal with that feature.

Secondly, let's talk a little bit about the risk associated with getting what you think you are going to get in retirement. As people have mentioned already, there of course is risk in the markets for someone with money in a 401(k) plan or other similar type of account. We know that, and sometimes it can be very bad for people. But let's not overlook the fact that there is political risk associated with benefits that are payable through the Social Security system because these depend on political and budgetary pressures on the system. There is no guarantee in the system we now have, so we really are talking about balancing and comparing risk. Our Social Security benefits are always going to be subject to change and to risk because of political and budget factors.

So we are talking about relative risk here. In the world of relative risk, it's important that we don't put all of our eggs in the political risk basket. Diversification is very important—which is why, if people must put some of their taxes into a system that is prone to political risk, they should at least have the opportunity, if they so wish, to put some of these taxes into another diversified, more market-based way of looking at their retirement. So that's another reason why we should look very carefully and debate how we should create some kind of personal individual element in the Social Security system.

The third reason that it's important to contemplate this kind of change is because under the way in which the Social Security system has matured over time, its shortcomings for many millions of people became much more apparent. In mature systems throughout the world, as the population ages, the amount going in continues to rise, while the return that one can expect, in the normal sense of the word "return," begins to decline. It was a great system at the beginning, of course, as these systems necessarily are, but as time has gone by, the return that people can expect, on average, has declined.

An average worker today retiring on Social Security, and with reasonable projections about life expectancy and other factors, will in real terms get a return for the money they put in of about 1.27 percent. It is a positive return, but certainly a very modest one. And it will decline over time under the current structure of Social Security. Somebody who is 25 years old today on average will get less in real terms than they paid into the system—and that situation will get worse as time goes by. And, unlike a system where you have any form of personal stake—a 401(k) plan or an IRA—if you die before retirement under the current Social Security system, you have nothing to pass on to your heirs. It is true, of course, that you get spousal and dependents' benefits—that's insurance, and that's an integral and proper part of the system. But what you don't get is any kind of buildup for what you have paid over time that could be used by your heirs, and that is a very important deficiency of any kind of retirement program. Not only does that reduce potential wealth for the retiree: it also reduces the intergenerational wealth buildup that has been so critical to the general growth of incomes in this country among certain populations.

When you start looking at particular populations, you see that the situation is even worse, which that is why so many people looking at reforming the Social Security system have focused on minority communities that have lower-than-average life expectancies, particularly in the African-American community, where life expectancy is sufficiently different that people in that community will get a far worse return from the contributions they make to Social Security than others will. This disparity is one of the reasons that while incomes for equally situated people in both populations may not be substantially different, there are dramatic differences between the two populations in terms of savings and wealth.

This disparity between population groups is one reason why so many of us believe that some form of personal account is critical within the system. Even if we're talking about additional steps to encourage savings beyond the Social Security system, personal accounts are important because so many people are unable to take advantage of those other alternatives for savings and right now and so are necessarily shortchanged by the system. It is important therefore, to start looking at reforms that will essentially recreate the original vision of Social Security as part of a multiple system aimed at retirement.

Now we can debate exactly how we should do that, and we can have honest disagreements about that. But it is very important to recognize this is the direction in which we must go if we are going to have truly secure retirement for Americans. We must have a multiple-based retirement system of insurance: a steady monthly income that can be counted on, and a system of insurance, savings, and wealth so that people can insulate themselves more readily from the vicissitudes of their retirement years. Wealth is important so that they can enjoy their retirement years beyond getting monthly checks, so they can have a nest egg they use for themselves or for their heirs. That requires moving towards a system with some partial ownership and direct control of those funds, even if there are tight restrictions on access to those.

I take Peter's points that you never know how the political system will work in the future—none of us knows that. But when somebody says we should just raise taxes today and reduce benefits in the future over time, it shows the political system is at least as risky as the market. Moreover, we get taxes now, and see benefits raised rather than reduced later on, and so we may be back where we started from in terms of a massive shortfall. Higher levels of taxes also have all kinds of implications for job creation and business creation. So this notion that there is uncertainty in the future about the political system is a fact of life about every proposal in this area. It is not unique to one or the other although clearly we should be looking at the politics and the public choice aspects of all these things.

So the debate we're having is a critical debate. People can have honest disagreements about certain features, but we should and can agree that we need to move forward to restructure a retirement system to achieve the original vision of that multipart program that we established in the 1930s.

Barbara Kennelly: Recently, I finished my day's work and left the office and went over to the gallery of the U.S. Senate to hear a debate. It was an excellent debate—two Senators for and against personal accounts were debating, but both absolutely believed that we should fix the current system. Illinois Senator Richard Durbin said something that struck me—that "the debate we're having in this country now about Social Security is not about the *solvency* of the system but about its *legitimacy*." What we are in the process of deciding is, do we keep the current system and fix it, or do we have a brand new system?

Let me tell you where I am coming from. The National Committee to Preserve Social Security and Medicare has 4.3 million members and supporters. That is nothing compared to John Rother's 35 million in AARP, but we are the second-biggest membership organization. Our members are older, no doubt about it. They understand the hazards and vicissitudes of life, and they think there should be a shared risk. They really like the insurance aspect of the Social Security system. And they really seem to understand that when you have personal accounts taken from the payroll tax, it is the beginning of the dismantling of the system.

Let me give you just a few reasons why our members and I are against private or personal accounts. When you read the current Social Security report, you learn that we can pay 100 percent of full benefits up to 2041, and that even if we did nothing—which no one is suggesting—74 percent of benefits could be paid because all of us are constantly working and paying into the system. So for me, the glass is half full. I feel very strongly that we should make the changes that would fix the current system now—and I think I have the credentials to address this issue because I was in the Congress in 1983, the last time we reformed the system.

Now, that was a crisis. We didn't know if we could pay benefits out for the next couple of months, and we had to make the very tough decisions that you heard Mr. Saving talk about. Raising the retirement age to 67 to get full benefits—we did things like that. We tackled Social Security for the first time, and let me tell you, I don't know how I got re-elected. But the reason I did get re-elected is that people really wanted to fix the system. So that is where we are now. But while I think we should fix the system, I do *not* think we should have personal accounts or private accounts, no, I do not. Even the President has agreed that carving personal accounts out of Social Security does not address the solvency problem.

In fact, what this does do is make the solvency problem very much worse. What is happening is that you are diverting money out of the payroll tax into these private accounts, and this accelerates the solvency problem. Almost immediately the surplus that we have now, where we have more money going into Social Security than we have paying benefits, would just disappear. There would have to be bigger cuts to the guaranteed benefits, and our nation would have to borrow more money. So one wonders, why the confusion? Why don't people understand this? One of the reasons could be because the administration says, well, you just take 4 percent of the payroll tax for the private accounts. That doesn't sound like very much, but 4 percent of payroll is two-thirds of what individuals pay and one-third of what businesses and individuals combined pay, and that is a massive transfer of money out of Social Security.

We are going to have to borrow trillions of dollars to bring the new system into being because we have a huge deficit right now. Your privatizers will say, don't worry about it, Mrs. Kennelly, it is okay because it is like prepaying your mortgage. But when we already have a deficit situation, and then we borrow that money up front, it is a very serious situation.

I follow this program, obviously, because I was on the Ways and Means Committee, and I was with Ken at the Social Security Administration. I have followed this program and watched some of the people who have long believed that we shouldn't have a Social Security system, that we should all be on our own. The Cato Institute and many others did a very good job of telling the younger generation that Social Security won't be there for them. Those who like the current system—maybe like myself—didn't say much because we knew that the system had been fixed in 1983. We knew the baby boomers were there, and that's why we had to raise the payroll tax to the extent we did because we wanted to have a soft landing for them. But young people are being told time and time again it is not going to be there. To me, the disappointing thing right now is that young people don't think Social Security is going to be there for them—but the more they learn about the privatized system that is being presented, the more they realize that under privatization they would to have to pay twice.

Social Security is a pay-as-you-go type of system. The people who are working today are paying for the retirees. Well, if you pay into your personal account, and you are also paying full benefits for the current retirees in the United States of America, you are going to have to pay twice. And the costs of this transition will last for generations. I have grandchildren who would be paying this cost well into their middle years. And think about personal accounts for those people 40 and 50 years old. The President says nobody under 55 will be touched, that you will be okay. Well, if you are 48 years old, I would begin to worry, because you are having this money go into your personal account, and the market goes up, and the market goes down, and if the market goes down, you are not going to have very many years to make up for what you lost—so 40- and 50-year-olds should worry about that.

However, I have another idea. People are working so hard these days, between the voicemail and the high-tech items that we carry around and the productivity that we are putting out. The 40- or 50-year-olds try to educate their kids and make things work for themselves, and they really haven't thought about all of these issues—so I cringe, excuse me Mr. Saving to say it, but I cringe when I hear the argument that these personal accounts are voluntary.

They are about as voluntary as a shotgun wedding, let me tell you. We knew when the President's Social Security commission report came out in 2001 that they had three plans. The second plan was the one that everybody was looking at, and the President of the United States has said that is the blueprint that he thinks we should have. But that plan proposed to change income indexing, as Peter Orszag explains so well, going from wages up to prices. That is where they found the money because, as Peter explained, the standard of living would not keep up with most of the people who were working. So here you have indexing that takes away half your guaranteed benefit because everybody gets that cut. That is one of the ways that they pay for the privatized system when we have a deficit. So this indexing idea plan takes away nearly half of the guaranteed benefit and then clawback takes away the other half of your benefit.

At the senate debate I mentioned seeing the other night, I was surprised. The senator who was arguing for personal accounts had a graph that showed how, eventually, by the time this got worked out, there would be trust in the market. But you look at it and you say, well, I don't know if that is such a good idea.

The Congressional Research Service report confirms these numbers. I don't know if you agree with the CRS, but they say when people who are 41 now have these personal accounts, they are going to lose a good deal of their account, but a child who is born this year will lose 91 percent of the account through indexation and the clawback. We are talking about a huge change in the system; we are talking about dismantling Social Security.

Let's talk a few minutes about risk. We have all mentioned risk—but as this plan was being presented, it began poorly in the polls because people realized that the risk was what was bothering them. The Social Security benefit is a very modest amount of money, but at least people know it is going to be there. The people who are promoting carve-out accounts decided to compare them to the thrift savings plan that federal workers have. But that analogy is specious because in a thrift savings plan, you don't lose any of your Social Security. When I decide to take my own thrift savings benefit, I knew that was a supplement on top of Social Security. So for proponents of the new Social Security plan to say it is like a thrift savings plan really is wrong.

Workers are also assured that "It is all going to be okay—don't worry about going into the market because the funds you're investing in are going to be indexed." Indexed funds might be a little safer than being in invested only in the company you work for or in a number of companies—but indexed funds are still in Wall Street. And when that market goes up or it goes down, the indexed funds go up or down, too. Many people in 1999 to 2001, when the market was going up, were in indexed funds—but if you stayed in past that time and you were planning to retire—well, chances are you are still working.

One of the most surprising things to the President, I am quite sure, was the negative reaction to the plan of people like my members, people who are 60 and up, because they were told, "Don't worry about it—if you are 55 and older, it is not going to hurt you." Yesterday, I appeared before the U.S. House Financial Services committee, and a congresswoman there really gave it to me about being for the traditional system because I have thousands of members in her district. She kept saying, "You have got to tell those members of yours that they won't be hurt." And I responded, "That is not the point." As I said earlier, older people understand what happens in life. If you were someone my age and you are looking at your daughter in her 40s and maybe things hadn't gone too well, are you saying that they are not going to need any help? What is going to change so much in the world?

We talk about the lack of poverty now among older people, and we say, "That is a generational thing—they have everything." Why do you think there is so little poverty now? It has gone from 35 percent in 1960 to 10 percent now, and why is that? Social Security—my members understand that, older people understand it. As I said earlier, I know what a crisis is, I know how hard it is to make these decisions, but we should not let the solvency debate be held hostage by the push for privatization.

I don't know what is going to happen in Washington. Our members join us and pay $10 a year for us to go lobby on Social Security and Medicare. Another reason why seniors are not accepting the fact that they are not going to lose anything: seniors are worried to death today about their Medicare Part B premiums, and next year they are going to have a Part D premium. And if you are living on a fixed income, you understand that if our nation is borrowing trillions of dollars more now, down the line, Medicare will be cut. Medicare will be cut if we continue this course.

So I stand here as a woman who talks to seniors all the time, travels around the United States meeting with my members, and they are worried. They are worried that a country like the United States of America is thinking about getting rid of their social retirement program. We can do better than that. I tell members of Congress, "Look, I made those tough decisions, and you can, too. But don't wait because we have that trust fund surplus—do it now, and it won't be as tough." You know, we are going to solve this problem down the line; come on, Social Security has been changed 11 times. It has 2,500 rules regarding the benefit formula. It is a very complicated program. However, Social Security has got the administrative costs down as low as you can get them. That is the sleeper issue.

Dr. Hoskins told us about what happened in England. If we copy that here we are going to have to pay for these things. I don't see why a country like the United States of America, where we have a good system and some ingenuity, can't fix the system we've got. Unfortunately, I think everybody is going to have to take a step back, take a big breath, and start debating that.

Maya MacGuineas: I really agree with Barbara's comment: the discussion that this country has gotten off to on Social Security reform is really an unfortunate one. Most of the focus has been on private accounts—whether private accounts will save the system or private accounts will ruin the system. I would argue that neither is correct—but that accounts really are not the central issue we should be discussing.

And the second false debate we are having is whether Social Security faces a crisis. I get questions from reporters all the time—"Is this a crisis? Is this not a crisis?" There is an obsession with certain words—"privatization," "crisis." If it is a crisis, that is not an argument *for* private accounts. And, if it is not a crisis, that is not an argument *against* private accounts. Pretty much the only thing all experts agree on is that we know there is a problem and that the sooner we make changes, the better. So it would be great if we could start having a discussion about the changes we really do need to make.

When it comes to reforming Social Security, three key issues need to be addressed, boiling down to what, when, and where. What changes are we going to make to the system? When are we going to make them? And where do we store the savings that are meant for Social Security?

So, to go through those quickly, when it comes down to it, the options are pretty well known. They are raising taxes and cutting benefits. We have heard a whole lot of promises from politicians about which ones they will *not* do. We have not heard so much about which one they would want to do.

On the revenue side, we have things like raising the payroll tax rate, raising the payroll tax cap, raising other revenues, and diverting other revenues into the Social Security system. On the benefits side, we could do across-the-board benefit reductions, we could do benefit reductions for some groups of people and not other groups of people, we could raise the retirement age, or we could get rid of some kinds of benefits.

Those are the possibilities, and we need to pick a sensible menu of all of them. Personally, just because I want to do what I preach, and talk about what I would do, not what I wouldn't do, the kind of plan that I think makes the most sense is the one that is a balanced package between both revenue and benefit reductions. I would look at raising the payroll tax cap and raising the retirement age. When we first started Social Security, the life expectancy was 63, and the retirement age was 65. The retirement age is gradually going up to 67, but I think it probably needs to go up more quickly in order for us not to expect people to support us in retirement for a good chunk of our lives. And then, finally, I would reduce benefits, and I would do so in a way that is progressive. I would reduce benefits for people who don't depend on them rather than for people who do.

The second question is when we make these changes. You can do it sooner or you can do it later. Almost everyone agrees there are reasons to do it sooner, but a lot of times that means making the decision to make those changes now, but phasing them in very gradually over time. That is what we did in 1983, and I understand the argument for that—it basically gives people the time to plan accordingly. You know that your tax rate will go up and your benefits will go down, and therefore you can adjust your behavior.

But I think there are actually better reasons to implement the choices now, not just to make them. This is a big enough problem that I think we have to talk about shared sacrifice. Everybody needs to be part of the solution. We've known about it for a long time, and continuing to delay is like a congressman who says, "I am going to raise taxes 20 years from now." I don't really think that is political courage. It is sort of like my saying I'll go on a diet in a year and half. That kind of decision is not really the hard part of it.

So what changes can we phase in as soon as possible in a way that will both spread the cost among generations—which I think is the fairest way to do it—and also build up the saving for Social Security in advance of when we know that those savings will be needed to pay for benefits? If such savings contribute to national saving, increasing saving in the macro economy can strengthen the economy along the way, which I think is certainly desirable.

The third issue is the where. Let's say that we make the courageous choices, and we make the changes sooner rather than later—we still have the question of what to do with those additional savings. Right now, we have Social Security surpluses that are saved and stored in the Social Security trust funds. And as Ken said in his opening remarks, a lot of this tension is whether you believe that the trust funds have worked or not. For me, personally, I fear that the trust funds have not been an effective way to save the money that is obligated to Social Security, because we have Social Security surpluses that are co-mingled with the rest of government, making politicians feel richer than they are. And so we have Social Security surpluses going to all other areas of government—defense, education, environment, and notably, in the past few years, a lot of tax cuts and the creation of a prescription drug bill, which arguably were there and were larger because we had these Social Security surpluses.

This is where private accounts come in. I am not a big fan of a lot of the arguments for private accounts. I don't think the ownership argument is a strong one. I don't think the higher returns argument is a strong one. But I do think that if we are courageous enough to make the choices up front that we need to fix Social Security, I worry about putting that money into the government trust funds. We will have the same problems that we've had in the past two decades when we have built those trust funds, and then money that is meant for Social Security gets diverted and used for other purposes. If there was a way to truly lock the money away from Congress, I would feel a lot safer about saying forget private accounts, they are not really important. But accounts may be the only true lock box that there is to keep it shored up.

That said, private accounts don't fix Social Security, and they do have issues that have to be addressed. You have to think about how to ensure that the investments are not risky. I really think this point about not giving people a lot of choices is a critical one. You want just a few broadly managed index funds both to regulate the risk and to minimize the costs. You want to acquire things like annuities so that people don't reach retirement with a pool of $100,000 or a few hundred thousand dollars that they then go and spend. You want to make sure that that turns into something like Social Security, where you have an inflation-adjusted benefit.

I don't think emphasizing, "This is your money and that is what is so important about it" is a very good idea, because I actually think that money needs to be highly regulated, but I do think the accounts can serve a very useful purpose in saving the money for Social Security. However, they do nothing to replace those tough choices of what you are actually going to do to fix Social Security.

Beyond those three key issues, I want to make an argument for why benefit reductions are an important part of the Social Security reform proposals. First, I think back to how the country is not having a very useful discussion about the tradeoffs involved. We have really compartmentalized the issues that are involved with how to finance the retirement of the baby boomers. There are a lot of major trends that are going on in our country that are dramatically different looking forward than they were looking backward. The two that jump out are the world of globalization and the demographic shifts we have, not just here but around the entire world. And yet, maybe because of how our policy thinkers are set up, we are very compartmentalized—you know, somebody is an expert on Social Security, someone on the budget, someone on taxes, someone on Medicare. We are sort of ticking at these issues one at a time rather than thinking holistically about what our budget will look like going forward.

What are the ways that we should be thinking about all these issues? What this compartmentalization has led us to is a discussion where we are focusing on Social Security and are completely ignoring Medicare. You say to an audience, "Social Security is not the real problem here; Medicare is," and they nod knowingly, "That's right, we shouldn't be doing Social Security; we should focus on Medicare." I don't think that is the right answer. I think Medicare is so much harder than Social Security, and given how poorly the discussion of Social Security is going right now, I am a little worried about even trying to fixing Medicare. This is sort of the warm-up to get people in Congress from different parties talking to each other, which they barely are doing right now.

But what we do know is that the problems with Medicare are a lot larger and are going to take a lot of revenues. So in my mind I would rather not overemphasize the tax increases now for fixing Social Security because we know we are going to have to put more money into Medicare. In fact, I am not too worried about the tax levels in the economy right now. They are well below where they should be to actually pay the bills of our budget. I would rather see taxes go up now. But I don't think we should plan for all of the financing of the retirement of the baby boomers through tax increases because you reach a point where they really are a drain on the economy, and if we were to go forward and pay everything that we promised, we know that we would certainly hit that point.

The second issue is that I am really worried about the way our budget works. We are pre-budgeting more and more of our budget so we are promising today what future people will pay. And that doesn't make sense. If there is one thing we have seen in the past couple of years, you never know what will happen. You never know about things like the new security issues that have come up in the past few years and what the demands on the budget will be down the road. So it worries me to lock ourselves into a system where we have pre-allocated a whole lot of resources, and we don't know if there will be new security needs, if there will be new environmental needs, if there will be other kinds of needs. Say we decided we want to start helping workers that are dislocated from the integrated markets that globalization is leading to; that could be a whole new kind of program we would want to start, and you want to have the resources in your budget to allow you to do that.

Finally, if we err on the side of cutting benefits too much, which is something that people worry about a lot, I don't worry that Congress would be willing to increase benefits. If you think about what Congress likes doing, they like cutting taxes and raising benefits, and they particularly like raising benefits for seniors. I was thinking that I am sitting between the leaders of the two senior citizens' groups, and the memberships of their organizations are a little intimidating when you have a group, The Committee for a Responsible Federal Budget, where I think I have 200 members, and they don't pay dues. So I know that if we make the mistake of under-indexing benefits, if benefits are too low, we will increase them in the future. And if we make the mistake of indexing taxes so that they go up too high, Congress would be happy to cut them in the future. I would rather err on those two sides and let Congress go to Washington and do what is easy, since that seems to be a little more likely for what we will actually see come out of any cooperation.

Finally, I want to talk specifically about one idea on the benefits side that is not getting much attention, but which deserves some conversation, and that is means-testing. In means-testing you would actually reduce the benefits for retirees based on higher levels of income or wealth. Clearly, this is not popular in Congress; again, the only thing that both parties have managed to agree on is that nobody over 55 would be affected by any reforms. And I understand that politically, but I am not sure that is the fairest policy out there. We have known about the problems facing Social Security and Medicare for years and probably decades, and we have continued to kick the can down the road. Saying, "Therefore we are going to grandfather all sorts of people out of the reforms" is really a way to reward that kind of political procrastination.

There are a lot of arguments for wanting to let people have time to make adjustments for the changes that would come from reducing any benefits, but there are some people who don't have the ability to adjust. For low-income workers, all of their money is going to the basic necessities. For 75 percent of families, the payroll tax is already the largest tax that they pay. So I worry about bumping the responsibilities onto that group of people even more. You can choose to cut benefits across the board and across generations, or you can exempt certain groups—and that means that the benefit reduction and/or tax increases have to be higher for other groups. My preference would be to reduce benefits for people who don't need them. So I just throw that out there as an idea that is not a politically popular one, but I think it helps the debate to have different kinds of tradeoffs on the table.

I don't particularly care that the kind of plan that I like is the one that is adopted. Again, just to be clear, a plan that does something on the taxes, something on the benefits, and certainly something on the retirement age makes sense. I like saving all the extra money that we create in private accounts, and I also like matching that saving with an add-on. A hybrid, add-on account, partially from the money that we have to fix the Social Security system, makes sense, but really all I want is to see that something gets done. I think we have an opportunity right now to do something because Social Security is on the political agenda. It would be a real loss if this whole sort of partisan and shrill discussion ends up meaning that we don't do anything, because the one thing we all know is that something has to be done so we can quickly move on and figure out how to fix Medicare.

Any plan that sounds too good to be true really is. We started this discussion off with a lot of people offering tremendous free lunches. We are going to borrow trillions of dollars, create accounts, and then, over time, that is going to fix the system. Won't happen—borrowing money to save money does not work. You can't borrow here and save here and say that you have somehow magically come out ahead. It doesn't work.

It is about tough choices. In the end there are a number of goals for reform that you want to think about. For me, they end up being: How do you protect the people that depend on Social Security? How do you make sure that our budget still allocates resources in a way that is fair and makes sense? Right now the federal government spends about $8 per senior on every $1 that it spends for children, and that ratio is going up. That may be the right ratio—it may even be that we are under-investing. But those are the kinds of choices we have to make. We have to look at the whole budget as a reflection of our national values. We have to look at it holistically and see whether we are really spending the money in the ways that makes the most sense both for today and for the future.

And finally, the third issue is how to make sure that we strengthen the economy while we are fixing Social Security. We can't grow our way out of this problem, but a stronger economy certainly will lessen the burden of paying for the retirement of the large baby boomer population that we know is right around the corner. So I hope that putting these ideas out there is helpful.

The thing that I most would like is that we could end the partisanship that is going on in the debate right now and somehow look to the other countries that we have heard about and see how to have a national discussion that actually moves the ball forward.

John Rother: I wish we could get more people, especially younger people, to tune into this debate. But I also want to recognize AARP members in the crowd—thank you for being here. And for the rest of you, we welcome you when you turn 50, and we know that you are coming, so we are paying attention to all of you.

I am going to say some of the same things that have been said before but maybe from a little different perspective, and that is the perspective not so much of the federal budget but of the family budget of people like you and like me and what this means to them.

To start with, I would like to go back to something I learned in third grade, which is that there are really only two questions in life, and one is "Oh yeah?" and the other is "So what?" For "Oh yeah," I think the point is not an isolated program; Social Security is part of a larger retirement picture that people have to face in terms of their own family economic security. And we should remember some of the things that Ken reminded us of earlier about what is really facing people today. For example, half of the jobs in America today do not have a pension. So how are people supposed to save without a regular payroll deduction mechanism to build for their future? For those who do have retirement savings in the boomer generation, people in the generation closest to retirement, the median level of savings—that means half have more but half have less—is just over $50,000 in retirement savings.

So we have a whole generation, the largest generation in American history, that is completely unprepared financially for what is ahead of them. We know that the average benefit in Social Security today is a little under a $1,000, and as Ken reminded us, it replaces about 40 percent of pre-retirement earnings. But when you start making those deductions and looking into the future, that starts to trail down under the current system without any further changes. We know that in the Medicare program—and let's remember that the Part B premium is deducted from that Social Security check—we are now looking at the third consecutive year of double-digit increases: 17 percent in 2004, probably at least 15 percent this coming year. So that is a grim picture, and I think it is important to keep that in mind as we talk about what changes we want in Social Security, because after all, the bottom line isn't really about solvency. The bottom line is what role we want this program to play in each of our lives, and our children's lives and parents' lives. So we have to really think in a larger context.

There are more goals than just solvency here. There is the goal of adequacy: are we treating everybody fairly? And there is the goal of what is good for us as individuals and for the economy, and that is the issue that Maya just spoke to—how can we increase savings? We aren't saving enough in this country today; we are actually living off the savings of people in China and other underdeveloped countries. They are putting their money into United States treasuries, and we are living off that. How long can that go on? And what is the morality of that? Shouldn't we be self-sufficient? Shouldn't we take care of our own fiscal future without having to depend on other people around the world? So that is the "Oh yeah" part of my answer to this question.

According to the trustees, the gap between what Social Security is likely to bring in and what it is likely to pay out over the next 75 years is 1.92 percent of payroll. That is a lot of dollars, but in terms of percentages, it is really a pretty small gap that we have got to fill. So over the 75-year period, can we afford to meet that gap? Of course we can—1.92 percent of payroll is not a big number.

So why are we having so much trouble here talking about what we need to do and how to do it? That is the second part of my talk today, the "So what" part, and what does this mean for how we go about addressing this issue, what does it mean for politics? Is there a way to get to a solution, given the political dynamic that we are in today? I actually think there is.

We have some successful examples of previous Congresses who stepped up to the plate and took a look at Social Security and made some major adjustments. The most recent was 1983, when they had about the same gap in terms of income and outgo. Congress looked 75 years down the road, and they made some changes. Half of those changes were on the revenue side, and half were on the benefits side. So it was truly a bipartisan solution. You might remember Senator Moynihan, Senator Dole, Claude Pepper, President Reagan—leadership of both parties agreed this was the right thing to do, and you know there was a little pain involved. Benefits were made subject to taxation. The COLA was delayed for six months, and the normal retirement age was increased, but not for a long time. It gave people a lot of time to plan ahead.

Today, the retirement age is going up based on a decision made in 1983, so that is a successful political template for how to get this issue resolved. It has to be bipartisan, it has to be shared between revenue and benefits, and you have to look way down the line and hopefully be very gradual in how you make changes because, after all, retirement is something that people have to plan ahead for way ahead, and you need to give people a chance to make adjustments over a working life. So how do we get this thing fixed? What does each side need to be able to agree to in order to reach a solution?

In my mind there are three things that each side needs. What does the Republican Party need, according to the President, to declare a success? They need to make the program solvent, certainly; number two, they need something in the way of individual accounts; and number three is that there can be no payroll tax rate increase. Does that sound right? That is kind of the bottom line as I see it from the Republican side.

And what do Democrats need to make this acceptable to them? They need a system that maintains adequacy, especially at the low end; they need to have a defined benefit reinforced so that we are not converting over to a system that puts more people at risk; and they don't want to see any additional debt.

So can we get there with those two kinds of bottom lines? Well, of course we can. This is not that hard to solve if it is a mathematical exercise. What makes it hard is the politics and being clear with ourselves about what we want the system to be in the future.

I would say that the way to get this thing solved is to stay with the 12.4 percent of payroll that we have dedicated to Social Security now, and do some things to raise some revenue by expanding the base, not the rate. In other words, lifting the cap up somewhat, maybe adding surtax as a small percentage, and then doing some things on the benefits side as well, which are going to be painful, certainly for AARP to talk about. But we can push those out until they happen later.

We can do things like longevity index benefits, so that if we live longer in the future, individuals would get the same amount of money that you would get before but over a longer period of time. We can adjust bend points in the system. I don't know how many of you know what bend points are, but the system today is progressive so that it pays a higher percentage back to lower income people. There is a formula that governs how that is done, and we could play with that formula a little bit. So contributions would still be related to benefits, but people who have more money and have the opportunity to save more and have the tax breaks to subsidize that saving might get a little bit less, relatively speaking, in benefits. You don't have to means test the system, you don't have to change the character of Social Security, but you do have to make some adjustment to bring some more revenue in and to pay a little less in the way of benefits out compared to the current schedule.

So would that do it? That would keep the system solvent. But what about individual accounts? Here I do think there is reason to talk about individual accounts as additions to Social Security, and there are good policy reasons, including that Americans aren't saving enough for retirement. People don't have pensions. Everyone should have the opportunity to have a payroll deduction system into a tax-favored retirement account. Every American who works should have that opportunity. That is easy to do. We could do that, and it does not cost that much. There are reasons to do it in order to promote savings and to promote individual family financial security. But there are also reasons to do it for the politics, because, as I have said before, for the President to win, he has to have those private accounts. I think the White House would accept private accounts in addition to Social Security as part of a total package.

So we have an answer or pretty close to one sitting in front of us, but no one is going to want to go right to that middle ground immediately. This is politics, and we are all going to go appeal to the bases, and we are going to continue to argue about this. But among the challenges that we face as a country, this is one of the easy ones. It is only money—money coming in and money going out. We can make those adjustments.

The real issue isn't the money, because we are a rich country and we can afford this. The real issue is what future do we want for ourselves, our children, our communities, and our country? What do we want it to look like? That is really the issue.

In conclusion, let me just say that if the questions are "Oh yeah" and "So what," then the "Oh yeah" is that we have to look at this in the broader context. This is not just about keeping a program solvent over 75 years. It is about the economic security of the American people. It is about what future we see for ourselves. And the "So what" is, can we have a solution that makes sense to both Democrats and Republicans so that they can be bipartisan and it can be balanced and can work for the American people? I think it can, but we are going to need your help. I look forward to your questions.

Pam Herd: Tom Saving and Peter Orszag, I am interested in a little bit of discussion from both of you on the implications of private accounts in terms of the insurance portions of Social Security, meaning disability, survivor, spousal benefits. And I know that is a hard question given that there hasn't been a lot of detail presented in many plans about exactly how to do that, but I am interested in what you all feel are some of the options and the implications of different approaches that we might take to deal with those benefits. I think particularly with spousal and survivor benefits, given that 60 percent of women are drawing on benefits as married women, I think it is worth talking about.

For Barbara Kennelly and Stuart Butler, I am interested in hearing both of you talk about more specifics on what compromises do you see in terms of benefit cuts versus tax increases. I probably have a guess about where each one of you might go, but I am curious to hear a little bit specifically about dealing with the fiscal problems with the program, and what balance you think is appropriate.

And for our final two panelists, John Rother and Maya MacGuineas: John Rother said, and I really agree with this, that the budgetary side is of course really easy, it is the political implications that are tricky. So I am interested in hearing both of you present the long-term political implications of any kind of fiscal solutions we make,

such as the long-term political implications of benefit cuts for high-income beneficiaries, and of increasing the wage cap on Social Security. Let's start with Tom Saving
and Peter Orszag.

Tom Saving: All right, let me respond to that because I think those are important
issues. One other thing about women is that when we were on the commission we
had a lot of people looking at the current distribution of retirees and elderly widows.
The issue of the low benefits they get was brought up once today. In one sense that
is a disappearing problem. If you look at the current retired women, they are much
less educated than retired men, and they have much less work history than men, on
average. But if you look at the world now, young women are much more educated
than men, and they are going to have a similar work history to men, and they won't
be retiring on their husband's retirement. That is not going to be happening in the
future, not in the long-run.

That is one part of this issue here, and the second part of it is what do you do
with survivor benefits? The first aspect was spousal benefits, and I think most of these
private account reforms want to give full property rights to spouses and to say that
that is an important aspect of any kind of private account, that is, each spouse should
have a private account even if one of them does not work, so that they have some
ownership in something. I think that is important because under the current system,
if you are a woman married to a man and you don't work for nine years and 364 days,
and you walk out, or you get dumped, you have zero property rights in any benefit
under the current system. And we tried to tackle that in the commission by making
sure that both spouses have equal title to retirement accounts. And I think that is an
important issue that you actually have legal title to your pension benefits.

FDR said in his press conference in 1937 that he put those contributions there
to give the contributors the legal, moral, and political right to their pension benefits.
You have no legal right now because you have a contract with Congress. You can't
change the terms, but they can change the terms of their contract anytime they feel
like it. You are helpless with them because they do what they want to. You wouldn't
sign a contract with any other individual in this room on that basis. So we wanted to
give people real property rights, and spouses in particular, because a lot of people on
the commission felt that was very important.

The second aspect of most of the private account returns is that survivor benefits
is really life insurance, in a sense, and it is declining in value as you age, of course,
because you only get survivor benefits if you have children under the age of 18. But
if you are going to have a real private system, you would have to completely cost that
out. Now the current systems that we are discussing weren't really affecting survivor
benefits nor were they about disability benefits because those were left alone.

In a changed system, you would want to perfectly account for those, as for example, in the Galveston system. They had an opportunity to totally privatize their
system and they did. They have these benefits, but it is still important that they cost

something. If you are going to claim that you have a reform that pays for everything then you have got to make sure that you are paying for the life insurance component and the disability insurance component.

Peter Orszag: First let me just say that the interaction of individual accounts with disability benefits, survivor benefits, and spousal benefits is very complicated. Ken Apfel co-chaired a panel that Maya and I were on that looked at a lot of those questions, and I would say that even a panel of very knowledgeable people had a lot of difficulty grappling with all of the complexities of introducing a system of individual accounts. I will be frank in saying that this has not been fully fleshed out, including by the good work that the commission did.

Let me just mention a couple of things. The President often talks about a spouse being able to inherit an account and that is true—but don't forget that the spouse would also inherit the debt back to Social Security. This really is like investing on margin. You owe a debt back to Social Security, so if your husband or wife passes away, you get the account, but you also get the debt. Let's hope that your spouse was a good investor, because if not, your debt is going to exceed your account, and you will actually wind up worse off—the President doesn't really talk about that piece.

The second thing is that under Social Security, the surviving spouse gets benefits as long as the surviving spouse is alive. That is a very important protection—we talked about how the widow poverty rate would be much higher without those survivors' benefits. The key question is, under an individual account, will the money last as long as the surviving spouse is alive? In order to get that, you would need to require that the account, upon retirement, is transformed in a joint survivor annuity that lasts not only as long as the worker is alive but the survivor is alive. The administration has said that those annuities would be required, but only up to the poverty line. So if you are a middle-class family, and you are used to a particular standard of living, and you have some money in the account and don't have to annuitize a big chunk of it, you may go off and have good time, not really thinking through everything. Or maybe one of you winds up being healthier than you thought, and the other dies earlier, and the survivor could wind up running out of money from the account because it had not been annuitized.

There are also very significant issues with regard to disability benefits. The expectation that you are going to accumulate an account doesn't really work if you become disabled at age 30 or 35. And in fact, under the proposed rules, you would not be allowed to withdraw whatever meager balance you had accumulated in that account if you became disabled at an early age. Furthermore, there are a lot of questions about what would be happening to the disability benefit itself under Social Security. Would those be reduced as part of a solvency plan or not? This is one area where I think the commission was not as straightforward as it should have been in the financial analysis of its plans. It assumed that benefits were significantly reduced, but then it had a statement in the report saying that that was not a policy recommendation—and yet it counted the savings towards restoring solvency.

So disability benefits also raise a series of questions. The model of a single worker reaching retirement and having the account is such an oversimplification. There is so much reality involving people who die before retirement, people who become disabled, surviving spouses, and all of that. It becomes much messier when you look under the hood and start to grapple with the way that the system would work.

And that brings me to my final point, which is that people often look at how complicated Social Security is and throw up their hands and put up an idealized version of what individual accounts would be like—they would be very transparent and simple and clear, and that would be a benefit. I don't know how many of you have ever looked at rules governing IRAs and 401(k)s, but they are incredibly complicated. The non-discrimination rules governing 401(k) plans, for example, are among the hardest section of the tax code. Once you grapple with all the realistic situations that you would need to deal with regarding individual accounts, in order to make sure that they did not end up harming surviving spouses or harming people who became disabled or harming all sorts of vulnerable beneficiaries, you again introduce a lot of that complexity. The complexity comes from real world complications.

Stuart Butler: Barbara and I were challenged to suggest some ways of reaching a compromise. I honestly think that it is quite possible for people of good will to imagine a compromise. A precondition to that is that anybody suggesting a change in any way in the system can't be denounced as dismantling the system. If President Roosevelt came back today and suggested transform the system back into the three-part structure that he first imagined, I'm sorry to say he would be accused by some people of dismantling the Social Security system that he set up. So it is very important to start from the premise that we are all trying to make retirement more secure. And if one does that, as John Rother said, there can be an outline about how one might go forward. I think it is also possible to put a little bit more meat on that outline.

The elements that would be critical would include the following. First, in order to carry out our obligations and recognize the huge fiscal imbalance that is in Social Security, let alone the bigger problem of Medicare, there must be substantial reductions in the promised benefits to upper- and probably middle-income people. I don't think Bill Gates needs Social Security. I don't think millions of Americans really need Social Security. I have been an observer at a number of discussions between people and their financial advisors. And the financial advisors at a point would say, "Oh, of course then you will also have Social Security." It was like, "Oh yeah, I had forgotten about that." People with middle and upper incomes hadn't even thought about that. So I think part of the equation has to be a substantial reduction for some Americans. I think that is absolutely critical, as they don't need Social Security if they have 401(k)s and other savings vehicles.

Second, I think it is essential to recognize the huge problems within the lower-income community associated with saving, wealth creation, and passing on from one generation to another. We need some kind of safe, personal account that allows savings and wealth creation within lower-income communities.

How would you structure that? You could say to the lower-income people, here is this great opportunity—we will match the money that you put into a personal account. As I said, a lot of people have nothing to put into it, so you have to think about how to finance that. That is where these issues of payroll tax and whether you divert tax and so on come in, but it is open to discussion about how one does that. I think it can be done, and it would address a fundamental need to essentially recreate the multi-leg system that President Roosevelt talked about, which has disappeared for lower-income people.

To the extent that any proposal involves any kind of transition to a personal account, we need to have some up-front taxes to pay for at least part of that transition, as opposed to debt financing. I have drawn the analogue—and I know it is not a perfect analogue when looking at these kinds of changes—of refinancing a mortgage. When you refinance a mortgage you aim to reduce your liabilities, or at least your finance charges, over time. Part of the package is an up-front charge. Some people say, "Let's just borrow that, stick it onto the mortgage, and I will pay it over 30 years." That would be like saying, "Let's finance transition in Social Security reform by just borrowing money." But other people say, "I'll write a check for those points." It is quite appropriate to say that a substantial amount of the transition cost has to be "points" in the form of upfront taxes.

But there must be guarantees that the taxes up front do go along with the reforms, including the reduction of benefits for upper-income people. That is why so many people on the conservative side are very leery of arguments like "Let's just raise taxes now to finance some of these changes, and we really will make the changes down the road." We are very concerned that you get the taxes now and you don't get the changes in the future, so there has got to be some assurance there.

In this kind of compromise, the difference between add-on accounts and carve-out accounts is more semantic than real. Without going into detail, I think a deal can be achieved.

I do agree that trimming benefits for upper-income individuals means you have to be concerned about maintaining the political constituency for Social Security. The fact is that the more reforms emphasize raising caps or tax rates and reducing benefits, the less and less it looks like social insurance and the less and less you have solidarity between different income people. So we need to be aware of that. But if you look at those three elements—the substantial changes in benefits for upper-income people, really making sure that lower-income people have some form of assured savings vehicle within the structure of Social Security, and recognizing that there should be some up-front taxes in order to finance any reform in the system—I think we can see a compromise that would work politically.

Barbara Kennelly: Stuart, I am not going to say that I won't use "dismantle" any more, because I sincerely believe that when you have a deficit situation, and you take money out of your Social Security system and put it into personal accounts, it is the beginning of the dismantling of the system. And I know that there are many who have been actively looking at these private accounts for years, and not wanting to have a social insurance system. So I think that debate has to continue to go on.

John Rother has a plan that AARP is working on, and they have thousands of bright people working there, so we are following that very closely. Peter Orszag here has a plan, and Bob Ball, who is the godfather of Social Security, has a plan. There are laundry lists in Washington about what can be done, and they have to be a lot of smaller things because people wouldn't be able to accept a high increase in taxes or a big cut in benefits. I got a kick out of John mentioning bend points—I think Peter is one who can explain to us the bend points, and Ken could too, of course—but I have been studying those for years, and it is just so intricate in Social Security—how you can raise dollars or spend dollars in the accounts.

But, let me just say something about women. I wish I could say down the line everything will be equal, but I have to tell you something. We women live a long time, and that is why we need to have Social Security insurance you can't outlive. The highest quintile of growth in population in the United States, as in many other places, is people over 85 years old. The poorest people in this country, the ones who are having some of the hardest times, are women. One out of five women has only Social Security. What they haven't figured out is how anybody besides us can have babies, and we are the caretakers. I have bright children who went to wonderful colleges and grad schools, but one of them has five kids, and she has had to drop out of the workforce to take care of those children. And women will continue to go in and out of the workforce.

We have seen studies where women are the caretakers of their in-laws. We are often the caretakers—so I just have to say that for women, it is terribly important that we have a Social Security system. As John Rother said earlier, we are not talking about huge amounts of money—the average payment is about $998 for men and $750 for women, so that is not a lot. I really think we can afford that.

And how are we going to have to do it? As I said, I can't do it, I don't have that Ways and Means staff anymore, but your representatives and your senators are going to have to make these decisions, and I hope we all hold them to make it very soon. Look at us all sitting, thinking about Social Security. Now is the time to do it—but they are going to have to make some difficult decisions, there is no doubt about it. And I am just hopeful that they will have the courage to make those decisions, and that we as voters should demand that they make those decisions—but I still am not for private accounts.

Maya MacGuineas: You asked me a different question, but I am going to take a quick moment to respond to the comments that were just made, because I was thinking, as you said, you have four million people, and they each paid $10 to be a member.

That is a $40 million budget, so I was comparing it to my budget. I am sure there is enough in that budget to find staff who would come up with a plan, and I say that only because I think it is so useful for everybody to be willing to put something out there. I don't think it is helpful just to say what is a bad idea. It is very helpful to move the ball forward and say what is a good idea—because none of the choices sounds very good.

But to answer the question you asked me about the long-term political ramifications, I would make the system a lot more progressive, and I would do so by raising payroll tax caps so that high-income earners would pay more into the system. I would also reduce benefits, and I would reduce them a lot more for high-income retirees.

Now there have been some concerns that are voiced pretty regularly. I am a die-hard political independent, so a lot of times in relation to what I think the parties are going to respond to, I am dead wrong. I thought my ideas would be something Republicans were not that friendly to, and Democrats would think, "That makes sense, let's make it more progressive." But it is actually generally a bit of the reverse, where there are a lot of progressives that are kind of worried that changes that make the system more progressive would undermine the political support for it—and that is something that is worth thinking about.

But it is not such a strong argument as to lead me to support regressive policies. The payroll tax is regressive; you know I am not going to want all benefits to be more progressive. Since people have to sacrifice, it is better to have those who sacrifice be people who can afford to than people who can't. So I don't worry so much that this leads to the undermining of the support of the system. Actually, what it does is let future people make choices about their own budget.

We shouldn't decide today what the budget should look like ten years from now. I have to trust Congress and the public in the future to know that for themselves, based on the fact that they are just as able as we are to figure out the right way to guide the country. More importantly, they will have very different conditions. So I want to leave the budget flexibility there for them. What I really see in the long-term political ramifications of scaling back benefits for people that don't need them is a freeing up of resources in the budget that will allow us to meet a lot of the unmet needs that are there.

Again, I don't necessarily think that the budget looks the way it should—I look at the budget and think we are doing a lot of under-investing in this country. There are so many areas, from education to basic infrastructure to research, that are being squeezed out of the budget as our entitlement programs grow larger and larger and our domestic discretionary spending, where so much of the investment takes place, grows smaller and smaller. I would like to leave more resources available so that in the future we can decide where that dollar goes. I think giving people political freedom over their own budget is the right thing to do.

John Rother: I want to speak to "the ownership society." Has everybody heard that phrase? There is a lot more to this debate than just how to fix the program. Part of the debate is really about political realignment, or at least an effort to get political realignment, and that is by taking a program that is a very successful program but clearly a government program and trying to move people away from that toward more of a market orientation.

So the ownership society, in part at least, is a very conscious effort to move people and their focus of attention away from government and toward the performance of investments. The theory is that once that happens, those people will then be Republicans and that they will vote that way for the rest of their lives. The data behind that is kind of soft, but there is some element of truth to it. So that is certainly a very conscious political aim that underlies this debate.

Now on the other side, if we would do what many of us are recommending, we would eliminate poverty at old age in America, and we could eliminate it very quickly, and that is a tremendous social accomplishment. The question is, who would get the credit for that? Would that be seen as a Democratic accomplishment? Or, if Bush were to sign this into law, would that be seen as a Republican accomplishment? Or does anyone care who gets credit for it? Can we just all acknowledge that that would be the right thing to do?

Another question is that if we make—and it is inevitable that we will make—the benefit more progressive, and we ask people with higher incomes to pay more, what is the political risk of that? Several of us have mentioned that there is a political risk that people who have more will no longer see Social Security as for them. That is a question that goes to whether we are a mature country or not, and whether we understand that this is not an investment program and that we do not measure the worth of the program in terms of whether you get a return on it. It is really an expression of community and your responsibility as a citizen who did very well to help assure that there is a standard of decency for everyone else in your community.

Now my saying that does not count for very much, but the question is, how would people feel about it if we went this direction and people who had more paid in more were reminded that they did not get a good return on their investments? But I didn't get a good return on my fire insurance last year—or maybe I feel that I didn't get a good return on the taxes that went to pay for wars and other things. It is a serious question of how do we gauge the worth of this program. Do we measure it in terms of investment return? Or do we measure it in terms of other social accomplishments? All of those questions are very much up in the air, and how they get resolved will then tell us what the political implications are for the future.

Pam Herd: Let's take some questions from the audience.

Audience Member: Thank you for the presentation. I like your comments about the community and thinking about it in those terms, perhaps giving back to the community if those people that have a higher income would pay more. I understand that it has to be fixed and I have been pondering why. I could not understand, because you can do your own individual 401(k)s, your own private plans. I finally found an article that says one reason why the current administration seems to be pushing for this. It is in *Harper's* magazine, and it is called "The $4.7 Trillion Pyramid"—below the title it says, "Why Social Security won't be enough to save Wall Street." Basically what it says is that the administration hopes to create a Wall Street bubble, which will probably help for the short term, but not for the long term. So I'll give this to Peter because it was written by an economist.

Peter Orszag: Thank you. Let me say there have been a lot of comments on this, and I actually do not think that bailing out Wall Street or trying to artificially influence stock market prices are important motivations for the administration economists that I know or for most of the administration officials. They don't call me that much, but when they do, they are not talking about that. I think, instead, it probably has more to do with other considerations that you have already heard about—things like the argument that Maya made that it is a way to try to save some of the funds, although I think there are analytical problems with that argument. But, I think that they believe in individual control and that way of looking at the world, and they are less motivated by bailing out financial firms, and you can actually see that in the design of the plan.

The plan is actually—I hate to say it—a big government plan. The plan would have the accounts administered by a government entity, just as is done in Sweden. The government would be choosing the index funds that you would be allowed to invest in. The government would be maintaining the records associated with the accounts. This plan, as proposed, would farm out only the investment management piece—the index funds themselves—to private firms. According to most of the estimates, there would be a very significant expansion of government bureaucracy to run the accounts; we are talking tens of thousands of new government workers—a significant expansion. Given that proposal, it is kind of hard to jive that with the thought that the main motivation here is some Wall Street one, so I think it probably isn't.

Audience Member: Thank you for this very interesting discussion. One thing that has not been mentioned much is broadening the base. Someone said that the way to do that was to remove the caps on the contributions. I was wondering, aren't there people who are not included within the Social Security system? I am particularly thinking of local governments and municipalities, school districts, people who somehow along the way have been exempted from being in the Social Security system. If we included everyone, wouldn't that help the system, or would that increase the problem? That is one question. The other is, would it not help increase or broaden our base if we raised the minimum wage and had more jobs for people to participate in the system and contribute more and pay more for Social Security?

Tom Saving: There is no marketing with an S&P index fund. Well, Fidelity is already marketing and it is 10 basis points total.

Peter Orszag: It is true that the administrative costs can remain low as long as the government, what the administration calls a "central administrative authority," is doing all of the inter-mediation and all the record-keeping and all of that. I don't know how people would respond in this room, but that is not going over very well with the American public. There are concerns about having the government play that role. If you move out of having the government play the role, then the advertising costs increase. We know from the United Kingdom and Chile too, for example, that as soon as you get private financial firms into the role and you have a decentralized system of accounts, the advertising costs, marketing costs, and administrative costs skyrocket. So it is correct that you can design a low-cost system, but it has a low number of funds, and it is centrally administered, and the government is at the heart of it.

Stuart Butler: I think that a government-managed system like that could be the basis of reform.

Tom Saving: The Fidelity index funds are not run by the government.

Pam Herd: Let's take one more question.

Audience Member: I am president of the Summit Oaks chapter of AARP. I am excited about being here for two reasons. One is my daughter is a graduate of the LBJ School, and the second is this is really a good panel. I have to congratulate you for having this panel. I'd like two things, one is I would like people on both sides to admit when someone says something and it is a crock. We need a "truth in crocks committee" and once we get rid of the crocks we go back to dealing with what we really need to deal with, which all of you are saying we need to do.

I happen to be very fortunate. I am an example of Social Security plus a private retirement account. I haven't retired yet, but I saw a drop between 1999 and 2001 of 38 percent in my 401(k)-type plan. If a person does not have the stability of Social Security as an insurance policy, and if they were expecting to retire in two years or the next five years, their plan wouldn't be back to where is was supposed to be. So I am totally supportive of Social Security stabilized, and the solvency of Social Security, and an effort bring on 401(k)s starting with people when they first start work.

So sitting here listening to you, I spontaneously came up with this. We all know that the minimum wage has not increased in a long time. It is a failure of Congress for many years, I would suggest, and in an expansion of what was stated, if you have the government decide that every three or four years it is going to raise the minimum wage for the next 40 years, business will know what is coming and out of that dollar take the 12.6 percent and put it in Social Security as it is now, the same tax rate from business as from the person. Actually it would only be 6.2 from the person, split the remainder, and 50 percent goes into an add-on retirement account, privatized, and the other half goes to the person. They don't lose, and we start at a young age, the most important age, to put mandatory money away—50 cents for 2080 hours is $1,000 a year that goes into an add-on private retirement account. In Texas we happen to have a state-run, administered system that has a few plans that you can invest in. The federal government can leave it up to states to do that, but you have mandatory contributions by the worker towards the worker's future privatized account, and they still get an increase in their minimum wage, and this happens every three or four years.

Peter Orszag: I think the basic concept is the right one. The evidence strongly shows that people are more willing to save out of increases in their pay, because you don't miss what you never had, but in terms of the specific proposal we may need to talk a little bit more. I am not sure it is actually practical to think that we are going to know exactly which workers were earning the minimum last year and will be earning it this year so we know that out of that increase we have to take a certain share out. But I think the basic concept of doing that kind of thing, maybe not that specific thing, but that kind of thing is exactly one of the directions that we should be moving in.

Part III

Civic Dialogue and Deliberation: What the Public Has to Say

Chapter 4

Big Choices: The Practice and Potential for Public Deliberation

by Taylor L. Willingham and Vanessa L. Davis

At the heart of the Big Choices facing the U.S. is the need for a public voice on the issues. Aside from elections, polling is the most common method of finding what the public thinks on any particular issue. But polls are often inadequate in that they represent what people think when confronted with a particular question, phrased in a particular way. A more useful, if less common, way of seeking public opinion is to ask, "What would people think if they were informed about the issues and had the chance to speak with other citizens about the advantages and disadvantages of different options?" This kind of interaction is known as "deliberation."

Deliberation is based on the premise that when people have a way to come together to talk about divisive issues, they can make sound decisions based on shared values. When citizens deliberate, they recognize their own and others' assumptions, acknowledge the validity of diverse perspectives, learn about the costs and consequences of public policy alternatives, move from "I" to "we" language, and define their shared interests and values.[1]

In order to engage in deliberation with others, people need to see the issue named and framed in terms that resonate with them—a reflection of their hopes, concerns and way of thinking about the issue. This is often different from the way the issues are characterized by the media, policymakers, and experts.

How Deliberation Differs from Other Forms of Public Discussion

Most opportunities for public discussion promote a "sound bite" approach that often further divides people with diverse perspectives. Media commentary, attuned to the standards of spectacle and diversion, is typically confrontational and ideological, consisting of exchanges among people who have already made up their minds. Media accounts tend to focus on personalities and not issues.[2]

In public hearings, for another example, comments usually consist of one-sided advocacy statements of an individual's position before a governing or public policy-making authority.

A third example of public conversation—formal debates—can provide the public with an opportunity to compare and contrast different views, but they do not help us explore common concerns or think together about how *we* as a public might act together to solve public problems.

Typical conversations among trusted friends, family members, and professional colleagues is a step toward an authentic conversation. However, these conversations may simply reinforce our own perspectives. Our professional and social networks are usually composed of like-minded individuals or at least individuals with similar interests and/or common experiences. These conversations lack the rich complexity of public deliberation because diverse perspectives may not be fairly represented within our existing social and professional circles. Public policy based solely on the outcomes of a conversation among like-minded individuals is bound to fail or at a minimum to have adverse effects on large populations not represented in the conversation.

In contrast, deliberation requires participants to weigh the consequences and costs of various options based on what is truly valuable. This kind of interchange helps citizens fully understand the implications of their own opinions—how they would affect others who may have life experiences very different from their own.

What is most valuable about these conversations is what they reveal about the struggles that citizens go through as they sort out the trade-offs and consequences of pursuing one option over another.

Framing the Issues

Using the methodology pioneered by the National Issues Forums Institute, Texas Forums[3] members created a framework for the Social Security issue using the following criteria:

- The issue must be named and framed in terms that reflect how people are experiencing the issue.

- The framework must propose various alternatives that do not allow the participants to resort to deeply entrenched and divisive positions.

- There must be more than two approaches (otherwise a debate will ensue), but usually no more than four approaches in order to keep the approaches and the conversation manageable.

- Each of the approaches must have elements that are appealing to the participants as well as potential trade-offs that might be unacceptable.

• The approaches are not mutually exclusive. The participants, through deliberation, may select actions within the approaches that are acceptable. At the same time they may determine possible outcomes that are not acceptable based on what they heard from heard in their interviews with stakeholders. The framework helps participants to talk through the "gray" aspects of the issue and narrow the range of options for moving forward together.

• The framing captures the most fundamental concerns behind the way people see the problem. In other words, everyone can see themselves in the approaches that they are asked to consider.

The framework was constructed with hope that it could be useful for any group that wished to create a deliberative dialogue on the big choices we all face in relation to Social Security.

Notes

1. Nancy Kranich, Michele Reid, and Taylor Willingham, "Civic Engagement and Academic Libraries," *College and Research Libraries News,* vol. 65, no. 7, July/August 2004.

2. Keith Melville, Taylor Willingham, and John Dedrick, "Different Approaches to Conducting National Issues Forums," in *The Deliberative Democracy Handbook: Strategies for Effective Civic Engagement in the Twenty-First Century,* ed. John Gastil and Peter Levine (San Francisco: Jossey Bass, forthcoming).

3. An initiative of the LBJ Library to train citizens in techniques of deliberation and to provide a support system for deliberative dialogues. See http://www.texasforums.org for more information.

Chapter 5

Framing the Issues for Public Discussion: Three Options for Social Security Reform

The Future of Social Security: How Can We Ensure Financial Security for Older Americans?

Social Security Overview

The Social Security Act of 1935 created a program to provide modest lifetime payments to retired workers. When it was passed, many elderly Americans had little financial security, and the nation was still recovering from the Great Depression. Upon signing the Act, President Roosevelt commented, "We have tried to frame a law which will give some measure of protection . . . against poverty-ridden old age."

Social Security is supported by a dedicated tax on the wages of current workers. In exchange, younger workers are entitled to receive retirement benefits based in part on the amount that they have paid in payroll taxes. It is an intergenerational agreement and a nearly universal retirement program. Almost all people aged 65 and over receive benefits and for a third of them, Social Security is virtually their only source of retirement. Because almost all workers contribute to Social Security and because it is a separate payroll tax, it has been regarded as an earned benefit, resulting in broad and continued support.

Some question whether we can afford to continue to support Social Security as it is currently structured and whether a program designed in 1935 is still appropriate in 2005.

When the first Social Security checks were paid out, many workers supported each retiree. With fewer workers and more retirees, it now takes three workers to support one retiree's benefits. This requires that current workers and employers each pay a 6.2 percent payroll tax, compared to the 1 percent workers contributed when the program began.

Note: This chapter was originally published in a pamphlet given to participants in the deliberative forums in order to frame the issues for discussion.

In 2008 the first wave of baby-boom retirees will be eligible for benefits, further stretching the current system. And these retirees are living longer, with an estimated retirement life of nearly two decades.

Although this discussion is about how to sustain Social Security as the influx of baby-boomers causes its cost to soar, it is also about questions of principle and purpose. In a highly charged debate, it is easy to get lost in the details and technicalities of Social Security, but our public discussions need to begin in a different place. We need to start first with conversations about principles and purpose. Who is this program for? What are our social obligations and our personal responsibilities to older Americans? Only then can we consider whether or not Social Security as it was conceived in 1935 is still relevant and the best way to ensure financial security for older Americans.

Option 1. Reaffirming Social Security: The Promise of Protection

Diagnosis of the situation and what should be done
Social security is a commitment to a common good and a promise to working Americans and retirees that we must keep. It took decades to fulfill the promise of income security for retirees. Social security is an American success story. In 1959, the poverty rate for people 65 and older was 35 percent. Forty years later, the poverty rate was less than 10 percent. Social security also provides a safety net for those unable to work: disabled persons, widows, children, and other relatives of deceased workers.

Few Americans—only 21 percent versus 40 percent back in 1980—have employer retirement benefits, and many are just a step away from great financial risk. About 65 percent of all beneficiaries depend on Social Security for more than half of their total income, and it is virtually the only source of retirement income for a third of all people. According to advocates of this approach, social security should and could be continued with minor adjustments such as higher payroll taxes and raising the income level eligible for payroll taxes.

What are the potential costs and consequences?
A growing elderly population will require more funds, but critics of this approach are concerned that our current course will impose a crushing burden on the young. Since Social Security pays benefits to Americans at all income levels, regardless of need, people living quite comfortably receive monthly checks paid for by taxes on current workers who are struggling. Maintaining current benefits is like making an expensive purchase on a credit card that the next generation will have to pay.

As Social Security benefits have become more generous, personal savings for retirement accounts have declined. Critics of the current system want individuals to take greater personal responsibility for their own financial security. Otherwise, young workers will have to shoulder larger financial burdens or other necessary public projects and expenses may go unfunded.

What do you think?

• How do we balance the increased cost to support a growing elderly population with other priorities?

• Do we have an obligation to continue the promise of Social Security through higher taxes, or should we consider alternative ways to support elderly Americans?

Option 2. Reconstructing Social Security: The Case for Personal Accounts

Diagnosis of the situation and what should be done

This approach asserts that the nation needs a retirement financing system that emphasizes personal accountability and freedom of choice. Individuals should decide how they invest their earnings to pay for their retirement. Under a partial privatization plan, employees could self-manage a portion of their payroll taxes in a private investment account. Each dollar put into a personal account would reduce the employee's claim to future Social Security benefits. Furthermore, any money in a personal account not used in retirement would be passed on to the retiree's heirs.

Advocates of private accounts want to transform the retirement system so that all Americans can reap the same benefits that current stockholders enjoy. Those who promote personal accounts are convinced that ownership has the power to transform people. This measure would encourage people to invest in personal savings, it would increase social mobility, and it would give people more control over their future income.

What are the potential costs and consequences?

Payroll taxes collected today are necessary to pay for current Social Security benefits. Diverting a portion of these funds away from Social Security and into personal accounts will result in a shortfall. This would require the federal government to borrow billions of dollars in the early phase of this plan to cover the existing commitments to retirees, an expensive proposition.

Critics are particularly concerned about the investment risk associated with private investment. There is no guarantee that the money invested in private accounts will have a positive return. This approach assumes that people are knowledgeable enough to make wise choices about complicated investment options. Furthermore, steep and extended stock market declines could reduce an investment portfolio. People who live into their 80s and 90s might live beyond the payout of their private accounts. Social Security at least guarantees a base minimum for life.

What do you think?

• Why shouldn't individuals be given more choices to save and invest for their own retirement?

• What should be done for individuals who make poor investment decisions or live beyond the payout of their investment?

Option 3. Renewing Social Security: Revising the Contract for a New Generation

Diagnosis of the situation and what should be done

Current Social Security policies are based on a previous generation that does not reflect today's realities. The creators of Social Security could not predict how different the last quarter of life is today compared to 70 years ago. Today, an ever-vigorous senior population spends their "golden years" living a life resembling an extended vacation or they continue working. One third of all men and one quarter of all women 65-69 continue working in gainful employment. People are more active in their senior years, and their senior years last longer.

In 1935, the life expectancy was only 61.7 years, and you were lucky to reach 65. Today, someone who is 65 can expect to live to 82 years of age and collect Social Security for 17 years. In addition, $15 billion Social Security dollars are paid to households with retirement incomes of more than $100,000. Advocates of this approach believe we should adjust the retirement age to reflect the longer, healthier life span we enjoy and target benefits to those who need them most.

What are the potential costs and consequences?

Many older Americans have to continue to work because of pension plans that did not deliver as promised or to get medical coverage. It is unreasonable and even dangerous to expect all Americans to continue working late in life, particularly those who work in low-income, physically demanding jobs.

Increasing the retirement age would shortchange older Americans. Compared to other wealthy nations, the United States has one of the highest eligibility ages for public pensions. Wage earners pay taxes over a 35-year career, expecting a return that will enable them to retire at a reasonable age and enjoy years of travel and leisure. This is a reasonable expectation Social Security should continue to support.

What do you think?

• Is it reasonable to expect someone to continue working later in life just because we are enjoying a longer life span?

• What would be the impact of changing the payout of Social Security to target those most in need?

Chapter 6
Social Security:
A Deliberative Dialogue

by Taylor L. Willingham

This is a summary of the deliberative discussions held at the Big Choices Symposium on Social Security held on April 21, 2005. The outcomes of these forums are examples of how citizens talk and think about a complex issue such as Social Security when they have an opportunity to deliberate various public policy options and to test the potential outcomes of those options against their deeply held values.

Participants
Deliberative forums challenge participants with diverse perspectives to explore their different experiences with others in order to uncover potential areas of common ground. A key requirement for this type of deliberative dialogue is that participants feel safe to discuss their deepest concerns. Ideally, participants in a deliberative dialogue would comprise a representative sample of the population.

But for most forum conveners, achieving that level of representative diversity is time-consuming, cost-prohibitive, and impractical. Given the age-related issues arising from Social Security, the Big Choices project chose to focus its resources on recruiting dialogue participants from various age groups, including those from UT's continuing education programs for seniors, the young professionals comprising the LBJ Library's Future Forum program, and UT students.

At the evening dialogue session, participants were randomly assigned to discussion tables to maximize diversity of age, ethnicity, and gender. There were eight small groups ranging in size from 6-11 participants—large enough to include different ages, but small enough to ensure adequate opportunity for everyone to participate. Each group was comprised of students, Social Security beneficiaries, and young professionals.

Moderators and Recorders
Each group was moderated and recorded by volunteers from the LBJ Library Texas

Forums network. These volunteers had each completed a two-day training session during which they had learned the theory that supports deliberation as well as practical skills in moderating, recording, and reporting on a deliberative forum.

The Forum Process

During the planning time of the Big Choices Social Security symposium, the symposium organizers learned that the National Issues Forums Institute (NIFI) was developing a 32-page discussion guide based on three different approaches to social security:

• Reaffirming Social Security: The Promise of Protection

• Reconstructing Social Security: The Case for Personal Accounts

• Renewing Social Security: Revising the Contract for a New Generation

Working closely with the author of the NIFI discussion guide, members of the Texas Forums network distilled the three approaches in the draft issue book into a tri-fold brochure. The information that Texas Forums presented for each approach included a brief diagnosis of the situation and what should be done from that approach's perspective; potential arguments against the approach; and a compelling question to stimulate conversation about the potential trade-offs, benefits, and consequences of the approach. Because the forums took place prior to the completion of the NIFI issue book, the results of these forums provided valuable feedback to the NIFI author about what worked and what aspects of the approach were difficult to understand.

In opening the forums, the table moderators invited participants to share a personal story or experience that illustrated why the topic of Social Security is important to them. Sometimes referred to as the "ice-breaker stage of the forum," these stories reminded the participants that they were not simply engaged in an intellectual discussion, but were undertaking a deliberation about an issue that deeply touches people. Stories build empathy and lay the groundwork for the group to work together.

The forums then moved into the deliberation phase, exploring the benefits and costs of each approach and the underlying values that motivate the participants to hold a particular perspective regarding that approach.

At the debriefing, participants were asked to reflect on the elements that should frame decisions about Social Security—for example, their group's common themes, overriding concerns, unacceptable outcomes, and deeply held values. Representatives from the various groups came forward to report on the common themes or public voice that emerged from their individual forums. They were specifically charged to report on the criteria they thought should drive how decisions about the future of social security are made.

What the Participants Said—Summary Notes

Participants were adamant that Social Security should be preserved, but were willing to be flexible and explore minor changes to the system. Social Security is not a substitute for retirement savings, but should be seen as a supplement.

While some people were concerned that the working poor are paying into a system that is benefiting wealthier retirees, participants were concerned that allowing people to opt out of the system could weaken support for it. Several participants expressed a willingness to accept trade-offs in order to preserve the current system—those with higher incomes were willing to pay more in and take less out.

Raising the age of retirement was an option participants were willing to explore, but they wanted to preserve the individual's right to choose their own retirement age and were concerned that forcing the retirement age upwards would unduly impact laborers.

Incentives to increase personal savings were well-received, but participants were concerned that personal accounts were impractical for lower wage earners and the majority of people who are not knowledgeable about how to manage their own investments.

The continued commitment to Social Security elicited the most passion and support among the participants. Young people who were skeptical that they would reap the benefits of Social Security and the elderly who were concerned about the undue hardship being imposed on young people were united in wanting to preserve Social Security, despite some of the challenges to the current system. But the participants, through their deliberation, did entertain possible changes to the Social Security system, provided those changes did not violate core values and priorities.

Understanding the reasons behind the widespread support for Social Security and the areas where people are willing to be flexible can provide a framework for understanding what courses of action might be supported by participants. This report will focus on the common themes and stated values that resulted from these deliberations.

Common Themes

1. Social Security is a Safety Net

Participants pointed with great pride to the role of Social Security in reducing poverty among the elderly and women. They even referred to Social Security as a great American success story. But several people said that Americans need to be educated about the role of Social Security as a safety net or supplement to personal savings for retirement, not a substitute for retirement savings.

Surprisingly, the loss of employer-provided pension plans for retirees did not generate the level of interest anticipated by the framers of the issue. This may speak more to the nature of the participants and the dominant industries in Austin rather than the importance of this growing shift away from employer-provided plans. Many of the younger forum participants are part of the new economy in which an individual may hold numerous short-term jobs with little possibility of employer-provided retirement, while many of the older participants expressed that they were well-situated for retirement. It was only briefly mentioned in one group when a retiree from IBM reflected on how the corporate world is changing in terms of the support that it gives to retirees.

2. Social Security is a Community Responsibility

The value of community—something we are all in together—came out very strongly in this first approach. From the perspective of many participants, "we are supporting a community and in a community, everyone has a responsibility to help the other community members." To many, Social Security is a compassionate requirement society must provide to its older citizens. They were particularly proud that Social Security is a system that everyone pays for.

Even those who might not have entered into the conversation with this perspective came to appreciate Social Security as a contribution to the common good. As one woman said, "When I came in here, I didn't think of Social Security as anything more than a retirement plan. Now I think of it as a community good."

3. Ensure Human Dignity

The issue of dignity echoed in every small group forum. Participants repeatedly advocated a basic level of comfort above poverty for all elderly Americans. Social Security is the insurance that guarantees dignity without want, essentially providing for the neediest in our society. A commonly held notion was that "no one should have to choose between filling their prescriptions and buying food." To say that this commitment to human dignity was unconditional may not be completely accurate because it was never tested. But the issue of whether or not to withhold support for any circumstance was never discussed. Even when discussing the second approach and the possibility that private accounts can go bust, leaving retirees without the requisite nest egg for survival, participants agreed that it is the responsibility of society to take care of them in old age.

4. Encourage Individual Saving for Retirement, but not as a Replacement for Social Security

Several participants spoke with dismay about the lack of savings in this country and were attracted by incentives to increase saving. Participants were attracted to the possibility that private accounts would encourage savings and personal responsibility.

But the appeal of private accounts lost luster when participants realized that personal accounts would enable people to opt out of a public system into a private system and violate the value of Social Security as a community responsibility. There was grave concern with the proposition that Social Security and private accounts would be an "either/or" system.

Even those who support private accounts admitted that they have been successful as investors, but were concerned about how dismantling Social Security would affect other people—people of low income, few resources for investment, and elderly grandparents who have taken on the responsibility of raising their grandchildren. As noted in the first approach, participants were attracted to the Social Security as safety net. Several people noted that no one should expect to get rich off of Social Security, but they should expect that it would prevent them from becoming destitute.

5. Educate, Educate, Educate

In discussing personal accounts, one major theme was the need for better education about finances. Personal responsibility was an attraction, but everyone agreed that it cannot be achieved without a better understanding of how to save, how to plan, how much is required for retirement, how to understand risk, and how to secure an income. Preparing young people to take personal financial responsibility for their future was perceived as an important first step.

6. Preserve Choice, Provide Opportunity

The issue of whether or not to change the contract by raising the retirement age was unresolved, but participants clearly did not want to mandate an increase for everyone without full consideration of the impact. The drawbacks that they noted included the impact it would have on volunteerism, and the impracticality of expecting someone in heavy labor and other physically demanding jobs to continue working. On the other hand, some people were willing to continue working until age 70, but wanted to preserve their right to make that choice for themselves, and they wanted to be supported in that decision. One group noted ironically that many companies encourage early retirement because aging employees are often seen as liability. One gentleman was frustrated that he was laid off at age 50 and was unable to find work because companies do not want to hire older workers. Companies see older workers as expensive because they may have greater health needs and problems that will drive up insurance costs.

Concluding Thoughts

Deliberation produces thoughtful acknowledgement of the difficult choices we face as a public and the possibility of new relationships, or, at a minimum, a new understanding about the reason for our differences and a willingness to continue to engage with each other. Keeping people at the table talking, despite their differences, is no small feat, and its benefits should not be underestimated. In fact, people also spoke of a desire to engage with others who hold different perspectives because that level of engagement was seen as a means to long-term, publicly supported solutions.

Throughout the forums on Social Security, participants articulated the criteria they would like to see used in making in our Social Security system. And they talked about the tensions inherent in decisions about how to encourage personal savings while preserving the commitment to the community good that Social Security engenders. They were willing to explore an increase in the retirement age, but not to mandate it for everyone.

No single forum can fully resolve the kind of complex problems that require public deliberation. But when people begin to see themselves as political actors working with others to find common ground, new possibilities emerge. The charge is to continue the deliberation, to continue to explore the areas of complexity and uncertainty, and to make difficult decisions together that can lead to sustainable action.

Part IV

Policy Alternatives: Additional Resources

Chapter 7
Background

Income Security for Older Americans: Assessing Social Security's Past, Present, and Future

by Kenneth S. Apfel and Lindsay Littlefield

This book addresses the future of what is perhaps America's single most important social program. It is hard to overstate the importance of Social Security, which provides a foundation of financial support for about one in six Americans, with benefit protections available over a lifetime. Our social insurance system is critically important not only for older Americans, but also for the disabled, survivors of deceased workers, and families.

Changes need to be made to our retirement system, given the aging of America. What does the future hold for Social Security? The future, in some ways, is in our hands. Ideally, an educated citizenry will help to shape the debate, with any changes made to the system reflecting the shared values of the American people.

To help the reader put the future Social Security challenge in context, this chapter begins with a discussion of the past. Why did we establish such a system and how has it evolved? What is the importance of Social Security today, and how does it fit in with the other components of retirement security? What are the dimensions of the challenge confronting the system and what are the key reform approaches? This chapter briefly frames all of these issues in order to set the stage for the balance of the book.

Social Security's Evolution

Income insecurity in old age existed long before the adoption of Social Security in 1935. Prior to 1935, older Americans not in the workforce relied primarily on familial support, though some found very limited support from private and public pensions as they emerged in the years following the Civil War. As the Great Depression and burgeoning social movements drew national attention to the income insecurity of the elderly, a window of opportunity emerged for President Franklin D. Roosevelt to propose a series of programs including a new social insurance program for the elderly. Social Security—even to this day—is very similar in intent and structure to the vision articulated by FDR in the 1930s.

Assistance in Retirement Prior to Social Security

Throughout early U.S. history, fears of destitution kept much of the aging population in the workforce or forced them to rely on the support of families. When pensions began to emerge in both the public and private sectors, certain groups benefited but coverage was very limited.[1]

Historically, family members provided the primary physical, economic, and social support for the elderly. Many elderly continued to work as long as they were able to avoid destitution.[2] Over 60 percent of men over age 65 were employed in 1900 and those unable to work relied on help from their children and other relatives.[3] Of those over age 65 in 1900, 16 percent of men and 34 percent of women lived in one of their children's households.[4]

Because the burden of supporting the elderly was primarily left to families, the problem of income security in old age was largely defined as a private matter. What little relief available was provided at the local level. Relief was inconsistent and based on English poor laws. Poorhouses (also known as workhouses) were the last safety net for the elderly, providing minimal support for about 2 percent of the elderly population,[5] though their use increased in the early 1930s.[6]

Private pension coverage was almost nonexistent until the 20th century. By 1900, only five major companies offered private plans, covering about 2 percent of the population.[7] By 1920, fewer than 5 percent of Americans had pension coverage.[8] Despite this, over the next several decades, especially after Social Security's passage, private pension plans became more common. The population covered by private pensions increased from 6 percent to 20 percent in the 15 years following Social Security's passage in 1935.[9]

Public support for certain constituencies also emerged in the post-Civil War era. In 1862, the federal government created a Civil War pension system administered to wounded soldiers and their dependents. Through a series of expansions in coverage, by 1910, 93 percent of Civil War veterans in the North and 25 percent of the total elderly population received limited benefits through this program.[10]

Other groups benefited from public pensions as well, including limited numbers of single mothers, the blind and disabled, and some elderly. "Mothers pensions" appeared in the Progressive Era to support single mothers, but benefits only covered about 50,000 women and were modest in size. At the state level, pensions were provided to the blind and disabled in 20 states, though the level of benefits varied.[11] Old-age pensions were available in 17 states in 1932, and by 1935, 30 states provided small benefits to about 3 percent of the elderly population.[12] The sizes of these benefits were modest, at $0.65 per day.[13]

Conditions Leading to Social Security's Passage

Social Security's passage occurred in the midst of the Great Depression, a time in which unemployment soared to 25 percent. Dire financial conditions existed for many, including older workers and retirees. The traditional supports for the elderly—primarily families and very limited employer and local supports—were clearly inadequate. In 1935, half of the elderly were poor and that number reached two-thirds by 1940.[14]

The dire economic conditions of the time spawned several social movements promoting dramatic changes in governmental economic assistance. Father Coughlin and his National Union for Social Justice argued for a living wage, greater unionization, and changes to the tax code and banking systems.[15] Huey Long's "Share Our Wealth" movement supported a guaranteed annual income of $5,000 for all families.[16] Dr. Francis E. Townsend also gained a large national following with his plan to provide a $200 monthly minimum pension to retirees, provided that they spent the sum within a month to revitalize the ailing economy.[17] Although far to the left of Roosevelt's vision for a social insurance program, the messages of these individuals and groups resonated with the American public and prepared the nation for an expanded federal government role in economic security.

Shortly after his election, President Roosevelt sought to implement a host of social programs to relieve the worst effects of the Depression and made Social Security a focal point in that strategy. In his inaugural address in 1933, Roosevelt asked the public for "as great as the power that would be given me if we were in fact invaded by a foreign foe."[18] In June 1934, the Committee on Economic Security, a five-person committee chaired by Labor Secretary Frances Perkins formed to provide recommendations to improve the nation's economy. The committee's recommendations supported Roosevelt's plan for pensions for retirees funded through a social insurance program that provided retirees with public benefits in retirement.

Representatives Doughton and Lewis and Senator Wagner introduced President Roosevelt's Social Security legislation in 1935. There were several potential threats to the bill's passage including the constitutionality of a federal social insurance program.[19] Congressional debates centered on the program's scope and the universal nature of the program. Treasury Secretary Henry Morgenthau and others testified that covering some groups of workers, such as domestic and agricultural workers, would be difficult administratively and cost-prohibitive.[20] The final legislation excluded not only these categories of workers but also many others, including the self-employed and non-profit workers. In addition, state and local employees were not required to participate in the system, which pre-empted a tenth amendment court challenge based on concerns about the federal government taxing state governments.[21]

A major attempt to modify the legislation was an amendment offered by Senator Joel Bennett Clark that would have enabled businesses with over 50 employees to opt out of Social Security as long as they operated private pension plans. The Clark Amendment, had it passed, would have dramatically affected the scope of Social

Security protections. Critics of the amendment argued that enabling companies to opt out of the national system would prevent the program from being financially viable because companies and workers left behind in the federal system would effectively create a pool of the "worst risks." Another concern was that in the absence of a universal system, individuals who moved or transferred jobs would lose benefits from former employers, increasing the risk of vulnerability in retirement. Opponents also charged that the Clark Amendment enabled abuse of the system; companies could create complicated eligibility rules such that no employees qualified for or actually received benefits. Though the amendment passed on the Senate floor, it was eliminated from the final bill in conference committee, assuring that Social Security would be more universal and not limited to persons not covered by employer-based pensions.[22]

President Roosevelt signed the Social Security Act on August 14, 1935. What President Roosevelt helped to create, to use his words, was "some measure of protection" in old age. Roosevelt predicted the expansion of Social Security, stating that "This law, too, represents a cornerstone in a structure which is being built but is by no means complete."[23]

The signing of the Social Security Act in 1935 represented a dramatic departure in the role of government in providing a foundation of economic support for older Americans. After its initial adoption and for the next half century, the Social Security system underwent a period of expansion, and despite fiscal and demographic pressures experienced over the past 30 years, the program still provides a solid but modest foundation of support for most Americans over their lifetimes. The key elements of the Social Security system that were adopted in the 1930s and 1940s have remained largely intact: intergenerational financing through payroll taxes paid by workers and their employers, a relatively modest and progressive benefit structure paid to workers and their dependents over their lifetimes, and excess tax revenues placed in a trust fund to be used solely to pay future benefits.

Expansion: the First Phase of Social Security's Evolution

While the main framework of the Social Security program has remained basically constant, considerable expansion occurred in three areas between 1935 and the 1970s: the proportion of the workforce covered by Social Security, the overall scope of benefit protections, and the level of benefits that people receive from the system. These expansions over the first 50 years of Social Security's history represented the first real phase of Social Security's evolution.

1) Expansion in Eligibility

About 60 percent of the workforce paid into Social Security in 1950.[24] Many government employees, railroad workers, domestic and farm workers, non-profit employees, and the self-employed were not covered.[25] In the following decades, several laws were enacted that expanded coverage. For example, in 1950 President Harry Truman signed legislation that extended coverage to 10 million domestic and agricultural workers, non-profit employees, and state and local employees that chose coverage over other public pensions.[26] Before this expansion, only 3.5 million individuals received benefits but by 1960, that number increased to 14.8 million individuals.[27] During the 1950s, coverage for the self-employed also expanded.[28]

In 1983, the last major changes to Social Security eligibility were enacted into law. At the recommendation of the National Commission on Social Security Reform (also known as the Greenspan Commission), Congress passed legislation incorporating new federal employees and all nonprofit employees into Social Security, and preventing state and local governments from opting out of Social Security.[29]

With these expansions in the number of eligible workers, Social Security became a nearly universal program for workers. Now nearly all workers pay into Social Security and become eligible for benefits. Only federal employees hired before 1984 and some state and local employees who previously selected to participate in state or local plans are excluded from the system.[30]

2) Expansion in Types of Coverage

In terms of the scope of benefit protections, the original act only provided retirement coverage for workers. Before the first benefits were administered, the Social Security Board and the 1938 Advisory Council issued recommendations that the system move from a worker-based plan to a family-based plan, leading to the adoption of a series of very important expansions. The 1939 amendments added provisions for family economic security by creating survivor and dependent benefits for spouses and children.[31] Widows over age 65 could receive three-fourths of their partners' pensions, while spouses and child dependents could receive half of their relatives' pensions.[32]

Other changes that took place in the 1939 amendments created monthly payments instead of lump sums, and created the trust fund for payroll taxes.[33] The significance of the 1939 amendments cannot be overstated. "The 1939 law is probably second in importance only to the original Act itself in shaping Social Security in America."[34] These amendments not only placed a focus on supporting families in addition to workers, but also provided more generous benefits for early recipients of the program who did not work sufficient years to build up sufficient accounts, thereby alleviating poverty for millions.[35]

Other key expansions were adopted in the 1950s. During the Eisenhower Administration and under the Congressional leadership of Lyndon Johnson, disability benefits were added to Social Security (see text box for more information about President Johnson and Social Security). Social Security contained no disability insurance provisions save that employees who had to exit the workforce temporarily due to disabilities could "freeze" their benefit levels, not receive a penalty for absence from the workforce, and thereby still receive benefits upon retirement.[36] Up to that point in time, government policy was focused on rehabilitating workers but not providing long-term income support for workers with major disabilities.[37] In 1956, the enact-

LBJ's Role in Social Security's Expansion

Significant expansions in the scope and size of Social Security benefits occurred during the 1950s and 1960s, largely through the Congressional and presidential leadership of Lyndon B. Johnson. These provisions resulted in greater income support for elderly and disabled Americans, and reveal the depth of Johnson's leadership.

Johnson's deal-making abilities as Senate Majority Leader are well-documented, and the 1956 passage of the legislation that created disability insurance is illustrative of his congressional powers. Though discussed as early as 1936, disability insurance did not gain momentum until after World War II.[1] In the late 1940s and early 1950s, the House passed several disability bills but all were rejected by the Senate. Influential interest groups including the U.S. Chamber of Commerce were mobilized against the bill.[2] The Senate Finance Committee and President Eisenhower tended to favor rehabilitation of disabled workers, as opposed to income support through social insurance.[3] Johnson was determined to achieve passage but knew that he needed a majority of the Senate since Vice President Richard Nixon would cast his vote against the bill if the Senate vote was tied. To secure the deciding vote, Johnson struck a deal with Molly Malone, a Republican senator from Nevada who authored a bill that would have the federal government purchase $69 million from Nevada's tungsten mines. The Eisenhower Administration and Senate Republicans opposed Malone's bill but Johnson delivered 28 Democratic votes, securing the bill's passage, in exchange for Malone's support for the disability insurance bill.[4] The disability insurance amendment passed 47-45, representing the first major expansion of the scope of Social Security benefits since 1939.

continued—

ment of Social Security Disability Insurance (SSDI) enabled workers with permanent disabilities aged 50 to 64 to receive SSDI benefits.[38] This program federalized disability benefits which had previously been provided by some states. Two years later, dependents of disabled workers became eligible for benefits and in 1960 the age requirements were eliminated so that insured disabled workers of all ages could receive benefits.[39]

Another major change in eligibility occurred during the Eisenhower and Kennedy Administrations, when an early retirement age option was authorized in law. In 1956 and 1961, women and then men were granted the option to retire at age 62 with reduced benefits.[40] This increased the number of individuals receiving benefits, as many retirees took advantage of the opportunity for early retirement.[41] This option increased flexibility for workers in deciding when to retire, albeit at reduced benefit levels.

This period of expansion culminated during Lyndon Johnson's presidency with

---

LBJ's Role in Social Security Expansion continued—

Once in the White House, Johnson focused on strengthening support for older Americans. He presided over a series of Social Security expansions. Amendments in 1965 and 1967 expanded and increased Social Security benefits. In 1965, disability benefits were expanded to cover all disabled workers, not just those over age 50, and benefit levels increased by 7 percent.[5] In 1967, Johnson asked Congress to approve a 20 percent benefit increase and Congress compromised by passing a 13 percent benefit increase.[6]

The most significant of LBJ's initiatives was the adoption of Medicare to provide health insurance for retired workers. Attempts to enact legislation to provide health care to the aged failed several times prior to the 1960s. A combination of large Congressional gains for Democrats in 1964, the window of political opportunity brought by President John F. Kennedy's death, and Johnson's legendary negotiations skills enabled Medicare's passage in 1965.

1. Edward D. Berkowitz, "Disability Policy and History, Statement before the Subcommittee on Social Security of the Committee on Ways and Means," July 13, 2000. Online. Available: http://www.ssa.gov/history/edberkdib.html. Accessed November 30, 2005.

2. Howard S. Erlanger, "Disability Policy: 'The Parts and the Whole,'" *American Behavioral Scientist*, vol. 28, iss. 3, Jan/Feb 1985. Available: PCI Full Text, p. 328.

3. Berkowitz, "Disability Policy and History."

4. Robert A. Caro, *The Years of Lyndon Johnson, Master of the Senate* (New York: Alfred A. Knopf, 2002), p. 680.

5. Daniel Beland, *Social Security History and Politics from the New Deal to the Privatization Debate* (Lawrence, KS: University of Kansas Press, 2005), p. 131.

6. Social Security Administration, "Social Security, A Brief History," p. 10. Online. Available: http://www.ssa.gov/history/pdf/2005pamphlet.pdf. Accessed: October 20, 2005.

---

the adoption of Medicare, which represented the second key pillar of social insurance for older Americans. In 1965, Johnson signed the Medicare legislation into law, providing health coverage to seniors covered by Social Security. At the time of Medicare's passage, almost half of older Americans lacked health insurance. Policymakers recognized that without medical coverage, retirees were unable to achieve a decent standard of living in old age, even with Social Security benefits. The provision of a modest level of universal acute health coverage, together with Social Security, helped retirees to achieve greater income security.[42]

Together, the creation of survivors' and dependents' pensions, benefits for the disabled and their dependents, and health benefits provided through Medicare to all retirees over age 65 resulted in significant transformation of the Social Security program from a modest pension for workers to a more substantial source of financial support for families. Additionally, with the creation of an early retirement age for women and men, the system created a more flexible arrangement for retirees to choose when to exit the labor force.

3) Expansion in Benefit Levels

Initially, Social Security benefit levels were very modest, but benefit levels for beneficiaries as well as new generations of retirees have been increased significantly. Prior to 1950, no cost of living adjustments were made to benefits. In recognition of the eroding purchasing power of retirees, President Truman signed a 77 percent increase of Social Security benefits in 1950 to account for higher living costs.[43] In 1972, legislation was adopted implementing automatic cost-of-living allowances so that benefit payments would grow with inflation and a person could count on the purchasing power of their benefits remaining constant over their lifetime.[44]

One way of measuring the adequacy of Social Security benefits is to consider the extent to which benefits replace earnings. As Table 7.1 indicates, the "replacement rate" of average Social Security benefits, defined as benefits divided by earnings during employment, has increased significantly. From 1940 to 2006, the replacement rate for workers earning median wages retiring at age 65 increased from 23 percent to 41 percent. Benefit levels for future generations of retirees were automatically increased to account for higher living standards and growth in the economy. While benefit levels continue to increase to this day, replacement rates peaked in the early 1980s, as fiscal and demographic pressures confronting the system forced modest retrenchments in the 1970s and 1980s (the next section discusses this in greater detail).

In sum, the first phase of Social Security's evolution was one of expansion—in the share of the workforce covered by the system, the types of benefits provided, and the dollar level of benefits. What was once a plan that originally only covered about half of U.S. workers today covers nearly all workers. What was once a plan that originally provided income security only for workers now provides family, disability and survivor benefits and offers retirees the option to exit the labor force at age 62. And what was a plan that originally provided very modest benefit levels now provides higher benefit levels as well as inflation protection through annual increases in benefits for all beneficiaries. These changes enabled Social Security to live up to the original promise of providing a foundation of economic support available over a lifetime.

Limits to Growth: the Second Phase of Social Security's Evolution

The ongoing expansion that occurred throughout the first several decades of the program's operation gave way to an understanding that tighter limits needed to be imposed on the system, given the demographic and economic changes underway in the U.S. This realization ushered in the second phase in Social Security's history, a period of modest contraction that started in the 1970s and continues to this day.[45] The U.S. therefore began making changes to its public pension system before many of its European counterparts that today are experiencing more acute demographic and fiscal pressures.

Table 7.1
Social Security Replacement Rates for Median Earners from 1939-2006

Year When Turn 65	Percent of Earnings*	Year When Turn 65	Percent of Earnings*	Year When Turn 65	Percent of Earnings*
1940	23.4	1962	28.2	1984	43.5
1941	22.8	1963	27.4	1985	41.5
1942	21.9	1964	27.3	1986	41.9
1943	19.9	1965	28.6	1987	42
1944	17.5	1966	28.4	1988	41.4
1945	16.1	1967	27.3	1989	42.1
1946	16	1968	29.5	1990	43.5
1947	17.6	1969	28.6	1991	43.1
1948	15.8	1970	31.7	1992	43.8
1949	15	1971	34.1	1993	42.8
1950	18.7	1972	35.6	1994	42.8
1951	26.3	1973	37.4	1995	43.2
1952	25.3	1974	39	1996	42.9
1953	26.3	1975	40.5	1997	43.1
1954	26.6	1976	41.6	1998	40.8
1955	29	1977	42.6	1999	39.4
1956	28.3	1978	44.2	2000	38.7
1957	26.9	1979	45.7	2001	39
1958	27.1	1980	48.9	2002	40.8
1959	29.4	1981	51.7	2003	41.5
1960	28.3	1982	49.2	2004	41.8
1961	28.2	1983	46.4	2005	42.2
				2006	41.3

Adapted from: Board of Trustees of the Old-Age and Survivors Insurance and Disability Insurance Trust Funds, "Single-Year Tables Consistent with 2005 OASDI Trustees Report, VI.F10—Estimated Annual Scheduled Benefit Amounts 1 for Retired Workers With Scaled Medium Pre-Retirement Earnings Pattern Based on Intermediate Assumptions Calendar Years 1940-2080," *2005 Annual Report of the Board of Trustees of the Federal Old-Age and Survivors Insurance and Disability Insurance Trust Funds,* March 23, 2005. Online. Available: http://www.ssa.gov/OACT/TR/TR05/lr6F10-2.html. Accessed: January 8, 2006.

*Assumes retirement at age 65.

Facing financial pressures, President Jimmy Carter's administration focused on raising revenues and slowing benefit growth. In 1977, reforms were enacted that increased payroll taxes and decreased future benefits in part by correcting for an error in benefit calculations caused by changes in laws enacted in 1972. A new system of calculating benefits was established and the recalibration of benefits was controversial for "notch" babies who did not receive as much as those who retired a few years before them.[46] Carter also supported amendments in 1980 to require disability recipients to undergo regular reviews to determine continued eligibility for benefits. Even with changes, Social Security's trust funds decreased significantly from 1974 to 1980.[47]

Despite the fact that many predicted that the changes of 1977 would lead to the creation of growing surpluses in the Social Security Trust Fund, inflation and slower wage growth in the late 1970s and early 1980s placed the system on the brink of insolvency, as trust fund balances became nearly exhausted.[48] During Ronald Reagan's presidency, a series of changes to Social Security were enacted into law. In 1981, with the passage of the Omnibus Budget Reconciliation Act, several changes were made to Social Security including phasing out Social Security student benefits and limiting the Social Security lump sum payment.[49]

In addition, President Reagan signed an Executive Order to create the Greenspan Commission to study the issue of long term solvency. In 1983, the Commission generated several recommendations that were enacted into law by Congress.[50] Changes included gradually raising the retirement age from 65 to 67, increasing payroll taxes, taxing part of benefits for upper-income retirees, expanding coverage for government and non-profit workers, and delaying cost-of-living increases for all beneficiaries to the end of December of each year instead of June.[51] Together, these balanced measures strengthened the long-term finances of the system. In some respects, 1983 is similar to today in that a financing shortfall existed as did a real disagreement among constituent groups on the appropriate policy remedies. The reforms of 1983 called for mutual sacrifice including benefit cuts, payroll tax increases, and increases in the retirement age.

In sum, after several decades of expansion (in terms of the proportion of the workforce covered, the types of benefits provided, and the level of benefits), Social Security's underlying fiscal problems emerged in the 1970s. Every president since Jimmy Carter has struggled to engage in reforms to ensure long-term stability of the system.

Conclusion

Social Security's enactment resulted in a much greater public role in providing basic economic security for America's elderly. Despite the limits and constraints adopted over the past quarter century, the system's main framework is basically the same as existed in 1940. Social Security remains remarkably successful in addressing FDR's original goal of providing "some measure of security" in retirement. The remainder of this chapter examines the impact of Social Security, how Social Security fits into the overall U.S. retirement system, the Social Security financing shortfall, and three general approaches now under consideration to change the system. These approaches include measures to *reaffirm* the existing system primarily through revenue increases, measures to *revise* the system through changes in benefits, and measures to *restructure* the system by creating personal/private accounts as a partial substitute to Social Security's current benefit structure.

Impact of Social Security

The impact of Social Security on Americans has been profound. Social Security has dramatically reduced the poverty rates of the elderly and disabled, expanded retirement security for the elderly and created disability and life insurance protections for workers and their families. At the same time, Social Security has created a significant spending responsibility for society as a whole.

Over the past several decades, the U.S. has witnessed significant declines in the poverty rates of older Americans. Poverty rates among the elderly rose to 50 percent during the Depression and as many as two out of three elderly individuals were poor in the early 1940s.[52] Even as recently as 1959, over one-third of all older Americans were living in poverty. Expansions in the scope and size of benefits, particularly during the 1950s to the early 1970s, contributed to greater financial security for the elderly, resulting in steady declines in elderly poverty rates to present levels of about 10 percent.[53] If Social Security benefits stopped tomorrow, about half of all seniors would be living in poverty the day after tomorrow. Social Security is now the foundation of support in retirement for almost all Americans.

While providing all entitled retirees with support, Social Security benefits are weighted progressively. By and large, low wage earners receive higher replacement rates because Social Security replaces a higher share of pre-retirement earnings for lower wage workers (see Figure 7.1), though higher wage earners receive larger benefits but at lower replacement rates. However, because lower wage earners on average live shorter lives, the progressive nature that is built into the formula is undercut to some extent.

The Social Security benefit structure greatly benefits women and minorities. Progressive benefits compensate in part for women's lower wages, time out of the workforce, and longer life expectancy.[54] Retired women have fewer sources of income support besides Social Security, as four in ten white women and six in ten minority women receive over 90 percent of their retirement incomes from Social Security.[55] Minority retirees also benefit from the system. Social Security is an income-equalizer across races, as it provides African Americans with incomes that are closer to the incomes of white individuals than at any other time in their lives.[56] Hispanics in particular benefit because their life expectancy as a group is the highest of all racial/ethnic groups and because their wages are often lower than average.

In addition to providing benefits to millions of retired workers, Social Security provides a substantial amount of support for widows, families, and disabled workers. Of system beneficiaries, 37 percent receive survivor and disability payments, including six million disabled workers, three million spouses and two million children of retired and disabled workers, and seven million survivors (almost two million children).[57] Given that women are three times more likely to out-live a partner, the current structure provides substantial survivor pensions to widows.[58] As a group, African Americans disproportionately receive disability and survivor benefits, at 17 and 22 percent of all recipients, respectively.[59]

Another major trend that took place during the 20th century relates to the age when workers enter retirement. In the early 1900s, workers often remained in the

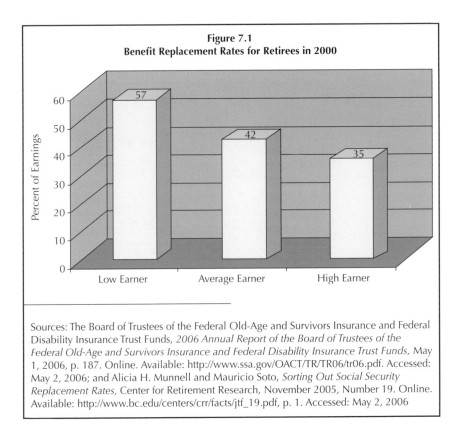

Figure 7.1
Benefit Replacement Rates for Retirees in 2000

Sources: The Board of Trustees of the Federal Old-Age and Survivors Insurance and Federal Disability Insurance Trust Funds, *2006 Annual Report of the Board of Trustees of the Federal Old-Age and Survivors Insurance and Federal Disability Insurance Trust Funds,* May 1, 2006, p. 187. Online. Available: http://www.ssa.gov/OACT/TR/TR06/tr06.pdf. Accessed: May 2, 2006; and Alicia H. Munnell and Mauricio Soto, *Sorting Out Social Security Replacement Rates,* Center for Retirement Research, November 2005, Number 19. Online. Available: http://www.bc.edu/centers/crr/facts/jtf_19.pdf, p. 1. Accessed: May 2, 2006

labor force until they died or became very disabled, with an average retirement age at about 74 years. The average retirement age has decreased considerably over the past century; it was 74 in 1910, 70 in 1940, 65 in 1970, and 63 in 1985 and 2000.[60] In the mid-1980s, the retirement age leveled off; the majority of workers choose to claim benefits at about age 62. On average, people now live longer, retire earlier and therefore spend more of their lives in retirement. Given that less than a century ago, retirement was not an option for most of the elderly and that old age often meant destitution, the ability now to retire and be assured of a modest income is a major change for our society.

In addition to creating retirement security and more options for workers and their families, Social Security has also created new fiscal responsibilities for the nation. Higher benefits, greater coverage, and earlier retirement all have costs. Historically, the Social Security system has been financed through a payroll tax. In the 1930s, the payroll tax was just 2 percent, half born by employers and employees. As the number of beneficiaries and the level of benefits increased, the payroll tax has increased. Today's tax is 12.4 percent, split equally by employees and employers. Payroll taxes for Social Security comprise about 5 percent of the nation's Gross Domestic Product (GDP), a share that will have to rise to over 6 percent by the latter half of this century if current benefit commitments are maintained.[61] Though some citizens might agree that these costs represent the price to be paid for a civil society, it must be recognized that a significant public price is paid for the benefits provided to the elderly.

Social Security and the U.S. Retirement System

Social Security is a sizeable source of income for older Americans. Figure 7.2 depicts the sources of income for all individuals over age 65 in America, with about 40 percent coming from Social Security, 20 percent from pensions, 25 percent from earnings, and about 14 percent from assets. Social Security is part of a multi-legged income "stool" for older persons, complemented by pensions and savings to support

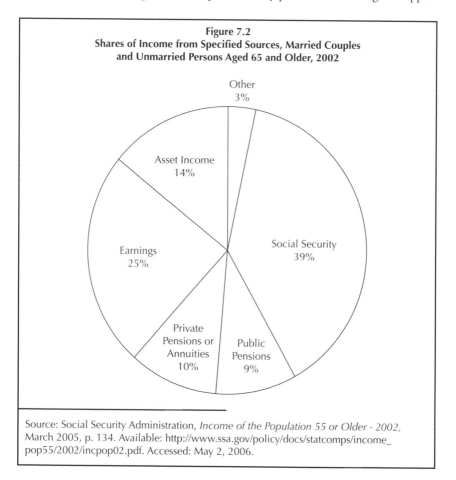

Figure 7.2
Shares of Income from Specified Sources, Married Couples and Unmarried Persons Aged 65 and Older, 2002

Other
3%

Asset Income
14%

Social Security
39%

Earnings
25%

Private
Pensions or
Annuities
10%

Public
Pensions
9%

Source: Social Security Administration, *Income of the Population 55 or Older - 2002*, March 2005, p. 134. Available: http://www.ssa.gov/policy/docs/statcomps/income_pop55/2002/incpop02.pdf. Accessed: May 2, 2006.

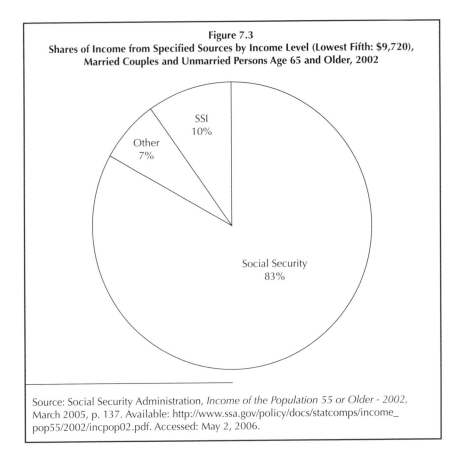

Figure 7.3
Shares of Income from Specified Sources by Income Level (Lowest Fifth: $9,720),
Married Couples and Unmarried Persons Age 65 and Older, 2002

SSI
10%

Other
7%

Social Security
83%

Source: Social Security Administration, *Income of the Population 55 or Older - 2002*, March 2005, p. 137. Available: http://www.ssa.gov/policy/docs/statcomps/income_pop55/2002/incpop02.pdf. Accessed: May 2, 2006.

people in retirement. In addition, income from continued work is another source of income for many older Americans.

While Social Security provides almost 40 percent of income for the average retiree, as Figure 7.3 illustrates, for the Americans in the bottom fifth of income, those with incomes below roughly $10,000, Social Security provides 83 percent of income. For the bottom two-fifths of the retired population, Social Security is not part of a three or four-legged "stool"; there is basically only a one-legged "stool" of support consisting of Social Security (coupled with Supplemental Security Income (SSI) payments for the very poor).

Figure 7.3 raises important questions about choices for the future. Should future Social Security benefits be cut for this group? Should Social Security continue to provide most of the support for people in the lowest income quintiles? Is the current system in which personal savings and pensions provide so little support for low-income individuals appropriate or should the federal government adopt policies to encourage more savings and/or less reliance on Social Security for this group?

Figure 7.4 provides data for middle income older Americans. Social Security still represents almost two-thirds of all income for the middle fifth of older Americans but pensions, earnings, and savings all comprise greater shares of support. It should be noted that income levels for the average older American household is still quite low, at about $20,000 a year.

Figure 7.5 highlights income sources for the elderly with the top fifth of income, those with incomes above about $40,000 a year. For this group, Social Security represents about 20 percent of income. Pensions are equally important, amounting to 20 percent of income. Earnings and assets and savings provide substantial resources to this group. For the upper income quintile, a strong four-legged "stool" of support exists. Given that earnings make up a significant share of support, it should be noted that many of the individuals in this group are in their 60s because there are few people over age 70 still in the labor force.

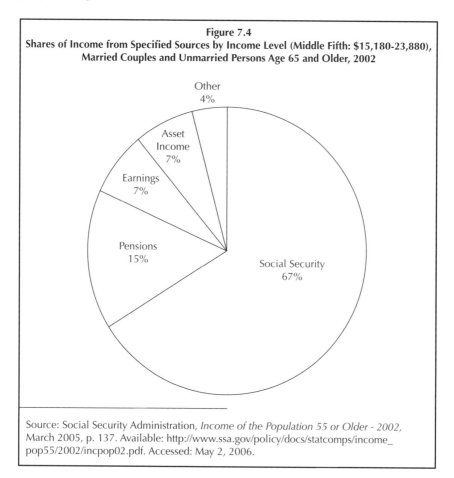

Figure 7.4
Shares of Income from Specified Sources by Income Level (Middle Fifth: $15,180-23,880), Married Couples and Unmarried Persons Age 65 and Older, 2002

Other
4%

Asset
Income
7%

Earnings
7%

Pensions
15%

Social Security
67%

Source: Social Security Administration, *Income of the Population 55 or Older - 2002,* March 2005, p. 137. Available: http://www.ssa.gov/policy/docs/statcomps/income_pop55/2002/incpop02.pdf. Accessed: May 2, 2006.

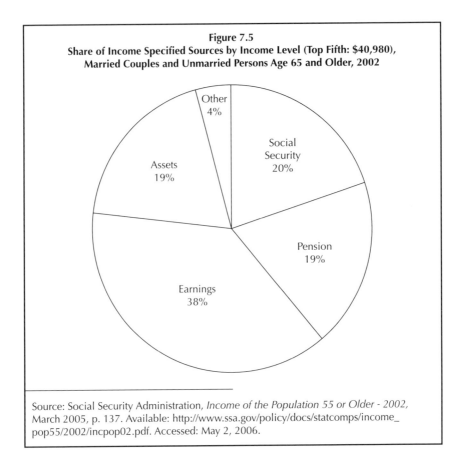

Figure 7.5
Share of Income Specified Sources by Income Level (Top Fifth: $40,980),
Married Couples and Unmarried Persons Age 65 and Older, 2002

Source: Social Security Administration, *Income of the Population 55 or Older - 2002,*
March 2005, p. 137. Available: http://www.ssa.gov/policy/docs/statcomps/income_
pop55/2002/incpop02.pdf. Accessed: May 2, 2006.

Figure 7.5 also raises a series of questions about choices for the future. Should
Social Security still be available at current levels for those with the highest incomes?
Should Social Security be means-tested to provide benefits only for those in financial
need of support? Should the federal government adopt policies to encourage this
group to save even more? Should more older Americans be encouraged or required to
stay in the workforce later in life?

This analysis of the share of support Social Security now provides to retirees brings to
light many of the important policy questions on the role Social Security could play in the
financial support of lower, middle, and higher income retirees, given the fiscal pressures
facing the system. The role that Social Security, savings, earnings, and pensions will play
25 or 50 years from now will be determined by the actions taken by current policymakers,
as they decide, with input from the public, how to change the system.

Future Challenges Confronting Social Security

While widespread agreement exists that the Social Security system will need changes, significant disagreement surrounds various proposals for change. Very different options emerge depending in part on how one perceives the problem. Data exist on several dimensions of the size and scope of the long-term financing shortfall, yet the data are interpreted differently. Points of contention include the extent of the pressures facing the system due to demographic changes, the challenges facing the other legs in the retirement income "stool," and magnitude of the changes needed to ensure long-term solvency of the system. This section explores these uncertainties to provide context to reform options.

Demographic Challenges

A major demographic change is taking place all over the world. As fertility rates decrease and longevity rates increase, the growth and share of the population over age 65 continues to increase. These trends exert substantial pressure on social insurance programs due to increasing demands for services, coupled with decreasing proportions of workers supporting these populations.

Like most nations, the U.S. faces demographic changes that complicate questions about the future of Social Security. The number of older Americans, defined as those over age 65, is increasing and people are living longer. In 1934, 5.4 percent of the population was 65 or older but today that number is 12.5 percent and is expected to be as high as 20 percent by 2030.[62] As Figure 7.6 indicates, in 1946 there were about 11 million Americans aged 65 and older. Currently, there are about 35 million older Americans and as the baby boomer generation retires, that number will increase to 70 million by 2030. The baby boomers mark the beginning of large waves of retirees, as population trends indicate that future generations will retire in roughly the same numbers.[63] Life expectancy at age 65 was 12 years in 1900, has increased to 18 years in 2001 and continues to grow.[64] It is likely that these future projections are relatively accurate, because the estimates are mostly of people who are alive today.

Though demographic changes are occurring worldwide, the U.S. faces a less severe challenge than its European and Japanese counterparts. In Europe and Japan, the population is aging but fertility rates are also declining, resulting in fewer individuals to support the aging population. Fertility rates have remained relatively high in the U.S.

While most demographers agree that the U.S. is an aging society, with an elderly population projected to roughly double in the next 25 years, there is disagreement on how big a challenge this represents in part because other factors such as future fertility rates are hard to project with any certainty. Other factors include the immigration rate, which has remained relatively high and has a beneficial impact on Social Security. Future immigration rates are also very hard to predict, as are future economic growth rates affecting Social Security revenues and benefit payments.

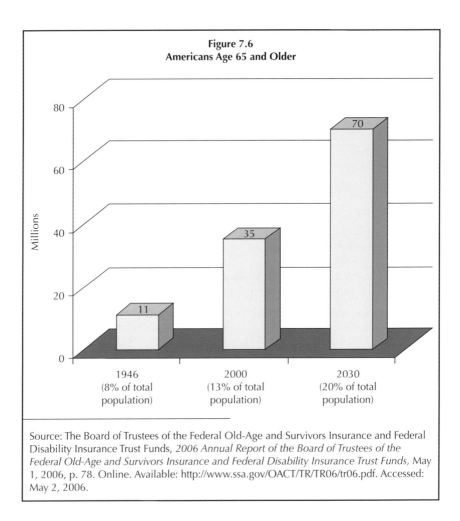

Figure 7.6
Americans Age 65 and Older

Source: The Board of Trustees of the Federal Old-Age and Survivors Insurance and Federal Disability Insurance Trust Funds, *2006 Annual Report of the Board of Trustees of the Federal Old-Age and Survivors Insurance and Federal Disability Insurance Trust Funds,* May 1, 2006, p. 78. Online. Available: http://www.ssa.gov/OACT/TR/TR06/tr06.pdf. Accessed: May 2, 2006.

Retirement System Trends

Social Security, pensions, and savings—three of the pieces of the retirement "stool" of support—as well as work practices will continue to shape the income security of the aged in the future. While it is difficult to predict the future with regard to any of these areas because they depend upon personal behavior and potential law changes, it is possible to outline trends, given the current legal structure.

1. Social Security

Under current law, Social Security benefit levels for future generations are projected to increase in real value, but under current laws, Social Security will not be replacing as much pre-retirement income as it does now. Social Security replaces about 40 percent of the average worker's earnings. The progressive structure of benefits ensures that low-income workers receive higher replacement rates (57 percent) than high-income workers (35 percent).[65] While workers do not require full replacement rates in retirement, as they usually pay fewer taxes and do not have to save, financial planners estimate that individuals need about 70 percent to 80 percent of pre-retirement income to maintain an adequate lifestyle in retirement.

Current retirees are experiencing relatively high Social Security replacement rates compared to retirees a half century ago.[66] By 2030, Social Security under current law will likely only be replacing about a third of income, after deducting future Medicare premiums, taxes, and planned benefit reductions now in law.[67] Many argue that further retrenchments would place future retirees in jeopardy, given declining replacement rates under current laws. How high replacement rates should be in the future will remain a central policy question in Social Security reform discussions.

It should be pointed out that although future replacement rates are decreasing, Social Security benefit levels for future generations are actually increasing in real dollar terms. Every generation's Social Security benefits are roughly tied to increases in wages, which increase faster than prices, so each generation receives higher benefits and greater purchasing power than prior generations.[68] Because benefit levels are projected to go up, some argue that slowing the rate of benefit growth is acceptable because benefits will still be increasing. The rate of increase in benefit levels in the future will also be a central policy question in Social Security Reform discussions.

2. Pensions

In FY 2001, the U.S. government tax expenditures amounted to $85 billion annually for incentives to encourage employers to provide pensions to their employees,[69] yet overall traditional pension coverage is declining and a major shift is underway in the type of pensions available. Under current policies, it is likely that traditional pensions will make up a diminishing share of retirees' income for future generations.

Two-thirds of retirees receive at least some of their retirement income from pensions,[70] though pension participation varies significantly by socio-economic status (see Figure 7.8). For the top income quintile, 65-70 percent of workers have pensions but in the bottom quintile, only 10-15 percent of workers have pensions.[71] Low-income workers are less likely to have pensions than other workers because they are more likely to work in jobs where pensions are unavailable such as part-time positions or for small employers. Even when pensions are available, these workers are less likely to take advantage of them because they lack the means to make contributions.[72] Over the past two decades, there has been a decrease in the availability of pension plans for all workers, but women's likelihood of working in jobs with pension access increased as their labor participation expanded.[73]

A major trend in pension coverage has been an erosion in coverage in traditional defined-benefit plans that provide monthly employer paid benefits in retirement in favor of defined-contribution plans like 401(k)s and Individual Retirement Accounts (IRAs) that

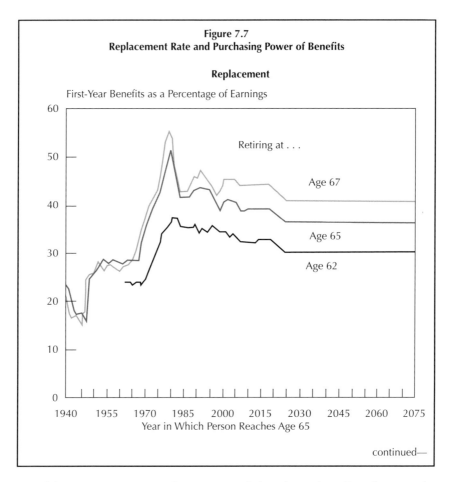

Figure 7.7
Replacement Rate and Purchasing Power of Benefits

Replacement

First-Year Benefits as a Percentage of Earnings

Retiring at . . .

Age 67

Age 65

Age 62

Year in Which Person Reaches Age 65

continued—

provide lump-sum payments, with investment risks born by workers. Contributing to the declining role of defined-benefit plans is the difficulty many employers, especially small firms, have in keeping their defined-benefit plans fully-funded and coping with high administrative costs.[74] As firms shift to defined-contribution plans, the percent of workers covered by defined-benefit plans decreased from 60 percent in 1980 to about 14 percent in 1999.[75] From 1975-1999, more people participated in and more contributions flowed into defined-contribution plans than defined-benefit plans, signaling a major change in the type of support provided to retirees.[76]

Today's defined-contribution plans differ from defined-benefit plans in several ways. Proponents of defined-contribution plans tout their portability and greater personal control as benefits for young, mobile workers. The tradeoff for this flexibility is an increase in risk. Defined-contribution plans shift the risk from the firm to the individual.[77] Defined-benefit plans use annuitized benefit distribution, meaning

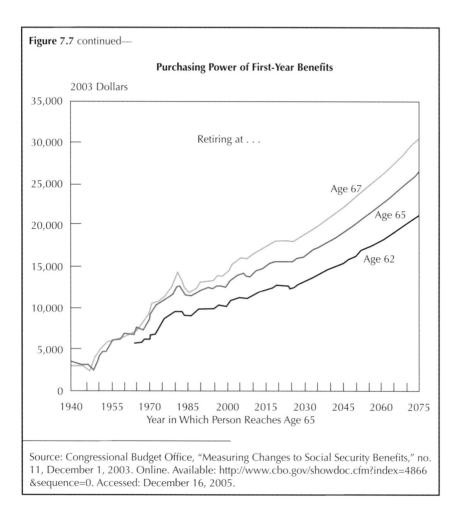

Figure 7.7 continued—

Purchasing Power of First-Year Benefits

2003 Dollars

Retiring at . . .

Age 67

Age 65

Age 62

Year in Which Person Reaches Age 65

Source: Congressional Budget Office, "Measuring Changes to Social Security Benefits," no. 11, December 1, 2003. Online. Available: http://www.cbo.gov/showdoc.cfm?index=4866 &sequence=0. Accessed: December 16, 2005.

that individuals can count generally on receiving payments of the same size until death. Under this system, firms bear the responsibility to maintain enough funds in their pension accounts to ensure benefit provision to all retirees. Under defined-contribution plans, firms and workers each contribute to individual accounts and funds are invested. The performance of the market dictates the returns; workers are not guaranteed a minimum monthly benefit. Aside from the original contributions, firms are not responsible for future contributions, even if workers experience losses in the market.

As a result of pension pressures, many firms are either choosing not to offer retirement plans or to convert to a system of defined-contribution plans. In addition, some firms are cutting costs by eliminating retiree health benefits because unlike pensions,

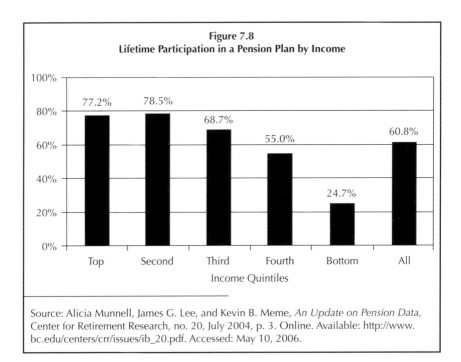

Figure 7.8
Lifetime Participation in a Pension Plan by Income

Source: Alicia Munnell, James G. Lee, and Kevin B. Meme, *An Update on Pension Data,* Center for Retirement Research, no. 20, July 2004, p. 3. Online. Available: http://www. bc.edu/centers/crr/issues/ib_20.pdf. Accessed: May 10, 2006.

laws do not regulate their operation.[78] Given these changes, most researchers predict that defined-benefit pensions will provide a shrinking source of support for retirees in the decades to come.

Savings
There have been dramatic changes in the personal savings habits of workers in the past half century (see Figure 7.9). Workers in the 1950s saved about 7 percent of their earnings. By 1982, that number climbed to 11.2 percent. Just two decades later, personal savings plummeted to 1.8 percent.[79] There are some problems with the way this savings rate is calculated, as pension savings are not counted toward its total. However, even with the inclusion of pensions into savings, many caution that these resources will not provide sufficient income for many for retirement.[80]

In terms of savings specifically designed for retirement, there has been a sizeable change in the rate of participation in 401(k) and IRA plans over the past several decades. Most of those participating in these plans are of higher incomes. Table 7.2 illustrates that the top ten percent of workers hold significantly more assets in their retirement accounts than low-income workers, whose contributions are only 1 percent of total retirement account assets. For the majority of workers, the amounts of their retirement savings are much more modest than for the top ten percent of workers.

Figure 7.9
Household Savings as a Percent of Income

Source: Bureau of Economic Analysis, *National Income and Product Accounts Table, Table 2.1, Personal Income and its Disposition,* National Economic Accounts, May 4, 2006. Online. Available: http://www.bea.gov/bea/dn/nipaweb/TableView.asp?SelectedTable=58& FirstYear=2004&LastYear=2006&Freq=Qtr. Accessed: May 10, 2006.

For workers aged 45-54, on the cusp of retirement, about 60 percent had retirement accounts and the average value of their retirement savings is about $50,000, a small amount in terms of the resources needed to sustain a family in retirement (See Table 7.3).

Some argue that these findings on generally low savings rates and minimal balances in retirement accounts call for significant efforts to strengthen retirement savings for the entire population. Others contend that given the small amount of support most retirees receive from savings, it is more crucial to preserve the foundation of support that Social Security provides to retirees. Others argue that we need both. These questions are large, not just for the debate about Social Security reform, but also for the entire retirement security system.

Work

Throughout most of the 20th century, workers have been retiring at increasingly ear-

Table 7.2
Participation in Tax-Favored Retirement Accounts by Family Income, 2001

Income Group	Median Income	Account Holder Median Value	Percent of Total Account Assets
Lowest fifth	$10,300	$4,500	1
Second fifth	$24,400	$8,000	4
Middle fifth	$39,900	$13,500	9
Next to highest fifth	$64,800	$31,000	19
Next to highest tenth	$98,700	$52,000	17
Top ten percent	$169,600	$130,000	50

Source: Peter Orszag, 2003 Tabulations using the 2001 Survey of Consumer Finances.

Note: Accounts include 401(k) plans, other defined-contributed plans, IRAs, and Keogh plans.

lier ages, despite longer life expectancies and fewer physically demanding jobs. Today, 74 percent of men and 78 percent of women retire before age 65.[81]

Work is an important element in the Social Security debate. Current laws set the parameters for current retirement practices but the retirement behavior of current workers remains uncertain. It is possible that many people will choose to work longer, given that two or three years of extra time in the labor force can make a profound difference in terms of economic security in retirement. For other workers, especially blue-collar workers and those with health problems, the option to work longer is less realistic and their behavioral practices may more closely mirror the status quo.

In sum, the future roles of Social Security, pensions, savings, and work in the retirement security of the elderly all remain open questions. Current retirees benefit from one of the strongest retirement systems in the world, but future retirees face

Table 7.3
Retirement Account Holdings

Age of the Head of Household	Percentage of Families Holding Retirement Accounts	Median Value
Less than 35	45.1	$6,600
45-54	63.4	$48,000
55-64	59.1	$55,000

Source: Federal Reserve Board, Ana M. Aizcorbe, Arthur B. Kennickell, and Kevin B. Moore, "Recent Changes in U.S. Family Finances: Evidence from the 1998 and 2001 Survey of Consumer Finances," *Federal Reserve Bulletin,* January 2003, p. 13. Online. Available: http://www.federalreserve.gov/Pubs/oss/oss2/2001/bull0103.pdf. Accessed: May 10, 2006.

more uncertainties, as each of the legs of the "stool" confront real challenges. If Social Security benefits are scaled back, personal savings, pensions, and work will have to compensate for lost benefits, or the income of older Americans will suffer.

The Size of the Social Security Challenge

How big is the Social Security financing problem? While there is agreement that the American society is aging and that the growing aged population will put pressure on the Social Security system, disagreement exists about the overall dimensions of the problem. Government projections show that Social Security payroll taxes are going to start falling behind spending in about a decade. Since 1983, payroll tax increases have ensured that funds have been coming in at a faster rate, and that excess funds have been deposited in the Social Security trust fund. By about 2017, the money going out in benefit payments will exceed money coming in from taxes (see Figure 7.10). At that point, the trust fund reserves will be needed to pay part of the benefits. To some, the looming date of 2017 is one for alarm and sets the stage for dramatic changes.

By about 2041, the trust funds are projected to be exhausted. That means that

Figure 7.10
Annual OASDI Cost Rates Under Intermediate Assumptions, Percentage of Taxable Payroll

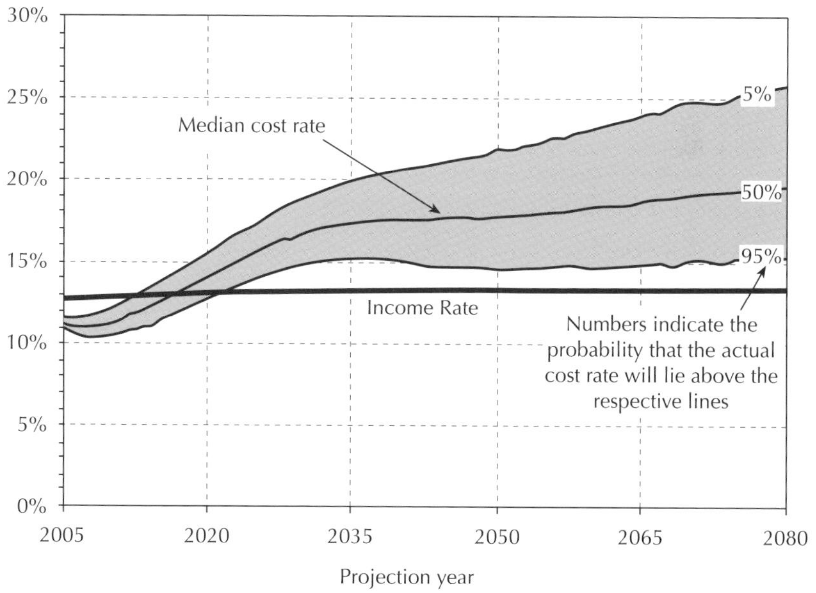

Source: Social Security Administration, *Summary of the 2005 OASDI Trustees Report,* March 23, 2005, p. 19. Online. Available: http://www.ssa.gov/OACT/TRSUM/ tr05summary.pdf. Accessed: May 10, 2006.

all the reserves that have been accumulating in the trust fund over the last 20 years, and will continue to build for the next 15 years or so, will be depleted. As specified by law, current Social Security benefits will therefore continue without any changes until about 2041. After 2041, payroll tax revenue will only be able to pay about three-fourths of the promised levels. For some, the date of 2041 allows for adequate time to make modest changes to ensure long-term solvency.

Should 2017, the year when expenditures may start to exceed revenues, or 2041, the year when benefit cuts may occur absent changes, be the focus? The types of policy options policymakers, advocates, and the public will consider depends on how they view the size and the immediacy of the problem. Differing opinions exist based on the same facts.

Another source of ongoing debate is the size of the shortfall. Over the next 75 years, the shortfall is considered to be about $4 trillion. Over the infinite horizon, the shortfall is considerably larger, about $11 trillion dollars. One way to make these numbers more understandable is to evaluate them as a share of the economy, but there are different ways to frame the size of the problem in these terms as well. Over the next 75 years, the funds needed to finance the system will comprise around 0.5 percent of GDP. Over the infinite horizon, the shortfall may be about 1.5 percent of GDP, clearly a bigger challenge.

It must be pointed out that the longer into the future one makes projections, the less reliable the projections become. Another source of constant debate is whether to set policies now based on Social Security projections generations into the future. Generally, those arguing for more dramatic changes to the system give more credence to the long term projections; those arguing for more modest changes often give less credence to the long term projections.

Conclusion

It is clear that we face uncertainties—demographic trends, changes in savings, pensions, work, and the overall dimensions of the Social Security financing problem—and whether one believes there is no crisis, or that we face a long-term manageable problem, or that a crisis exists now depends in part on how one evaluates the information available. In addition, one's perceptions of the problem also determine in part the options that one will consider to change the system. The next section frames three main approaches to change the Social Security system.

Options for Reform

A large and diverse range of options has been proposed to change Social Security. To assist the reader in better understanding the various options, this section frames the various policy options for Social Security into three general approaches. These three approaches have been under development by the National Issues Forum to help the public to be more informed about the issue.

The first approach would keep Social Security in its overall current form, achieving solvency of the system by making a variety of relatively moderate changes. This approach includes options to increase the payroll tax rate and to moderate future benefit increases. Also included here are options eliminating or raising the cap on taxable income above the current level of about $90,000 as well as investing some of the surplus trust funds in higher-yielding investments instead of government bonds.

The second approach would significantly revamp future Social Security benefits by making sizeable increases in the retirement age, by means-testing the program, or by instituting major changes in the calculation of future benefits.

The third approach would be to create personal/private savings accounts as a replacement for part of Social Security. This approach, usually coupled with substantial reductions in benefits, would represent a significant departure from the current program—in effect, a third stage in the evolution of the Social Security system.

There are various ways to structure each of these approaches and none of them are entirely mutually exclusive. The various approaches presented here can be viewed from many different perspectives. Will the three approaches that frame the current discourse strengthen or weaken the Social Security system? Some believe that any one approach strengthens the system and others believe the very same approach weakens the system. In addition, the issue of income adequacy will emerge in any discussion about the future of the Social Security system. If the fundamental goal of government policy in the area of retirement security is to assure adequate income in retirement, what are the strengths and weaknesses of the various approaches? Lastly, what are the values that underlie these approaches and what is the role that government should play in the lives of older Americans? There are no straightforward answers to these questions.

Table 7.4 summarizes a series of commonly discussed policy solutions, grouped by the three general approaches. This series of tax and spending options are outlined and critiqued in subsequent sections. The first column shows the traditional actuaries' projection regarding share of the financial deficit solved over the next 75 years. The second column illustrates the possible savings projections 75 years from now. Again, it must be pointed out that uncertainty in the estimates increases the further out into the future one goes.

Approach 1: Reaffirming Social Security: The Promise of Protection

Supporters of this approach argue that the best strategy to strengthen Social Security is to make modest modifications within the existing structure of the program that will enable it to remain solvent over the long-term and continue to play as integral a role for future generations as it does now. Perhaps the key value underlying this approach is that the public has a collective responsibility in providing basic economic security for retirees and that an important role exists for the government to play in the provision of security to retirees.

Social Security's success in lifting the elderly, disabled, and dependent spouses and children out of poverty is well-documented. One analyst concluded that without

Table 7.4
Effects of Policy Changes on Solvency

General Policy Options	Specific Initiatives	Actuarial Balance Over 75 Years	Actuarial Balance In 75th Year
Approach 1: Reaffirming Social Security	Raise the Payroll Tax 2% (for employers and employees combined)	102%	35%
	Eliminate the Wage Tax Cap and Cap Benefits	115%	51%
	Benefit Reductions for newly eligible (5%)	32%	16%
	Invest 40% of the Trust Fund in Equities (with 6.5% rate of return)	46%	0%
Approach 2: Revising Social Security	Raise the Normal Retirement Age to 70	36%	28%
	Means-Testing Benefits[1]	50%	50%
	Major Benefit Reductions: Price Indexing	124%	138%
Approach 3: Reconstructing Social Security	Personal/Private Accounts with Offsets[2]	-26%	37%
	Combination of Personal/Private Accounts with Offsets Couple with Sliding-Scale Benefit Reductions[3]	100%	100%

Source: Social Security Administration, Chris Chaplain and Alice H. Wade, *Estimated OASDI Long-Range Financial Effects of Several Provisions Requested by the Social Security Advisory Board,* August 10, 2005, pp. 3-5. Online. Available: http://www.ssab.gov/documents/advisoryboardmemo—2005tr—08102005.pdf. Accessed: March 8, 2006.

Note: Table assumes an actuarial balance of -1.92 percent of taxable payroll over 75 years and -5.7 percent of taxable payroll in the 75th year.

1. Source for means-testing estimate is the authors.

2. Source for these two numbers is Stephen C. Goss and Alice H. Wade, *Estimates of Financial Effect for Three Models Developed by the President's Commission to Strengthen Social Security,* January 21, 2002, Memo to Daniel Patrick Moynihan and Richard D. Parsons. Online. Available: http://www.ssa.gov/OACT/solvency/index.html. Accessed: July 20, 2006.

3. Source for these two numbers is Stephen C. Goss, *Estimated Financial Effects of a Comprehensive Social Security Reform Proposal Including Progressive Price Indexing,* February 10, 2005, Memo to Bob Pozen. Online. Available: http://www.ssa.gov/OACT/solvency/RPozen_20050210.pdf. Accessed: July 20, 2006.

Social Security, ". . . there has never been any real possibility that individual middle- and low-income workers could finance their own financially comfortable retirements at what most people consider a normal retirement age."[82] Given the success of the program and the dependence of retirees on benefits, proponents of this view argue that altering the program dramatically will unnecessarily put this population at risk, and because the program establishes a link between funds contributed to the system and benefits received, elderly across all class and racial lines benefit. Changes in the universal component of the program risk eroding the broad base of support for the program. Key options under this general approach are as follows.

Raise the Payroll Tax Rate

Employees and employers each contribute 6.2 percent of wages up to about $90,000 through the Federal Insurance Contributions Act (FICA). Raising the payroll tax by 1 percent for both employees and employers would resolve Social Security's 75-year financing shortfall.[83] This solution is also viewed by proponents as the simplest administrative way to rectify the funding shortfall. Opponents of this proposal have argued against tax increases generally as economically harmful, resulting in fewer new hires and stagnation of the economy. By choosing the path of payroll tax rate increases to fund Social Security, critics insist that this approach will ensure that the payroll tax burden would have to continue to increase over time given the longer term projections, indicating a significant shift of the tax burden of future genera- tions.[84] Given these potential disadvantages, alterations within this option could be pursued to mitigate the effects but still raise some revenue, including smaller tax in- creases or a delayed tax increase to occur closer to the point at which Social Security will be facing funding shortfalls.

Modify the Wage Tax Cap

Wages are currently taxed up to a capped amount, at $94,200 for 2006.[85] As recently as two decades ago, the cap taxed about 90 percent of aggregate earnings of workers, but over time a growing share of wages has been exempted from the tax. Currently about 15 percent of aggregate pay of workers is above the cap,[86] a share expected to grow to 17 percent in a decade.[87] The entire 75-year financing shortfall would be eliminated if all wages were taxed and wages above the cap did not count toward benefit provision.[88] Proponents argue that this approach is beneficial because it re- stores solvency and ensures that wealthier workers contribute a higher share to Social Security.

Opponents of this approach argue that practically, the proposal will have negative economic effects and that symbolically it represents a break in the link between pay- ments into and benefits received from the system. Critics project a significant cost to small businesses and argue that the tax would result in less investment and reductions in hiring of new workers.[89] They identify this increase as the "largest tax increase in the history of the United States" and an action that would reduce worker earnings, hurt personal savings, and reduce jobs.[90] Depending on how policymakers structure this option, if all wages are taxed but benefits are only paid up to salaries of $94,200, this approach could risk public backlash because it transforms one of Social Security's earliest promises, that workers would be able to trace a clear link between what they pay into the system and what they receive in benefits.

Some options exist to mitigate some of these criticisms, including taxing all wages and allowing all or some income to count toward benefits or creating a cap higher than $90,000—perhaps $145,000—a figure that contains 90 percent of today's earnings, the same level that existed two decades ago. Raising the cap over time to about $145,000 would resolve about 43 percent of Social Security's 75-year financing deficit.[91]

Benefit Reductions for Newly Eligible Retirees

Relatively modest reductions in benefits would clearly help to stabilize financing for the Social Security system. Cutting benefits by 5 percent for newly eligible beneficiaries would eliminate about one-third of the 75-year financing shortfall.[92] Given rising levels of real wages, future retirees receive greater benefits than their predecessors, meaning that with moderate benefit cuts, future benefit levels will still grow, but not as fast as increases in wages. This approach is criticized by some who argue that retirees have planned on a certain level of benefits and that reductions for lower income beneficiaries, in particular, would be unfair. Others argue that benefit cuts alone should not be a complete solution to the solvency problem. Because benefit reductions would have to be large to eliminate the entire deficit, modest benefit reductions are often discussed in conjunction with increasing taxes. Some plans for solvency would raise taxes slowly over several decades, coupled with reductions in future benefit levels, with greater cuts for higher income workers and smaller cuts for lower income workers.

Invest the Trust Fund in Equities

In the current system, by law, Social Security trust funds are invested in low-risk and low-yield special Treasury securities, or if the Treasury Secretary deems appropriate, in marketable Treasury securities. Some analysts argue that in order to strengthen long-term solvency, a portion of the Social Security trust funds should be invested in equities, which have historically earned a higher rate of return. This approach would not eliminate the entire 75-year shortfall but could resolve up to about half of it.[93]

One advantage of this approach is that it lessens the need for benefit cuts or tax increases to resolve the shortfall. In addition, proponents argue that it creates greater equity between Social Security and other pension plans, both public and private. Workers who receive public pensions at the state or local levels, and those who hold private pensions benefit from the market's growth through a diversified portfolio of investments.[94] A third reason that supporters advocate investment in equities is that it might spread the risk of financing benefits across generations. This approach converts the pay-as-you go plan in part to a plan of building assets now for future use in paying benefits.[95] The current system places the burden of financing Social Security on current and future workers, who will have to pay larger payroll taxes in order to keep the system operational absent other reforms. Using current trust funds to build greater funds corrects this imbalance of responsibility.[96]

Critics contend that this proposal involves greater risk than status quo investments. In addition, increases in returns are not "magic"; the result of this proposal would depend on market performance.[97] Some argue that the government is better able to survive ebbs and flows in the market as opposed to individuals investing their own funds who might be forced to retire in a market low.[98] Others contend that the government cannot "'invest' [its] way out of a funding problem," and that the government has to be prepared to make significant financial contributions to salvage Social Security.[99]

Aside from whether investing the trust fund will improve Social Security's financial position, a major concern raised by critics of this proposal is the level of uncertainty surrounding how investing the trust fund in the market will affect the market's performance and the national economy.[100] Predictions of effects of the initial investment vary. Some fear that if the government signaled that it was going to take this action, the effects would be extremely disruptive, while others believe that a major effect is unlikely because participants in the market would have had time to adjust their investments.[101] Some contend that there will be no major disruptions in the market and overall interest rates and stock prices will not increase over the long-term because even though stock prices might increase temporarily, other actors in the market would make adjustments in their investments, thereby nullifying the effects of the new investment.[102] A more optimistic scenario posits that investing the trust fund could actually fuel economic growth through the investment of new private capital.[103]

A final concern raised by critics of investing the trust fund is that it is inappropriate for the federal government to intervene in the markets. There are also the risks that special interests will influence where funds are invested and that the investments will influence actions of other market actors including corporations.[104]

In light of the concerns raised by critics of this idea, several alternate proposals have been offered to mitigate these risks including using the private sector and not the government to make investment decisions and restricting investments to reduce risk. For example some argue for the trust funds to be initially invested solely in government insured mortgages ("Ginnie Maes"). These funds are guaranteed by the government and have higher rates of return than Treasury bonds.[105] Such an approach could have a modest positive improvement on financing the system.[106]

Criticism of this Overall Approach

Taken together, the various approaches outlined in this section have been opposed on several grounds. Some contend that the changes are too minor to enable the program to remain viable for the long-term and that by cutting benefits or increasing taxes, they only succeed in burdening retirees and employers.[107] Critics also argue that similar reforms adopted in the past (as in 1983) enabled the system to stay solvent but unpredictably and unfairly affected workers.[108] Another group of analysts report that the current situation differs significantly from the environment in which Social Security was created and that only a revamped program will meet the needs of current retirees.

Opponents of this approach have differing views on how best to proceed. Some argue in favor of revising the program to provide benefits for the neediest and/or oldest beneficiaries, possibly curtailing the universal nature of the program, and others support greater individual control and less government responsibility in the provision of resources for the elderly. The next two sections explore these two approached in greater detail.

Approach 2: Revising Social Security: A New Contract for a New Generation

A second general approach to changing Social Security affirms Social Security's past role in providing basic economic security for the elderly but argues that certain subsets of the retired population do not require as much assistance as in the past—the "young" elderly and persons with higher incomes. Proponents of this approach argue that major benefit changes are necessary, given the facts that life expectancy and quality of life continue to improve for most Americans and that significant sums of government funding supports higher income elderly families. Proponents of this approach believe that major changes to the program, such as the current Social Security retirement age and the universal nature of benefits, should not be off limits to change. Specific policy prescriptions addressed in this section include increasing the retirement age, providing means-tested benefits only to the elderly with low or moderate incomes, and making major changes to the benefit structure through a new system of sliding-scale benefit reductions/ progressive price indexing.

Raise the Normal Retirement Age

Though the normal retirement age for full Social Security benefits is gradually increasing to 67, some advocate further increases in the age. One specific proposal would raise the age to 70 for people born in 2021, a measure that would eliminate 36 percent of the funding shortfall.[109] Proponents of this strategy base their case on demographic trends and on the benefits of increased work for individuals in retirement and the economy. Primarily, they argue that the current retirement age is not in line with today's population and labor trends. Most retirees receive benefits for almost a third of their lifetimes and that to receive benefits for the same number of years today as retirees did in the 1950s, workers would have to delay retirement until age 74.[110] Not only has life expectancy at age 65 increased by six years since 1900,[111] but more people are living active, healthy, independent lives.[112] In 2004, 73.3 percent of people aged 65 reported that their health was good or excellent, compared to 26.7 percent people that reported it to be fair to poor, though some variations exist by gender and race.[113] Along with changes in the elderly population, the nature of work is changing, with fewer individuals working in physically demanding jobs (a 12.8 percent decrease between 1950 and 1996).[114] In 2000, only 17 percent of male workers stayed in the labor force after age 65.[115] Proponents argue that the current tax system creates financial incentives to retire because the gains of working between the ages of 60-65 are outweighed by guaranteed receipt of Social Security benefits and diminishing returns from income due to Social Security and Medicare taxes.[116]

Aside from the demographic case, proponents of this approach contend that raising the retirement age has individual and societal economic benefits. Delaying retirement for only a relatively short time significantly increases the resources workers have for retirement, though the benefits of work begin to diminish over time.[117] By keeping workers in the workforce longer, workers would pay into the system longer and delay receipt of benefits. This yields economic benefits for individuals in retirement and helps to strengthen the sustainability of the program.

The case against increasing the age of retirement consists of arguments of fairness, feasibility, and inequality. Critics point to the disparate implications of this policy change on low-income and minority persons whose life expectancy is below the national average. These retirees—whose health and job types often make extra working years difficult—would receive even fewer benefits under this approach. In 1993, a study reported that a quarter of early retirees exited the workforce because frailty prevented them from completing their work.[118] One study noted significant health disparities between blue and white-collar workers, indicating, ". . . blue-collar workers are more likely to have musculoskeletal problems, respiratory diseases, diabetes, and emotional disorders than white-collar workers. Blue-collar workers are 58 percent more likely to have arthritis, 42 percent more likely to have chronic lung disease, and 30 percent more likely to have a foot or leg problem."[119] The likely result of increasing the retirement age is that some of these workers would go on Social Security Disability Insurance, but others in need of support might not qualify for disability benefits.[120]

Also, age-based discrimination in the workforce makes it difficult for many people over 67 to remain in the workforce, even if they want to work. Studies document employer fears of extending health care coverage to older workers and perceptions about the lower productivity of older workers as barriers to hiring elderly workers.[121] Another recent study in Massachusetts found that younger workers received callback interviews 40 percent more frequently than those over age 50, resulting in significantly longer job searches for older workers.[122]

A related option would be to couple an increase in the normal retirement age with an increase in the early retirement age from 62 to 64. Currently, 56 percent of workers who become eligible to retire at age 62 choose to retire.[123] About 10 percent of those who choose to retire at age 62 retire due to disabilities or reduced capacity to perform their jobs and have few sources of income support.[124] Programs like Social Security Disability Insurance and Supplemental Security Income might have to be modified to assist this population.

Some people who retire at age 62 have other sources of income (pensions or work-ing spouses) and may be able to absorb the partial loss of benefits incurred due to early retirement. Some analysts project that three-fifths of workers would conform by delaying retirement to age 64.[125] Most retirees make the decision about when to cease working rationally, based on whether they have earned enough to support themselves in retirement,[126] though some retirees operate without perfect information because they are misinformed about the amount of benefits they are scheduled to receive from Social Security.[127]

Means Testing

Some reformers believe that Social Security provides support for many Americans who do not require assistance, prompting them to argue in favor of means-testing benefits, or eliminating benefits for those above a certain income threshold. Great diversity exists among the elderly, with Social Security comprising 40 percent of in-come for most Americans, but nearly 100 percent of income for the poorest 20 per-cent of the elderly.[128] Social Security payments amount to about $15 billion each year for elderly with incomes above $100,000. One approach would be to eliminate all benefits for upper income elderly. If benefits were eliminated for the elderly with the top 10 percent of income, the long term shortfall could be roughly cut in half. This option positions Social Security more as a "safety net" but not a universal source of support for retirees.[129]

Opponents of this strategy argue that means-tested policies will be perceived as punishing upper-income elderly who have worked to earn their income, undermin-ing the support for the entire program that exists because of its universality.[130] They also charge that Social Security's current promise to workers is that all workers pay into the system and have a right to benefits. This policy would change a key ele-ment of the program by eliminating the link between taxes paid and benefits to be received.

Some oppose means-tested programs because of the added administrative costs that come with establishing new eligibility criteria, and for the potential of fraud.[131] One outcome might be a disincentive to save or a disincentive to work to a level that would guarantee retirement security.[132] Workers could spend most of their assets to remain eligible for greater benefits or take lump sums of benefits from their 401(k) or employer pension plans and spend them before retirement so that they can qualify for Social Security benefits in retirement.[133] Some empirical evidence exists to evalu-ate this scenario. Australia has adopted some form of means-testing, though frequent changes in eligibility rules make it difficult to determine if individuals adjust their financial decisions or deliberately spend assets to qualify for benefits.[134] There is some evidence that when income but not assets were tested to determine benefits, indi-viduals shifted funds to private bank accounts.[135]

Some evidence from the U.S. suggests that a means-tested program could discour-age work. Men close to receipt of SSI benefits have been found to be less inclined to remain in the workforce, though these findings might not be applicable to a future means-tested Social Security system because old behaviors and attitudes might not translate with the adoption of a new system.[136]

Major Benefit Reductions by Changes in Indexing

In 1977, amendments to the Social Security program were adopted that tied benefit growth for new retirees to changes in average wages. This ensured that future benefits would replace about the same levels of pre-retirement wage income for future generations as they do for current retirees.[137] Because wage inflation rises more quickly than price inflation, benefit levels for future retirees continue to rise by about 1 percent a year faster than inflation. Some argue for adopting a system of "price indexing" to slow benefit growth. In effect, under this approach, future generations of retirees would receive about the same level of benefits in real terms as current retirees. Tying benefit increases to price inflation through the Consumer Price Index rather than wage growth would yield savings large enough to eliminate the entire long-term financing shortfall.[138]

Many analysts dismiss a plan of purely price indexing because the resulting benefit reductions would be significant for all retirees, particularly for workers with low and average wages who would experience a greater relative loss of income. For example, a 65 year-old in 2022 would receive 10 percent fewer benefits than today. A 65 year-old in 2075 would receive a 46 percent benefit cut.[139] Another way of conceptualizing this loss is that an average earner retiring in 2080 would only receive Social Security benefits that replace 16 percent of wages instead of 39 percent.[140] Eventually, benefits will be miniscule compared to workers' earnings, with future retirees seeing reductions in their quality of life because of their ability to purchase fewer goods.[141] Some groups including the disabled and survivors of beneficiaries might be especially vulnerable.

Given the concern about indexing all workers' benefits to prices, a plan of "sliding-scale benefit reductions/progressive price indexing" has been suggested by some analysts who argue that it would produce cost savings without regressive effects.[142] Under this proposal, benefits for middle and upper-income workers would be tied to price increases, but low-income workers' benefits would be tied to wage increases. This proposal acknowledges that low-income retirees depend heavily on Social Security but that retirees with other sources of retirement security do not need the level of benefits currently provided to them through Social Security. Although not as extreme as "means-testing" by eliminating benefits for upper-income workers, this approach weights benefit provision toward the poorest 20-30 percent of workers by exempting them from price indexing, while reducing the benefits of the upper 70 percent of workers by linking the growth in their benefits to prices instead of wages.

Critics argue that such a system would entail drastic reductions in future benefits for most future retirees, as all workers who earn over $20,000 per year and some workers who earn near $20,000 will lose benefits.[143] Benefits for workers now earning about \$60,000 would be reduced by 28 percent in 2045 and 42 percent in 2075.[144] Critics charge eroding the value of middle and high-income retirees' benefits will ensure that eventually, everyone would end up receiving pensions identical to low-income workers,[145] despite the fact that they put much more into the system.

Approach 3: Reconstructing Social Security: Personal/Private Accounts

A third approach to changing Social Security makes the case that the Social Security system is an inadequate and unsustainable form of support for retirees and that the U.S. government should systematically restructure the system by gradually moving Social Security over to a system of personal/private accounts. To replace part of Social Security's benefit protections, proponents of reconstructing the Social Security system maintain that the status quo does not offer individuals control over their retirement funds or the opportunity to make profitable investments. Proponents of this approach stress the importance of shifting from "dependency" of government to an "ownership society," in which Americans of all income levels retain control over their retirement security and have the ability to participate in stock market system.

Though plans for privatization or semi-privatization of the Social Security system have existed for decades, recent debates have centered on the recommendations issued by the Commission to Strengthen Social Security, created by President George W. Bush in 2001. The Commission issued three plans, all of which include personal/private accounts.[146] Some of the proposals made by the Commission would allow workers to invest up to 4 percent of wages (up to \$1,000 per year) in personal/private accounts. Workers would receive reduced benefits from the current Social Security system based on the amount contributed to personal/private accounts. In addition, benefit growth would be further strained by indexing benefits to prices instead of wages. This combination of personal/private accounts and benefit reductions has gained the endorsement of President Bush.[147] This section will first evaluate the arguments for and against personal/private accounts with corresponding offsets in Society Security benefits, and then a proposal for a combination of personal/private accounts coupled with offsets and sliding-scale benefit reductions/progressive price indexing.

Before analyzing these specific options, it is important to note that many questions remain about how these accounts will operate. Uncertainties include whether contributions will be mandatory or voluntary, how funds will be distributed after retirement (ranging from annuitized payments or unlimited withdrawals), and whether individuals will be able to withdraw funds early, as with 401(k) accounts. These are important questions that could determine whether individuals will be able to amass enough resources for retirement and whether they will have adequate income later in life.[148] These issues are beyond the scope of this chapter.

Personal/Private Accounts Coupled with Social Security Offsets

The President's Commission to Strengthen Social Security developed three plans, all

An International Comparison: The Chilean Case

While much of the private/personal accounts debate in the U.S. remains hypothetical in terms of how much such accounts will increase national savings or what size returns will be produced, several international examples exist that provide empirical evidence of how private accounts operate. One often-cited example is Chile and though its system is not exactly analogous to the U.S., it provides some lessons on the operation of private accounts. Chile's defined-contribution plan, implemented by Augusto Pinochet in 1981 and financed by workers, produced high average returns of over 11 percent between 1981 and 1999 and resulted in an increase in national savings.[1]

Critics argue that the system did not decrease the state's financial obligations or improve the security of retirees. Transition costs were high and because the state established a minimum pension, it supplied funds whenever workers could not generate sufficient pensions.[2] Because contributions are not required, only 44 percent of workers make regular payments to their accounts,[3] and many require state assistance. In total, the state has spent $66 billion since 1981 financing benefits to the 1.4 million retirees still under the old system, providing recognition bonds to workers who switched from the old to the new system, and supplementing pensions of those unable to earn the minimum pension.[4] According to some accounts, the system also did not improve many workers' situations, and as much as 41 percent of the benefit-receiving population is forced to work to survive.[5] Many low-income and seasonal workers struggle to make payments and cannot generate sufficient funds with what they do invest.[6]

1. Barbara E. Kritzer, "Social Security Privatization in Latin America," Social Security Bulletin, 2000, vol. 63, no. 2, p. 21. Online. Available: http://www.ssa.gov/policy/docs/ssb/v63n2/index.html. Accessed: May 10, 2006.

2. Greg Anrig Jr. and Bernard Wasow, 12 Reasons Why Privatizing Social Security is a Bad Idea, The Century Foundation, December 14, 2004. Online. Available: http://www.socsec.org/publications.asp?pubid=503. Accessed: September 27, 2005.

3. John Lear and Joseph Collins, "Retiring on the Free Market: Chile's Privatized Social Security, 20 Years After" in NACLA: Report on the Americas, January 2002, p. 8.

4. James H. Hennessey, "Keeping the Promise: Will the Bush Administration's Plan to Privatize the Social Security System Actually Work?" Connecticut Insurance Law Journal, 2004/5 (11 Conn. Ins. LJ 433), Retried: Lexis-Nexis Academic Universe, 10/11/2005, p. 462.

5. Century Foundation, Social Security Reform, revised 2005 edition, p. 33. Online. Available: http://www.epinet.org/content.cfmissueguide_socialsecurity. Accessed: October 4, 2005.

6. Lear and Collins, "Retiring on the Free Market," p. 8.

of which include personal/private accounts. Under one plan, individuals could redirect 2 percent of the 12.4 percent payroll tax into an individual account. The only change made to Social Security is that Social Security benefits are "offset" (reduced) to compensate for the receipt of the account.

These two changes alone do not ensure solvency of the Social Security system. Indeed, the redirection of Social Security revenues would increase the size of the shortfall over the next 75 years by about a quarter. That is why private accounts proposals often include additional benefit reductions and general revenue transfers to make up for losses and to restore solvency. The next section includes more detailed analysis of a more comprehensive private account proposal along these lines.

All forms of personal/private accounts dramatically change the Social Security system. Proponents argue that given the problems facing the current system, now is the time to convert to a restructured system of personal/private accounts. Supporters of private accounts list many reasons for their adoption, including decreasing the government's long-term financial obligations, building national and individual savings, and creating an "ownership society."

Proponents contend that a system of personal/private accounts will significantly reduce the federal government's financial obligations to future retirees. In the current Social Security system, the government bears a majority of financial responsibility of ensuring retirement security for elderly Americans and though the size of this future financial obligation is debatable, it is clear that the current system necessitates growing tax payments from future workers. Under a system of private accounts, individuals would make contributions to their own accounts and be responsible for managing their accounts. This system would not offer retirees the guarantee of a certain level of benefits, thereby decreasing future fiscal pressures on the government.

Advocates of personal/private accounts also argue that that they will increase national savings. Over the past 50 years, national savings has decreased from about 8 percent of GDP to 1 percent of GDP.[149] Lower rates of national saving are problematic to many who argue that national savings enables the U.S. economy to grow by making capital available for investment.[150] For these reasons, proponents argue that shifting from the pay-as-you-go Social Security system to a pre-funded system would build greater savings at the national level.[151]

Proponents also argue that personal/private accounts will enable more individuals to accumulate greater retirement savings and that these accounts enable workers— especially younger workers—to earn greater returns on their investments.[152] While market returns sometimes fluctuate, a survey of 226 financial economists forecasted 5 percent annual returns (real) from equities during the next 30 years,[153] though some supporters of privatization caution against adopting such accounts purely due to high projected rates of return, given that the system will also have high costs during the transition and increased risk.[154]

A final reason proponents provide in support of personal/private accounts is that they further the values of responsibility, liberty, and property by giving all individuals, regardless of income, the means to participate in capital markets and the task of ensuring their own security in retirement.[155] Further, because accounts are assets that belong to individuals, family members of deceased workers can inherit personal/private accounts.[156]

Critics of personal/private accounts raise several concerns with the approach. First, they argue that personal/private accounts do not address the financing shortfall and will have significant transition costs. New government spending will be required for the first half century of implementation to set up the accounts.[157] Many proposals for personal/private accounts have surfaced in recent years but most necessitate general revenue transfers in some form.[158] As much as $5 trillion may be required to finance these accounts.[159]

A second criticism is that personal/private accounts increase the risk of financial insecurity in retirement by decreasing the level of risk carried by government and increasing the risk born by individuals. If people do not receive returns as large as projected or retire in an economic downturn, they will likely be at added risk in retirement. Market performance over the past 75 years supports the fact that returns are highly variable.[160] While overall performance was strong, "for any given 10-year period, investors have a 25 percent chance of realizing lower returns from a portfolio of Standard and Poor's stocks than from a portfolio of government bonds."[161] Many forecast that future economic growth will be lower due to labor shortages and reduced productivity, and the returns on stocks and bonds may decrease accordingly.[162]

Third, opponents of privatization argue that personal/private accounts disproportionately place risk on vulnerable groups including low-income persons, women, minorities, and the disabled. The current system provides somewhat higher returns for lower wage workers. Under a system of personal/private accounts, the redistributive effects of Social Security might be eroded. These populations have fewer resources to invest, but much more to lose under a system of private accounts. Stable income in retirement is important for all retirees, yet the loss of the guarantee of a certain level of benefits for the duration of one's life is especially threatening for women who, given their longer life expectancies, risk outliving their private accounts. Also, because discussions of survivor and disability benefits are often lost in the discussion of Social Security reform, critics of privatization are concerned about how these benefits will be affected. Specific strategies for protecting disability and survivor benefits are rarely articulated fully.[163]

Personal/Private Accounts Coupled with Sliding-Scale Benefit Reductions/Progressive Price Indexing

A very wide range of comprehensive proposals have been put forward that combine private accounts with other major changes to Social Security benefit payments. Some of these proposals, such as one by Robert Pozen, resolve the entire Social Security financing shortfall, albeit utilizing major transfers of general tax revenue to Social Security. Other proposals, such as the one outlined by President Bush, establish private accounts and make other changes that resolve part of the financing shortfall.

President Bush's approach contains two key parts: personal/private accounts with corresponding cut-backs (offsets) in Social Security benefits, coupled with reductions in remaining Social Security benefits for most workers earning over $20,000 annually through the adoption of a system of sliding-scale benefit reductions/progressive price indexing.[164] Proponents of the combined approach point to two related benefits: resolving part of the long-term financing shortfall and preventing low-income individuals from experiencing large benefit reductions.

Though creating a system of personal/private accounts alone does not address the financial shortfall of Social Security, combining them with sliding-scale benefit reductions accomplishes two of the President's goals, converting the system of Social Security to individual accounts, and resolving some of the system's financing shortfall.

Proponents argue that sliding-scale benefit reductions spare the lowest-income retirees from large benefit cuts. Given that current benefit levels are not sustainable absent changes, proponents of President Bush's plan argue that this approach makes the changes necessary to restore solvency while enhancing the progressive structure of the current system. Benefits for the lowest 30 percent of earners, or those making $20,000 or less, would be protected by tying benefits to changes in wages, while the benefits of the remaining 70 percent will be reduced by tying benefit levels to changes in prices.[165]

Opponents point to several flaws with the President's plan including a failure to resolve the Social Security shortfall, instituting significant benefit reductions for most beneficiaries, and paving the way for a long-term unraveling of the Social Security system. Critics conclude that the combination of personal/private accounts and progressive price indexing is more harmful than either option alone.

The first objection with the combined approach is that it only resolves part of the shortfall, necessitating other strategies to resolve the remaining deficit. To opponents, the fact that this approach does not resolve the entirety of the problem makes the large benefit cuts proposed by the President especially problematic. Additionally, even with billions in savings from benefit reductions, the plan is not enough to mitigate the net transition cost, projected to be as high as $4.9 trillion.[166]

A second concern with this overall strategy is that the Social Security benefit reductions are dramatic, resulting in a situation in which all benefits over time will become similar in size; the amount of taxes paid into the system will be divorced from benefit receipt. Individuals are affected by two reductions in benefits, once from the mandatory sliding-scale reductions and also from funding personal/private accounts. Upon retirement, workers would not have the amount they invested in their accounts subtracted from their benefits, but also funds to cover an interest rate 3 percent above inflation, making it possible that if their accounts did not earn enough benefits, they could lose all of their benefits.[167] Estimates vary as to the size of the cuts, ranging from 16 percent for 2022 retirees to 40 percent for 2042 retirees to 62 percent for 2075 retirees.[168] Others project more severe reductions and that cuts for those with incomes above 60 percent of the average wage will lose 97 percent of benefits by 2075.[169] Further, because rising Medicare premiums are deducted from Social Security benefits, millions of retirees could receive few or no benefits.[170]

Opponents of privatization also argue that these benefit cuts will result in the unraveling and potential dismantling of the Social Security system. Because all but the lowest-income retirees will experience great benefit losses, the support of moderate to high-income retirees for Social Security could decrease. These individuals are likely to perceive greater benefit from their accounts as opposed to their small Social Security benefit.[171] In the past, the foundation for Social Security's appeal was its universality, and the combination of accounts and sliding-scale benefit reductions undermines this aspect of Social Security's design and the broad support that currently exists for the program.[172]

The Future of Social Security

America's democratic institutions came together 70 years ago and forged our Social Security system, reflecting the shared societal notion that old age should not mean destitution. While there have been substantial changes in the program's size and scope, Social Security remains the foundation of today's retirement system—a foundation critically important to tens of millions of Americans.

The Social Security system has evolved over the decades and the system will continue to change in the years ahead. It is clear that the demographic pressures confronting the system necessitate some changes. However, because substantial disagreement exists about the extent of the Social Security problem and the most appropriate policy remedies, Congress has not yet enacted changes.

The three broad approaches for Social Security reform outlined in this chapter present very different ways to change the system. These approaches differ sharply on the role that Social Security should play in the future. Policymakers will have to reconcile competing visions and values, and they will have to acknowledge the fact that reforms will affect certain subsets of citizens differently. These are tough but important choices that affect the well-being of future generations of Americans.

The quandary that confronts policymakers today is how to design a system in light of these emerging challenges and points of strong disagreement. It is important for all Americans—our parents and grandparents, our children and grandchildren—that we find common ground on the future of Social Security, because the actions taken to change Social Security will shape not only retirement security for future generations, but also the collective vision defining our roles and responsibilities to one another.

Notes

1.   Jacob S. Hacker, *The Divided Welfare State* (New York: Cambridge University Press, 2002), p. 92.

2.   Carolyn L. Weaver, "Support of the Elderly Before the Depression: Individual and Collective Arrangements," *Cato Journal,* vol. 7, no. 2 (Fall 1987), pp. 503-525, p. 507. Online. Available: http://www.cato.org/pubs/journal/cj7n2/cj7n2-15.pdf. Accessed: January 11, 2006.

3.   Tim Heaton and Caroline Hoppe, "Widowed and Married: Comparative Change in Living Arrangements, 1900 and 1980," *Social Science History,* vol. 11, no. 3. (Autumn 1987), p. 266. Available: JSTOR. Accessed: November 1, 2005.

44. Martin and Weaver, "Social Security: A Program and Policy History," p. 5; and Harper, *Social Security Reform, Timeline* (online).

45. Martin and Weaver, "Social Security: A Program and Policy History," p. 10.

46. Beland, *Social Security, History and Politics,* p. 147.

47. Harper, *Social Security Reform, Timeline* (online).

48. Martin and Weaver, "Social Security: A Program and Policy History," p. 9; and Kollmann, "Summary of the Major Changes," p. i (2).

49. SSA, *Chronology, 1980s.* Online. Available: http://www.ssa.gov/history/1980.html. Accessed: October 20, 2005.

50. Ibid.

51. Social Security Reform Center, *History of Social Security* (online); and National Committee to Preserve Social Security and Medicare, *Social Security Primer,* par. "History of the Social Security Program."

52. Fleming, Evans, and Chutka, "A Cultural and Economic History of Old Age in America" (online).

53. Keith Melville, "The Social Security Struggle, Fixing the Retirement System," National Issues Forum, 2005, p. 16.

54. Peter Fronczek, "Income, Earnings, and Poverty, from the 2004 American Community Survey" (August 2005), p. 10. Online. Available: http://www.census.gov/prod/2005pubs/acs-01.pdf. Accessed: October 13, 2005.

55. Maya Rockeymoore, "Testimony Before the Subcommittee on Social Security of the House Committee on Ways and Means," May 17, 2005. Online. Available: http://waysandmeans.house.gov/hearings.asp?formmode=printfriendly&id=2660. Accessed: October 4, 2005.

56. Ross Eisenbrey and William Spriggs, "Two Steps Back, African Americans and Latinos Will Lose Ground Under Social Security 'Reform,'" EPI Issue Brief #212 (July 14, 2005), p. 4. Online. Available: http://www.epinet.org/issuebriefs/212/ib212.pdf. Accessed: October 4, 2005.

57. Social Security Advisory Board, *Social Security: Why Action Should be Taken Soon* (September 2005), p. i. Online. Available: http://www.ssab.gov/documents/WhyActionShouldbeTakenSoon.pdf. Accessed: October 11, 2005.

58. Older Women's League, *Social Security Privatization, a False Promise for Women* (2002), p. 6. Online. Available: http://www.owl-national.org/owlreports/MothersDay2002.pdf. Accessed: October 14, 2005.

59. Rockeymoore, "Testimony Before the Subcommittee on Social Security of the House Committee on Ways and Means" (online); and Maya Rockeymoore, *Social Security Reform and African Americans: Debunking the Myths,* National Urban League, Policy Brief No. 2 (August 2001), p. 2. Online. Available: http://www.ourfuture.org/docUploads/NUL%20Debunking%20the%20Myths.doc. Accessed: October 4, 2005.

60. Gary Burtless and Joseph F. Quinn, *Is Working Longer the Answer for an Aging Workforce?,* Center for Retirement Research, Number 11 (December 2002), p. 3. Online. Available: http://www.bc.edu/centers/crr/dummy/issues/ib_11.pdf. Accessed: May 2, 2006.

61. Social Security and Medicare Boards of Trustees, *A Summary of the 2005 Annual Reports* (2005). Online. Available: http://www.ssa.gov/OACT/TRSUM/trsummary.html. Accessed: December 2, 2005.

62. Melville, "The Social Security Struggle, Fixing the Retirement System," p. 21; and Federal Interagency Forum on Aging-Related Statistics, "Table 1b1. Percentage of the Population Age 65 and Over and 85 and Over, Selected Years 1900-2000," *Older Americans 2004: Key Indicators of Well-Being* (2004). Online. Available: http://www.agingstats.gov/chartbook2004/CBpopulation.xls. Accessed: September 27, 2005.

63. Robert Clark, Richard Burkhauser, Marilyn Moon, Joseph F. Quinn, and Timothy M. Smeeding, *The Economics of an Aging Society* (New York: Blackwell Press, 2004), p. 23.

64. Federal Interagency Forum on Aging-Related Statistics, "Table 13 A. Life Expectancy, By Age and Sex, Selected Years 1900-2001," *Older Americans 2004: Key Indicators of Well-Being* (2004). Online. Available: http://www.agingstats.gov/chartbook2004/CBhealth%20status.xls. Accessed: September 27, 2005.

65. Alicia H. Munnell and Mauricio Soto, *Sorting out Social Security Replacement Rates,* Center for Retirement Research, Number 19 (November 2005), p. 1. Online. Available: http://www.bc.edu/centers/crr/facts/jtf_19.pdf. Accessed: December 16, 2005.

66. Alicia H. Munnell and Mauricio Soto, *How Much Pre-Retirement Income Does Social Security Replace?,* Center for Retirement Research, Number 36 (November 2005), p. 4. Online. Available: http://www.bc.edu/centers/crr/issues/ib_36.pdf. Accessed: December 16, 2005.

67. Alicia H. Munnell, *A Bird's Eye View of the Social Security Debate,* Center for Retirement Research, Number 25 (December 2004). p. 5. Online Available: http://www.bc.edu/centers/crr/issues/ib_25.pdf. Accessed: December 16, 2005.

68. Congressional Budget Office, *The Future Growth of Social Security: It's Not Just Society's Aging,* No. 9 (July 1, 2003). Online. Available: http://www.cbo.gov/showdoc.cfm?index=4380&sequence=0. Accessed: December 16, 2005.

69. Government Accountability Office (GAO), *Private Pensions, Issues of Coverage and Increasing Contribution Limits for Defined Contribution Plans* (September 2001), p. 1. Online. Available: http://www.gao.gov/new.items/d01846.pdf. Accessed: December 18, 2005.

70. Alicia H. Munnell and Mauricio Soto, *How do Pensions Affect Replacement Rates?,* Center for Retirement Research, Number 37 (November 2005). p. 3. Online. Available: http://www.bc.edu/centers/crr/issues/ib_37.pdf. Accessed: December 16, 2005.

71. Alicia H. Munnell, James G. Lee, and Kevin B. Meme, *An Update on Pension Data,* Center for Retirement Research, Number 20 (July 2004), p. 3. Available: http://www.bc.edu/centers/crr/issues/ib_20.pdf. Accessed: December 16, 2005.

72. GAO, *Private Pensions, Issues of Coverage and Increasing Contribution Limits for Defined Contribution Plans,* pp. 10-11.

73. Munnell, Lee, and Meme, *An Update on Pension Data,* p. 2.

74. Employment Policy Foundation, Shifting Trends in Pension Plan Coverage (April 28, 2005), p. 1. Online. Available: http://www.epf.org/pubs/factsheets/2005/fs20050428a.pdf. Accessed: December 18, 2005 (no longer available online); and Victor A. Canto, *Pension Problems, Pension Politics,* National Review (July 25, 2003). Online. Available: http://www.nationalreview.com/nrof_canto/canto072503.asp. Accessed: December 9, 2005.

75. Munnell, Lee, and Meme, *An Update on Pension Data,* p. 5.

76. Ibid.

77. Ibid., p. 6.

78. Ken Apfel, "Retirees Losing a Benefit," *Dallas Morning News,* August 11, 2002, p. 5J.

79. Alicia H. Munnell, Francesca Golub-Sass, and Andrew Varani, *How Much are Workers Saving?,* Center for Retirement Research, Number 34 (October 2005), p. 2. Online. Available: http://www. bc.edu/centers/crr/issues/ib_34.pdf. Accessed: December 16, 2005.

80. Munnell, Golub-Sass, and Varani, *How Much are Workers Saving?,* p. 7.

81. Munnell and Soto, *Sorting out Social Security Replacement Rates,* p. 3.

82. Patricia E. Dilley, "Hope We Die Before We Get Old: The Attack on Retirement," *The Elder Law Journal,* no. 12 (2004), p. 245. Retrieved on Lexis-Nexis Academic Universe, October 11, 2005.

83. SSA, *Estimated OASDI Long-Range Financial Effects of Several Provisions Requested by the Social Security Advisory Board* by Chris Chaplain and Alice H. Wade (August 10, 2005), p. 4. Online. Available: http://www.ssab.gov/documents/advisoryboardmemo--2005tr--08102005.pdf. Accessed: March 8, 2006.

84. Melville, "The Social Security Struggle, Fixing the Retirement System," p. 20.

85. SSA, *Contribution and Benefit Base* (October 14, 2005). Online. Available: http://www.ssa.gov/ OACT/COLA/cbb.html. Accessed: December 16, 2005.

86. Lawrence Mishel, "Lifting Cap on Social Security Taxes Would Rescue Retirement Program," Economic Policy Institute, from *The Journal Star* (May 15, 2005). Online. Available: http://www.epi. org/content.cfm/webfeatures_viewpoints_lifting_cap_on_SS_taxes. Accessed: October 4, 2005.

87. Virginia P. Reno and Joni Lavery, *Options to Balance Social Security Funds Over the Next 75 Years,* Social Security Brief, National Academy of Social Insurance, No. 18 (February 2005), p. 3. Available: http://www.nasi.org/usr_doc/SS_Brief_18.pdf. Accessed: September 26, 2005.

88. SSA, *Estimated OASDI Long-Range Financial Effects,* p. 5.

89. Norbert J. Michel and J. Scott Moody, *Raising the Social Security Wage Cap Would Hurt Small Business,* Heritage Foundation, WebMemo #694 (March 17, 2005). Online. Available: http://www.heritage.org/Research/SocialSecurity/wm694.cfm. Accessed: September 29, 2005.

90. Rea S. Hederman, Jr., Tracy L. Foersch, and Kirk A. Johnson, *Keep the Social Security Wage Cap: Nearly a Million Jobs Hang in the Balance,* Heritage Foundation (April 22, 2005). Online. Available: http://www.heritage.org/Research/SocialSecurity/cda05-04.cfm. Accessed: September 27, 2005.

91. SSA, *Estimated OASDI Long-Range Financial Effects,* p. 5.

92. Ibid., p. 3.

93. Ibid., p. 5.

94. Alicia H. Munnell and Pierluigi Balduzzi, *Investing the Social Security Trust Fund in Equities,* American Association of Retired Persons (March 1998), pp. 6-7. Available: http://assets.aarp.org/rgcenter/ econ/9802_sstrust.pdf. Accessed: October 25, 2005.

95. American Academy of Actuaries, *Social Security Reform: Trust Fund Investments* (December 2000), p. 2. Available: http://www.actuary.org/pdf/socialsecurity/sstrustfund_1200.pdf. Accessed: December 16, 2005.

96. Munnell and Balduzzi, *Investing the Social Security Trust Fund in Equities,* pp. 7-8.

97. Joseph J. Cordes and C. Eugene Steuerle, *A Primer on Privatization,* The Privatization Project, Urban Institute, Occasional Paper Number 3 (November 1999), p. 10. Online. Available: http://www. urban.org/UploadedPDF/retire_3.pdf. Accessed: September 27, 2005.

98. Thomas N. Bethell, *What's the Big Idea,* AARP Bulletin (April 2005). Online. Available: http://www.aarp.org/bulletin/socialsec/ss_ideas.html. Accessed: September 27, 2005.

99. David S. Blitzstein, "An Organized Labor Perspective on Social Security Reform," in *Prospects for Social Security Reform,* eds. Olivia S. Mitchell, Robert J. Myers, and Howard Young (Philadelphia: University of Pennsylvania Press, 1999), p. 353.

100. Munnell and Balduzzi, *Investing the Social Security Trust Fund in Equities,* pp. 8-9; and American Academy of Actuaries, *Social Security Reform: Trust Fund Investments,* pp. 2-3.

101. Munnell and Balduzzi, *Investing the Social Security Trust Fund in Equities,* pp. 8-9.

102. American Academy of Actuaries, *Social Security Reform: Trust Fund Investments,* p. 3.

103. Ibid., p. 4.

104. Daniel J. Mitchell, *Government-Controlled Investment: The Wrong Answer to the Wrong Question,* Heritage Foundation (February 16, 2005). Online. Available: http://www.heritage.org/Research/SocialSecurity/draft-govinvest.cfm. Accessed: November 11, 2005.

105. Thomas Hungerford, *The Effects of Investing the Social Security Trust Funds in GNMA Mortgage-Backed Securities,* AARP Issue Paper 2006-05 (2006), p. i. Online. Available: http://www.aarp.org/research/socialsecurity/reform/2006_01_ss_gnma.html. Accessed: March 9, 2006.

106. Ibid.

107. David C. John, *No, Retirees, Workers Would be Hurt,* AARP Bulletin (June 2002). Online. Available: www.aarp.org/bulletin/faceoff/a2003-06-25-cansocialsecurity.html/page=2. Accessed: September 27, 2005.

108. Salvador Valdes-Prieto, *Market-based Social Security as a Better Means of Risk-Sharing,* Pension Research Council Working Paper (2005). p. 3. Online. Available: http://www.pensions-institute.org/workingpapers/ WP2005-16.pdf. Accessed: October 11, 2005.

109. SSA, *Estimated OASDI Long-Range Financial Effects,* p. 4.

110. C. Eugene Steuerle, "Social Security—A Labor Force Issue," Statement Before the Subcommittee on Social Security, Committee on Ways and Means, U.S. House of Representatives (June 14, 2005), p. 2. Online. Available: http://www.urban.org/uploadedPDF/900819_Steuerle_061405.pdf. Accessed: September 27, 2005.

111. Federal Interagency Forum on Aging-Related Statistics, "Table 13 A" (online).

112. Melville, "The Social Security Struggle, Fixing the Retirement System," pp. 22-3.

113. Federal Interagency Forum on Aging-Related Statistics, "Table 20 1. Respondent-Assessed Health Status Among People 65 and Older," *Older Americans 2004: Key Indicators of Well-Being* (2004). Online. Available: http://www.agingstats.gov/chartbook2004/CBhealth%20status.xls. Accessed: September 27, 2005.

114. Eugene Steuerle, Chris Spiro, and Richard W. Johnson, *Can Americans Work Longer?,* Urban Institute, No. 5 (August 15, 1999), p. 1. Online. Available: http://www.urban.org/UploadedPDF/Straight5.pdf. Accessed: September 27, 2005.

115. Melville, "The Social Security Struggle, Fixing the Retirement System," p. 23.

116. Barbara A. Butrica, Richard W. Johnson, Karen E. Smith, and Eugene Steuerle, *Does Work Pay at Older Ages?,* Urban Institute (December 2004), p. 17. Online. Available: http://www.urban.org/UploadedPDF/411121_DoesWorkPay.pdf. Accessed: September 27, 2005.

117. Ibid., pp. I, 17.

118. Melville, "The Social Security Struggle, Fixing the Retirement System," p. 27.

119. Cynthia Fagnoni, *Implications of Raising the Retirement Age*, General Accounting Office (August 1999), p. 25. Online. Available: http://www.gao.gov/archive/1999/he99112.pdf. Accessed: September 27, 2005.

120. Ibid., pp. 9, 12.

121. Urban Institute, *Working Longer to Make Retirement More Secure* (January 4, 2005). Online. Available: http://www.urban.org/urlprint.cfm?ID=9141. Online. Accessed: September 27, 2005; and Fagnoni, *Implications of Raising the Retirement Age*, pp. 20-21.

122. Joanna N. Lahey, *Do Older Workers Face Discrimination?*, Center for Retirement Research at Boston College, Number 33 (July 2005), p. 3. Online. Available: http://www.bc.edu/centers/crr/issues/ib_33.pdf. Accessed: October 4, 2005.

123. Century Foundation, *The Basics: Social Security Reform*, Revised 2005 edition, p. 24. Online. Available: http://www.tcf.org/Publications/RetirementSecurity/SocialSecurityBasicsRev2005.pdf. Accessed: October 4, 2005.

124. Alicia H. Munnell, Kevin B. Meme, Natalia A. Jivan, and Kevin E. Cahill, *Should We Raise Social Security's Earliest Eligible Age?*, Center for Retirement Research at Boston College, Number 18 (June 2004), p. 4. Online. Available: http://www.bc.edu/centers/crr/issues/ib_18.pdf. Accessed: October 4, 2005.

125. Alan Gustman and Thomas L. Steinmeier, "The Social Security Early Entitlement Age in a Structural Model of Retirement and Wealth," National Bureau of Economic Research, Working Paper 9183, (September 2002), pp. 27, 32. Online. Available: http://www.nber.org/papers/w9183.pdf. Accessed: October 11, 2005 (No longer available online).

126. Andrew Au, Olivia S. Mitchell, and John W.R. Phillips, *Savings Shortfalls and Delayed Retirement*, University of Michigan Retirement Research Center, Research Brief 2005- 78, p. 2. Online. Available: http://www.mrrc.isr.umich.edu/publications/briefs/pdf/rb078.pdf. Accessed: October 14, 2005.

127. Alan Gustman and Tom Steinmeier, *Imperfect Knowledge, Retirement, and Saving*, University of Michigan Retirement Research Center (June 2001), p. 4. Online. Available: http://www.mrrc.isr.umich.edu/publications/briefs/pdf/ib_012.pdf. Accessed: October 14, 2005.

128. Melville, "The Social Security Struggle, Fixing the Retirement System," p. 16.

129. David Neumark and Elizabeth Powers, "Means Testing Social Security," in *Prospects for Social Security Reform*, eds. Olivia S. Mitchell, Robert J. Myers, and Howard Young (Philadelphia: University of Pennsylvania Press, 1999), p. 244.

130. Melville, "The Social Security Struggle, Fixing the Retirement System," p. 29.

131. American Academy of Actuaries, *Means Testing for Social Security*, American Issue Brief (January 2004), p. 4. Online. Available: http://www.actuary.org/pdf/socialsecurity/means_0104.pdf. Accessed: September 29, 2005, p. 4.

132. Neumark and Powers, "Means Testing Social Security," p. 246.

133. American Academy of Actuaries, *Means Testing for Social Security*, pp. 2-3.

134. Neumark and Powers, "Means Testing Social Security," p. 247.

135. Ibid., p. 248.

136. Ibid., p. 261.

137. Patrick Purcell, *'Progressive Price Indexing' of Social Security Benefits*, Congressional Research Service (April 22, 2005), p. 3. Online. Available: http://www.tcf.org/Publications/RetirementSecurity/CRS_Price_Indexing_04-22-05.pdf. Accessed: October 4, 2005.

138. SSA, *Estimated OASDI Long-Range Financial Effects*, p. 3.

139. Reno and Lavery, *Options to Balance Social Security Funds*, p. 6.

140. Purcell, *'Progressive Price Indexing' of Social Security Benefits*, p. 6.

141. Alicia H. Munnell and Mauricio Soto, *What Does Price Indexing Mean for Social Security Benefits*, Just the Facts on Retirement Issues, Center for Retirement Research at Boston College, Number 14 (January 2005), p. 1. Online. Available: http://www.bc.edu/centers/crr/facts/jtf_14.pdf. Accessed: October 4, 2005.

142. Robert Pozen, *The Route to Real Pensions Reform*, Economist.com Opinion (January 6, 2005). Online. Available: http://www.economist.com/opinion/displayStory.cfm?story_id=3535838. Accessed: January 10, 2006.

143. Jason Furman, "Evaluating Alternative Social Security Reforms," Testimony Before the Full Committee of the House Committee on Ways and Means," May 12, 2005, p. 8. Online. Available: http://www.cbpp.org/5-12-05socsec-test.pdf. Accessed: October 13, 2005.

144. Ibid., p. 9.

145. Purcell, *'Progressive Price Indexing' of Social Security Benefits*, p. 10.

146. President's Commission to Strengthen Social Security, *Strengthening Social Security and Creating Personal Wealth for All Americans* (December 21, 2001), pp. 14-16. Online. Available: http://www.csss.gov/reports/Final_report.pdf. Accessed: January 13, 2006.

147. "Bush's Plan Dies Quickly, Leaving Lessons for Next Time," *USA Today*, October 10, 2005. Online. Available: http://www.usatoday.com/news/opinion/editorials/2005-10-10-social-security-edit_x.htm. Accessed: October 11, 2005.

148. Kenneth S. Apfel and Michael J. Graetz, *Uncharted Waters: Paying Benefits From Individual Accounts in Federal Retirement Policy, Study Panel Final Report*, National Academy of Social Insurance (2005), pp. i-ii. Online. Available: http://www.nasi.org/usr_doc/Uncharted_Waters_Report.pdf. Accessed: December 16, 2005.

149. N. Gregory Mankiw, *Social Security Reform: National Saving and Macroeconomic Performance in the Global Economy*, Council on Foreign Relations (January 18, 2005), p. 2. Online. Available: http://www.whitehouse.gov/cea/20050118-Mankiw--CFR.pdf. Accessed: December 16, 2005.

150. Mankiw, *Social Security Reform*, p. 2.

151. "Greenspan: Private Accounts OK But . . . ," *Money*, February 16, 2005. Online. Available: http://money.cnn.com/2005/02/16/retirement/fed_socialsecurity. Accessed: December 16, 2005; and Jeffrey R. Brown, "Would Private Accounts Improve Social Security?" *Journal of Policy Analysis and Management*, vol. 25, iss. 3 (Summer 2006), pp. 680-683.

152. David C. John and Stuart Butler, *Bush's Progressive Indexation Plan: A Key Step to Preserve Social Security*, Heritage Foundation, WebMemo #733 (May 2, 2005). Online. Available: http://www.heritage.org/Research/SocialSecurity/wm733.cfm. Accessed: September 27, 2005.

Chapter 8

Reaffirm Social Security: The Promise of Protection

Meeting Social Security's Long-Range Shortfall: How We Can Cope Calmly with a Readily Manageable Challenge

by Robert M. Ball

All is momentarily quiet on the Social Security front. So this may be an opportune time to take a calm look at the long-term financing shortfall facing the system.

As everyone surely understands by now, the aging of the baby boom generation will greatly swell the ranks of Social Security beneficiaries over the next 30 years, with the total, including children and disabled beneficiaries, increasing from about 48 million today to about 88 million in 2035. The numbers will continue to grow after that, although more slowly, and are projected to reach 110 million by 2080—the end-point of the trustees' current 75-year cost estimates, which also assume, with good reason, that the elderly of the future will live longer and thus receive benefits longer than their predecessors.

How should we meet this sharply increasing cost?

Social Security has traditionally had two sources of income: the contributions of workers and their employers plus the investment income earned by the trust funds, which hold the accumulating excess of income over expenditures. Since 1983, when the most recent major amendments were enacted, the program has had a third source of income: taxation of the benefits of higher-income beneficiaries. In 1983 it was estimated that the income from these three sources would meet estimated costs over the following 75 years and leave a reserve equal to about one year's benefits.

Because of changes since 1983 in some of the assumptions governing their long-range

(Updated March 28, 2006; used with permission)

projections, Social Security's trustees now anticipate a deficit over the current 75-year estimating period of about 2 percent of payroll. It is this long-term shortfall—which I believe should be seen as neither trivial nor overwhelming—that needs to be addressed. Moreover, we should not view the next 75 years as a closed period during which we build up the trust funds and then spend them down again. We need rather to keep building the funds throughout the 75 years so that future earnings on the funds will contribute to financing the system during the current 75-year period and beyond.

We can do the job with three modifications of present law which are desirable in themselves in any event—and, very importantly, without further benefit cuts.

1. Restore the Maximum Earnings Base to 90 Percent of Earnings

Our goal, as before, should be to build up and maintain an invested reserve that can help meet future costs—costs which, if covered on a strictly pay-as-you-go basis without the earnings from a reserve, would require a substantial increase in contribution rates (rising from today's 12.4 percent of payroll to an estimated 18.15 percent in 2080 and even more beyond). Building the reserve, therefore, is very important. We should start by getting back to the practice of collecting the Social Security tax on 90 percent of all covered earnings, the goal affirmed by Congress in 1983.

Present law contains a provision which was intended to keep the coverage level at 90 percent: an automatic annual increase in the maximum annual earnings base (now $94,200) by the same percentage as the increase in average wages. But this adjustment mechanism hasn't worked as planned because over the past 20 years the earnings of the higher paid have been rising much more than average wages—so an increasing proportion of earnings exceeds the maximum earnings base and thus escapes Social Security taxation. Today only about 83 percent of earnings is being taxed. That seemingly small slippage translates into billions of dollars in lost revenues each year.

I propose to get us back to 90 percent, but to do so very gradually so that the additional tax on the 6 percent of earners with wages above the cap would increase very little year by year. I would increase the maximum earnings base by 2 percent per year above the increases occurring automatically as average wages rise. Thus, for example, the maximum next year would go up $1,884 (2 percent of $94,200) beyond the automatic increase, and the maximum tax increase beyond present law would be $116.81 ($1,884 times the Social Security tax rate of 6.2 percent). In practice, this would mean that deductions from earnings for the highest-paid 6 percent of workers would simply continue for a few days longer into the year, and for their additional contributions would receive somewhat higher benefits. For the 94 percent of covered workers with earnings below the cap there would be no change at all.

With this approach it is estimated that we would get back to the 90-percent level in about 40 years. Such a gradual adjustment would be virtually painless—but this seemingly small change would reduce the projected 2 percent of payroll deficit by almost a third, to about 1.3 percent of payroll.

We could, of course, speed up the timetable in order to reach the 90-percent level sooner—in, say, 10 years instead of 40. That would reduce the deficit a bit more (just over 0.1 percent of payroll more) but because it would require adding 8 percent rather than 2 percent per year to the automatic adjustment we would substantially increase the burden of taxation on workers earning not much above the present maximum. For example, someone earning only $7,500 above the cap next year would pay an additional tax of $465. The slower timetable accomplishes nearly as much deficit reduction without such sharp increases in cost for anyone.

2. Earmark the Estate Tax for Social Security

In addition to restoring the taxable earnings base, I propose to establish a new source of funding by changing the estate tax into a dedicated Social Security tax beginning in 2010.

Present law gradually reduces the estate tax so that by 2009 only estates valued above $3.5 million ($7 million for a couple) will be taxed. President Bush then wants to abolish the estate tax permanently from 2010 on. Instead, I would freeze the tax at the 2009 level and earmark the proceeds for Social Security from 2010 on, thereby converting the residual estate tax into a dedicated Social Security tax just like the tax on employers' payrolls.

Such a tax would be an appropriate way to partially offset the deficit of contributions that was unavoidably created in Social Security's early years—the so-called "legacy cost." At that time the sensible decision was made to pay higher benefits to workers nearing retirement age than would have been possible had their benefits depended entirely on the relatively small contributions that they and their employers would have had time to make.

Like most of the founders of Social Security, I once assumed that general revenues would eventually be used to make up for this initial deficit of contributions. The idea still makes sense, since there is no good reason why the cost of getting the system started should be met entirely by the contributions of workers and their employers in the future. But there are no general revenues available because the President's policies have resulted in projections of deficits rather than surpluses as far as the eye can see. Therefore I favor substituting for general revenues this new dedicated Social Security tax based on the residual estate tax, which otherwise appears destined for repeal.

I believe we will have to earmark the estate tax in order to save it. And we should. Carving a modest tax on large estates out of general revenues, to help pay off part of the cost of establishing a universal system of basic economic security, would be a highly progressive way to partially offset the original deficit of contributions—in other words, before any further tax cuts, I believe, like President Clinton, that we should "Save Social Security first."

Moreover, to allow the transfer of huge estates from one generation to another without paying a tax to the common good is undemocratic in principle (as Tom Paine, among other early advocates of an inheritance tax, recognized). And an analysis by the Congressional Budget Office found that a $3.5 million exemption would almost totally protect against the risk of having to break up small family farms or businesses in order to pay the tax, an alleged result that has frequently been used as an argument against the estate tax.

This change reduces Social Security's projected long-term deficit by about 0.5 percent of payroll. When combined with restoration of the earnings base, it cuts the projected deficit slightly more than in half, to 0.8 percent of payroll.

These two changes bring the deficit to the outer margin of close actuarial balance—that is, the point where income and costs are projected to be within 5 percent of each other over 75 years. The concept of close actuarial balance, which recognizes the impossibility of making exact forecasts so far into the future, has long been used by Social Security's trustees to help determine whether financing changes are needed. The cost of the program today is estimated to average about 15.8 percent of payroll over the next 75 years, so a deficit of about 0.8 percent of payroll would just meet the close actuarial balance test, using the trustees' middle-range estimates.

Although I favor judging the adequacy of long-range financing according to the trustees' projections, it should be noted that the Congressional Budget Office anticipates a long-term deficit only about half as large as the deficit forecast by the trustees. Thus these two changes alone might well be sufficient to bring the system into long-term balance according to CBO's assumptions.

3. Invest in Equities

To further strengthen Social Security's financing and bring the system well within close actuarial balance for the next 75 years, I would diversify the trust funds' investments—putting some of the accumulated funds into equities, as is done by just about all other public and private pension plans. Several other government-administered programs (including part of the Railroad Retirement program as specifically authorized by Congress) already make such direct investments in stocks, as does Canada's social insurance system. There is no good reason to continue to require Social Security to invest only in low-yield government bonds.

Investment of a portion of Social Security's assets in stocks should be done gradually. I would propose starting with 1 percent in 2006, 2 percent in 2007, and so on, up to 20 percent in 2025 and capped at that percentage of assets thereafter, with investment limited to a very broad index fund (such as the Wilshire 5000) that reflects virtually the entire American economy. A Federal Reserve-type board with long and staggered terms would have the limited but important functions of selecting the index fund, selecting the portfolio managers by bid from among experienced managers of index funds, and monitoring and reporting to the trustees and public on Social Security's investments.

Among other things, reliance on a board with long and staggered terms will guard against any risk that Social Security's investments could become subject to political manipulation. Social Security would not be allowed to vote any stock or in any other way influence the policies or practices of any company or industry whose stock is held by the index fund. (In any case, there would be no more reason to expect government interference under this plan than under President Bush's proposal, which would give government the responsibility for investing the individual accounts he advocates. So the argument against letting Social Security invest in stocks because of the alleged risk of market interference has lost some traction lately. But the more important point is that concerns about political interference can be addressed by limiting the amount of assets invested, requiring passive investment in a total-market index fund, and providing for oversight by a board structured to ensure its impartiality and autonomy.)

Investment by the trust funds has a major advantage over individual investment account proposals. Investing one's basic retirement funds in stocks is very risky for individuals because, among other reasons, they will ordinarily need the money upon retirement, and in order to be sure of making the income last until death will need to buy an annuity with the proceeds. But that could mean having to sell stocks and buy an annuity during a market downturn. As Gary Burtless of the Brookings Institution has demonstrated (by examining what would have happened if an individual-accounts system had been in effect in the past), timing is everything. A variation of just a few years—even months—in the time of buying an annuity can make a huge difference in its value. In contrast, investment by the trust funds is largely protected against this risk, since Social Security would be able to ride out market fluctuations.

As with the investments of a private retirement plan, the goal of trust fund investing would be to build up and hold on to a reserve whose earnings would help meet future costs. This proposal is estimated to save about 0.4 percent of payroll. When combined with the other two changes outlined above, it brings the 75-year deficit anticipated by the trustees to an estimated 0.4 percent of payroll, well within the range of close actuarial balance (based, as noted above, on the trustees' middle-range estimates).

It bears emphasizing that all three of these proposals are desirable in themselves regardless of their importance in reducing the long-range deficit. And if their adoption should result in overfinancing the program, it would still be desirable to enact them—and then provide for a reduction in Social Security tax rates.

At the same time, it is important to ensure that the build-up of the trust funds is maintained so that earnings on the funds continue to contribute to future financial stability during and beyond the current 75-year estimating period. I therefore favor providing for a contingency contribution rate increase that may or may not be needed, depending on the accuracy of the long-range estimates. With this approach the law would provide that if short-term estimates showed that the trust funds would begin to decline within the next five years, a tax rate increase would go into effect to prevent such a decline. If the need for this increase were to occur before the maximum earnings base had been restored to fully cover 90 percent of earnings, I would accelerate the timetable for restoration of the base and then determine whether there is still a need for the tax rate increase.

And there are other potential sources of income that would make it less likely to need a rate increase to prevent a decline in the trust funds' assets from the maximum achieved. If, for example, Social Security coverage were to be extended, as it should be, to all newly hired state and local government employees, the 75-year deficit anticipated under the middle-range estimates would be reduced by about another 0.2 percent of payroll. And adoption of the more accurate Consumer Price Index recently developed by the Bureau of Labor Statistics would result in slight reductions in Social Security's annual Cost of Living Adjustment, thereby saving about an additional 0.4 percent of payroll and bringing the balance of the system below close actuarial balance to exact balance.

It's also possible, of course, that because of productivity increases greater than previously assumed and other favorable factors, the trustees' middle-range estimates may prove to be too pessimistic and actual experience may be closer to their low-cost estimates. In that case just the three changes that I am proposing to make immediately effective—restoring the maximum wage base, earmarking the residual estate tax as a new dedicated Social Security tax, and diversifying the trust funds' investment portfolio—might well be sufficient to maintain the trust funds at the highest point achieved and produce a surplus beyond the next 75 years.

The Trust Funds: Real Money

How does this analysis square with President Bush's doomsday proclamations of a current crisis for Social Security? It doesn't. And there is no basis for such alarms, since the middle-range cost estimates—the set on which the trustees depend—show the system able to pay full benefits as defined under present law until 2041.

Although the cost of benefits is expected to exceed income from contributions plus taxes on benefits in 2017, the only way for the Administration to predict a crisis at that point is to ignore the existence of the trust funds and count only contributions and taxes on benefits against the system's costs. To do so, however, requires repudiating 70 years of depending on earnings from a fund build-up invested in United States bonds and held by the trust funds. Most experts believe to the contrary that these bonds held by the trust funds and bought by the dedicated Social Security contributions of the past are protected by the full faith and credit of the United States, just like all other bonds issued by the government.

If the only money available for Social Security payments is to come from current Social Security contributions and taxes on Social Security benefits, then there will be, of course, a big gap between the program's rising costs and its income—a gap which the president would close with benefit cuts so large that they would convert Social Security from a modest retirement and family income protection system for everyone to a narrowly targeted welfare program for very low wage earners. But to predict a near-term crisis requires being able to argue with a straight face that the government cannot keep books—that all previous Social Security contributions have vanished without a trace because the money has been spent on other government programs, with the bonds held by the trust funds meaning nothing at all.

If that's true, the federal government has been lying to workers covered by Social Security for 70 years—and that would be a scandal of staggering proportions. But it's not true.

To be sure, the Social Security contributions of the past have been invested in government bonds—and just as the government has used the money it has borrowed from selling bonds generally, so it has used the money it has borrowed from selling bonds to the Social Security trust funds. And it is true that if the bonds held by Social Security were called in, it would be necessary for the Treasury to borrow money or raise taxes to redeem them—just as would be the case in redeeming any other bonds issued by the government and held by the public.

In practice, however, it is unlikely that Social Security would ever want to cash in the government bonds it will hold. After all, the object is to build up an earnings reserve and use the interest on the reserve to pay benefits, just as is done with private pensions—not build up a reserve and then cash it in again.

A Balanced Approach

This plan addresses Social Security's long-term shortfall solely by increasing income to the system. Why not achieve balance by trimming benefits too? The problem is that benefits are already being cut in two significant ways—first by changing the retirement age, which alters the benefit formula in a way that has the effect of an across-the-board benefit cut, and second by the ongoing deduction of Medicare premiums from Social Security benefits. So a truly balanced solution to the long-term shortfall must call for more income, not more benefit cuts.

We simply can't afford to reduce the protection that Social Security currently provides. Social Security benefits are the major source of support for two out of every three beneficiaries and are vitally important to nearly all the rest. Benefit levels need to be maintained or even improved, particularly in light of the increasingly uncertain future faced by private pension plans— with traditional defined-benefit plans (many of them underfunded) now covering only about 20 percent of the private-sector workforce, and with the 401(k) individual savings plans that are to some extent replacing the traditional plans subject to the vagaries of individual investment experience and vulnerable to being cashed out before retirement.

It's in this context that we have to assess Social Security's long-term financing challenge. I believe that an accurate assessment can lead to only one conclusion. Radical changes are unwarranted. And the changes I propose are anything but radical. As noted, the first three are desirable in themselves—and vastly preferable to the drastic benefit cuts proposed by the president or the major tax rate increases that would be required in a strictly pay-as-you-go-system.

Perhaps, in this moment of relative calm, we can make the case for common sense.

Robert M. Ball served as Commissioner of Social Security under Presidents Kennedy, Johnson, and Nixon, and has subsequently served on many statutory advisory councils as well as on the bipartisan commission that produced the 1983 amendments. His latest book is Insuring the Essentials: Bob Ball on Social Security *(Century Foundation, 2000). For additional discussion of the proposals described here, see* The Battle for Social Security: From FDR's Vision to Bush's Gamble, *by Nancy J. Altman (Wiley, 2005).*

Saving Social Security (Part 1)

by Peter A. Diamond and Peter Orszag

For almost 70 years, Social Security has provided retirees with a basic level of income that is protected against inflation, financial market fluctuations and the risk of outliving one's assets. It protects against other risks as well, such as disability or the death of a family wage earner. In addition, through its progressive structure, Social Security provides some protection against one's career not turning out well. Social Security plays a critical role in providing financial security during retirement: It provides the majority of income for two-thirds of elderly beneficiaries, and all income for 20 percent of elderly beneficiaries.

Over the next 75 years, Social Security costs are projected to rise by about 2.5 percent of Gross Domestic Product (GDP), while revenues are projected to decline slightly as a share of GDP. Social Security's long-term financial health can be restored through either minor adjustments or major surgery. In our view, major surgery is neither warranted nor desirable—sustainable solvency and improved social insurance can be accomplished by a progressive reform that combines modest benefit reductions and revenue increases (as presented in more detail in Diamond and Orszag, 2004).

We begin by describing some benefit improvements for vulnerable groups for which there appears to be wide support, including from the President's Commission to Strengthen Social Security (2001) appointed by President Bush. We then discuss our proposed benefit and tax changes to close the underlying Social Security deficit and finance these important social insurance improvements. We also examine plans that replace part of Social Security with individual accounts, explaining why, in our view, such a course would not represent sound policy.

Improving Social Insurance

We begin by focusing on a small number of particularly vulnerable beneficiary types, following the lead of President Bush's Commission to Strengthen Social Security (2001) and others.[1]

First, workers with low lifetime earnings often live in poverty during retirement despite Social Security's progressive benefit formula. In 1993, taking into account all sources of income, 9 percent of retired worker beneficiaries lived in poverty. Of these

(originally published in Journal of Economic Perspectives, vol. 19, no. 2, Spring 2005, pp. 11-32; used with permission)

Note: The first half of this article appears here, and the second half is included in Chapter 10 where Personal Accounts are discussed. The references appear at the end of the second half.

poor retired worker beneficiaries, 10 percent had worked for 41 or more years in employment covered by Social Security, and more than 40 percent had worked between 20 and 40 years. In other words, many workers who have had substantial connections to the work force throughout their careers nonetheless face poverty in retirement. Our plan includes a benefit enhancement for low earners that applies to workers with at least 20 years of covered earnings at retirement, along the general lines of Sandell, Iams and Fanaras (1999).

Second, Social Security should strengthen its protection of widows and widowers. A widow typically suffers a 30 percent drop in living standards around the time she loses her husband (Holden and Zick, 1998). This decline is a challenge for many widows, pushing some into poverty. Indeed, while the poverty rate for elderly married couples is only about 5 percent, the poverty rate for elderly widows is more than three times as high (Favreault, Sammartino and Steuerle, 2002). To address this problem, we raise the survivor benefit under Social Security so that it equals at least three-quarters of the couple's previous combined benefits.[2]

Third, despite Social Security's protections, disabled workers and their families have higher poverty rates and are more financially vulnerable than the general population. For example, in 1999, 22 percent of disability insurance beneficiaries lived in poverty (Martin and Davies, 2003-2004). It is unclear whether the rules governing eligibility for disability insurance are optimal, given the tradeoff between inappropriately awarding benefits and inappropriately denying them. But redesigning the entire disability program, to the extent changes are warranted, would represent a massive and complex task beyond the scope of our immediate attention.

Although we do not explore a wider reform of the disability program, we are concerned about the elevated rates of poverty among disabled workers. We therefore propose that, in the aggregate over the next 75 years, disabled workers be held harmless from the benefit reductions that would otherwise apply under our plan. Instead of merely maintaining the current disability benefit formula, however, our approach reduces initial benefits upon disability but then increases annual benefits in force faster than inflation. The result raises lifetime benefit levels for workers who become disabled earlier in their careers and reduces them for workers who become disabled later in their careers—redistribution that seems advantageous, since workers who begin receiving disability benefits at younger ages seem more needy and are locked into lower real benefits than workers who become disabled at older ages. We apply the same system to benefits for young survivors.

Restoring Actuarial Balance

In the 2004 trustees' report, Social Security's 75-year actuarial imbalance was estimated at 1.9 percent of taxable payroll, or 0.7 percent of GDP. One of the primary goals of a Social Security reform plan should be to eliminate this 75-year actuarial deficit, since failing to address this long-term deficit would result in large, sudden changes to the program and/or to the federal budget. A reform that begins sooner can spread the costs over a longer period of time, avoiding the possibility of having to make substantial changes to benefits for people already receiving benefits or soon to start.

Social Security reform plans should go beyond eliminating the 75-year deficit, however, because of the "terminal year" problem. Merely restoring 75-year actuarial balance while preserving the current structure of benefits and revenue could result in the rapid reappearance of a 75-year imbalance. For example, the 1983 reform of Social Security made the program solvent for 75 years at that time. But by 2004, when the terminal year for 75-year projections had moved two decades later, more than 60 percent of the actuarial deficit in the program was because of the added years. Thus, reforms should not only close the 75-year deficit, but also ensure a stable or rising trust fund relative to expenditures at the end of the 75-year projection period. This result—of eliminating the 75-year deficit and ensuring a rising trust fund compared to expenditures at the end of the period—is referred to as "sustainable solvency."

Sustainable solvency can be achieved through different combinations of specific policy changes. Some proposals would close the entire actuarial shortfall through benefit reductions. In our view, however, this approach would result in replacement rates—that is, benefits as a share of previous earnings—that would be too low from a social insurance perspective. Replacement rates for an average earner at age 62 (the most common age for claiming benefits) are scheduled to fall from 33 percent to 29 percent between now and 2030 as changes enacted as part of the 1983 reforms come into effect. Furthermore, Medicare Part B premiums are automatically deducted from Social Security benefit payments; as those premiums rise faster than income over time, the net replacement rate will decline further (Munnell, 2003). Looking back on the 1983 legislative process (Light, 1985), a balanced approach combining benefit reductions and revenue increases seems a helpful starting place for obtaining a political compromise.

In restoring long-term balance, our reform plan focuses on three areas, all of which contribute to the actuarial imbalance: improvements in life expectancy, increases in earnings inequality, and the burden of the legacy debt resulting from Social Security's early history.

Increasing Life Expectancy

Life expectancy at age 65 has increased by four years for men and five years for women since 1940 and is expected to continue rising. Since Social Security retirement benefits are paid as an annuity, any increase in life expectancy at retirement age increases the cost of Social Security. To examine how Social Security should react to the costs associated with longer life expectancy, consider how a worker would sensibly react to learning that he or she will live longer than previously expected. The worker can adjust by consuming less before retirement (that is, saving more), consuming less during retirement or working longer. A sensible approach would likely involve all three. The Social Security system already increases benefits for retirees who start benefits later. The other two elements of individual adjustment correspond to an increase in the payroll tax rate (consuming less before retirement) and a reduction in benefits for any given age at retirement (consuming less during retirement). Our approach includes both of these.

To offset the projected cost from further increases in life expectancy, we propose a balanced combination of benefit and tax adjustments, which would be phased in starting in 2012. Specifically, in each year the Office of the Chief Actuary would calculate the net cost to Social Security from the improvement in life expectancy observed in the past year for a typical worker at the full benefit age. Half of this cost would be offset by a reduction in benefits, which would apply to all workers age 59 and younger. The other half would be financed by an increase in the payroll tax rate. This life expectancy adjustment reduces the 75-year actuarial deficit by 0.55 percent of taxable payroll, slightly less than a third of the currently projected deficit.

Another way of indexing the system to life expectancy involves raising the age for receipt of full retirement benefits (the so-called "normal retirement age"). This approach, however, is merely an alternative method of reducing benefits, one that affects workers retiring at different ages in somewhat different ways. Since we favor adjusting to longer life expectancies through a combination of lower benefits and higher revenue (rather than exclusively through lower benefits), since the pattern of benefit reductions associated with increases in the full benefit age does not seem inherently desirable, and since changes to the full benefit age are a less transparent mechanism for reducing benefits than a direct reduction, our approach to life expectancy indexing seems preferable.

Increasing Earnings Inequality

Social Security's financing is also affected by the increase in the share of earnings above the maximum taxable earnings base ($90,000 in 2005), and therefore untaxed, and by the widening difference in life expectancy between lower earners and higher earners.

Over the past two decades, the fraction of aggregate earnings above the maximum taxable earnings base has risen from 10 percent to 15 percent. One impact of this shift is a widening of the Social Security deficit: The loss in revenue more than offsets the reduction in benefits to be paid on high earnings. In our view, Social Security should offset some of the shift that has occurred in this area since 1983 for two reasons. First, in our view, a tax system should respond to such an increase in pre-tax income inequality by becoming more progressive. Second, it could be argued that policymakers implicitly accepted the 1983 share of untaxed earnings by not making changes to the maximum taxable earnings base when a major reform was implemented then, especially since changes had been made in 1977 and could presumably have been made again in 1983.

Our plan raises the maximum taxable earnings base so that the percentage of aggregate earnings above the taxable maximum returns about halfway to its 1983 level—that is, to 13 percent. We phase in this reform smoothly through 2063 to allow workers time to adjust. Increasing the maximum taxable earnings base would raise

the payroll tax only for the 6 percent of workers in each year with highest earnings, and marginal tax rates for even fewer (for example, if the change were fully in effect today, under three million workers would experience an increase in their marginal tax rate). An increase in taxable earnings raises subsequent benefits as well—albeit by less, in present value, than the additional revenue. The net effect reduces the 75-year actuarial imbalance by 0.25 percent of payroll.

A second piece of our earnings inequality adjustment addresses differential trends in life expectancy. People with higher earnings and more education tend to live longer than those with lower earnings and less education, and these mortality differences by earnings and education have been expanding significantly over time (Elo and Smith, 2003). This increasing gap in mortality rates by level of education has two implications for Social Security. First, to the extent that projected improvements in average life expectancy reflect disproportionate improvements for higher earners, the adverse effect on Social Security's financing is larger than if the projected improvement occurred equally across the earnings distribution. Second, the changing pattern of mortality tends to make Social Security less progressive on a lifetime basis than it would be without such a change, since higher earners will collect benefits for an increasingly larger number of years, relative to lower earners.

To offset the growing gap in life expectancy and so offset the decline in lifetime progressivity that has occurred from this trend, our plan increases the progressivity of the monthly Social Security benefit formula. In particular, we gradually lower the marginal benefit in the top tier of the benefit formula, affecting approximately the highest-earning 15 percent of workers: an extra dollar of career-average monthly earnings increases monthly benefits by 10 cents rather than 15 cents by 2031. This benefit reduction lowers the 75-year deficit by 0.18 percent of payroll.

The Burden of the Legacy Debt

Benefits paid to almost all current and past cohorts of beneficiaries exceeded what could have been financed with the revenue they contributed (Leimer, 1994). That is, if earlier cohorts had received only the benefits that could be financed by their contributions plus interest, the trust fund's assets today would be much greater. Those assets would earn interest, which could be used to finance benefits. This history imposes an ongoing burden on the Social Security system, which we refer to as a "legacy debt" and see as providing another lens through which to view Social Security's financing challenges. The legacy debt reflects the absence of those assets and thus directly relates to Social Security's funding level.

The decisions, made early in the history of Social Security and continued until legislation enacted in 1977—to provide the early generations of beneficiaries benefits disproportionate to their contributions—was a humane response to a history that included World War I, the Great Depression and World War II, and it helped to reduce unacceptably high rates of poverty in old age. Moreover, the higher benefits not only helped the recipients themselves but also relieved part of the burden on their families and friends and on the cost of the Old Age Assistance program.

Today, we cannot take back the benefits that were given to Social Security's early beneficiaries, and most Americans seem unwilling to reduce benefits for those now receiving them or soon to receive them. Those two facts largely determine the size of the legacy debt. Assuming that benefits will not be reduced for anyone age 55 or over in 2004, the legacy debt—the net amounts already transferred plus those projected to be transferred to all of these cohorts—amounts to approximately $11.6 trillion.

The key issue is how to finance this legacy debt across different generations, and across different people within generations.[3] We propose three changes that alter how the program's legacy debt is financed: universal coverage under Social Security; a legacy tax on earnings above the maximum taxable earnings base; and a universal legacy charge that applies to workers and beneficiaries in the future.

First, about six million state and local government employees were not covered by Social Security in 2002 (25 percent of total state and local employees). It is unfair to workers who are covered by Social Security (including the great majority of state and local government workers) that many other state and local government workers, by virtue of being outside the program, do not bear any of the legacy debt. More precisely, the benefit from not bearing the legacy debt is shared between some state and local governments and their employees, neither of whom deserve to be excluded from bearing part of the burden. Our plan therefore brings all newly hired state and local workers into the Social Security system.

Second, in an actuarially balanced system, roughly 3 to 4 percentage points of the 12.4 percent payroll tax would be devoted to financing the program's legacy debt (Geanakoplos, Mitchell and Zeldes, 1998). Those with earnings above the maximum taxable earnings base do not bear a share of this legacy cost proportional to their total earnings. Thus, we propose a tax on all earnings above the taxable maximum; the tax rate begins at 3 percent (1.5 percent each on employer and employee) and gradually increases over time, along with the universal charge to be described next, reaching 4 percent in 2080.

Third, future workers and beneficiaries must contribute toward financing the legacy debt, so we propose a universal legacy charge on both benefits and tax rates that applies to all workers from 2023 forward. The benefit adjustment reduces initial benefits by 0.31 percent a year for newly eligible beneficiaries in 2023 and later.[4] The revenue adjustment raises the payroll tax rate to balance the benefit reductions from this component of our plan. The result is that the tax rate increases by 0.26 percent of itself each year starting in 2023 (that is, if there were no other changes, the current rate of 12.4 percent would become 12.43 in 2023).

Taken together, this approach to financing the legacy debt represents a balance between burdening near-term generations and burdening distant generations, between burdening workers and burdening future retirees, and between burdening lower-income workers and burdening higher-income workers. The phased-in nature of the universal legacy cost adjustment also helps the Social Security system to adjust to the reduced fertility rates that have occurred since the 1960s and further eases the terminal year problem.

Summary

Our three-part proposal restores 75-year actuarial balance to Social Security, as summarized in Table 1. These proposals were designed to achieve actuarial balance while also ensuring a stable ratio of the trust fund balance to annual expenditures the following year (called the "trust fund ratio") at the end of the projection period, thereby addressing the terminal-year problem.[5]

	Table 1 Summary of Effects of Proposed Reforms	
	Effect on actuarial balance	
Proposed reform	**As percentage of taxable payroll**	**As percentage of actuarial deficit**
Adjustments for increasing life expectancy		
Adjust benefits	0.26	13
Adjust revenue	0.29	15
Subtotal	0.55	29
Adjustments for increased earnings inequality		
Increase taxable earnings base	0.25	13
Reduce benefits for higher earners	0.18	9
Subtotal	0.43	22
Adjustments for fairer sharing of legacy cost		
Make Social Security coverage universal	0.19	10
Impose legacy tax on earnings over taxable maximum	0.55	29
Impose legacy charge on benefits	0.45	24
Impose legacy tax below taxable maximum	0.52	27
Subtotal	1.71	89
Reforms to strengthen social insurance functions		
Enhanced benefits for lifetime low earners	-0.14	-7
Increased benefits for widows	-0.08	-4
Hold-harmless provisions for disabled workers and young survivors	-0.21	-11
Subtotal	-0.43	-22
Interactions of above reforms	-0.26	-14
Total effect	2.00	104
Alternative: reform existing estate tax*	0.60	31

Source: Authors' calculations based on analysis from the Office of the Chief Actuary.

*This reform could be enacted in place of one of the other proposed reforms that affect primarily higher earners.

Under our plan, the trust fund ratio peaks somewhat higher and somewhat later than under current law and then begins a steady decline. This decline is relatively rapid at first, as the continued financing of benefits to baby-boomer retirees draws the trust fund down. Over time, however, as the baby-boomers die and our changes to both taxes and benefits are slowly phased in, the decline in the ratio slows. By the end of the projection period, as shown in Figure 1, the trust fund ratio is again beginning to rise.[6]

What do these various changes imply for the benefits that individual workers will receive and for the taxes they will pay? Workers who are 55 years old or older in 2004 experience no change in their benefits from those scheduled under current law. For younger workers with average earnings, our proposal involves a gradual reduction in benefits from those scheduled under current law for successive cohorts. For example, a 45-year-old average earner experiences less than a 1 percent reduction in benefits; a 35-year-old, less than a 5 percent reduction; and a 25-year-old, less than a 9 percent reduction. Reductions are smaller for lower earners and larger for higher ones.

These modest reductions in benefits for average earners are in line with the tradition set in the 1983 Social Security reforms, which reduced benefits by about 10 percent for those 25 years old at the time, slightly more than under our plan for average earners age 25 in 2004. It is also worth noting that even with the modest benefit

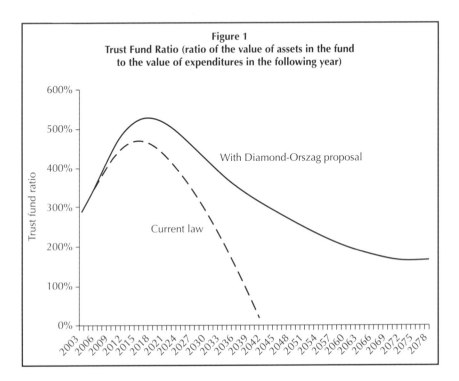

Figure 1
Trust Fund Ratio (ratio of the value of assets in the fund to the value of expenditures in the following year)

reductions in our plan, average inflation-adjusted benefits rise from one generation to the next.

Our plan combines its gradual benefit reductions with a gradual increase in the payroll tax rate. The combined employer-employee payroll tax rate rises from 12.4 percent today to 12.5 percent in 2015, 13.2 percent in 2035, 14.2 percent in 2055 and 15.4 percent in 2078; it would continue to rise slowly over time thereafter. This gradual increase in the payroll tax rate slows the decline in replacement rates for any given retirement age.

The provisions that affect average earners are closely balanced between benefit reductions and revenue increases. Analyzing the balance between benefit and revenue changes for the overall plan, however, is more complicated. Expanded coverages (for state and local workers and those above the maximum covered earnings) both bring in new revenue and create new benefit obligations for Social Security. We think the best approach is to divide the accounting into three categories: revenue changes, benefits changes and changes in coverage. In achieving both actuarial balance and financing of our social insurance improvements, 33 percent of the deficit is eliminated by benefit reductions, 51 percent by revenue increases and 16 percent by coverage expansions.[7]

A final dimension along which our plan can be examined is the degree to which it places the burden of closing the deficit on higher earners. Three of our changes apply specifically to higher earners: the increase in the maximum taxable earnings base, the reduction in benefits that applies only to the top tier of the benefit formula and the tax applied above the maximum taxable earnings base. These three provisions account for 36 percent of the total deficit reduction provisions in our plan—that is, 0.98 percent of payroll out of 2.69 percent of payroll. To be sure, higher earners will also share in the more universal changes that we propose. But someone must bear the burden of closing the deficit, and having slightly more than one-third of the deficit reduction coming from provisions specifically aimed at higher earners does not strike us as grossly unfair. We also note that just as our benefit increases for vulnerable beneficiaries parallel those of the President's Commission to Strengthen Social Security (2001), so too, two of our three changes for high earners were included in the earlier Commission's report.[8]

(For the rest of this article, including the discussion on Personal Accounts, the conclusions, and the references, please see Chapter 10.)

Notes

1. The Commission to Strengthen Social Security (2001) included protections for lifetime low earners and widows and widowers. The Commission also ended its report by calling for a disability insurance commission and stating that the benefit cuts for the disabled in the report "should not be taken as a Commission recommendation" (p. 149).

2. For survivors whose benefit would be higher than that of the average worker, the increase would be financed by reducing the couple's own combined benefits while both are alive, with no effect on the

couple's combined expected lifetime benefits. For lower-benefit survivors, we finance the increase from the program as a whole. The shift from the system applying to above-average benefits to the one applying to below-average benefits could be gradual, with a phase-in range in between. Increasing survivor benefits under Social Security could disqualify some people from Medicaid, since low retirement income is part of eligibility for that program (and the Supplemental Security Income program). Most states would therefore need to adjust Medicaid rules for the elderly if an increased Social Security benefit is not to eliminate Medicaid eligibility.

3. To be sure, the legacy debt does not ever have to be fully paid off, just as there is no need ever to pay off the entire public debt. But ongoing legacy debt, like other outstanding public debt, does impose a cost for financing it. And just as a continuously rising public debt-to-GDP ratio would eventually become unsustainable (as doubts arise over repayment), so, too, the legacy debt cannot grow faster than taxable payroll indefinitely without disrupting the functioning of Social Security or the federal budget as a whole.

4. We select this starting date because under current law, the increases in the full benefit age continue until 2022. After 2023, we smoothly increase the legacy charge, since the growth rate in taxable payroll declines thereafter, requiring an increasing offset to the legacy cost. The benefit reduction would increase for newly eligible beneficiaries in 2024 to 0.62 percent relative to current law, and so on. The benefit reduction would be calculated as $1 - 0.9969 t{-}2022$, where t is the year in which the worker turns 62.

5. This proposal stays within the tradition of using the payroll tax (and the income taxation of benefits) as the only sources of tax revenue for Social Security. One could consider dedicating an additional tax in place of some of the tax increases described here. For example, dedicating the estate tax to Social Security could change the politics of whether that tax should be eliminated. Moreover, since the yield on the estate tax depends strongly on returns to capital, substituting a capital-income based tax for a wage-based tax would further diversify the bearing of capital risk in the economy, offering a partial substitute for trust fund investment in equities.

6. A number of observers have claimed that the buildup of the trust fund is irrelevant when the time comes to cash in the bonds held by the trust fund. In one uninteresting sense, the argument is factually accurate: unless it simply prints money, the government finances all of its activities through increasing taxes, cutting spending for other purposes, or borrowing. But this insight is not helpful. To the extent the Social Security surpluses contributed to reducing overall budget deficits, they have reduced interest costs and increased the government's ability to borrow, and so made it easier for the government to operate. To the extent that building up the trust fund has added to national saving, it has made more resources available in the future.

7. The total deficit-reducing steps in our plan amount to 2.69 percent of payroll. Of this, 1.36 percent is revenue increases, 0.89 percent is benefit reductions and 0.44 percent is coverage expansions. We do not attempt to divide the 0.26 percent of payroll in interactions among these three categories.

8. The increase in the maximum taxable earnings base was mentioned in a footnote to Model 3 in the Commission to Strengthen Social Security (2001), but not formally included in that plan. The footnote reads: "Some members of the Commission believed that a substantial portion of this 0.63% should come from an increase in the payroll tax base, while leaving the payroll tax rate the same. They suggested that the payroll tax base should be stabilized as a percentage of the total U.S. wage bill closer to its level during the last two decades. However, this suggestion was deemed inconsistent with the principles in the executive order establishing the Commission and was therefore not included in the final version of this plan.

Chapter 9

Revise Social Security for a New Generation

Raising the Pensionable Age in Social Security

by John Turner

In most countries, the life expectancy of workers is increasing. Increases in life expectancy raise the value of lifetime benefits workers receive from traditional defined benefit Social Security plans because workers collect benefits for more years. In countries with pay-as-you-go Social Security systems, this trend raises the costs of providing benefits and may force the systems towards insolvency.

A possible policy response to the social security financing problems that arise in part because people are living longer could be to raise the retirement age. The Member states of the European Community have committed to raising the retirement age (European Commission 2002).

Policy analysts discussing the option of raising the retirement age have given that concept at least four different meanings. First, it can mean the age at which workers actually retire. Second, it can mean the age at which workers can receive "full" Social Security benefits, technically referred to as the normal retirement age. Third, it can mean the early retirement age in the Social Security program. Not all countries, however, have an early retirement age, with some having the earliest age be 65. Fourth, it can mean the earliest age at which workers can receive Social Security old-age benefits, sometimes referred to as the pensionable age.

This paper focuses on issues related to raising the pensionable age in traditional defined benefit Social Security plans. The term "pensionable age" is used here to distinguish from the other concepts of retirement age. It is a preferable here to the term the "earliest retirement age" because workers generally need not fully retire at the pensionable age in order to receive benefits. This age is often referred to in the

(AARP Public Policy Institute, January 2003; used with permission)

literature on Social Security as the early retirement age, or sometimes it is called the early entitlement age.

This paper examines the extent to which countries have raised the pensionable age in their Social Security programs. It first discusses the desirability of this policy. Second, it discusses likely effects of the policy. Third, it surveys countries that have raised the pensionable age in their Social Security program. The survey provides a number of examples where countries have raised their pensionable age, with a view towards what lessons can be learned from experience as to how these countries put that policy into effect.

This paper considers social security plans where workers qualify for old age benefits based on their age and years of work. It focuses on changes in the minimum age requirement, but also considers changes in the minimum requirement concerning years of work.

Background Issues

The Changing Demographic and Work Environment

By the year 2050, demographic projections suggest that Europeans will live at least four to five years longer than in 2000 (European Commission 2002). Life expectancy in the United States increased over the 20th century and is forecast to continue to do so. Combined with earlier retirement, the amount of time U.S. men spend in retirement has risen about 2 years a decade, increasing almost 12 years since 1940 (Burtless and Quinn 2002). In 1940, 54 percent of U.S. males survived from age 21 to age 65. By 1990, that figure had risen to 72 percent (Social Security 2001). No slowdown in the rate of improvement in life expectancy has occurred, even in countries with life expectancies well above those in the United States, such as Japan (Population Reference Bureau 2002).

One of the concerns in raising the pensionable age is for people with disabilities who are unable to postpone their retirement and who are not seriously enough disabled to qualify for disability benefits. Recent research, however, indicates that disability among all age groups in the United States declined throughout the 20th century (Costa and Steckel 1997). This finding was confirmed by data for the past 20 years, where the issues of data comparability are less a concern (Cutler 2001).

Another concern is for workers in physically demanding jobs. The percentage of jobs in the U.S. that require strenuous physical effort has declined (Manton and Stollard 1994 and Baily 1987). Many workers in physically demanding jobs, for example fire fighters, have pensions that allow them to retire earlier than age 62, which is the pensionable age in the United States. Further, it is significant to note that many of those pensions are raising their retirement age, so that the difference between their retirement age and age 62 is shrinking. Raising the pensionable age may not affect the age at which those workers actually retire, and it would be supported by the increase in the pensionable age in the occupational pension plans for many of those workers.

Policy Analysis

This section analyzes issues related to the benefits and costs to society of raising the pensionable age.

Benefits of Raising the Pensionable Age

Raising the pensionable age may have a several positive effects on the economy. It may increase national output and material living standards due to the increase in the size of the labor force. It may reduce the burden on social security and pension systems.

Raising the pensionable age could be done so as to both improve the financing of Social Security and raise annual benefits to retirees. If benefits are adjusted in an actuarially fair manner, however, so that when they are received at the higher pensionable age, they are larger by an actuarially fair increase, there would be no cost savings to the Social Security program. If the benefits received at the higher pensionable age are larger by less than an actuarially fair increase, there would be a cost savings to the Social Security program. For example, in the United States benefits are increased at about 7 percent per year for workers who postpone benefit receipt from age 62 to 63. If the pensionable age were raised one year, for the majority of workers who are currently taking benefits at age 62 and would be taking them at age 63, age 63 benefits could be raised by half that amount—to about 3 percent above their age 62 level. Workers retiring at age 63 who had been retiring at age 62 would receive higher annual benefits, while at the same time the financing of Social Security would be improved. If the workers worked the additional year, their annual benefits would increase by more than 3 percent in real terms due to the added work. While their lifetime benefits would be reduced, the annual level of benefits is also an important measure of wellbeing, and they would be better off in that regard. A pensionable age of 63 would still be two years younger than the earliest age at which U.S. workers can receive Medicare benefits, which is age 65.

Raising the Pensionable Age Versus Raising the Normal Retirement Age

Within the range of traditional policy options, perhaps the leading competing alternative to raising the pensionable age is to raise the normal retirement age, with a reduction in benefits received if the worker retires at the current pensionable age. Raising the normal retirement age and raising the pensionable age are quite different in their likely economic effects. Raising the normal retirement age is equivalent to an across the board benefit reduction and may have little effect on the ages at which workers retire. Raising the early retirement age, however, while also a way of reducing benefits very likely will have an important effect on the age at retirement for some workers. Raising the normal retirement age would result in reducing the level of monthly benefits that workers actually receive if workers continue to retire at the earliest possible age, while raising the pensionable age could be done so as to raise the level of benefits received, although lifetime benefits would be reduced.

With an increase in the normal retirement age, people could still continue to retire at the original pensionable age but with a greater reduction in benefits than previously, or could choose to postpone retirement. A similar policy to raising the normal retirement age is to index benefits to increases in life expectancy, so that benefit levels fall as life expectancy increases. These policies may be preferable to raising the pensionable age if people would adequately weigh the effects of the reduction in pension benefits when they considered at what age to retire. However, if some people with high discount rates automatically chose to take retirement benefits at the earliest age, it could be argued that raising the pensionable age would be preferable.

Rather than being alternative policy options, increases in the normal retirement age may raise the desirability of increasing the pensionable age. If the normal retirement age in the U.S. were increased to age 70, and the pensionable age were unchanged, workers claiming benefits at age 62 would receive 52 percent of a full pension if the reduction were actuarially fair, which is probably too little for low-wage worker who generally have few other sources of income. It thus seems advisable to increase the pensionable age if the NRA is increased above age 67 (Burtless and Quinn 2002). To implement this reform, it might be advisable to liberalize eligibility requirements for DI benefits starting at age 62. People who have worked in physically demanding occupations and are in impaired health could be given access to benefits (Burtless and Quinn 2002).

As well as economic considerations, there are also political considerations. Politicians may be more uneasy about reforms that deny benefits to an identifiable group of people who would be forced to retire at a later age than about reforms that reduce benefits modestly to a much wider population (Burtless and Quinn 2002).

The "Math" of Raising the Pensionable Age

Often analyses of the pensionable age under Social Security look for a mechanical formula tied to life expectancy for prescribing what the pensionable age "should" be. For example, in the United States, life expectancy at age 65 is now five years longer than it was when that age was originally set as the pensionable age in 1940 (Verma and Rix 2002). Thus, life expectancy during retirement at the current pensionable age of 62 is 8 years longer than it was originally at the pensionable age of 65. If the ratio of working years to retirement years remained at the level it was when old-age benefits were first paid, the earliest retirement age would be 70 or 71, rather than 62 (Social Security Advisory Board 1998).

As suggested by these statistics, a simple way to think about the pensionable age would be to determine an appropriate ratio of retirement years to work years for the average pensioner. The lower the ratio, the lower the savings or contribution rate needed by the worker to fund retirement. In developed countries, the ratio of retirement to work years is roughly one to two, for full career workers there being roughly 20 years of retirement and 40 years of work. In these countries, many people have the luxury of retiring while still in good health so that they can enjoy an active retirement.

Because of their lower income, people in developing countries are less able to afford retirement. The ratio of retirement to work years is generally less in developing than in developed countries, with both lower retirement ages and lower life expectancy because of the greater difficulty paying for retirement (Gillion, Turner, Bailey and Latulippe 2000). Thus, the ratio between retirement years and work years in a country appears to be higher the higher is the level of worker income.

Effects of Raising the Pensionable Age

The effects of raising the pensionable age influence the desirability of doing so. In considering the option of raising the pensionable age, at least two comparisons can be made concerning its effects on older workers. First, life expectancy, disability rates, pension coverage, and other factors that affect the feasibility of raising the pensionable age can be compared for the time period at which the pensionable age is to be raised as opposed to those conditions at some earlier time. Such comparisons tend to support the feasibility of raising the pensionable age. A second comparison is for the cross section of workers affected by an increase in the pensionable age. Such a comparison tends to indicate the extent that hardship may result from such a policy.

Workers Hurt by Raising the Pensionable Age. In the United States, a little over half of workers claim Social Security benefits at the pensionable age of 62 (Panis et al 2002). The primary criticism to raising the pensionable age is that doing so places an unfair burden on certain vulnerable groups of workers retiring at the pensionable age who have a short life expectancy, who are unable to work at older ages because of physical limitations, or who become unemployed at older ages and are unable to find another job.

Raising the pensionable age may pose problems for workers forced to take early retirement or who are fired in the few years before the pensionable age because of the greater difficulty older workers have in leaving unemployment and finding a job.

The best solution for retirement for occupational groups unable to continue working into old age because of the physical demands of their work may be occupational pension plans that permit early retirement. For example, in countries as different as the Russian Federation and the United States, police, fire fighters, the military, and miners—occupations with physically demanding jobs-- all have occupational pension plans that permit early retirement (Turner and Guenther 2002). Perhaps because of longer life expectancy, there is a trend for plans that offer early retirement to offer it at later ages. For example, Washington, DC firefighters currently can retire at age 50, but new firefighters will not be able to retire until age 55.

Measuring the extent to which raising the pensionable age would hurt vulnerable groups, one study found that fewer than ten percent of men who take Social Security benefits at age 62 in the United States are both in poor health and have no source of pension income other than Social Security. For women, the figure is 20 percent (Burkhauser, Couch and Philips 1996). A more recent study for the United States found that 5 percent of workers taking benefits at the current pensionable age were vulnerable to an increase in the pensionable age due the combination of poor health, lack of a pension, and a physically demanding job (Panis et al 2002).

Disability Benefits. A higher pensionable age may increase the demand for disability benefits and poverty benefits, which would reduce the savings in benefit expense to the government. One study estimated that 22 percent of U.S. Old Age and Survivors Insurance (OASI) beneficiaries aged 62-64 have health problems that substantially impair their ability to work, and that 12 percent would qualify for Disability Insurance benefits (Leonesio, Vaughn and Wixon 2000). Because more workers will need to withdraw from labor force activity due to increases in disability rates with age, an increase in the pensionable age will increase the demand for disability benefits. It may reduce the stringency of requirements to qualify for disability benefits, providing an alternative pathway for some workers to early retirement.

Reactions by Employers and Government. Raising the pensionable age may cause employers to change the structure of pensions they provide. Employers may support the increase by also raising the minimum age that they offer pension benefits. The pensionable age in Social Security may be viewed by employers as a signal as to the age at which it is reasonable to expect that workers will retire. Raising the pensionable age raises the cost to employers of providing benefits for early retirement, which would tend to reduce the extent to which employers provide early retirement benefits. Alternatively, employers may feel they need to encourage some workers to retire at earlier ages, and they may increase the generosity of their early retirement pension benefits in order to make that possible.

Government policy in other areas may support or weaken the effect. Government may raise the minimum age at which occupational pension benefits can be received. Moving in the opposite direction, it may develop other programs to facilitate early retirement, which may be the result of political pressures arising from the postponement of the pensionable age in Social Security.

Labor Supply Effects. While some workers may retire earlier than the pensionable age, an increase in the pensionable age will cause some workers to postpone retirement. The pensionable age provides a standard when people think about retirement age. Also, some workers may be liquidity constrained, having insufficient funds to retire until the minimum age for retirement under Social Security, and being unable to borrow against their future Social Security benefits.

Some workers, however, already retire before Social Security benefits are available, and may continue to do so. In some countries, many people retire at the minimum age or earlier. In western Europe, however, most workers retire before the minimum age at which Social Security retirement benefits can be received (Gillion, Turner, Bailey and Latulippe 2000).

Workers who have high discount rates will place little value on the increase in benefits with postponed retirement and will tend to retire at the earliest date possible. Gustman and Steinmeier (2002) estimate that about three-fifths of those workers in the U.S. retiring at age 62 would postpone their retirement to age 64 if that were the new pensionable age.

International Survey

This section surveys countries that have raised the pensionable age in their Social Security programs. It also considers countries that have raised the requirements for receiving benefits at the pensionable age, which effectively raises the pensionable age for some workers.

This section surveys countries that have raised the pensionable age for both men and women (Tables 1 and 2). The following section considers countries that have raised the pensionable age for women only because it had been lower than that for men. Some countries have effectively raised the pensionable age by eliminating special early retirement for some occupations. Those countries are not considered here. Some countries appear in these surveys more than once because of having different programs providing old-age benefits.

Countries that Have Raised the Pensionable Age for Both Sexes

During the 1990s, many countries increased the pensionable age, although often the effective date of the increase was a decade or more later (Gillion, Turner, Bailey and Latulippe 2000).

Australia. In 2000, a retiree could receive the mandatory superannuation benefits at age 55. This age is scheduled to rise gradually to age 60, with the phase in beginning in 2015. By 2025, all persons born after June 1964 will be required to wait to age 60 to receive their superannuation benefits.

Austria. Up to 2000 the pensionable age was 60 for men and 55 for women. In May 2000, a stepwise increase in the pensionable age was legislated. Starting in October 2000 and ending in September 2002 in quarterly steps, the early retirement age has increased to 61.5 for men and 56.5 for women.

China. In 1951, when China established its Social Security system, the pensionable age was 50 for women and 60 for men. Since at least the early 1990s it has been 55 for women (50 for blue collar workers) and 60 for men (55 for blue collar workers, 65 for executive level workers) (Sin 2000).

Estonia. Under the Soviet system, the pensionable age for most pensioners was 55 for women and 60 for men. A number of countries that were formerly Republics of the Soviet Union have raised their pensionable ages. In Estonia, the ages have been raised over several years to 63 for men in 2001. The pensionable age for women will be gradually raised until it reaches age 63 for women in 2016 (Leppik and Männik 2002).

Germany. In Germany, workers could retire at age 60, 63 or 65, depending on meeting certain qualifying conditions. Legislation passed in 1989 and effective in 1992 stipulated an increase of both the age 60 and age 63 pensionable ages to age 65, starting in 2001.

Greece. Greece is raising the pensionable age to 65 for men and women who first

Table 1
Delay, Transition Period, and Annual Increase in Raising the Pensionable Age

Country	Change (number of years)	Legislated	Length of phase in from year of first increase to year completed (year completed)	Average increase in pensionable age per year over transition period
Australia	For mandatory-superannuation benefits from 55 to 60 (5 years)		10 years (2025)	0.5 years
Austria	From 60 to 61.5 for men and 55 to 56.5 for women (1.5 years)	2000	3 years (2002)	0.5 years
Hungary	60 to 62 for men, 55 to 62 for women (2 years men, 7 years women)	1996	3 years – men (2000), 10 years women (2009)	0.67 years men, 0.7 years women
New Zealand	60 to 65 for both men and women (5 years)	1991	10 years (2001)	0.5 years
Portugal	62 to 65 for women (3 years)		6 years (1999)	0.5 years
Switzerland	62 to 64 for women (2 years)	1997	5 years (2005)	0.4 years
United Kingdom	Increase from 60 to 65 for women (5 years)	1995	10 years (2020)	0.5 years

Source: Author's compilation.

start working after 1993. In 2000, it was age 58 for men and women with long careers of work.

Hungary. In Hungary, where the pensionable age had been age 55 for women and age 60 for men under the Soviet-type retirement income system, in 1996 it was increased to 62 for both sexes, to be phased in over a transition period to be completed in 2002 for men and 2009 for women (Augusztinovics et al.2002).

Table 2
Pensionable Age Increases in Selected Central and Eastern European Countries

Country	Current law	Men (years increase)	Women (years increase)
Czech Republic	1995	Increasing from 60 to 62 with 25 years of service, at a rate of 2 months. per year between 1996 and 2006 (2 years)	53-57, depending on no. of children, increasing to 57-61 at a rate of 4 months per year between 1996 and 2007 (4 years)
Estonia	1996	62.5, increasing to 63 in 2001 (0.5 years)	57.5, increasing to 63 in 2016 (5.5 years)
Hungary	1997	62	57, increasing to 62 in 2009
Latvia	1998	60 with 10 years of insurance	57 with 10 years of insurance, increasing to age 60 by increments of six months each year (3 years).
Lithuania	1990	61, increasing in increments of 2 months per year to 62.5 in 2009 (1.5 years)	57, increasing in steps of 4 months per year to 60 in 2009 (3 years)
FYR Macedonia	2000	Increasing from 63 to 64 with at least 15 years of service by 31/12/2001 (1 year)	Increasing from 60 to 62 with at least 15 years of service by 31/12/2007 (2 years)
Slovenia	2000	Increasing from 61 to 63 for full retirement with 40 year qualifying period, minimum retirement age 58 (2 years)	Increasing from 53-58 to 58-61 for full retirement with 38 year qualifying period, minimum retirement age 58 (5 years)

Source: Fultz and Ruck (2001).

Italy. Italy, which among OECD countries had low pensionable ages of 55 and 60 for women and men is raising pensionable ages to 60 for women and 65 for men. It formerly also had a seniority pension that a retiree could receive based solely on years of work, but that pension provision is being terminated.

Japan. Beginning in 2000, Japan is gradually raising its pensionable age in its social security Employees' Pension Insurance program from 60 to 65 for both men and women.

Lithuania. Starting in 1995, the pensionable age was raised annually by four months for women and by two months for men. The goal is for the pensionable age to be 62 and 6 months for men and 60 years for women. This is up from the Soviet standard of 60 and 55 for men and women (Medaiskis 2002).

New Zealand. The pensionable age in New Zealand rose from 60 in 1991 to 65 in 2001. Those who turned age 60 before 31 March 1992 were eligible at age 60. From

1 April 1992 eligibility was at age 61. The initial one-year increase reflected a general acceptance that age 60 was too low. From 1 July 1993, eligibility rose by 3 months for each 6 month period until 1 April 2001, when the pensionable age reached age 65. A Transitional Retirement Benefit was paid over this period to those affected by the changes, with the age of eligibility for this benefit also rising until it was paused out on 1 April 2001.

Poland. Poland reformed its retirement income system in 1999, replacing a system that offered early retirement to many workers based on their occupation with one that set a pensionable age of 65 for men and 60 for women. Under the old system, the actual average ages of retirement were 59 for men and 55 for women. Workers born after 1968 were required to participate in the new system (Chłoń-Domińczak 2002).

South Korea. In 2000, the pensionable age was 60 for both men and women. It will be increased to age 65 by 2033 (US SSA 1999).

Sweden. When the Swedish pension system was reformed in 1999, the pensionable age for the old-age pension was raised from 60 to 61 (US SSA 1999).

Increases in the Pensionable Age Designed to Equalize the Treatment of Men and Women

Most OECD countries have at some point permitted women to receive Social Security old-age benefits at younger ages than men. Most of these countries, however, are moving to equalize pensionable ages for men and women. Countries in the European Union are required to equalize the Social Security pensionable age for both men and women. Equalizing the pensionable age for the sexes does not necessarily imply an increase for women, but in practice it has generally occurred that way.

Australia. Australia is raising the minimum age at which a woman can receive its means-tested age pension by six months every two years, from age 60 in 1995 to age 65 in 2013. The legislation making this change was enacted in 1994. The pensionable age for the means-tested program has been age 65 for men for a number of years.

Austria. Legislated in 1992, but starting in 2018, the pensionable age for women, which is age 56.6, will be increased to that of men, which is age 61.5. The change will occur stepwise until it is completed in 2034.

Denmark. The pre-early retirement plan, which provided a transitional benefit for people aged 50-59 who had become unemployed and had contributed to the unemployment benefit program for at least 30 years, was closed to new entrants in 1996, and will be fully phased out by 2006 (Commission of the European Communities 2002).

Japan. Social Security reform in 1985 in Japan raised the pensionable age for women for the national Employee's Pension Insurance from 55 to 60 over a 15-year period. It reached age 60 in 2000, the same age for men (Liu 1987). Beginning in 2000, the pensionable age for both men and women started increasing to age 65, which is the pensionable age for the National Pension Insurance program.

Portugal. Portugal raised the pensionable age for women from 62 to 65 over the period 1994 to 1999.

Switzerland. Switzerland, by contrast has decided not to equalize the treatment of the sexes, raising the pensionable age for women from 62 to 64. The pensionable age for women increased from 62 to 63 on 1 January 2001 and to 64 on 1 January 2005. The pensionable age for men is 65.

United Kingdom. The pensionable age is currently 65 for men and 60 for women. As a result of legislation passed in 1995, it will be gradually raised for women over a ten-year period, starting in 2010 for women who reach age 60 that year, until it is equalized for all in 2020 at age 65 (O'Connell 2002).

Increases in the Requirements for Receiving Benefits at the Pensionable Age

Increasing the requirements for receiving benefits at the pensionable age effectively raises the pensionable age for some workers. This policy has gender implications since workers with career breaks will have to wait longer to accumulate the required years unless career credits apply.

Belgium. The eligibility requirements for early retirement social security benefits were raised in 1997 from a minimum contributory career of 20 years up to 35 years in 2005 (European Commission 2002).

Countries with Pensionable Age of 65 or Higher

Some countries have not legislated future increases in their pensionable age because they already have a pensionable age of 65 or older (Table 3).

Table 3
Selected OECD Countries with Current or Future Legislated
Pensionable Ages of 65 or Older for Social Security Old-age Benefits

Country	Age	Effective date if later than 2003
Australia	65	2013 (women)
Germany	65	2004 (women)
Greece	65	Workers starting work after 1993
Iceland	65	
Ireland	65	
Netherlands	65	
New Zealand	65	
Norway	67	
Poland	65 (men only)	
Portugal	65	
Switzerland	65 (men only)	
United Kingdom	65	2020 (women)

Source: U.S. Social Security Administration, 1999.

Denmark. In Denmark, the universal flat-rate old age pension benefit, that is financed from general tax revenue, is available at age 65. The minimum age for receipt of tax-favored pension benefits is age 67, but other programs facilitate early retirement.

Iceland. In Iceland, the universal pension is available at age 65.

Ireland. In Ireland, the Social Security retirement pension is available at age 65, and the old-age contributory pension is available at age 66.

Netherlands. In the Netherlands, the basic Social Security old age pension is available at age 65. However, the early retirement VUT program was developed in the early 1980s as a way to allow earlier retirement. With at least 10 years of uninterrupted employment, a worker age 60 could retire with a replacement rate of at least 80 percent. The government plans to phase out gradually the present system.

Norway. In Norway, the pensionable age for both the universal and the earnings-related Social Security old-age benefit are age 67 (US SSA 1999).

Countries That Have Raised the Pensionable Age for Occupational Pension Plans

Belgium. In Belgium, the age at which private sector workers can receive an occupational pension was raised to 60 in 2002, previously it had been in the fifties (Reid 2002).

India. In India, the pensionable age for government workers was 55 at the time of independence in 1947. That age was raised to 58 in the 1960s, and to 60 in 1996 (Subrahmanya 2002).

Switzerland. To harmonize the pensionable age for social security pensions and occupational pensions, in 2001, Switzerland increased the pensionable age for occupational pension plans from age 62 to age 64, with the increase from 62 to 63 taking place in 2001 and the increase from 63 to 64 taking place in 2005.

United States. In the Civil Service Retirement System for U.S. government employees hired in 1983 or earlier, the pensionable age is 55. In the Federal Employees Retirement System, which covers federal government employees hired after 1983, the pensionable age is 55 for workers born before 1948. The pensionable age is increased to age 57, phased in over a 22-year period, so that workers born in 1970 and later have a minimum retirement age of 57. Workers must have 30 years of service to be eligible to retire at the pensionable age.

Summary of Policies to Raise the Pensionable Age

The data presented in the previous section on policies countries have followed to raise the pensionable age can be analyzed for similarities in the policies. The following points apply generally, but with exceptions. First, a number of countries have raised the pensionable age in their Social Security programs. Second, in almost all cases the increase is by more than one year. Third, in a number of cases the increase is as long as 5 years. Fourth, the increase almost always involves raising the pensionable age for women to that of men if it initially had been lower. Fifth, the increase is almost always in less than one year increments. Sixth, a common rate of increase is 0.5 years per year. Seventh, the increase usually occurs after a delay. Eighth, the delay period is often only a few years. Ninth, more than a dozen countries have legislated an increase in the pensionable age to at least 65 for at least men or already have the pensionable age set at 65. Tenth, higher income countries whose populations have higher life expectancies tend to have higher pensionable ages than do lower income countries.

Conclusions

Because of increases in life expectancy, a number of countries have raised the pensionable age in their Social Security program as a way of dealing with problems of Social Security financing. Raising the pensionable age can be viewed as restoring the system to a previous state with respect to the probability of workers surviving to retirement and the length of time they will spend in retirement. Alternatively, it can be viewed in comparison to the current situation without such a change, which would mean that fewer people will survive to pensionable age and the average length of time spent receiving a pension will fall.

Though the pattern has exceptions, the pensionable age tends to be higher in high income countries than in low income countries. While a pensionable age of 65 may appear to be politically infeasible in some OECD countries, more than a dozen countries have legislated an increase in the pensionable age to at least 65 for at least men or already have the pensionable age set at 65.

References

Augusztinovics, Mária; Gál, Róbert; Matits, Agnes; Máté, Levente; Simonovits, András; and Stahl, János. "The Hungarian Pension System Before and After the 1998 Reform." In *Pension Reform in Central and Eastern Europe*, volume 1, edited by Elaine Fultz. Budapest: International Labour Office, 2002, pp. 25-93.

Baily, Martin N. "Aging and the Ability to Work: Policy Issues and Recent Trends." In *Work, Health, and Income among the Elderly*, edited by Gary Burtless. The Brookings Institution Press: 59-96.

Burkhauser, Richard V.; Couch, Kenneth A.; and Philips, John W. "Who Takes Early Social Security Benefits? The Economic and Health Characteristics of Early Beneficiaries." *The Gerontologist* 36(6) (1996): 789-99.

Burtless, Gary and Quinn, Joseph F. "Is Working Longer the Answer for an Aging Workforce?" Issue Brief No. 11, Center for Retirement Research at Boston College, December 2002.

Castello Branco, Marta de. "Pension Reform in the Baltics, Russia, and Other Countries of the Former Soviet Union." International Monetary Fund, IMF Working Paper WP/98/11. February 1998.

Chłoń-Domińczak, Agnieszka. "The Polish Pension Reform of 1999." In *Pension Reform in Central and Eastern Europe*, volume 1, edited by Elaine Fultz. Budapest: International Labour Office, 2002, pp. 95-205.

Commission of the European Communities. "Joint Report to the Commission and the Council on Adequate and Sustainable Pensions." Brussels, 2002.

The views, opinions and judgments expressed here are solely the responsibility of the author and do not represent the position of AARP. I have received helpful comments from Elaine Fultz, Jay Ginn, Alois Guger, Robert Stephens, Roland Sigg, and Wolfgang Scholz.

Congressional Budget Office. "Raising the Earliest Eligiblity Age for Social Security Benefits." January 1999. www.cbo.gov.

Costa, Dora and Steckel, R. "Long-Term Trends in Health, Welfare, and Economic Growth." In *Health and Welfare During Industrialization,* eds. R. Steckel and R. Floud. Chicago, IL: The University of Chicago Press, 1997.

Cutler, David M. "Declining Disability Among the Elderly." *Health Affairs* 20 (November/December 2001): 11-27.

European Commission. "Joint Report by the Commission and the Council on Adequate and Sustainable Pensions." Commission of the European Communities, 2002.

Fultz, Elaine and Ruck, Markus. "Pension Reform in Central and Eastern Europe: An Overview of Restructuring in Selected Countries." International Labour Office, Central and Eastern European Team (ILO CEET) Policy Paper No 25, 2001.

Gillion, Colin; Turner, John; Bailey, Clive; and Latulippe, Denis, eds. *Social Security Pensions: Development and Reform.* Geneva, Switzerland: International Labor Office, 2000.

Gustman, Alan L. and Steinmeier, Thomas L. "The Social Security Early Entitlement Age in a Structural Model of Retirement and Wealth." NBER Working Paper 9183.

Leonesio, Michael V.; Vaughn, Denton R. and Wixon, Bernard. "Early Retirees Under Social Security: Health Status and Retirement Resources." *Social Security Bulletin* 63(4) (2000): 1-16.

Leppik, Lauri and Männik, Georg. "Transformation of Old-Age Security in Estonia." In *Transformation of Pension Systems in Central and Eastern Europe.* Edited by Winfried Schmähl and Sabine Horstmann. Cheltenham, UK: Edward Elgar: 2002.

Liu, Lillian. "Social Security Reforms in Japan." *Social Security Bulletin* 50 (August 1987): 29-37.

Manton, Kenneth G. and Stollard, Eric. "Medical Demography: Interaction of Disability Dynamics and Mortality." In *Demography of Aging,* edited by Linda G. Martin and Samuel H. Preston. National Academy Press, pp. 217-279.

Mitchell, Olivia S. and Phillips, John W. R. "Eligibility for Social Security Disability Insurance." Working Paper No. 2001-011. Ann Arbor, MI: University of Michigan Retirement Research Center, 2001.

O'Connell, Alison. "Raising State Pension Age: Are We Ready?" London, England: Pensions Policy Institute, 2002.

Panis, Constantijn; Hurd, Michael; Loughran, David; Zissimopoulos, Julie; Haider, Steven; and StClair, Patricia. "The Effects of Changing Social Security Administration's Eraly Entitlement Age and the Normal Retirement Age." Report prepared for the Social security Administration. RAND, June 2002.

Population Reference Bureau. "How Much Better Can It Get?" 2002.

Reid, Dickon. "Belgian Occupational Pensions Law Finalised." *IPE Newsline* September 9, 2002. http://www.ipe-newsline.com/article.asp?article=13426.

Sin, Yvonne. "Country Profile for China." World Bank, 2000.

Social Security Administration. "Life Expectancy for Social Security." Social Security Online, History Page, November 28, 2001.

Social Security Advisory Board. "Forum on Implications of Raising the Social Security Retirement Age." Washington, DC: Social Security Advisory Board, 1998. http:www.ssab.org.

Subrahmanya, RKA. "Income Security for Older People: An Asian Perspective." *International Social Security Review* 55 (January-March 2002): 49-65.

U.S. Social Security Administration (US SSA). *Social Security Programs Throughout the World*. SSA Publication No. 13-11805. August 1999.

Verma, Satyenda and Rix, Sara E. "Retirement Age and Social Security Reform: The Macroeconomic Effects of Working Longer." AARP Issue Brief, 2002.

Should we Raise Social Security's Earliest Eligibility Age?

by Alicia H. Munnell, Kevin B. Meme, Natalia A. Jivan, and Kevin E. Cahill

Introduction

Social Security's Earliest Eligibility Age (EEA) allows one to claim reduced benefits as early as age 62. For full benefits, individuals must wait until the Normal Retirement Age (NRA), which was traditionally 65 but is gradually increasing to 67. So, Americans have a choice to make when they reach their early 60s: claim a reduced Social Security benefit right away or delay until some further date and receive a larger benefit. The reduction for claiming benefits early is designed to be actuarially fair, i.e. monthly benefits are lowered by an amount that offsets the longer period for which they will be received. The total amount that the average person can expect to receive over his or her lifetime thus does not depend on when benefits are claimed.

In recent years some have suggested raising the EEA. Proponents say that such a move could make Social Security a more adequate source of income later in life by preventing people from taking benefits so early that their monthly check is too low. In addition, they say, raising the EEA may encourage people to work longer. Increasing labor force participation among those in their early sixties is possibly the best solution to guaranteeing a more financially secure retirement.

Not everyone is so convinced, though. Opponents claim that many individuals can neither work longer nor save more for retirement. Raising the EEA could impoverish these groups as well as strain social programs like Disability Income (DI) and Supplemental Security Income (SSI) that would likely end up serving more people. Finally, they contend that withholding benefits until a later age hurts those with shorter life expectancies, and shifts more retirement wealth to those with longer lives.

Despite these negatives, raising the EEA may well be desirable policy. But it is a hard sell politically. It does nothing to eliminate Social Security's long-term financing gap and would probably require greater current outlays on DI and SSI. The best that could be said on the financing side is that it may pave the way for future increases in the Normal Retirement Age, which does improve solvency. Raising the EEA thus is probably a realistic option only as part of a package of other changes that restore financial balance and maintain equity in the Social Security program.

(Center for Retirement Research at Boston College, Issue Brief #18, June 2004; available at http://www.bc.edu/centers/crr/issues/ib_18.pdf; used with permission)

Raising the EEA: Pros and Cons

Proponents of increasing the EEA argue that such a change would safeguard the fundamental purpose of Social Security's Old Age and Survivors Insurance (OASI) program—to counteract myopia and assure an adequate income across an individual's entire old age.[1] The Normal Retirement Age (NRA) for Social Security is currently rising from its traditional age of 65 to 67 for those born in 1960 or later.[2] This change means that benefits claimed at age 62 will fall from 80 percent to 70 percent of benefits claimed at the NRA.[3] This 12.5 percent reduction in monthly benefits can have a profound impact as retirees age, since the elderly tend to spend down their other retirement assets and rely increasingly on Social Security. By keeping the EEA at 62, the program allows workers to elect two more years of retirement today—when they are relatively young and when their non-Social Security retirement incomes are typically at their peak—but at the price of risking very low incomes at the end of their lives. In essence, as life expectancies lengthen, keeping the EEA at 62 shifts more Social Security benefits toward "middle age."[4]

Raising the EEA to, say, 64—in step with the two year increase in the NRA—would counteract this shortsightedness and prevent incomes from falling to inadequately low levels. Furthermore, an increase in the EEA would help set the stage for future increases in the NRA, one option for maintaining the solvency of the Social Security program. An EEA of 62 makes any additional increase in the NRA highly unlikely, since a higher NRA would produce an even steeper reduction in benefits at age 62. A higher EEA would signal that retiring in one's early 60s is no longer economically feasible, preparing the way for a higher NRA.[5] Of course, any increase in the EEA would need to be implemented slowly, as is being done with the NRA.

Finally, given that Social Security will provide less replacement income in the future than it does today, and that the income provided by employer-sponsored pensions has become less certain with the rise of 401(k) plans, the only way most individuals can secure adequate resources for their retirement is by working longer. The impact of working an additional two years can have a profound impact on the resources available to finance retirement. Opponents of increasing the EEA argue that many individuals are unable to work past age 62, either because they are in poor health, because their jobs are physically demanding, or because they have been displaced later in life and cannot find work. Many of these individuals are dependent on Social Security, and an increase in the EEA would eliminate their only source of income. Opponents also note that raising the EEA is unfair to individuals with shorter life expectancies—particularly blacks and low-income workers. These people are clearly better off claiming benefits as soon as they become available.

Finally, an increase in the EEA does nothing, in and of itself, to improve the financial outlook of the Social Security system as a whole. In fact, such a change may actually increase costs. Programs such as SSI and DI are likely to pick up those who cannot work past 62 or support themselves for the additional two years until they can begin receiving benefits from Social Security.

Future Retirement Income Sources Will Fall Short

The traditional sources of retirement income will not be sufficient for most people in the future. Going forward, Social Security's already modest benefit amounts will decline due to four factors: the scheduled rise in the NRA (equivalent to an across-the-board benefit cut for retirement at any given age), rising Medicare Part B premiums, increased taxation of benefits, and benefit cuts to restore long term balance to the system. The cumulative effect of these four factors will lower the benchmark Social Security replacement rate for average earners who retire at age 65, net of Medicare Part B premiums, from 38.5 percent today to about 26.3 percent by 2030 (Table 1). Average earners who claim benefits at the early retirement age of 62 will see their replacement rate decline from 30.2 to 19.9 percent. Using today's average earnings of $36,200 as an example, for a 62 year-old retiree, this would yield a monthly cash income of $600, as opposed to $911 currently.

The increase began with individuals born in 1938, for whom the NRA is 65 plus two months, and increases two months per year until it reaches age 66. Then, after a 12-year hiatus, the NRA again increases by two months per year until it reaches age 67 for individuals born in 1960 or later.

Employer-sponsored pensions, too, are becoming less secure. Since the early 1980s, there has been a pronounced shift in coverage away from traditional defined benefit plans towards defined contribution plans, such as 401(k)s. The key distinction between the two plans is the role individual responsibility plays. In 401(k) plans,

Table 1
Estimated Social Security Replacement Rates, 2003 and 2030

	Percent of Pre-Retirement Earnings			
Development	Retire at Age 62	Retire at Age 65	Retire at Age 62	Retire at Age 65
2003				
Reported replacement rate (RR)	44.5	55.6	33.0	41.3
After Medicare Part B deduction	41.7*	52.8	30.2*	38.5
Net replacement rate	41.7	52.8	30.2	38.5
2030				
RR after extension of Normal Retirement Age	38.7	48.9	28.7	36.3
After deduction for Medicare Part B	35.0*	45.2	25.0*	32.6
After personal income taxation	35.0	45.2	22.8	29.9
After hypothetical 10% benefit cut	31.1	40.3	19.9	26.3
Net replacement rate	31.1	40.3	19.9	26.3

Source: Munnell (2003) and authors' calculations.

*For the individual retiring at age 62, the Medicare Part B premium will not begin until age 65.

participation is voluntary; investment risk is borne by the individual; workers must decide what to do with their balances when they change jobs; and retiring workers need to determine how to convert final balances into a stream of old-age income.

While 401(k) plans can work well in theory, in practice they fall short in many ways.[6] In 2001, median 401(k)/IRA account balances of households age 55-64 were about $55,000—not much to support a couple for 20 years or more in retirement. The reason balances are so low is because workers make poor choices at each step. One-quarter of eligible workers choose not to participate in their plan. Of those who do participate less than 10 percent contribute the maximum. Many workers fail to diversify their assets, over-invest in company stock, and do not rebalance their portfolios as they age. Furthermore, many short-change their retirement assets by cashing out when changing jobs rather than rolling their balances into an IRA or a plan with their new employer.

Individual saving seems unlikely to compensate for the eroding income from Social Security and employer-sponsored pensions. Saving as a percent of personal disposable income, which includes saving in employer plans, declined precipitously—from above 10 percent to just over 2 percent—between 1980 and 2000, a rate not seen since the Great Depression. Saving has increased somewhat in the last year or so, but still remains below 4 percent. This savings rate does not include capital gains but, even after including them, most people end up at retirement with few assets outside of their home and pension.

How will people manage with significantly less retirement income in the future? One obvious answer is working longer. Working longer can have a significant impact on an individual's retirement finances. Social Security benefits will be higher and retirement will be shorter, which makes the starting point for dissaving later. Thus the savings needed at retirement to supplement Social Security can be substantially reduced (Table 2). A higher EEA is likely to keep individuals in the labor force longer, since most people claim benefits and exit the labor force at the same time. The CBO finds that 75 percent of men and 80 percent of women aged 62 and 63 who claimed Social Security retirement benefits were also out of the labor force.[7] Since about half of all people claim benefits at age 62, raising the EEA could increase labor force participation for about 40 percent (75 percent of 50 percent) of 62 year olds.

Vulnerable Groups and a Higher EEA

While working longer is indeed an effective way to improve individuals' retirement income pictures, it is important to look at various groups of the population (especially the most vulnerable) and ask how many people would be affected by a change, and in what way.

Vulnerable Groups and the Decision to Work

Opponents to increasing the EEA argue that many of those that claim benefits at 62 are either dependent on Social Security, would not be able to work longer due to

Table 2
Representative Assets Needed at Retirement,
by Retirement Age and Earnings Status, 2003 Dollars

Retirement Age	Low Earner	Average Earner	High Earner
62	$58,840	$155,438	$267,133
63	48,412	136,055	238,858
64	38,574	117,581	211,744
65	29,354	100,059	185,849
66	20,419	82,940	160,427
67	12,197	66,925	136,424

Source: Authors' calculations based on methodology presented in CBO (2003). Wages for low, average, and high earners are based on the SSA average wage index (AWI) for 2002, which was equal to $33,477. Low earners have career average earnings equal to 45 percent of AWI; average earners have career-average earnings equal to 100 percent of the AWI; and high earners have career-average earnings equal to 160 percent of AWI. Base assumptions are as follows: income replacement in retirement is 80 percent of preretirement earnings, life expectancy at 62 is 21 years, and the real rate of return on assets is 3 percent. Tax rates are calculated using the National Bureau of Economic Research's TAXSIM model (http://www.nber.org/~taxsim/taxsim-calc5/). Social Security benefit amounts are based on earner-specific replacement rates given in SSA (2003a), Table VI.F11.

some work-limiting condition, or both. Thus, they maintain that moving back the EEA will harm the most vulnerable. How large of a segment of the population are those who are "Social Security-dependent" (SSD) and unable to work past age 62?

Three studies all find that the majority of workers who claim benefits early have significant non-Social Security income, suggesting that, if the EEA were raised, they could use their own assets during ages 62 and 63.[8] Among those without alternative income sources, many could remain at work beyond age 62.[9] Nevertheless, a sizable minority—about 10 percent of early claimers, or 4 percent of all those aged 62—is in poor health and does not have a source of income, other than work or Social Security, that would keep them out of poverty. These are the people that would be hurt.

We use data from the Health and Retirement Study (HRS) to expand upon these findings. The HRS is a nationally-representative longitudinal sample of Americans aged 51-61 in 1992. It contains detailed information on labor force participation, income, health status, retirement expectations, and perceptions about work and retirement.[10] We split our sample into two groups: those who claim Social Security early ("Takers") and those that do not ("Postponers").[11] The Takers are clearly the group we are interested in as they are the ones who would be affected by raising the EEA. In our sample, a little more than half of all individuals can be classified as Takers. About three-quarters of these Takers have enough other financial resources beyond Social Security to fall back on so that they could still retire early if they wanted. And, in return for waiting until 65 to claim Social Security, they would have higher monthly benefits throughout the rest of their retirement. Although the higher EEA would limit flexibility in choosing one's retirement age, we see this change as a clear gain since retirees would receive a higher benefit that is guaranteed and inflation-proofed for life.

The remaining one-quarter of Takers receive 80 percent or more of their income from Social Security. We call these people "Social Security Dependent." This group would clearly be affected by a higher EEA—especially if they were not able to work.[12] Using a regression equation, we estimate the probability of HRS respondents being employed based on a number of factors, including educational attainment, health status, and the physical demands of previous jobs. We find that the majority of SSD Takers are able to work past age 62, but about 26 percent of men and 34 percent of women are not (Table 3).[13]

For those SSD Takers who could continue to work, a higher EEA would eliminate the opportunity for them to retire at 62, but it would also improve their long-term financial situation. Each year of delayed retirement increases monthly Social Security benefits in two ways. Wages later in life can be used to fill in any gaps in the person's earnings history or to substitute for lower wages earlier in life. This can be particularly important for women, who typically retire with fewer than the 35 years of earnings included in the Social Security benefit calculation. In addition, a higher EEA prevents individuals from accepting monthly benefits that are substantially reduced due to the actuarial reduction. The net result is that if these individuals delay benefit receipt until age 64, their poverty rate at age 67 drops by 4 percentage points (20.3 percent for those who retire at 62 versus 16.2 percent for those who retire at 64). The financial outlook of these retirees becomes even better if they work until age 67. In this case, poverty at that age drops to about 11 percent.

In contrast, those SSD Takers who *cannot* work would face serious hardship for a few years; for example, their poverty rates would soar (see Table 4, middle column). However, by age 65, poverty rates would actually be lower for this group than they would be under current law due to the higher monthly benefits that they would receive (see Table 4, last column).

Table 3
Predicted Ability to Work at Age 62, Takers Classified as Social Security Dependent

Ability to Work	Male Takers	Female Takers
Able to work	68.4%	64.3%
Not able to work	26.3	33.5
Undetermined	5.3	2.3

Source: Authors' calculations based on the Health and Retirement Study matched to restricted Social Security administrative data.

Table 4
Poverty Rates by Age, SSD Takers Who Cannot Work

Earliest Eligibility Age	61	Age 63	65
62- Current Law	50.4%	40.8%	39.4%
64- Proposed	50.4.	56.6	34.9

Source: Authors' calculations based on the Health and Retirement Study matched to restricted Social Security administrative data. Ability to work is estimated based on multivariate linear probability model with health status, physical job, education and interaction terms on the righthand side (see Table 4 and Table 5 for details). Poverty rates are based on income derived from Social Security, private pensions, assets, and social programs such as DI and SSI.

Three key findings emerge from this analysis. First, the size of the most vulnerable group is very small—about 4 percent of all individuals aged 62. Second, this group would experience negative effects only for a short time; indeed, in the long run, many of them would be better off. And, third, ensuring that these individuals could cover basic living expenses between ages 62 and 64 would require an expansion of social programs such as DI or SSI.

The Impact of a Higher EEA on the Oldest Old

Another way to assess the impact of a shift in the EEA is to look at the oldest old. A higher EEA would increase incomes among this group, primarily by preventing workers from locking into very low monthly benefits at the early retirement age. The actuarial reduction in benefits plays a key role in the well-being among the oldest old since Social Security benefits become increasingly important as retirees age. In 2000, for example, Social Security accounted for 28 percent of income among 65-69 year olds, but 57 percent of income among individuals 85 years and older.[14] If the EEA remains at 62, however, longer life expectancies will mean that benefits will be more evenly distributed across an individual's lifespan rather than concentrated at the end of life.

Data from the Asset and Health Dynamics of the Oldest Old (AHEAD) survey, a nationally representative dataset of Americans born between 1890 and 1923, provides information on retirees age 75 and older in 1998. We divide the AHEAD sample into those who worked since age 62 and those who did not. We find that men who did not work since age 62 have lower Social Security benefits, lower levels of financial wealth, and were more likely to be receiving SSI (Table 5).[15] The descriptive results are consistent with the story that work at older ages provides for a more secure future into the latest stages of retirement.

As Social Security replacement rates decline and income from employer plans and individual saving becomes increasingly uncertain, especially toward the end of life, allowing workers to continue claiming benefits at age 62 risks a sharp increase in poverty at older ages. This outcome could easily lead to a significant expansion of SSI benefits, further stressing the government's social welfare budget.

The Equity Issue

Finally, when analyzing the impact of a higher EEA on various groups, there is an important equity issue that must be taken into consideration. Raising the EEA means that early claimants with shorter-than-average life expectancies will experience a reduction in benefits received over their lifetimes. Their "Social Security wealth"—the present value of their expected stream of benefits—goes down because they will not live long enough to have the higher monthly benefits, which begin at 64, make up for the loss of benefits at ages 62 and 63.

Consider the example of a single individual, with a history of average earnings. Assuming a 3 percent real rate of return on assets, if the worker claims benefits at age 62 and dies on his 64th birthday, his Social Security wealth is $21,787. If the EEA were raised to age 64, his Social Security wealth would be zero. For people who live to be 90, their Social Security wealth would be greater if they postponed benefit receipt to age 64. The present value of lifetime benefits is $226,526 for the age-64 claimer compared to $216,241 if benefits were claimed at 62. More generally, anyone who dies before age 79 (the "break-even" life expectancy) would receive more in Social Security wealth by claiming benefits early; anyone who dies later would be better off postponing. A person who dies at age 79 would receive the same amount of Social Security wealth regardless of when they claimed.

Given the different life expectancies across gender and race in the United States, different groups can expect an increase in the EEA to produce different gains and losses of Social Security wealth with a high degree of certainty. Table 6 estimates these changes in total Social Security wealth at age 62, per 100,000 beneficiaries, using two different discount rates.

Table 5 Financial Condition of American Males Age 75 and Over		
Retirement Outcome	**Exit at, or prior to, 62**	**Work since 62**
Percent who:		
—Expect financial help from friends or family	7.9	10.3
—Receive SSI	6.2	3.8
—Own their own home	77.4	76.2
Social Security income (monthly)	$700	$800
Financial wealth	$25,000	$41,250
Sample size	261	876

Source: Authors' calculations based on the HRS. (HRS and AHEAD individuals were interviewed at the same time in 1998.)

Table 6
Estimated Change in Total Social Security Wealth at Age 62
per 100,000 Beneficiaries, by Gender and Race, 2001

	Discount Rate	
Gender and Race	**3.0**	**4.0**
Males		
White	+0.4	-1.0
Black	-1.5	-3.0
Females		
White	+2.1	+0.7
Black	+1.0	-0.4

Source: Authors' calculations for average earners. Average earners have career average earnings equal to the SSA average wage index. Monthly Social Security benefits are equal to $922 if they are claimed at age 62 and equal to $1,074 if they are claimed at age 64. Aggregate Social Security wealth is the sum across all ages of a worker's benefit discounted at 3.0 (4.0) percent and multiplied by life expectancy at that age. Mortality rates at each age are from the 2001 United States Life Tables in Arias (2004).

Such knowledge of an inequitable outcome across different groups makes it difficult to enact legislation to increase the EEA. However, this impact should be considered in the context of the entire Social Security program. Many of those who would be hurt by a higher EEA tend to have lower earnings. As such, they gain from the progressivity of the Social Security benefit formula, which awards proportionately greater benefits to low earners.

Financial Issues

Raising the EEA brings up two important financial issues. The first is whether enacting an increase would have any effect on the financing of the Social Security program as a whole. The second is the question of what new financial obligations would have to be taken on to deal with the groups that would be adversely affected by an increase in the EEA.

Raising the EEA Does Not Improve Social Security Financing

Raising the EEA does not help the OASI program. This should not be surprising given that benefits are actuarially reduced to keep lifetime payments constant, on average, regardless of when they are claimed.

This intuitive result was documented in a recent study that considered two behavioral responses to calculate the impact on the OASI program of raising the EEA by one year, from 62 to 63.[16] The authors assumed that all workers who claim at age 62 under current law instead claim at age 63. They then modeled the two extreme responses: that no one works the additional year and that everyone works the additional year.

They estimated that continued employment would allow Social Security to receive additional payroll taxes equal to 0.66 percent of lifetime benefits for men and 0.40 percent for women. But more work means that many beneficiaries will have higher average earnings, which will raise benefits. The combined effect of the additional payroll taxes and the change in lifetime benefits results in a net loss for men of -0.82 percent and a gain for women of +0.80. Considering men and women together, the overall effect on the OASI fund is virtually zero.[17]

Increased Cost to Support Vulnerable Groups

Given the extremely high poverty rates for SSD Takers who cannot work, raising the EEA would also require additional finances to improve their condition. Two social programs, Social Security DI and SSI, are currently in place and could provide a safety net for these individuals. The DI program pays benefits to disabled workers and their families; the SSI program provides benefits for the blind and disabled and the elderly (aged 65 and older) with very low incomes and virtually no assets (less than $2,000 for an individual and $3,000 for a couple).[18]

If the EEA were raised to 64, older workers who are unable to work past age 62 could apply for DI benefits.[19] Of course, they might not get DI benefits at age 62 either because of delays in determining eligibility or because they are not classified as disabled according to existing program rules.[20] To broaden the current safety net, Congress could change the law and allow low-income individuals to claim SSI old-age benefits at age 62.[21]

Both options require increased public expenditures. One study estimates that the net change in OASDI spending from an increase in the EEA, primarily an increase in DI, would be about $9 billion a year.[22] Assuming that 4 percent of 62 year olds would require SSI benefits, beyond the assistance offered by DI, the cost of the expanded safety net would rise by another $1.4 billion.[23]

Conclusion

A higher EEA, by increasing the labor force participation of older workers, could have substantial benefits with respect to retirement income policy. More work means more income from earnings and shorter retirements to finance out of Social Security and private resources.

Critics charge that many households would be ill equipped to deal with a higher EEA. But we find that most of these Social Security-dependent people can work longer. Yet, about 30 percent of the Social Security Dependent population—or 4 percent of each age cohort—would need assistance from some other program such as DI or SSI.

A higher EEA would reduce lifetime Social Security wealth for those with lower-than-average life expectancies. Since blacks and low-wage workers have lower-than-average life expectancies, a higher EEA might be considered unfair. Nevertheless, this argument frames the debate in a rather narrow way, given that the progressive nature of Social Security in general is beneficial to low earners and the short-lived (who benefit from early survivors' and DI pensions).

On balance, an increase in the EEA might be a good idea from a retirement-income perspective. But it is a tough sell politically, particularly given that it does nothing to improve Social Security's long-term financial picture. It might become a more realistic option as part of a package of other changes to restore financial balance to the Social Security program. For example, raising the EEA might be considered in conjunction with some change to Social Security's progressive benefit formula that boosts replacement rates for low-wage individuals. The way in which a higher EEA might be implemented is important as well. It must be done gradually in order to give people enough time to alter their career and savings plans.[24] A logical approach is to have the EEA mimic the already legislated increase in the NRA.

Notes

1. The Social Security program consists of two separate trust funds, the Old-Age and Survivors Insurance (OASI) Trust Fund and the Disability Insurance (DI) Trust Fund. In addition, the Social Security Administration runs the Supplemental Security Income (SSI) program, although funding for SSI comes from general revenues. Throughout this *brief,* the term "Social Security" refers to the OASI program unless otherwise noted.

2. The increase began with individuals born in 1938, for whom the NRA is 65 plus two months, and increases two months per year until it reaches age 66. Then, after a 12-year hiatus, the NRA again increases by two months per year until it reaches age 67 for individuals born in 1960 or later.

3. Benefits are reduced by 5/9th of 1 percent for each month they are received prior to the normal retirement age (NRA) up to 36 months and 5/12th of 1 percent for each month thereafter. This is equivalent to a 6.67 percent reduction for the first three years prior to the NRA and 5 percent thereafter.

4. Steuerle and Spiro (1999).

5. An increase in the NRA is equivalent to an across-the-board benefit cut. Thus, increasing the NRA should not be thought of as the only approach to maintaining Social Security solvency. There are certainly other (and perhaps more desirable) options, which might give more protection to low earners and widows. For more details on reform options, see Diamond and Orszag (2004).

6. Munnell and Sundén (2004).

7. CBO (1999).

8. See Burkhauser, Couch, and Phillips (1996); CBO (1999); and Panis, et al. (2002).

9. Steuerle, et al. (1999).

All the authors are currently or formerly affiliated with the Center for Retirement Research at Boston College. Alicia H. Munnell is the director of the Center and the Peter F. Drucker Professor of Management Sciences at Boston College's Carroll School of Management. Kevin B. Meme is a research associate. Natalia A. Jivan is a graduate research assistant. And Kevin Cahill was formerly the associate director for research. The authors would like to thank Gary Burtless, Peter Diamond, Steven Sass, and Eugene Steuerle for helpful comments on a draft version of the full study from which this brief is derived.

10. More on the HRS can be found in the Appendix.

11. Takers include those who claim benefits at either age 62 or 63, but for simplicity throughout the rest of this study we refer only to age 62.

12. This cutoff is consistent with findings from other sources: CBO (1999) and Grad (2002).

13. See Appendix for details on the model, and for regression results.

14. Grad (2002).

15. These results do not prove causation. For example, it may be that males who are less successful retire earlier, and thus those who work longer are inherently more financially secure. This correlation effect is likely the case for females, whose results seem to tell the opposite story from the data for males, i.e., women working after age 62 are worse off financially than those who are not working. We believe this says more about the *types* of women who remain in the labor force than about the impact of work on income later in life. Perhaps women who continued to work were single or widowed with few alternative sources of income, while those who did not work were married or more financially secure.

16. Panis, et al. (2002).

17. It should also be noted that additional years of work will add some amount of tax revenue not only to Social Security and Medicare, but to federal income tax collections, state tax revenues, etc. These additional taxes certainly add up to additional funds that may be spent in a variety of ways.

18. Assets include cash holdings, real estate other than the individual's primary residence, and other assets, including stocks and bonds.

19. Older workers who were on DI prior to age 62 would presumably continue receiving DI benefits until the new EEA.

20. Some applicants will apply for DI and be denied benefits, and this process may entail lost earnings because of the program's five-month waiting period.

21. In addition, both the DI and SSI programs are linked to other federal health insurance programs, which would further dampen the impact of increasing the EEA. Most SSI recipients are currently eligible for Food Stamps and Medicaid benefits, while DI beneficiaries qualify for Medicare benefits, with a two-year waiting period.

22. See Panis, et al. (2002) and SSA (2003c).

23. This cost estimate is based on the size of the age 62 and age 63 population as reported by Census (2003) and the 2003 SSI payment rates reported by the Social Security Administration (2003b). As with DI enrollment, there would be additional costs to an expanded SSI program due to increased eligibility for Medicaid benefits.

24. In comments on an earlier draft, Eugene Steuerle suggested that it would also be logical to institute a project of detailed data gathering as any increase was phased in, to evaluate the change as it happens.

References

Arias, Elizabeth. 2004. "United States Life Tables, 2001." *National Vital Statistics Reports* 52, no. 14. [Available at: http://www.cdc.gov/nchs/data/nvsr/nvsr52/nvsr52_14.pdf].

Burkhauser, Richard V., Kenneth A. Couch, and John W. Phillips. 1996. "Who Takes Early Social Security Benefits? The Economic and Health Characteristics of Early Beneficiaries." The Gerontologist 36, no. 6: 789-799.

Cahill, Kevin E. and Alicia H. Munnell. 2004 forthcoming. "What Would Be the Effect of Raising the Earliest Eligibility Age for Social Security?" New York: Russell Sage Foundation.

Congressional Budget Office. 1999. *Raising the Earliest Eligibility Age for Social Security Benefits*. Washington, D.C.: U.S. Government Printing Office.

Congressional Budget Office. 2003. *Baby Boomers' Retirement Prospects: An Overview*. Washington, D.C.: U.S. Government Printing Office.

Diamond, Peter A., and Peter R. Orszag. 2004. *Saving Social Security: A Balanced Approach*. Washington, D.C.: Brookings Institution Press.

Grad, Susan. 2002. "Income of the Population 55 or Older, 2000." SSA Publication No. 13-11871. Washington, D.C.: Social Security Administration, Office of Research, Evaluation, and Statistics.

Juster, F. Thomas and Richard Suzman. 1995. "An Overview of the Health and Retirement Study." *Journal of Human Resources* 30, no. 5: S7-S56.

Munnell, Alicia H. 2003. "The Declining Role of Social Security." *Issue in Brief* 6. Chestnut Hill, MA: Center for Retirement Research.

Munnell, Alicia H., and Annika Sundén. 2004. *Coming Up Short: The Challenge of 401(k) Plans*. The Brookings Institution Press.

Panis, Constantijn, Michael Hurd, David Loughran, Julie Zissimopoulos, Steven Haider, Patricia St. Clair, Delia Bugliari, Serhii Ilchuk, Gabriela Lopez, Philip Pantoja, and Monika Reti. 2002. "The Effects of Changing Social Security Administration's Early Entitlement Age and the Normal Retirement Age." Report conducted by RAND for the Social Security Administration (June).

Steuerle, C. Eugene, and Christopher Spiro. 1999. "Adjusting for Life Expectancy in Measures of Labor Force Participation." *Straight Talk on Social Security and Retirement Policy* 10. Washington, D.C.: Urban Institute. [Available at: http://www.urban.org/url.cfm?ID=309271].

Steuerle, C. Eugene, Christopher Spiro, and Richard W. Johnson. 1999. "Can Americans Work Longer?" *Straight Talk on Social Security and Retirement Policy* 5. Washington, D.C.: Urban Institute. [Available at: http://www.urban.org/ url.cfm?ID=309228].

U.S. Bureau of the Census. 2003. *United States: 2000—Summary Social, Economic, and Housing Characteristics*. PHC-2-1 (July). Washington, D.C.: U.S. Government Printing Office. [Available at: http://www.census.gov/prod/cen2000/phc-2-1-pt1.pdf].

U.S. Social Security Administration. 2003a. *The 2003 Annual Report of the Board of Trustees of the Federal Old-Age and Survivors Insurance and Disability Insurance Trust Funds*. Washington, D.C.: U.S. Government Printing Office. [Available at: http://www.socialsecurity.gov/ OACT/TR/TR03/tr03.pdf].

U.S. Social Security Administration. 2003b. *SSI Monthly Statistics*. [Available at: http://www.ssa.gov/policy/docs/statcomps/ssi_monthly/2003-10/index.html#editions].

U.S. Social Security Administration. 2003c. *Understanding the Benefits*. [Available at: http://www.ssa.gov/pubs/10024.html#rates].

Social Security Reform: Statement before the Senate Committee on Finance

by C. Eugene Steuerle

Social Security Reform

Mr. Chairman and Members of the Committee:

Thank you for the opportunity to testify on achieving sustainable balance in Social Security. Since Social Security was first enacted, vast changes have occurred in the economy, life expectancy, health care, the physical demands of jobs, the labor force participation of women, and even the age at which one can be considered old. Yet, we often debate Social Security as if the type of system we want in 2080 should be determined by perceptions and measures of society's needs in 1930, or 150 years earlier. Much of my testimony will deal with our increasing inability to protect the young, the truly old, and the vulnerable when Social Security morphs into a middle-age retirement system.

The Social Security debate could and should be part of a larger one in which we engage our fellow citizens in figuring out how to take best advantage of new opportunities created by longer lives and better health. How can we spread the gains from this increased level of well-being and wealth to create a stronger nation with opportunity for all? And how should we share the costs?

Unfortunately, as now scheduled, the legacy we are about to leave our children is a government whose almost sole purpose is to finance our own consumption in retirement. We who are middle-aged or older come nowhere close to paying for the government transfers we are scheduled to receive, especially once health benefits are added in. More important, we plan to pay for them by shrinking almost to oblivion the rest of government that would serve our children and grandchildren.

The impact on the budget is especially large beginning around 2008 because that is when so many start moving from the working-age population into the retired population. Assume merely that Social Security, Medicare, and Medicaid continue on automatic pilot, that interest on the debt is paid, and that as a percentage of GDP existing levels of revenues are allowed to rise only moderately and defense expenditures decline only modestly. Then by about 2015 no revenues are left for anything else—not for justice or transportation or education, not for wage subsidies or education or environmental clean-up or community development, not for the IRS or

Statement of C. Eugene Steuerle before the Committee on Finance, United States Senate, May 25, 2005 (available at http://www.urban.org/UploadedPDF/900815_Steuerle_052505.pdf)

national parks—not even to turn on the lights in the Capitol. The pressure on the budget is not awaiting some magical date like 2018 or beyond. Social Security and Medicare are already spending much more than the Social Security tax for Social Security and Medicare, and even this accounting does not include all the other programs for the retired and elderly in the budget. The pressure on programs for children and working families is being felt right now, and the fight over the fiscal 2006 budget makes this glaringly apparent.

Clearly, retaining a necessary share of the budget for our children and grandchildren means that we must pare the growth rate in elderly entitlement programs. Nonetheless, I believe that *it is possible under existing tax rates to build a Social Security system that would do a better job than the current one at removing poverty (measured by relative living standards) and serving the majority of the population when they are truly old.* If we start with that type of base, then we can move onward to the other debates—those over how to increase private retirement saving, how many benefits should be provided to those who are middle-aged, and how much higher benefits need to be for those who are better off.

Measuring Lifetime Benefits

Looking at Social Security reform through an annual lens often distorts the impact of longer lives and more years of benefits on the costs of the system and the rate of benefit growth. A more comprehensive and more revealing approach, I believe, is to look at the lifetime package of benefits.

Define "lifetime benefits" as the value, at age 65, of Social Security and Medicare benefits as if they were sitting in a 401(k) account that would earn interest but be drawn upon over retirement. In today's dollars, lifetime benefits for an average-income couple have risen from about $195,000 in 1960 to $710,000 today ($439,000 in Social Security and $271,000 in Medicare) to over $1 million for a couple retiring in about 25 years (over $1/2 million in both Social Security and Medicare—see figure 1). These numbers quickly reveal what is happening to the budget as a whole. We cannot provide a very large portion of American couples $1/2 to $1 million of benefits and simultaneously encourage them to drop out of the workforce for the last third of their adult lives without affecting dramatically the services that can be provided through the budget to our children and to working families.

The Simple Arithmetic Driving Social Security Reform

Despite the confusing aspects of trust fund accounting, rates of return, and financial measures of solvency, the arithmetic behind Social Security's current problems is simple. Once the baby boomers starting hitting retirement, there is a scheduled drop in workers per beneficiary from more than 3-1 to less than 2-1. To simplify our arithmetic, let us assume that the drop is exactly from 3-1 to 2-1, and imagine that this drop were to occur instantaneously. Recall that Social Security is almost entirely a pay-as-you-go system, despite a slight and temporary buildup in trust funds

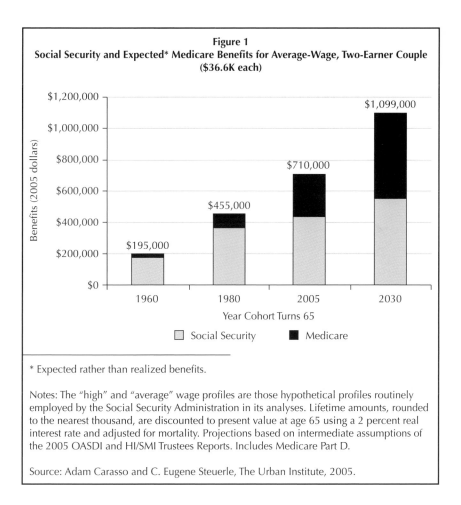

Figure 1
Social Security and Expected* Medicare Benefits for Average-Wage, Two-Earner Couple ($36.6K each)

* Expected rather than realized benefits.

Notes: The "high" and "average" wage profiles are those hypothetical profiles routinely employed by the Social Security Administration in its analyses. Lifetime amounts, rounded to the nearest thousand, are discounted to present value at age 65 using a 2 percent real interest rate and adjusted for mortality. Projections based on intermediate assumptions of the 2005 OASDI and HI/SMI Trustees Reports. Includes Medicare Part D.

Source: Adam Carasso and C. Eugene Steuerle, The Urban Institute, 2005.

that ultimately would pay for only around one-tenth of liabilities under current law. Now consider three workers, A, B, and C, who each transfer $3,333 and 1/3 to pay $10,000 of benefits to D (figure 2). All of a sudden C disappears, so only A and B must pay the benefits of D. A and B can continue to pay $3,333 each. But then D would receive only $6,666 in benefits. Thus, her benefits would fall by one-third. Or D can be held harmless, so that she still receives $10,000. But then A and B would have to increase their payments to $5,000 each. If we must hold at least one group harmless, then what is required is either a benefit cut of 33 percent or a tax rate increase of 50 percent.

Figure 2
Simple Example: Effect of a Drop in Workers to Beneficiaries from 3-to-1 to 2-to-1

	Taxes Paid by Taxpayers		Benefits per Beneficiary
A	B	C	D
	Pre-Baby Boomer Retirement		
$3,333	$3,333	$3,333	$10,000
	Post-Baby Boomer Retirement—Hold Taxpayers Harmless		
$3,333	$3,333	$0	$6,666
			(33 percent reduction in annual benefits)
	Post-Baby Boomer Retirement—Hold Beneficiaries Harmless		
$5,000	$5,000	$0	$10,000
(50 percent increase in tax rates	(50 percent increase in tax rates		

Source: C. Eugene Steuerle, "The Simple Arithmetic Driving Social Security Reform."
Economic Perspective Column, Tax Analysts. April 20, 1998. Available online at http://
www.urban.org/url.cfm?ID=1000085.

A Middle-Age Retirement System
Serving the Vulnerable Less Each Year

Social Security's current dilemma centers almost entirely on the drop in scheduled
workers per retiree—a labor force issue. Although more saving would be nice, whether in trust funds or retirement accounts, we are not going to save our way out of this
problem. Consider some of the consequences of the current system.

The system has morphed into a middle-age retirement system

• Close to one-third of the adult population is scheduled to be on Social Security
within about 25 years. Including adults on other transfer programs, we are
approaching the day when the majority of the adult population will depend upon
transfers from others for a significant share of its support.

• People already retire on average for close to one-third of their adult lives.

• The average Social Security annuity for a man retiring at 62 lasts 17 years, for a
woman 20 years, and for the longer living of a couple at least 25 years. The life
numbers are even higher for those with above-average lifetime earnings because
they have above-average life expectancies.

• When Social Security was young—for instance, in 1940 and 1950—the average
worker retired at about age 68. To retire for an equivalent number of years on

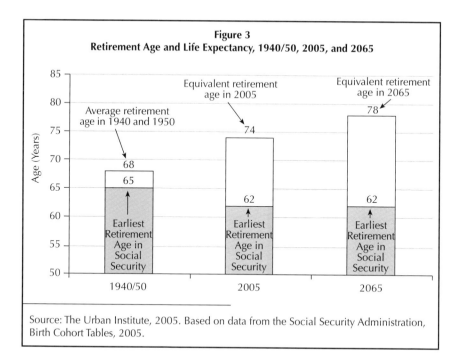

Figure 3
Retirement Age and Life Expectancy, 1940/50, 2005, and 2065

Source: The Urban Institute, 2005. Based on data from the Social Security Administration, Birth Cohort Tables, 2005.

Social Security, a person would retire at age 74 today and age 78 in another 60 years (figure 3).

Almost every year a smaller share of Social Security benefits goes to the most vulnerable

- By constantly increasing benefits to middle-age retirees, at least as defined by life expectancy, smaller and smaller shares of Social Security benefits are being devoted to the elderly (figure 4). If progressivity is defined by how well the vulnerable are served, the system is becoming less progressive every year.

The economy gets hit several ways, not just in terms of costs

- Among the most important, but ignored, sides of the Social Security budget equation is the decline in growth of the labor force (figure 5), with its additional effect on slower growth in national income and revenues.

- When a person retires from the labor force at late middle age, national income declines. But the decline is borne mainly by other workers, not by the retiree. For instance, when a $50,000-a-year worker retires a year earlier, national income declines by approximately $50,000, but most of those costs are shifted onto other workers as the retiree starts receiving about $23,500 in Social Security and

Figure 7
Labor Force Participation Rates: Males and Females
Aged 55+ vs. the Adult Population, 1948-2004

——— All 20+   ······ Males 55+   ·-·-· Males 55+

Source: U.S. Bureau of Labor Statistics, 2005.

Re-Orienting Benefits Toward the Old

Restoring Social Security to an old-age, not a middle-age, retirement program can be done partly by increasing the retirement ages (including the early retirement age—else it is just an across-the-board benefit cut). A related move would be to backload benefits more to help those who are older. Whatever the level of lifetime benefit settled upon in a final reform package, actuarial adjustments can provide more benefits later and fewer earlier. These adjustments can take various forms: adjust benefits upward when Social Security predicts that average life expectancy has fallen below, say, 12 years (about age 74 in 2005 and indexed for life expectancy in later years) and downward in earlier ages; or provide a lower up-front benefit in exchange for post-retirement wage indexing.

A related adjustment would be to provide a better actuarial adjustment for working longer. Currently we subsidize people to retire early. While lifetime benefits are about the same for a worker retiring at, say, age 62 or 65 or 68, the worker who stays in the workforce contributes much more in the way of tax. A greater differential between earlier and later retirement would be appropriate both from a fairness and an efficiency standpoint.

These changes in retirement ages and in the lifecycle distribution of benefits have many positive effects. They progressively move benefits to later ages when people have less ability to work, lower income, and less help from a spouse to deal with impairments. Support in old age WAS the original purpose of the program. They put labor force incentives where they are most effective—in late middle age, including the 60s, when most people report being in fair, good, or excellent health. When cuts in benefit growth rates are required, they cause less hardship than almost any across-the-board benefit cut for two reasons: first, they are more likely to increase revenues, thus making it possible to afford a better benefit package, and second, they don't affect the benefits of the truly old as long as they adjust their work lives in line with the changes in the retirement ages.

I recognize that some people are concerned about groups with shorter-than-average life expectancies. But attempting to address their needs by granting many of us who are healthy a 20th and 21st and 22nd year of transfer support and tens, if not hundreds, of thousands of dollars in extra benefits for retiring early is a very bad form of trickle-down policy.

An increase in the retirement age can be combined with other provisions that help, rather than hurt, groups with shorter life expectancies. One way to do this is to provide a minimum benefit aimed at lower-income households and at reducing poverty rates (using a poverty standard adjusted for living standards or wage- indexed) among the elderly. With such a minimum benefit in place, any of the age-of-retirement adjustments can actually increase, rather than decrease, the relative share of benefits for groups with lower life expectancies, since their life expectancies are correlated with lower lifetime earnings. In fact, with a good minimum benefit, we can increase the income of low-income people and reduce poverty rates, even relative to current law.

One warning is in order here, however. Some minimum benefit packages end up more symbol than substance. For instance, they may not be indexed for wages, so don't cost much in the long run. Or they have so many years of work requirement that they don't help some groups of low-income people, especially women. We need Social Security and other agencies to provide estimates of the effectiveness of different alternatives if we want to provide a base of protection.

Evidence on Ability to Work

One question that often arises is whether Social Security needs to provide an increasing share of benefits every year to those further and further from date of expected death. Three pieces of evidence are provided here: (1) health trends among old and near-old; (2) physical demands of jobs; and (3) the ability of people to work at similar ages in the years before early retirement options and other benefits were made available.

First, older Americans over age 55 seem to be reporting that their health has improved. Figure 8 reports the share of older adults reporting fair or poor health in two groups: those age 65–74 and those age 55–64 between 1982 and 2002. Even among those age 65–74, the fraction reporting fair or poor health is less than one-quarter. The fraction actually reporting poor health is much smaller still. The rest report being in good or excellent health.

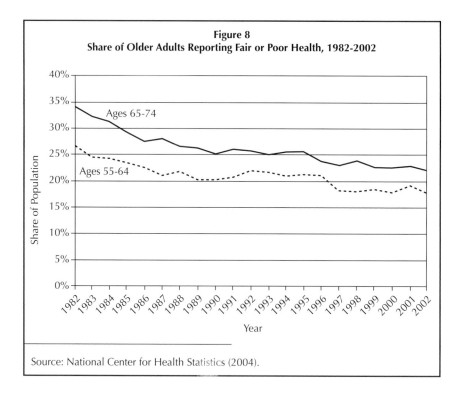

Figure 8
Share of Older Adults Reporting Fair or Poor Health, 1982-2002

Source: National Center for Health Statistics (2004).

Similarly, among those age 55 to 59, the share with work limitations has declined from 27.1 percent in 1971 to 19.5 percent in 2002 (figure 9). Note that a work limitation does not mean inability to work but, rather, a limitation to do certain types of jobs. In any case, the trend moves in the same direction: as years pass, fewer people of a given age have been reporting work limitations.

Survey results such as those just reported, of course, involve qualitative data. We need to check alternative evidence. A second approach is to try to find trends in physical limitations of jobs using a similar measure over the years. One source, shown in figure 10, indicates that the share of U.S. workers in physically demanding jobs has declined from over 20 percent in 1950 to about 8 percent in 1996.

Finally, let us compare the labor force participation of males with a similar life expectancy from 1940, when Social Security first paid benefits, until 2001. In figure 11, we see that about 86 percent of men with about 16 years of life expectancy participated in the labor force in 1940. That figure remained high until the late 1960s, a few years after men with a similar life expectancy became eligible for early retirement benefit and after Medicare benefits were enacted into law. After those enactments, labor force participation began a very rapid descent to less than 35 percent. It is now beginning to rise slowly—one more piece of evidence that demand for labor is shifting to older workers.

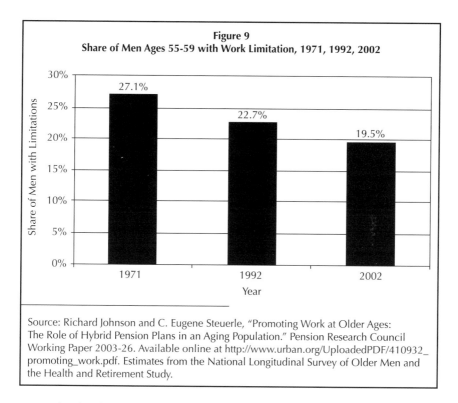

Figure 9
Share of Men Ages 55-59 with Work Limitation, 1971, 1992, 2002

Source: Richard Johnson and C. Eugene Steuerle, "Promoting Work at Older Ages:
The Role of Hybrid Pension Plans in an Aging Population." Pension Research Council
Working Paper 2003-26. Available online at http://www.urban.org/UploadedPDF/410932_
promoting_work.pdf. Estimates from the National Longitudinal Survey of Older Men and
the Health and Retirement Study.

It is hard to believe that as the physical demands of jobs have declined, people have become that much less capable of working. It is more likely that the higher levels of benefits in Social Security and Medicare, increasingly available for more and more years before expected death, have been the major factors driving the drop in labor force participation.

Changing the Default

Under current policy, federal government spending grows automatically, by default, faster than tax revenues as the population ages and health costs soar. These defaults threaten the economy with large, unsustainable deficits. More important, they deny to each generation the opportunity to orient government toward meeting current needs and its own preferences for services. Only by changing the budget's auto-pilot programming can we gain the flexibility needed to continually improve government policies and services.

Rudolph L. Penner (also a senior fellow at the Urban Institute and a former director of the Congressional Budget Office) and I have come to believe that there is no way to get the budget in order without addressing the issue of these defaults. Budget-irresponsible defaults apply to many programs of government, but the largest are linked to Social Security and Medicare. As currently structured, these programs are

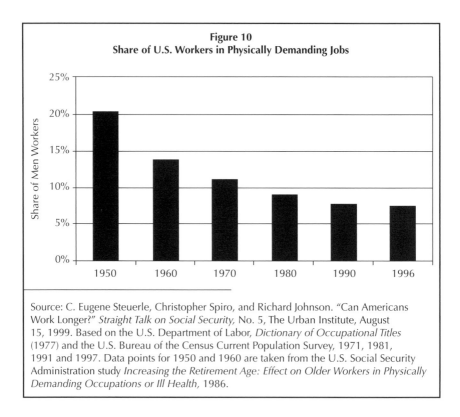

Figure 10
Share of U.S. Workers in Physically Demanding Jobs

Source: C. Eugene Steuerle, Christopher Spiro, and Richard Johnson. "Can Americans Work Longer?" *Straight Talk on Social Security,* No. 5, The Urban Institute, August 15, 1999. Based on the U.S. Department of Labor, *Dictionary of Occupational Titles* (1977) and the U.S. Bureau of the Census Current Population Survey, 1971, 1981, 1991 and 1997. Data points for 1950 and 1960 are taken from the U.S. Social Security Administration study *Increasing the Retirement Age: Effect on Older Workers in Physically Demanding Occupations or Ill Health,* 1986.

designed to rise forever in cost faster than national income and revenues—an impossible scenario. In Social Security, the problem is caused by the combination of more years of retirement support over time and wage indexing for annual benefits.

Regardless of what Social Security reform is undertaken, some rule should be adopted that would put the program back into balance over the long term when, for instance, the trustees report for three consecutive years that the program is likely to be in long-run deficit. This trigger should force the system's automatic features to move responsibly back toward budgetary balance.

With the trigger pulled, two of many options at that point strike me as particularly simple and easy to implement. First, the early and normal retirement ages could be automatically increased two months faster per year than under current law for everyone younger than, say, 57 in the year the trigger is pulled. Second, in those years, the benefit formula could be indexed to the lower of price or wage growth in a way that allows average real benefits to increase but more slowly than wages.[1] This approach could be supplemented by a new special minimum benefit indexed to wage growth. Other approaches to this option can also be devised to reduce the growth rate of benefits more for high earners than for low earners.[2]

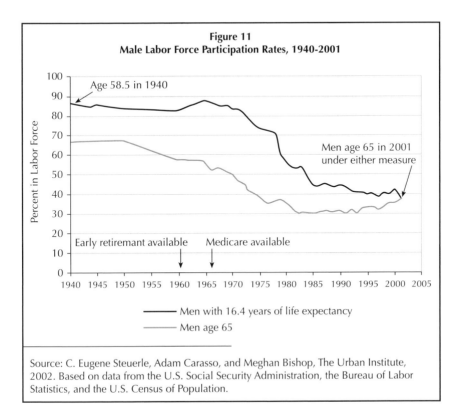

Figure 11
Male Labor Force Participation Rates, 1940-2001

Source: C. Eugene Steuerle, Adam Carasso, and Meghan Bishop, The Urban Institute, 2002. Based on data from the U.S. Social Security Administration, the Bureau of Labor Statistics, and the U.S. Census of Population.

Of these two options, I prefer increasing the retirement ages since that allows more revenues for the system and, consequently, higher lifetime benefits for the same tax rate. Other benefit reductions, as noted, hit the oldest beneficiaries with their greater needs as well as everyone else. For similar reasons, among the "progressive price indexing" options, I prefer creating a wage- indexed minimum benefit since that is more likely to protect the more vulnerable, including survivors, than is a form of progressive price indexing that continues to spend larger shares of revenue on increasing benefits for succeeding generations of those with well-above-median lifetime earnings. But, regardless, the system must be redesigned so that, when on automatic pilot, the default option leads to a responsible and sustainable budget.

There is, of course, no reason to believe that such automatic changes will alone lead to a socially optimum Social Security system. For instance, they do not deal with the discrimination in current law against single heads of households. The point of changing the defaults is, rather, to migrate from a system in which the Congress has little choice but to enact painful benefit cuts to one in which Congress has the opportunity to provide more generous benefits from time to time—that is, to play tax Santa Claus rather than Scrooge sometimes, as politics requires.

Social Security will not be changed for those 55 or older (born before 1950). Today, more than 45 million Americans receive Social Security benefits and millions more are nearing retirement. For these Americans, Social Security benefits are secure and will not change in any way.

Social Security is making empty promises to our children and grandchildren. For our younger workers, Social Security has serious problems that will grow worse over time. Social Security cannot afford to pay promised benefits to future generations because it was designed for a 1935 world in which benefits were much lower, life-spans were shorter, there were more workers per retiree, and fewer retirees were drawing from the system.

With each passing year, there are fewer workers paying ever-higher benefits to an ever-larger number of retirees. Social Security is a pay-as-you-go system, which means taxes on today's workers pay the benefits for today's retirees. A worker's payroll taxes are not saved in an account with his or her name on it for the worker's retirement.

- **There are fewer workers to support our retirees.** When Social Security was first created, there were 40 workers to support every one retiree, and most workers did not live long enough to collect retirement benefits from the system. Since then, the demographics of our society have changed dramatically. People are living longer and having fewer children. As a result we have seen a dramatic change in the number of workers supporting each retiree's benefits. According to the *2004 Report of the Social Security Trustees* (page 47):

  - In 1950, there were 16 workers to support every one beneficiary of Social Security.

  - Today, there are only 3.3 workers supporting every Social Security beneficiary.

  - And, by the time our youngest workers turn 65, there will be only 2 workers supporting each beneficiary.

- **Benefits are scheduled to rise dramatically over the next few decades.** Because benefits are tied to wage growth rather than inflation, benefits are growing faster than the rest of the economy. This benefit formula was established in 1977. As a result, today's 20-year old is promised benefits that are 40% higher, in real terms, than are paid to seniors who retire this year. But the current system does not have the money to pay these promised benefits.

- **The retirement of the Baby Boomers will accelerate the problem.** In just 3 years, the first of the Baby Boom generation will begin to retire, putting added strain on a system that was not designed to meet the needs of the 21st century. By 2031, there will be almost twice as many older Americans as today—from 37 million today to 71 million. (*http://www.ssa.gov/pressoffice/basicfact*).

Social Security is heading toward bankruptcy. According to the Social Security Trustees, thirteen years from now, in 2018, Social Security will be paying out more than it takes in and every year afterward will bring a new shortfall, bigger than the year before. And, when today's young workers begin to retire in 2042, the system will be exhausted and bankrupt. (*Summary of the 2004 Annual Report of the Social Security Trustees*, p. 1). If we do not act now to save it, the only solution will be drastically higher taxes, massive new borrowing, or sudden and severe cuts in Social Security benefits or other government programs.

As of 2004, the cost of doing nothing to fix our Social Security system had hit an estimated $10.4 trillion, according to the Social Security Trustees. (*2004 Report of the Social Security Trustees*, p. 58). The longer we wait to take action, the more difficult and expensive the changes will be.

• $10.4 trillion is almost twice the combined wages and salaries of every working American in 2004.

• Every year we wait costs an additional $600 billion. (*2004 Report of the Social Security Trustees*, p. 58).

• Today's 30-year-old worker can expect a 27% benefit cut from the current system when he or she reaches normal retirement age. (*2004 Report of the Social Security Trustees*, p. 8). And, without action, these benefit cuts will only get worse.

Strengthening Social Security Permanently

"We must pass reforms that solve the financial problems of Social Security once and for all."

President George W. Bush
State of the Union Address
February 2, 2005

In the State of the Union Address, President Bush called for an open, candid review of the options to strengthen Social Security permanently for our children and grandchildren.

The President pledged to work with Members of Congress to find the most effective combination of reforms. Former and current Members of Congress and a former President have suggested a variety of solutions to fix Social Security permanently, including limiting benefits for wealthy retirees, indexing benefits to prices rather than wages, increasing the retirement age, discouraging early collection of retirement benefits, and changing the way benefits are calculated. All of these ideas are on the table. The President recognizes that none of these reforms would be easy and has said he will listen to anyone with a good idea to offer.

The President believes that we must move ahead with reform, because our children's retirement security is more important than partisan politics.

In the State of the Union, the President laid out basic principles to guide reform:

- We must make Social Security permanently sound, not leave it for another day.

- We must not jeopardize our economic strength by raising payroll taxes—higher taxes would slow economic growth.

  - Increasing payroll taxes is a band-aid, not a permanent solution. Payroll taxes have been increased more than 20 times since 1935, and we still have not fixed the problem. The Social Security payroll tax, which was once 2%, is now 12.4%. To meet the needs of the 21st century, payroll taxes would have to be raised over and over and over again on American workers, stifling economic growth and job creation. Economists calculate that under the current system, the payroll tax would have to rise to more than 18% if our children and grandchildren are to receive their scheduled benefits. (*2004 Report of the Social Security Trustees,* p. 165).

- We must ensure that lower income Americans get the help they need to have dignity and peace of mind in their retirement. Any reform should maintain the system's progressivity.

- We must guarantee that there is no change for those now retired or nearing retirement. For those Americans 55 and older (born before 1950), nothing will change, and nobody is going to take away or change their check.

- We must take care that any changes in the system are gradual, so that younger workers have years to prepare and plan for their future.

- And, we should make Social Security a better deal for younger workers through voluntary personal retirement accounts.

Personal Retirement Accounts

"As we fix Social Security, we also have the responsibility to make the system a better deal for younger workers. And the best way to reach that goal is through voluntary personal retirement accounts."

President George W. Bush
State of the Union Address
February 2, 2005

The President believes personal retirement accounts must be part of a comprehensive solution to strengthen Social Security for the 21st century.

Under the President's plan, personal retirement accounts would start gradually. Yearly contribution limits would be raised over time, eventually permitting all workers to set aside 4 percentage points of their payroll taxes in their accounts. Annual contributions to personal retirement accounts initially would be capped, at $1,000 per year in 2009. The cap would rise gradually over time, growing $100 per year, plus growth in average wages.

Personal retirement accounts offer younger workers the opportunity to build a "nest egg" for retirement that the government cannot take away.

• Personal retirement accounts provide ownership and control. Personal retirement accounts give younger workers the opportunity to own an asset and watch it grow over time.

• Personal retirement accounts could be passed on to children and grandchildren. The money in these accounts would be available for retirement expenses. Any unused portion could be passed on to loved ones. Permitting individuals to pass on their personal retirement accounts to loved ones will be particularly beneficial to widows, widowers, and other survivors. According to the non-partisan analysis by the Social Security Administration's Office of Retirement Policy, the ability to inherit personal accounts provides the largest gains to widows and other survivors.

• Personal retirement accounts help make Social Security better for younger workers. A personal retirement account gives a younger worker the chance to save a portion of his or her money in an account and watch it grow over time at a greater rate than anything the current system can deliver. The account will provide money for the worker's retirement in addition to the check he or she receives from Social Security. Personal retirement accounts give younger workers the chance to receive a higher rate of return from sound, long-term investing of a portion of their payroll taxes than they receive under the current system.

Personal retirement accounts would be voluntary. At any time, a worker could "opt in" by making a *one-time* election to put a portion of his or her payroll taxes into a personal retirement account.

• Workers would have the flexibility to choose from several different low-cost, broadbased investment funds and would have the opportunity to adjust investment allocations periodically, but would not be allowed to move back and forth between personal retirement accounts and the traditional system. If, after workers choose the account, they decide they want only the benefits the current system would give them, they can leave their money invested in government bonds like those the Social Security system invests in now.

• Those workers who do not elect to create a personal retirement account would continue to draw benefits from the traditional Social Security system, reformed to be permanently sustainable.

Personal retirement account options and management would be similar to that of the Federal employee retirement program, known as the Thrift Savings Plan (TSP). A centralized administrative structure would be created to collect personal retirement account contributions, manage investments, maintain records, and facilitate withdrawals at retirement. The structure would be designed to facilitate low costs, ease of use for new investors, and timely crediting of contributions. This centralized investment structure would help minimize compliance costs for employers.

• Contributions would be collected and records maintained by a central administrator. Similar to the TSP, private investment managers would be chosen through a competitive bidding process to manage the pooled account contributions.

• The central administrator would answer questions from account participants and distribute periodic account statements.

• The central administrator would also facilitate withdrawals and the purchase of annuities with account balances.

• Like TSP, we expect participants to have easy access to investment information and to their accounts. Participants could easily check account balances and adjust investment allocations.

Personal retirement accounts would be invested in a mix of conservative bonds and stock funds. Guidelines and restrictions would be put in place to provide sound investment choices and prevent individuals from spending the money in these accounts on the lottery or at the race track. Workers would be permitted to allocate their personal retirement account contributions among a small number of very broadly diversified index funds patterned after the current TSP funds.

• Like TSP, personal retirement accounts could be invested in a safe government securities fund; an investment-grade corporate bond index fund; a small-cap stock index fund; a large-cap stock index fund; and an international stock index fund.

• In addition to these TSP-type funds, workers could choose a government bond fund with a guaranteed rate of return above inflation.

• Workers could also choose a "life cycle portfolio" that would automatically adjust the level of risk of the investments as the worker aged. The life cycle fund would automatically and gradually shift the allocation of investment funds as the individual neared retirement age so that it was weighted more heavily toward secure bonds.

Personal retirement accounts would be protected from sudden market swings on the eve of retirement. To protect near-retirees from sudden market swings on the eve of retirement, personal retirement accounts would be automatically invested in the "life cycle portfolio" when a worker reaches age 47, unless the worker and his or her spouse specifically opted out by signing a waiver form stating they are aware of the risks involved. The waiver form would explain in clear, easily understandable terms the benefits of the life cycle portfolio and the risks of opting out. By shifting investment allocations from high growth funds to secure bonds as the individual nears retirement, the life cycle portfolio would provide greater protections from sudden market swings.

Personal retirement accounts would not be eaten up by hidden Wall Street fees. Personal retirement accounts would be low-cost. The Social Security Administration's actuaries project that the ongoing administrative costs for a TSP-style personal account structure would be roughly 30 basis points or 0.3 percentage points, compared to an average of 125 basis points for investments in stock mutual funds and 88 basis points in bond mutual funds in 2003. (*www.ici.org/issues/fee/fm-v13n5*).

• The low costs are made possible by the economies of scale of a centralized administrative structure, as well as limiting investment options to a small number of prudent, broadly diversified funds.

• Most of these administrative costs are for recordkeeping which would be done by the government, not investment management done by Wall Street. (*Report of the 1994-1996 Advisory Council on Social Security,* p. 171, and January 31, 2002 Memorandum from the Social Security Actuary in the *Final Report of the President's Commission on Social Security,* p. 19).

Personal retirement accounts would not be accessible prior to retirement. American workers who choose personal retirement accounts would not be allowed to make withdrawals from, take loans from, or borrow against their accounts prior to retirement.

Personal retirement accounts would not be emptied out all at once, but rather paid out over time, as an addition to traditional Social Security benefits. Under a system of personal retirement accounts, procedures would be established to govern how account balances would be withdrawn at retirement. This would involve some combination of annuities to ensure a stream of monthly income over the worker's life expectancy, phased withdrawals indexed to life expectancy, and lump sum withdrawals. Individuals would not be permitted to withdraw funds from their personal retirement accounts as lump sums, if doing so would result in their moving below the poverty line. Account balances in excess of the poverty-protection threshold requirement could be withdrawn as a lump sum for any purpose or left in the account to accumulate interest. Any unused portion of the account could be passed on to loved ones.

Personal retirement accounts would be phased in. To ease the transition to a personal retirement account system, participation would be phased in according to the age of the worker. In the first year of implementation, workers currently between age 40 and 54 (born 1950 through 1965 inclusive) would have the option of establishing personal retirement accounts. In the second year, workers currently between age 26 and 54 (born 1950 through 1978 inclusive) would be given the option and by the end of the third year, all workers born in 1950 or later who want to participate in personal retirement accounts would be able to do so.

The President's personal retirement account proposal is fiscally responsible. The President's proposal is consistent with his overall goal of cutting the deficit in half by 2009. Based on analysis by the Social Security Administration Actuary, the Office of Management and Budget estimates that the President's personal retirement account proposal will require transition financing of $664 billion over the next ten years ($754 billion including interest). This transition financing will not have the same effect on national savings, and thus the economy, as traditional government borrowing. Personal retirement accounts will not reduce the pool of savings available to the markets because every dollar borrowed by the Federal government to fund the transition is fully offset by an increase in savings represented by the accounts themselves. Moreover, the transition financing for personal retirement accounts should be viewed as part of a comprehensive plan to make the Social Security system permanently sustainable. Publicly released analysis by the Social Security Administration has found that several comprehensive proposals including personal accounts would dramatically reduce the costs of permanently fixing the system (*www.ssa.gov/OACT/ solvency/index*).

Establishing personal retirement accounts does not add to the total costs that Social Security faces. Personal retirement accounts effectively pre-fund Social Security benefits already promised to today's workers and do not represent a net increase in Federal obligations. The obligation to pay Social Security benefits is already there. While personal retirement accounts affect the timing of these costs, they do not add to the total amount obligated through Social Security.

Thrift Savings Plan Background

The Thrift Savings Plan (TSP) is a voluntary retirement savings plan offered to Federal employees, including members of Congress.

It offers comparable benefits and features to those available to private sector employees in 401(k) retirement plans, including pre-tax contributions through convenient payroll withholding.

The TSP currently has 3.4 million participants, and their investments have grown to $152 billion. Participants voluntarily add $1.3 billion per month in new contributions to their accounts.

Participants have the choice to invest in any or all of five broad-based investment funds:

• A stable value fund invested in U.S. Treasury securities

• An index fund comprising investment grade bonds

• Small and mid-cap stock index fund

• Large cap stock index fund

• International stock index fund

These funds have the following 10-year compound annual rates of return:

• G Fund (government securities fund)—6.04% (3.67% real)

• F Fund (bond index fund)—6.95% (4.58% real)

• C Fund (common stock index fund)—10.99% (8.62% real)

• S Fund (small capitalization stock index fund)—9.70% (7.33% real)

• I Fund (international stock index fund)—4.32% (1.95% real)

Beginning this summer, the TSP will offer lifecycle portfolios, each with a designated ratio of investments among the five TSP funds. This balanced, diversified portfolio will automatically reallocate as the participant's retirement date approaches.

Administration and investment costs for the TSP are low at 6 basis points, or 60 cents per $1,000 of account balance. A Senate hearing in 2004 discovered that many "low cost" funds have expense ratios between 20 and 65 basis points. Other funds' costs are significantly higher.

The TSP is administered by the Federal Retirement Thrift Investment Board. Governance of the Board is carried out by five independent part-time Presidential appointees and a full-time Executive Director whom they select. TSP funds are held in trust. As fiduciaries, the Board Members and the Executive Director are required to act prudently and solely in the interest of TSP participants and beneficiaries.

The Board provides training and develops educational materials including publications, forms and videos. It maintains an interactive web site (*www.tsp.gov*) and a toll free telephone center for participants to obtain these materials, check account balances, change contribution levels, adjust investment allocations or request withdrawals.

The Demographics of Social Security

• *1950:* 16 Workers paying for every 1 Beneficiary

• *Today:* 3.3 Workers paying for every 1 Beneficiary

• *When Younger Workers Retire:* Only 2 Workers paying for every 1 beneficiary

---

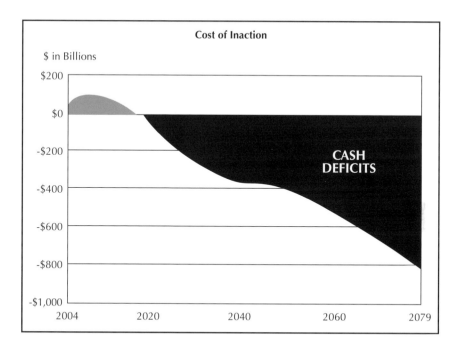

Cost of Inaction

$ in Billions

CASH DEFICITS

Social Security Reform Proposals that Incorporate Private Accounts

by Thomas R. Saving

The fundamental problem facing Social Security is summarized in Figure 1. Most of those familiar with Social Security know that its costs, in the form of benefit payments, will exceed its dedicated tax revenues beginning in 2017. The gap between cost and revenues grows in every year thereafter as the graph clearly shows. The present value of the difference between projected costs and revenues is $12.8 trillion. Closing this financing gap is the task of all reformers.

Before going any further, I must note that some analysts do not think this graph correctly summarizes the problem. They argue that the system is sound until the Trust Fund is exhausted in 2041 and even then, 72% of current benefits could still be paid. They are absolutely correct in asserting that the Trust Fund would last until 2041 if currently scheduled benefits are paid and only currently scheduled taxes are collected. However, drawing on the Trust Fund requires that general revenues be used to pay Social Security benefits. So while the Trust Fund is projected to last until 2041, in the context of the budget as a whole, the Trust Fund provides no revenues to the Treasury. If the system is allowed to continue as is, the challenge will be to find the resources required to pay benefits.

Given that there is general agreement that the Social Security system must be fixed, what is the solution? Can't we just stay with the current system? To put this question into perspective, consider the following. In just 12 years, payroll taxes will fall short of what is needed to continue paying Social Security benefit checks. At that point, the Treasury must begin transferring funds from general revenues to Social Security. The transfers will increase rapidly so that by 2022, the transfer will reach the equivalent of five percent of total federal income tax revenues.

Importantly, there have been only two previous times when significant general revenue transfers were required to pay Social Security benefits, 1978 and 1983. In 1978 the payment of Social Security benefits required a general revenue transfer of just over four percent of federal income tax revenues. The response of Congress to this transfer was to change the benefit formula, effectively reducing scheduled benefits for future retirees. The positive effect of this change was short-lived so that by 1983 the system once again required large general revenue transfers to pay benefits. The 1983 general revenue transfer was equal to four and one-half percent of income tax revenues. Once again the response of Congress was to cut

(August 8, 2005; used with permission)

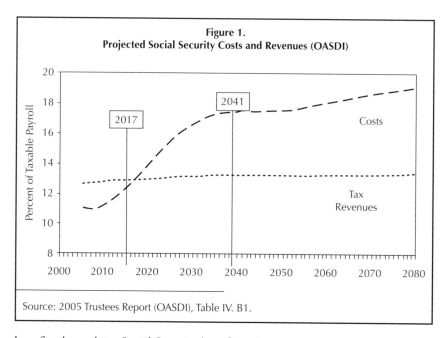

Figure 1.
Projected Social Security Costs and Revenues (OASDI)

Source: 2005 Trustees Report (OASDI), Table IV. B1.

benefits, by making Social Security benefits subject to income taxation. In 1983 Congress also raised taxes and increased the retirement age. Importantly, in 2017, within five years of its first deficit since 1983, the Social Security system will require greater general revenue transfers than Congress has ever allowed before cutting benefits. If the past is any indication of the future, we can expect benefits cuts as early as 2021, in just 16 years.

This imbalance between payroll tax rates and benefit levels will cost the nation an additional $12.8 trillion in today's dollars to keep the current benefit structure in place. Thus, keeping the current system afloat will cost almost as much as the entire GDP of the U.S. The unpleasant truth is that if we pay promised benefits and only collect scheduled taxes from the current generation, the next generation will have to come up with this $12.8 trillion. The current funding arrangement implies real and huge obligations that the system has no way to pay. Thus, the current system has its own and very significant "transition costs." The real issue dividing those who define the current financing arrangement and those who support personal accounts is the timing of the payment of these so-called transition costs.

Given that we are committed to reform, how can the various proposals be compared? Let me present a blueprint for such a comparison consisting of six elements that you should ask of anyone proposing to reform the system. First, who participates in the reformed system? Second, is participation voluntary? Third, are participants compensated for accrued benefits and if so how? Fourth, how does the benefit structure compare to current Social Security? Fifth, are there any guarantees, and if so, what do they cost? Sixth, how much of the current Social Security debt does the reform pay off?

Three Personal Account Based Reforms

In light of these six elements let me review three proposals that have been put forth beginning with the plan 2 of the President's Commission to Strengthen Social Security as presented to the President in December of 2001. The principle elements of that proposal answer each of the six questions posed above.

• First, all individuals younger than 55 years may elect the new system, i.e., all those currently 55 years of age and older remain in the current system.

• Second, participation is voluntary, individual participants are allowed to invest 4 percentage points of their Social Security taxes in private accounts up to $1,000 per year.

• Third, defined benefits are fixed in purchasing power rather than being a constant replacement rate by indexing benefits beginning in 2009.

• Fourth, at retirement the annuity value of private accounts offset the defined benefit payments by assuming a 2% rate of return.

• Fifth, while the total retirement benefit is not guaranteed, the combination of the private account and the benefit received from the new defined benefit is approximately equal to currently scheduled benefits into the indefinite future.

• Sixth, the Commission Plan 2 pays off 34% of current generation debt, or about $4.4 trillion.

President Bush has taken some of the components of Commission Plan 2 and is pressing Congress to act his plan. The components of the President's plan that are currently available are the following.

• First, all individuals currently 55 years and older must stay in the old system.

• Second, participation is voluntary, at any time workers can "opt in" by making a *one-time* election to enter the new system. Beginning in 2009 individual participants under age 59, will be allowed to invest 4 percentage points of their Social Security taxes in private accounts up to $1,000 per year. The $1,000 cap on contributions will grow $100 per year, plus growth in average wages.

• Third, those who stay in the existing system will draw benefits from a reformed and sustainable Social Security system.

• Fourth, at retirement the annuity value of private accounts offset the defined benefit payments by assuming a 3% real rate of return.

• Fifth, the total retirement benefit is not guaranteed but the combination of the private account and the new defined benefit can be expected to equal currently scheduled benefits.

• Sixth, without specifics concerning the reformed and sustainable Social Security system, no estimate can be made of the amount of the current debt that this reform will pay off.

Both the Commission's and the President's plans result in a dual system, part of which is a personal account and the remainder is a defined benefit just as current Social Security. One of the goal's of the Commission was to maintain the same benefit structure as current Social Security and the President's plan has the same goal in mind, however, the details are not fully specified. In contrast to the dual approach taken by the Commission and the President, consider a transition to a fully prepaid system based on personal accounts. Such a system can have the same level of redistribution inherent in the current system through a contribution subsidy for those with lower wages. The particulars of such a system are the following.

• First, workers 64 years of age and under contribute 10% of first $7,650, 3% above $7,650 and $55,000 and then 1% from $55,000 to taxable maximum. (Thresholds are adjusted by the Social Security Wage Index.)

• Second, participation is not voluntary.

• Third, workers would receive a share of their scheduled Social Security benefits based on a pre-announced formula.

• Fourth, the system is fully financed using the current system's surpluses, the trust fund, and additional contributions from workers and employers beginning at 2.5% and rising to 3.5% in 8 years.

• Fifth, total benefits for all groups of workers are not guaranteed but are approximately equal to the scheduled benefits of the current system, workers who have 35 years of full time work are guaranteed 150% of poverty level.

• Sixth, this reform pays off 48% of current generation debt, or about $6.2 trillion.

Why is it important to include personal accounts as part of any reform of Social Security? As I have pointed out, the past history of Social Security shows that whenever the payment of scheduled benefits required significant transfers from general revenues, so that the system impinged on the ability of Congress to fund its other programs, Congress changed the system. In effect, it is as if citizens have a contract with Congress the terms of which are subject to a clause that allows Congress to change the contract terms whenever they please, and citizens are required to abide by these new terms. Would anyone willingly enter into a contract that is so one-sided? Of course not! The question is, how can we design a contract that forces Congress to hold up its side of the bargain? The answer is, personal accounts. Only through personal accounts can individuals have the legal rights to their pension benefits. As President Franklyn D. Roosevelt said in an April, 1937, press conference: "They [taxes] are politics all the way through. We put those payroll contributions there so as to give the contributors a legal, moral, and political right to collect their pensions and unemployment benefits. With those taxes there, no damn politician can ever scrap my social security program."

The design of the Social Security system was to give participants a legal right to their benefits. Unfortunately, a system with Congress as one party to the contract, cannot be legally secure. It amounts to a contract you have with another, the terms of which cannot be changed by you, but can be changed by the other party however and whenever they choose. No individual would knowingly enter into such a contract. What reform can change the nature of this contract? Only personal accounts can give participants a legal right to their pension benefits. With personal accounts, participants would have standing in a court of law should Congress attempt to change the terms of the Social Security system.

Some Fundamental Issues of Reform

Regardless of the reform, any change will affect the fundamental tradeoff between generations. To illustrate this tradeoff, Figure 2 shows the Baby Boomers' prime working years, between 35 and 55 years of age, and prime retirement years, between 62 and 80 years of age. These years are shown along with the Social Security program's cost and revenues as a percent of taxable payroll.

Consider the option of paying the costs as scheduled. This option imposes the burden of paying future benefits squarely on the shoulders of future workers and taxpayers. The Baby Boomers pay a tax rate of about 12 percent during their working lives, while future workers must ultimately pay the 18 percent cost rate. Now consider scaling back future benefits to the level that can be sustained assuming the tax rate does not change. This means that the Baby Boomers will receive only the benefits that can be supported by the current tax rate, but these benefits are ultimately 25 percent less than those scheduled. Such a reform results in the Baby Boomers bearing the brunt of the cost. The next generation of workers would pay the same tax rate as the Baby Boomers now pay and receive

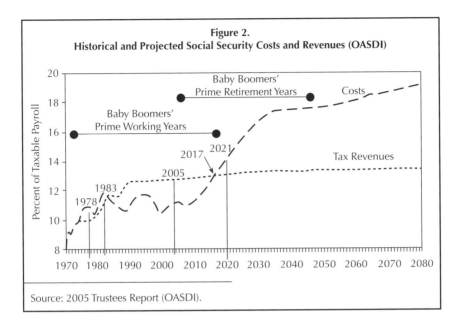

Figure 2.
Historical and Projected Social Security Costs and Revenues (OASDI)

Source: 2005 Trustees Report (OASDI).

comparable benefits, though these benefits are scaled back relative to the benefits the current generation of retirees is receiving.

A reform that cuts benefits and increases taxes to balance the system's finances results in the Baby Boomers receiving lower benefits than those that are scheduled and future workers paying higher taxes. Thus, both generations bear part of the burden of the reform.

Do the prepayment alternatives have different generational burdens? The answer depends on the extent to which benefits are prepaid. Suppose we start today with a program which prepays some or all future scheduled benefits. Prepayment of benefits requires additional resources from current workers. As the graph shows, the Baby Boomers, as a group, have about 15 years remaining of their prime working years. The additional resources from the Baby Boomers would come in the form of contributions to personal retirement accounts, and thus, they would bear some of the costs of the reform. The greater the extent to which benefits are prepaid, the greater is the reduction in the burden borne by future workers.

Note however, that if the accounts are funded through additional borrowing rather than additional savings, then future workers must pay off the additional debt, and we are back to a situation that is similar to simply paying the cost rate and the associated generational burdens.

Transition Costs

The previous discussion provides the backdrop for understanding transition costs. Recent media reports have stated that the transition costs of the personal retirement accounts reform, favored by the president, amount to between $1 and $2 trillion. What exactly do these estimates quantify? Do transition costs quantify the costs of shifting from the current financing arrangement to a partially prepaid system? As we will see, prepayment and paying scheduled benefits with future tax revenues have the same costs. An example will illustrate.

Suppose you have a $200,000 mortgage that has a series of monthly payments for the next 30 years. If you decide to step up your payments so as to retire the note sooner, is there a transition cost to doing so? For simplicity, assume that the rate you can receive on any savings is exactly the same rate as your mortgage rate. Well, you would have to consume less now to make the higher payments, but in the future you will be able to consume more than you would if you were still making the monthly payment. Thus, you have just changed the timing of the financial burden. Regardless of the option you take, you have to pay the $200,000 mortgage.

Similarly, prepaying Social Security partially or totally simply changes the timing of the financial burden and thus changes the generational burden of the program. However, if the goal of the reform is to pay scheduled benefits as depicted in the graphs, then the present value of those scheduled benefits are the basic costs of the program. The current financing arrangement cannot pay these costs and so the system must be reformed, but the costs are the same for all reforms. As pointed out above, the distinguishing characteristic of the reforms are the way in which they distribute the burden of the program across generations.

Benefit Cuts

Another misleading criticism of Social Security reforms that include personal retirement accounts is the claim that they involve benefit cuts. Such claims result from either a misunderstanding of how prepayment works or scare tactics. Personal retirement accounts provide a means by which individuals partially or totally prepay the benefits they are scheduled to receive from Social Security. Personal retirement account reforms are typically coupled with a pre-announced reduction in the defined benefits that will be paid by the Social Security Administration.

With a personal retirement account reform, workers save more and accumulate a fund from which they will purchase an annuity. The goal of most reforms is for the sum of the annuity and the reformed defined benefits to equal the benefits that are currently scheduled. Thus, the reforms do not reduce the total combined benefits retirees will receive. However, the reforms do reduce the share of total benefits that will be paid by future taxpayers, and as a result, future taxpayers have a lower burden than they would if all benefits had to be paid for through contemporaneous tax payments.

Some Concluding Remarks

All Social Security reforms must deal with the fact that benefits, as currently scheduled, cannot be paid for with the current tax rate. Comparing reforms essentially boils down to identifying how different generations will be affected. In addition to reducing the burden on future generations, prepayment with personal retirement accounts has two other collateral benefits. Workers become the owners of their retirement accounts, and increased savings will increase the nation's income relative to the current financing arrangement. For these reasons, such reforms offer a promising alternative in the current policy discussion.

Finally, when coupled with the pending Medicare shortfalls, we must find a way for the working generation to pay for some of their retirement consumption, while they are working. If we pay current law benefits for Social Security and Medicare and only collect current law taxes and premiums, the shortfalls will use up large parts of future federal income tax revenues. Figure 3 illustrates the shortfalls projected by the Trustees as a share of federal income tax revenues assuming that such revenues remain at their fifty-year share of Gross Domestic Product. Within just fifteen years, 2020, we will have to transfer more than 28% of federal income tax revenues to these two programs. The problem worsens rapidly so that just ten years later, more than one-half of all federal income tax revenues will be consumed by Social Security and Medicare. Clearly, these transfers cannot and will not happen. The real issue how will these programs be changed? The establishment of personal accounts as part of the reform of Social Security can form the basis for beginning the prepayment of all retirement benefits.

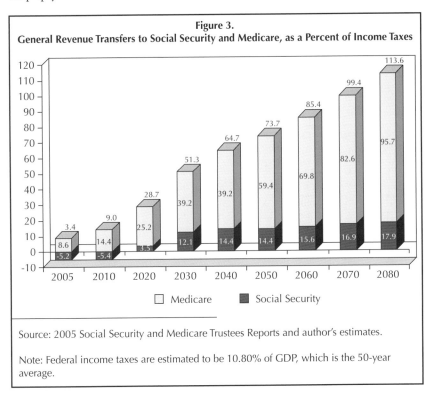

Figure 3.
General Revenue Transfers to Social Security and Medicare, as a Percent of Income Taxes

Source: 2005 Social Security and Medicare Trustees Reports and author's estimates.

Note: Federal income taxes are estimated to be 10.80% of GDP, which is the 50-year average.

How to Fix Social Security

by David C. John

There are only three real solutions to Social Security's rapidly approaching fiscal problems: raise taxes, reduce spending, or make the current payroll taxes work harder by investing them through some form of personal retirement account (PRA).

Establishing PRAs is the only solution that will also give future retirees the option to receive an improved standard of living in retirement. These accounts would give them more control over how to structure their income and allow them to build a nest egg that could be used for emergencies during retirement, used to start a business, or left to their families. However, establishing PRAs will be complex and—as experience from other countries shows—will require careful planning.

How can such a reform be achieved? Whatever emerges from Congress and is signed into law will not be identical to any one proposal presented to Congress. It may contain key elements from a number of specific proposals. As this process unfolds, however, it is critical that lawmakers committed to reform maintain a clear picture in their minds of the framework needed for reform and what variants of basic ideas can be accommodated without undermining the basic goals of reform.

What should such a framework look like? What choices within this framework would still achieve the goals of reform? This paper lays out a practical framework for establishing a successful PRA program that will improve the retirement incomes of future retirees and reduce the huge unfunded liability of the current Social Security system.

A Framework for Reform

A practical framework for establishing a successful PRA program would:

Create an account structure that uses a portion of existing payroll taxes and allows workers of all income levels an opportunity to build family nest eggs. The PRAs would be voluntary and would not affect current retirees or those close to retirement in any way. The Social Security PRAs should be funded by directing a portion of their Social Security retirement taxes into their PRAs. About 5 percent of income would be best, but the directed portion should not be less than 2 percent or more than 10 percent.

Create a simple, low-cost administrative structure for the accounts that uses the current payroll tax system and professional investment managers. Using the existing payroll tax system would reduce costs. Rather than having the government invest PRA money, the agency overseeing the accounts should contract out fund management to professional fund managers.

(November 17, 2004; available at http://www.heritage.org/Research/SocialSecurity/bg1811. cfm; used with permission)

Create a carefully controlled set of investment options that includes an appropriate default option. Initially, workers would be allowed to put their PRA contributions into any one of three balanced and diversified mixes of stock index funds, government bonds, and similar pension-grade investments.

Adjust current Social Security benefits to a more sustainable level. Despite promises from both the left and the right to pay promised benefits in full, this is simply not realistic. While current retirees and those close to retirement should receive every cent that they are due, future benefit promises must be scaled back to more realistic levels.

Create a realistic plan for paying the general revenue cost of establishing a PRA system. The necessary general revenue will have to come from some combination of borrowing additional money, collecting additional taxes, reducing other government spending, and reducing Social Security benefits. While some Representatives and Senators will be tempted to cover Social Security's deficits with higher taxes, this is the wrong approach. The necessary amounts are so large that such a tax increase would consume enough resources to stall economic growth.

Create a system that allows workers flexibility in structuring their retirement benefits while ensuring that they receive an adequate monthly benefit. A PRA plan should require all retirees to use some of that money to purchase an annuity that would guarantee at least a minimal level of income for life, including an adjustment for inflation. This requirement would protect taxpayers against retirees who could otherwise spent their entire PRAs and then expect some form of government handout to meet their monthly expenses.

The Challenges Facing Today's Social Security

According to the Congressional Budget Office, approximately 80 percent of Americans pay more in payroll taxes than in federal income taxes.[1] Today's Social Security system provides retirees with a stable retirement income and a level of protection against poverty caused by disability or the premature death of a parent or spouse.

Despite the presence of private methods to invest for retirement, in 2001 approximately one-third of retirees on Social Security received at least 90 percent of their income from that program. Almost two-thirds of them depended on Social Security for at least 50 percent of their retirement income.[2] These workers would likely benefit the most from a PRA that allowed them to invest some of their payroll taxes.

Today's Social Security faces four major problems that threaten its ability to provide future retirees the same type of retirement security that was available to their parents and grandparents:

Massive future deficits. In less than 15 years (approximately 2018), Social Security's retirement program will begin to spend more per year in benefits than it receives in taxes. Within a few years, these deficits will exceed $100 billion annually and will continue to grow from there. Social Security has a "trust fund" drawer full of government bonds, which are nothing more than pledges to use ever-larger amounts of general revenue taxes to pay benefits. When it comes time to repay those bonds, the federal government will have to reduce spending on other government programs, increase taxes, and/or increase government borrowing. By about 2042, the drawer of paper promises will be empty. From that point forward, the benefits paid to retirees will be cut—first by 27 percent and then by ever-greater amounts—as Social Security's deficits grow larger.

The inability of workers to build a nest egg and the lack of property rights to their benefits. Today's Social Security not only fails to provide workers with any way to build a family nest egg, but also actually discourages savings by absorbing a large proportion of earnings that moderate-income and low-income workers could otherwise use to save for retirement or other purposes.[3] In addition, workers have no property right to their benefits. This is a key flaw because, even if the program was reformed to allow workers to build a family nest egg, without property rights the government could reclaim that money at any time. Two Supreme Court cases dealing with Social Security confirm this lack of property rights.[4] The decisions in both cases explicitly state that workers have no level of ownership of their Social Security benefits.

A poor rate of return on their payroll taxes. Younger and lower-income workers will receive relatively little in benefits for their Social Security taxes because they will have to pay substantially higher taxes than older workers do. A 25-year-old male with an average income is predicted to receive a -0.82 percent rate of return on his Social Security taxes. In other words, he will pay more into the system in taxes than he will receive back in benefits. The situation is even worse for low-income workers. A 25-year-old male living in a low-income section of New York City would receive a -4.46 percent rate of return on his Social Security taxes.[5]

No choice of how benefits are paid. Under the current inflexible system, all workers receive a monthly payment that starts when they retire and ends when they die or when their spouses or dependents die. This one-size-fits-all approach especially hurts the one-fifth of white males and the one-third of African–American males who die between the ages of 50 and 70.[6] These workers face the prospect of paying a lifetime of Social Security taxes in return for little or no retirement benefits. A more flexible system would give them the comfort of knowing that at least a portion of their taxes will go to their families in the form of a nest egg.

Goals for Fixing Social Security

To focus the reform debate on real solutions, it makes sense to develop several overarching goals to ensure that all of Social Security's problems are fixed both for the next few years and for the foreseeable future. An unfocused debate would fix only certain problems while leaving the others to worsen. An incomplete or poorly considered reform would result in the same debate being replayed in a few years in an atmosphere in which there will be even less flexibility to resolve the system's financial crisis.

We therefore owe it to our children and grandchildren to get reform right the first time. When reforming Social Security, policymakers should keep the following goals in mind:

Goal #1: Improve the retirement income of future retirees without reducing the benefits of current retirees or those who are close to retirement.
Social Security reform should not reduce the benefits of current retirees or those who are close to retirement. These workers have spent a lifetime paying their payroll taxes in exchange for the promise that they will receive a set level of benefits. Americans have a moral obligation to pay them every cent that has been promised, including an annual cost-of-living increase to replace the loss of buying power caused by inflation.

At the same time, younger workers should have the opportunity to receive a higher retirement income than the current system will be able to pay by the time they can retire. Workers retiring after about 2042 can really expect to receive only about 73 percent or less of what they are being promised. A reasonable reform would allow them the opportunity to improve their retirement incomes by investing a portion of their current payroll taxes.

Goal #2: Add voluntary PRAs that include a savings/nest egg component to the current system.
In the future, Social Security retirement benefits should come from both the current government-paid program, which would become Social Security Part A, and from the individual worker's PRA, which will be known as Social Security Part B. Workers should be able to choose whether to rely totally on Part A or to invest a portion of their retirement taxes through Part B. As shown by the experience of over 25 countries, including the United Kingdom, Sweden, Switzerland, and Australia, PRAs can help workers to improve their retirement incomes without unreasonable risks.

At the same time, simply establishing PRAs is not sufficient. Social Security Part B should be designed to give workers more control over how their retirement income is structured by allowing them to build nest eggs. Upon retirement, these nest eggs could be used to increase monthly income, reserved for an emergency, or left to family members. In the event that the worker dies before retirement, these nest eggs would remain a part of the worker's estate and could be passed on to heirs.

Goal #3: Reduce the unfunded burden that today's Social Security system will impose on future generations.
Social Security has promised future generations far more in retirement benefits than its current funding sources will be able to pay. Meeting these obligations without reforms will force our children and grandchildren to pay crushing payroll taxes, which will sharply reduce their standard of living. In addition, because payroll taxes are essentially a levy on jobs, substantial payroll tax increases will reduce economic growth and kill jobs.

This also applies to the amount of additional general revenue money that will be required to pay full benefits under a PRA plan. Even though this cost will be substantially lower than the amount that would be required to pay full benefits under the current system, reformers should not repeat the mistake of trying to build political support today by pushing substantial costs onto future generations.

A sensible reform would reduce the benefits promised to younger workers to more reasonable levels while also giving them the time and tools necessary to make up the difference through investment earnings. Continuing to promise those who are a long way from retirement more than Social Security can realistically deliver only makes the system unstable by pushing the burden of paying for it onto future generations.

Six Steps to Creating a Workable PRA System

Step #1: Create an account structure that uses a portion of existing payroll taxes and allows workers of all income levels an opportunity to build family nest eggs.
Who Could Participate? PRAs would be voluntary. Younger workers would have the opportunity either to open a PRA or to continue in the current system and accept whatever benefits it could afford to pay at their retirement. Because the PRA plan would allow the worker the opportunity to receive higher retirement benefits than the government-paid system could afford to pay, workers would automatically have a PRA unless they opt out of the system.[7] Opting out could be accomplished by filing a simple form with the Social Security Administration or even by checking a box on the workers' income tax forms.

Current Retirees Would Not Be Affected. No system of PRAs would affect current retirees in any way. They would receive every cent that they have been promised, including an annual cost-of-living increase. This would also be true for workers nearing retirement. Because they would not have the ability to alter their retirement savings significantly, all workers above a certain age (which would be determined in part by the structure of the specific PRA plan) would also receive their full promised Social Security retirement benefits, including cost-of-living increases. Depending on the plan, this age could be as high as 60 or as low as in the 40s. In most cases, it would reflect the worker's age on the date that the plan goes into effect, even if it is announced well before then.

Workers Would Own Their Accounts. A key feature of this system is that workers would own their accounts. Every cent that goes into the PRA would benefit either the worker or the worker's family. Although the worker would not be able to use this money until retirement, the fact that he or she owns it and is able to see how the money is being used would help to prevent future Congresses from attempting to seize retirement money for some politically motivated purpose. In addition, if the worker dies before retirement, amounts left in the PRA after providing for any survivors' benefits would go into the worker's estate and could be left to the family, a church, or any other worthy cause designated by the worker.

Where Would the Money Come From? The money that would go into Social Security PRAs should come from directing a portion of workers' Social Security retirement taxes. Because money in these PRAs would earn higher returns than the current government-paid Social Security benefit, this structure would help the worker to get more for his or her taxes.

Hypothetically, PRAs could be funded by higher payroll taxes, mandatory additional savings, or even some form of general revenue transfer. It would also be possible to find the money for PRAs through some combination of these methods, either with or without directing some of the existing payroll tax. However, every method except using some of the existing Social Security retirement taxes essentially boils down to a tax increase and would require taxpayers to pay more for their Social Security benefits. This, in turn, would reduce the already low return that workers get for their retirement taxes to an even lower amount. In addition, higher payroll taxes would negatively affect the economy by reducing employment and curbing economic growth.

How Large Would the Accounts Be? Currently, workers pay a total of 10.6 percent of their income for Social Security retirement and survivors' benefits.[8] To fund PRAs that have a chance of paying for substantial portions of workers' retirement benefits, an amount of payroll taxes equal to about 5 percent of income should be deposited into their PRAs.

In theory, PRAs could be any size, ranging from about 2 percent of earnings to as much as 10 percent. However, in order to have any effect on future liabilities, these accounts should not be any smaller than 2 percent of income.

Because larger accounts—about 5 percent of income or more—create useable pools of money much faster than smaller ones, they are more likely to be able to pay for a higher proportion of the owners' Social Security benefits. This would sharply reduce costs for future generations and make it more likely that the reformed system could pay benefits closer to the level promised by today's system. The higher shorter-run general revenue requirements of establishing a system of larger personal retirement accounts would be more than offset by the reduction in the system's unfunded liability.

However, larger accounts will also require larger amounts of general revenue to make up the difference between the remainder of Social Security's payroll taxes and what the program owes in benefits. While the necessary general revenue transfers would be less than under the current Social Security system, they would still be significant.[9] As a result, if the additional general revenue costs of a system of larger PRAs is beyond Congress's ability to finance for now, it may choose to establish smaller PRAs.

"Progressive" Accounts. Today's program recognizes that low-income workers are much more likely than those with higher incomes to have no retirement benefits other than Social Security. As a result, those workers are currently given a higher monthly benefit relative to their earnings.[10] A PRA system could duplicate or exceed the current program's progressivity by allowing low-income workers to save a higher proportion of their payroll taxes. For instance, a minimum-wage worker might be allowed to save up to 6 percent to 8 percent of income each year, while the highest-income worker could save only about 2 percent to 4 percent. Because the amount of each worker's contributions would be calculated by the Department of the Treasury based on the worker's tax forms, it would be no harder for the Treasury to use this sliding scale than it would be to administer a system under which everyone contributes the same proportion of his or her salary.

There are two other benefits to this approach. First, because younger workers almost always start in fairly low-income jobs, it would allow them to build up account balances more rapidly than a flat contribution level would. These balances would grow throughout the remainder of the workers' careers. Second, a sliding scale that allows lower-income workers to place a higher proportion of their incomes in a PRA should help to lower administrative fees by reducing the number of very small annual contributions that the system would need to handle.

Another feature that could be added to a PRA system would be to give workers the option to make additional contributions up to a certain amount. Ideally, these additional contributions would receive the same tax treatment as contributions to individual retirement accounts (IRAs) and other retirement savings plans currently receive.

Building Nest Eggs for the Future. A well-designed retirement system includes three elements: regular monthly retirement income, survivors' and dependents' insurance, and the ability to save. Today's Social Security system provides a stable level of retirement income and provides benefits for survivors and dependents, but it does not allow workers to accumulate savings to fulfill their own retirement goals or to pass on to their heirs. Workers should be able to use Social Security to build a cash nest egg that can be used to increase their retirement income or to build a better economic future for their families.

A PRA system should be designed to allow every worker at every income level the opportunity to leave a nest egg to his or her family. Today, less than 13 percent of all households making less than $20,000 have ever received inheritances.[11] Only among families making over $100,000 does the frequency of inheritance exceed 25 percent. However, a properly designed PRA system would not limit inheritances to the rich. Everyone would be able to use his or her PRA to build a cash nest egg that could become an inheritance.[12]

Step #2: Create a simple, low-cost administrative structure for the accounts that uses the current payroll tax system and professional investment managers.

A simple and effective administrative structure is essential to the success of a PRA system. Probably the simplest and cheapest structure would be to use the existing payroll tax system. Under today's Social Security, the employer collects and sends to the Treasury Department both the payroll taxes that are withheld from an employee's check and those that are the responsibility of the employer. The payroll tax money from all of the firm's employees is combined with income taxes withheld from their paychecks and sent to the Treasury. The money collected is allocated annually to individual workers' earnings records after worker income tax records have been received.

Adapting this existing administrative structure to a PRA system would be easier to implement than other options. Under a PRA system, the employer would continue to forward to the Treasury Department one regular check containing payroll and income taxes for all of the firm's employees. The Treasury would continue to use its existing formula to estimate the amount of receipts that should be credited to Social Security and to reconcile this amount annually with actual tax receipts.

Once the Treasury determines the amount to be credited to Social Security, it would estimate the portion that would go to PRAs and forward that amount to a holding fund managed by professionals who would invest the amount in money market instruments until it is credited to individual taxpayers' accounts. The money would go to individual workers' accounts upon receipt of their tax information. It would then be invested in the default fund, except for workers who have selected (on their income tax forms) one of the other investment options, in which cases it would be invested accordingly.[13]

Using Professional Fund Managers. Rather that having the government trying to invest PRA money, the agency overseeing the accounts (which could be the Department of the Treasury, the Social Security Administration, or an independent board) should contract out fund management to professional fund managers. This investment management system is currently used by the Federal Employees Thrift Investment Board, which administers the Thrift Savings Plan, a part of the retirement system for federal employees.

Under this system, management of the specific investment pools would be contracted out to professional fund managers, who would bid for the right to manage an asset pool of a certain size for a specified period of time. The manager could invest the money only as directed by the agency. The agency would also contract out to investor services such tasks as issuing regular statements of individual accounts, answering account questions, and handling transfers from one investment option to another.

Advantages of this Administrative Structure. Building on existing structures and contracting out investment management and services should keep costs to the lowest level possible. In addition, employers would not have to change their current payroll practices. Using one central government entity to receive PRA funds also means that employers would not bear the cost of writing individual checks or arranging for individual fund transfers for each employee. In addition, this method allows the PRA contributions of workers who have multiple jobs to be based on their total income without placing any additional burden on either the worker or the employers.

From a worker's standpoint, this should be the lowest-cost structure available. In addition, because workers' PRA contributions would be distributed to their chosen investment plans only after their tax information has been received, workers with several jobs during a year should see contributions based on their total annual incomes.

Step #3: Create a carefully controlled set of investment options that includes an appropriate default option.

The investment options available to PRA owners should be simple and easily understood. While an increasing number of Americans are investing their money for a wide variety of purposes, a voluntary PRA system would bring in millions of new investors who may not have any previous investment experience. In addition, experience from both the 401(k) retirement plans and federal employees' Thrift Savings Plan shows that costs are far lower if the plan starts with only a few investment options and then adds more once the plan is fully established.

Carefully Controlled Investment Options. All investment options available under a PRA plan should be limited to a diversified portfolio composed of stock index funds, government bonds, and similar assets. Even if they so desire, workers would not be allowed to invest in speculative areas such as technology stocks or to choose specific stocks or bonds. Money in a PRA is intended to help to finance a worker's retirement security, not to be risked on speculative investments with the hope that taxpayers will support the worker if the investment fails.

Initially, workers would be allowed to put their PRA contributions into any one of three balanced and diversified mixes of stock index funds, government bonds, and similar pension-grade investments. Although the exact mix of assets would be determined by the central administrative agency, one fund might consist of 60 percent stock index funds and 40 percent government bonds, while another might be 60 percent government bonds and 40 percent stock index funds.

The third fund, which would also act as the default fund for workers who failed to make a choice, would be a lifestyle fund. These are funds in which the asset mix changes with the age of the worker. Younger workers would be invested fairly heavily in stock index funds, but as they age, their funds would automatically shift gradually toward a portfolio that includes a substantial proportion of bonds and other fixed-interest investments. This is designed to allow the portfolios of workers who are far from retirement to grow with the economy and to allow older workers to lock in that growth by making their portfolios predominantly lower-risk investments.

Workers would be allowed to change from one investment fund to another either annually (by indicating their choice on the income tax form) or at other specified times (by completing a form on the Internet). They would also receive quarterly statements showing the balance in their accounts. As with today's Social Security, PRA accounts are intended strictly for retirement purposes, and no early withdrawals would be allowed for any reason.

Keeping Fees Low. Under a successful PRA plan, all investments must be approved by the central administrative agency as being appropriate for this level of retirement investment. That agency would also ensure that administrative costs are kept as low as possible by awarding contracts to manage investment pools through competitive bidding and through direct negotiation with professional funds managers.

Research by State Street Global Investors[14] shows that administrative costs are lower if workers put all their money in one diversified pool of assets rather than attempting to diversify their portfolio by dividing it among several types of assets. For example, a worker who puts all of his or her money in one fund consisting of 50 percent stock index funds and 50 percent government bonds would earn the same as a worker who places half of his or her money in a government bond fund and half in a separate stock index fund. However, the first worker would incur significantly lower administrative costs.

Additional Choices for Larger Accounts. Once a worker's PRA account reaches a certain size threshold (determined by the central administrative agency), he or she would have the option to move its management to another investment manager if that manager offered better service or potentially higher returns. However, only investment managers who had meet strict asset and management quality tests would be allowed to receive these accounts, and the managers would be sharply limited in the types of investments they could offer. In the event that the worker is dissatisfied with either the fees or the returns from these individually managed accounts, he or she could switch back to the centrally managed funds at any time.

Step #4: Adjust Social Security Part A benefits to a more sustainable level.
The sad fact is that today's Social Security promises younger workers much more in retirement benefits that it can possibly hope to pay. Although the program should be able to pay full benefits from its own cash flow until about 2018, after that it will rely on increasingly larger amounts of general revenue taxes to pay the promised benefits. Initially, these amounts will be paid to retire the bonds in the Social Security trust fund, with the annual amount of general revenue needed to pay full benefits rising from approximately $20 billion in 2018 to over $600 billion by the time the last bond is redeemed in about 2042.[15] After that, the existing law requires Social Security to reduce its benefits to the amount that it can pay using payroll taxes. After about 2042, that would require a 27 percent cut in benefit payments.

Despite promises from both the left and the right to pay the promised benefits in full, this is simply not realistic—in part because the benefit levels of new retirees are increased each year beyond the rate of inflation. While current retirees and those close to retirement should receive every cent that they are due, future benefit promises must be scaled back to more realistic levels.

At the same time that benefits are becoming more realistic, it is essential that PRAs be established to allow workers the opportunity to restore—and even improve—their benefits through a carefully controlled investment program. The combination of realistic government-paid benefits and a PRA would be far more secure than the current system of empty promises.

Ideally, aggregate Social Security Part A benefits should be reduced gradually to a level that could be sustained by the program's income. However, this would have to take place over a substantial time so that workers can adjust their retirement planning. In the interim, Social Security's cash flow would have to be supplemented by general revenues, but a reformed Social Security plan using PRAs would cost substantially less than what the current system will need to pay for its promises.

Changing How Social Security Benefits Are Calculated. One of the reasons that today's system will be unable to pay all of its promised retirement benefits without substantial tax increases is the way benefits are calculated. When retirement benefits are calculated, workers' pre-retirement earnings are increased by both inflation and the growth rate of wages across the entire economy. The total of the two is higher than using an inflation index alone. As a result, benefits for new retirees grow each year, even after adjusting for inflation. In addition, retirees receive an annual cost-of-living adjustment increase to reduce the effect of inflation on their benefits.

One way to bring Social Security's benefits into line with what it can afford to pay would be to change how new retirees' benefits are calculated so that their past earnings are increased only by the rate of inflation.[16] If PRA earnings supplemented these results, workers would receive an improved level of retirement income, which would generally be above what today's Social Security could afford to pay. In addition, this would sharply reduce the program's annual deficits.

Improved Benefits for Lower-Income Workers. Another advantage of a PRA system would be a minimum benefit that would protect all workers from retiring into poverty after working a full career. Because today's Social Security pays benefits based strictly on past income, it is possible for the lowest-paid workers to work a full career and then receive retirement benefits that are significantly below the poverty level.

A PRA system should be designed to pay these lowest-income workers a minimum benefit that is *at least* the poverty level, or perhaps even twice the current poverty level.[17] These minimum benefits would be paid through a combination of government-paid Social Security Part A and PRA-financed Social Security Part B. In the event that the combinations would still be below the designated minimum benefit, the difference would be added to the government-paid amount.

Benefits Calculation Under a PRA System. The way that the two parts of Social Security interact with each other is crucial. Probably the simplest method would be to have Part A pay a monthly amount based on workers' average earnings while they were working, much as the current system does. To this amount would be added the amount that could be paid through the PRA-funded Part B. If that amount does not equal the system's minimum benefit, the government would pay the difference by adding to the amount paid by Part A.

Under a PRA system, workers would have more control over their retirement options and could choose not to take the full monthly benefit that could be paid through the PRA. This would be allowed as long as the worker chooses at least a certain minimum level of income so that he or she does not become dependent upon government welfare payments for daily living.

An alternate and slightly more difficult way to calculate monthly benefits would be to reduce the Part A benefits by a set amount based on either the monthly income that could be generated by the PRA or the level of contributions to the PRA plus some level of interest. Using this method assumes a somewhat higher Part A base benefit than under the preceding method. In this case, either the Part A benefit could be offset by a proportion of the amount payable by the PRA, or the PRA contributions could be assumed to grow by a certain annual amount and the Part A benefit reduced by the result. If the worker's account earned more than the assumed growth rate, he or she would have either higher monthly benefits or a larger nest egg.

An Alternative to Means Testing. Establishing a PRA system is far better than means testing as a way to keep the program solvent. While both changes would reduce benefit costs below what today's system has promised to pay future retirees, means testing begins the process of turning Social Security into a welfare program by denying benefits to workers with incomes above a certain level, even though they have paid Social Security taxes throughout their working lives.

Introducing PRAs would allow Social Security to continue to provide benefits for workers of all income levels. While upper-income retirees are much more likely to have alternate sources of income other than Social Security, as the system becomes unable to pay a higher and higher proportion of benefits from payroll taxes, a means-tested system would be forced to deny benefits to workers at lower and lower income levels.

Changing to an Appropriate Benefit Tax System. Contributions to PRAs should be taxed in the same way that contributions to Roth IRAs and similar retirement savings plans are taxed. Workers should pay income taxes on the money that goes into their PRAs, but both the growth of the account through interest and investment earnings and all withdrawals should be tax-free.

This treatment sharply contrasts with today's Social Security, under which workers pay income taxes on contributions to Social Security and then pay income taxes on up to 85 percent of their monthly benefits (if their total retirement income exceeds $34,000 for single workers or $44,000 for married retirees).[18] While the money raised from this additional tax on certain benefits helps to fund both Social Security and Medicare, it is also a form of means testing. To make matters worse, because the income level subject to income tax is not indexed to inflation, an increasing proportion of retirees are subjected to this tax each year.

Improved Benefits for Those Who Most Need Them. Some workers and their families, particularly spouses who stay at home to raise children and widows and widowers, are treated especially badly by the current system's benefit structure. One of the goals of a PRA system should be to improve benefits for these groups.

Spouses who remain at home to raise children should not be penalized. Their benefits could be enhanced through a combination of improved spousal account options and including at least some of the years spent raising children full-time in the benefit formula. Providing generous incentives to families to continue to put money in the spouse's PRA would pay large dividends. Because most families have children at a fairly young age, that money would have the opportunity to grow for some time and could significantly increase the retirement benefits available to the stay-at-home spouse. The increased spousal PRA could, in turn, reduce the amount of benefits that spouse would receive through Part A.

Improving benefits for surviving spouses who have no income other than Social Security should be another priority. Today, widows and widowers often see major reductions in their Social Security benefits after the death of their spouses. Under current law, a surviving spouse's benefits are usually between 50 percent and 67 percent of what the couple received when both were alive. Surviving spouses should receive at least 75 percent of the benefits the family received when both spouses were alive. That seemingly small amount would make a large difference in their standards of living.

Coordinating Retirement and Disability Benefits. Currently, both Social Security's retirement and survivors' program and its disability program use the same benefit formula. That means that any benefit changes in one program automatically affect the other. However, these two programs are vastly different. One is essentially a retirement savings program for older workers, and the other is a straight insurance program that protects younger workers and their families.

Therefore, when a PRA system is established, Congress should create separate benefit formulas for each program, preserving the current benefit formula for the disability program and adjusting the retirement and survivors' formula to allow for PRAs. This would allow disabled workers to continue to receive the same benefits they receive now. Once they reach retirement age, their benefits would be paid through a combination of any funds available in their PRA and an amount paid by the government. Retirement and disability benefit amounts for older workers would be coordinated to reduce any incentive to receive disability benefits instead of retirement benefits.

Step #5: Create a realistic plan for paying the general revenue cost of establishing a PRA system.

Both the current Social Security system and every plan to reform it will require significant amounts of resources in addition to the money collected through payroll taxes. This additional money, most likely from general revenue taxes, is necessary to reduce the difference between what Social Security currently owes and what it will be able to pay. Under the reform plans, the transition cost represents a major reduction in the unfunded liability of today's program. Even though the reform plans are expensive, all of them require significantly less additional money than today's Social Security system.

Paying for either today's Social Security or any of the reform plans will require Congress to balance Social Security's needs against other pressing needs such as paying for Medicare. In general, as additional dollars are needed for either the current system or a reform plan, fewer will be available for other government programs and the private sector. As the annual amount required grows, Congress will find it increasingly difficult to come up with the money. Additionally, the longer that a plan needs large annual amounts of additional money, the less likely that its benefits will be paid on schedule. This is especially true for the current Social Security system, which will need massive amounts of general revenue funds for an extended period in order to pay all of the promised benefits.

The necessary general revenue will have to come from some combination of four sources: borrowing additional money, increasing taxes, reducing other government spending, and reducing Social Security benefits more than is called for under current law or in the reform plans.

Some plans attempt to specify sources for the general revenues needed, but these are handicapped by the fact that no Congress can bind the hands of a succeeding Congress because the succeeding Congress could change the plan at any time by a majority vote.

The most important thing to remember is that both the existing Social Security system and all known reform plans have this problem. This weakness is not limited to personal retirement account plans or any other reform plan. The only questions are when the cash-flow deficits begin and how large they become.

Creating a Spending Reduction Commission. Given the above limitations, the best way to deal with either the cost of today's system or the smaller amount required to establish a PRA system would be to create a bipartisan spending reduction commission modeled after the successful military base closing commissions. The commission would examine federal programs to identify ones that are wasteful and duplicate, do not accomplish their purposes, or simply can no longer be afforded. It would then report its findings to Congress as a legislative proposal to end, combine, or trim specific programs.

Assuming that Congress gives the spending reduction commission the same powers as the base closing commissions, Congress would then have to consider the report as a whole. Individual committees could examine spending reductions that fall within their jurisdictions, but they would have no authority to amend the proposal, and the entire package would go to the House and Senate floors under an expedited procedure that included an up-or-down vote. An alternative would be to allow amendments, but only if each amendment reduces spending enough to pay for the program that it seeks to preserve. Since, at best, the Social Security deficits will persist for several decades, a series of these commissions would be necessary.

Borrowing. Even under the best of circumstances, some of the costs of either the current Social Security system or a PRA system will likely have to be handled through borrowing. If Congress acts responsibly to reduce spending, borrowing may be necessary simply because some deficits either are larger than expected or occur before they were expected.

However, it would be a serious error to attempt to cover all of the costs through borrowing. This is especially true for the deficits that the current system will begin to incur after about 2018. Not only would the necessary amounts be huge (potentially several times that of the existing federal debt held by the public), but the annual interest costs would rapidly grow to consume a major portion of the federal budget. Debt should be used only to supplement a transition plan, which should be funded mainly through spending reductions.

Structuring Accounts to Reduce Transition Costs. One way to reduce the costs of establishing a PRA system would be to have the accounts invest partly in U.S. government bonds. That way, a portion of the money that moves between Social Security and the PRA would move back to the government account, thus reducing cash-flow deficits. This essentially requires the people who will benefit the most from PRAs to bear a significant part of the cost of establishing the system. In addition to reducing the cost of PRAs, this investment structure also reduces the accounts' risk level.

However, in order for this structure to be more than a financial maneuver, the accounts must be structured so that future generations not only repay the bonds in earlier workers' accounts, but also require a smaller proportion of them in their own accounts. For example, workers born around 1990 might have 40 percent of their accounts in government bonds, while those born in the 2010s would have only 38 percent.

Transition Bonds. Another approach to the costs of shifting to a PRA system would be to use transition bonds, such as those used in Chile's reform during the early 1980s. In this case, workers are given bonds that, when mature, represent the retirement benefits they have already earned in the current system. They are free either to deposit the bond in their PRA or to sell it on the open market and deposit that money in the account.

The bond effectively cashes the individual out of the current system and bases his or her benefits on the amount in that worker's PRA. The specific budgetary consequences depend on when the bond matures, its interest rate, and whether it is paid off in one lump sum (when the worker reaches retirement age) or over time.

Raising Taxes Must Be Avoided. While some Congressmen and Senators will be tempted to cover Social Security's deficits with higher taxes, this is the wrong approach. For one thing, the necessary amounts are so large that such a tax increase would consume enough resources to stall economic growth. In addition, workers already receive an extremely low return on their taxes, and such a tax hike would only make matters worse.

Step #6: Create a system that allows workers flexibility in structuring their retirement benefits while ensuring that they receive an adequate monthly benefit.
Although the savings portion of PRAs receives most of the attention, what happens after an individual retires is equally important. A successful PRA plan can give the worker the ability to tailor his or her retirement income to meet specific goals. Today's Social Security requires all workers to take the equivalent of a lifetime annuity regardless of their health, needs, or financial circumstances.

Annuitization. In order to protect both the retiree and the taxpayer, a PRA plan should require all retirees to use some of their PRAs to purchase annuities that would guarantee at least a minimal level of income for life, including an adjustment for inflation. This requirement would protect taxpayers against retirees who would otherwise spend their entire PRAs and depend on some form of government handout to meet their monthly expenses.

Annuities would be available from private companies through the central administrative agency, as is currently done with the federal Thrift Savings Plan. Workers could also buy them directly from companies if the annuities meet certain financial safety standards. Companies seeking to offer them would be required to have insurance or some other safeguard that would allow the annuity to be paid even if the company ran into financial difficulty. While today's annuities have fairly high administrative costs, these are expected to decline sharply once demand for the product becomes more widespread. The central administrative agency would be able to negotiate with providers to ensure that retirees are charged the lowest fees possible.

However, workers need not convert their entire PRAs into annuities. Ideally, a worker would only be required to purchase a minimal-level annuity that, combined with any government-paid benefit, would meet basic living needs.[19] Of course, a worker could also choose to purchase an annuity that pays a much higher benefit. Married workers would have to purchase an annuity that included a spousal benefit, which would continue to pay monthly income to the surviving spouse.

Workers who chose a minimal-level annuity could use a programmed withdrawal system (similar to those available for today's IRA accounts) to supplement their monthly income. As mentioned above, PRAs would be designed to produce both retirement income and a nest egg that could be used for emergencies during retirement, used to provide a higher retirement income, or left as a legacy to the worker's family. In addition, the worker could retire early if his or her PRA was large enough to purchase an annuity that would pay the minimal-level income for the rest of his or her life.

Conclusion

It is not fair either to force senior citizens into poverty because of low Social Security benefits or to beggar their children and grandchildren by requiring them to pay for unrealistic promises. Establishing Social Security PRAs is the one way that avoids both of these extremes.

Because PRAs would earn higher returns than the current 100 percent government-paid system can afford to pay, they could preserve retirement benefits at a sustainable level and also reduce the unfunded promises that future generations will have to pay. However, they are not a magic bullet. In order to work properly, a PRA system must be carefully structured and administered. Whether reformed with PRAs or not, the system must neither promise more than it can reasonably be expected to deliver in benefits nor attempt to hide its true cost through budget tricks.

The experience of over 25 countries shows that PRA systems can be structured to deliver improved benefits in a cost-effective way. Rather than waiting for the inevitable crisis to arrive, Congress should establish a Social Security Part B that includes PRAs. Delay just makes the eventual cost higher while denying younger workers increased control over their own retirements and the ability to create nest eggs for their families.

David C. John is Research Fellow in Social Security and Financial Institutions in the Thomas A. Roe Institute for Economic Policy Studies at The Heritage Foundation.

Notes

1. "Economic theory and empirical evidence suggest that workers bear much of the employer's portion of the payroll tax through lower wages and reduced fringe benefits. If the employer-paid portion of payroll tax receipts is counted as the contribution of the worker, roughly 80 percent of taxpayers pay more in payroll taxes than in income taxes." The 80 percent figure includes payroll taxes for Social Security Disability Insurance and a portion of Medicare in addition to Social Security's retirement and survivors program. Congressional Budget Office, Economic Stimulus: Evaluating Proposed Changes in Tax Policy, January 2002, p. 12, footnote 7, at ftp.cbo.gov/32xx/doc3251/FiscalStimulus.pdf (January 26, 2004).

2. Social Security Administration, Income of the Aged Chartbook, 2001, May 2003, p. 10, at www.ssa.gov/policy/docs/chartbooks/ income_aged/2001/iac01.pdf (November 15, 2004).

3. All taxes reduce income and thereby reduce the ability to save or consume. Social Security also reduces the incentive to save because it provides retirement benefits that substitute for private savings. Virtually all of the research in this area identifies this "substitution effect" as the source of Social Security's impact on savings. See Congressional Budget Office, "Social Security and Private Saving: A Review of the Empirical Evidence," CBO Memorandum, July 1998, at www.cbo.gov/ftpdocs/7xx/doc731/ssprisav.pdf (November 15, 2004).

4. Helvering v. Davis, 80 U.S. 1367 (1937), and Flemming v. Nestor, 57 U.S. 904 (1960).

5. These calculations were made using The Heritage Foundation's Social Security Calculator, at www.heritage.org/research/features/socialsecurity. These values are consistent with the calculations of the Government Accountability Office (formerly the General Accounting Office) and others. See U.S. General Accounting Office, Social Security and Minorities: Earnings, Disability Incidence, and Mortality Are Key Factors That Influence Taxes Paid and Benefits Received, GAO–03–387, April 2003, at www.gao.gov/new.items/d03387.pdf (November 15, 2004), and Lee Cohen, C. Eugene Steuerle, and Adam Carasso, "Social Security Redistribution by Education, Race, and Income: How Much and Why," paper prepared for the Third Annual Conference of the Retirement Research Consortium on "Making Hard Choices About Retirement," Washington, D.C., May 17–18, 2001, at www.bc.edu/centers/crr/papers/Third/Cohen-Steuerle-Carasso_Paper.pdf (November 15, 2004).

6. Robert N. Anderson and Peter B. DeTurk, "United States Life Tables, 1999," in National Center for Health Statistics, National Vital Statistics Reports, Vol. 50, No. 6 (March 21, 2002), pp. 15–16 and 21–22, at www.cdc.gov/nchs/data/nvsr/ nvsr50/nvsr50_06.pdf (November 16,2004).

7. It would be easier to administer the PRA system if workers have only one opportunity to opt out of it.

8. Half of this amount (5.3 percent) is deducted from the worker's paycheck, and the employer pays the other half. As far as the employer is concerned, the employer-paid share is really part of the worker's salary because the tax is incurred for employing that particular worker. In addition, other payroll taxes totaling 1.8 percent of wages pay for Social Security's disability program, and a further 2.9 percent pays for Medicare.

9. The amount of general revenues required would depend on the plan's design and the extent to which it offsets future promised benefits.

10. However, a recent study suggests that the progressivity of the current Social Security program is overstated and that lower-income workers actually do worse than is popularly believed. For more details, see Alan L. Gustman and Thomas L. Steinmeier, "How Effective Is Redistribution Under the Social Security Benefit Formula?" Journal of Public Economics, Vol. 82, No. 1 (October 2001), pp. 1–28. An electronic version of an earlier draft is available at www.dartmouth.edu/~agustman/ Redistr6.pdf (November 10, 2004).

11. Calculated by the Center for Data Analysis using data from Federal Reserve Board, "2001 Survey of Consumer Finance," at www.federalreserve.gov/pubs/oss/oss2/scfindex.html (February 17, 2003). In this analysis, any major inheritance, gift, or bequest is considered an inheritance. Income figures represent adjusted gross income.

12. William W. Beach, Alfredo B. Goyburu, Ralph A. Rector, Ph.D., David C. John, Kirk A. Johnson, Ph.D., and Thomas Bingel, "Peace of Mind in Retirement: Making Future Generations Better Off by Fixing Social Security," Heritage Foundation Center for Data Analysis Report No. CDA04–06, August 11, 2004, at www.heritage.org/Research/SocialSecurity/CDA04-06.cfm.

13. A similar administrative structure was developed during the Clinton Administration by experts from the Department of the Treasury and the Social Security Administration. State Street Corporation also developed this model independently in 1999.

14. State Street Corporation, "Administrative Challenges Confronting Social Security Reform," March 22, 1999.

15. Both figures are in 2004 dollars (i.e., adjusted for inflation).

16. Slightly reducing the bend points in the benefit formula each year would be an equally valid method to offset benefit increases due to the growth of average wages.

17. This level of guaranteed benefits would be payable only to low-income workers who work at least a specified number of years.

18. Single retirees with total incomes over $25,000 and married workers with total retirement incomes over $32,000 pay income taxes on 50 percent of their Social Security benefits.

19. If this is not politically feasible, an alternative might be to require that the annuity and any government-paid benefit must equal the promised benefits under the PRA system.

Testimony before the
House Ways and Means Committee

by Robert C. Pozen

Mr. Chairman and Committee Members:

Thank you for this opportunity to testify before the Committee on Ways and Means. I strongly support the Committee's efforts to reach a bipartisan consensus on solvency for Social Security. We must first address solvency and then focus on what type of personal accounts (including add-on as well as carve-out accounts) might be appropriate as part of a legislative package.

Our best chance of developing a viable legislative package is to link Social Security reform with enhancements to private retirement accounts, such as the 401(k) plan and the individual retirement account (IRA). In the past, Social Security and private retirement plans have been treated as separate legislative subjects; yet these are two sources of retirement income that are considered together by most workers. In 1933 when Social Security began, the 401(k) plan and IRA were unknown; today, these programs play an important role in helping to provide retirement security. So today we should evaluate the Social Security system in light of the existing incentives for private retirement programs, and we should consider possible expansions of these programs in connection with any Social Security reforms.

In this testimony, I will first explain progressive indexing and respond to a few early observations about the proposal; second, evaluate the impact of progressive indexing on the middle class viewed from different perspectives; third, outline several alternatives for adding revenue to Social Security in connection with milder benefit reforms; and fourth, discuss a few approaches to increasing retirement income by enhancing different types of personal accounts.

I. Summary of Progressive Indexing

Progressive indexing is a strategy to move toward Social Security solvency (with or without personal accounts) by reducing its long-term deficit from a present value of $3.8 trillion to $1.1 trillion. In general, progressive indexing would change the formulas for computing initial Social Security benefits at retirement for different

Statement of Robert C. Pozen, Chairman, MFS Investment Management, Boston, Massachusetts, Testimony before the Full Committee of the House Committee on Ways and Means, May 12, 2005 (available at http://waysandmeans.house.gov/hearings.asp?formmode=view&id=2628)

groups of earners. In specific, progressive indexing would divide earners into three main groups as of 2012 (when progressive indexing begins): low earners with average career earnings of $25,000 per year and lower; high earners with average career earnings of $113,000 per year and higher; and, middle earners with average career earnings between $25,000 and $113,000 per year.

Under progressive indexing, all low-wage earners (as well as all those retiring before 2012) would receive the current schedule of initial Social Security benefits—which increases average career earnings by the rate that American wages have risen over their working careers. By contrast, under progressive indexing, all high-wage earners would receive initial Social Security benefits that grow more slowly than the current schedule because their average career earnings would be increased by the rate at which prices have risen over their working careers. The initial Social Security benefits of median-wage workers would be increased by a proportional blend of price and wage indexing.

The rationale for progressive indexing is simple. Low-wage workers are almost entirely dependent on Social Security benefits for retirement income; they have minimal participation in 401(k) plans and IRAs. On the other hand, almost all high-wage workers as well as most middle-wage workers do participate in private retirement plans. In 2004, the federal tax revenues forgone for 401(k) plans and IRAs were $55 billion.

Several technical concerns about progressive indexing have been raised. First, it has been observed that a flat benefit would result if progressive indexing were continued into the 22nd century. My proposal for progressive indexing runs until 2079, the end of the conventional period for measuring system solvency, at which time the benefits of the top-paid workers would still be 20% higher than the benefits of low-wage earners.

Second, some have questioned whether wages will continue to rise on average 1.1% faster than prices over the next century, as they have over the last century. This concern can be met by applying to the initial Social Security benefits of the top earners an index designed to reflect the historic difference between wage and price growth—for instance, the average annual increase in wages over their careers, minus 1.1% per year.

Third, the argument has been made that progressive indexing is not progressive since its benefit reductions would constitute only a small fraction of the pre-retirement income of a millionaire. In fact, the reductions in Social Security benefits for a maximum earner would be significantly larger, in both dollar and percentage terms, than those of a median-wage worker under progressive indexing. These larger benefit reductions are justifiable precisely because they constitute only a small fraction of the income of any millionaire before or after retirement.

II. Impact on Median Workers

Others have expressed a more substantive concern about the impact of progressive indexing on the median-wage worker, who will earn $47,000 in 2012 ($36,500 in

2005). It has been noted that such a worker retiring at age 65 in 2045 would receive 16% less under progressive indexing than scheduled benefits—$16,417 rather than $19,544 (in 2004 constant dollars). Is this reduction from the schedule a "benefit cut"? The schedule represents the benefits we have promised but do not have the money to deliver—this is why the long-term deficit of Social Security has a present value of $3.8 trillion. If the test of a politically viable reform plan is not reducing scheduled benefits for median-wage workers as well as for low-wage workers, then every politically viable plan to restore Social Security will fail.

One relevant criterion is how a reduction in scheduled benefits compares to the reduction that would occur if the Social Security system goes into default. If Congress does not enact Social Security reform of a major nature, the system will default in 2041 and benefit levels will automatically be reduced by roughly 27% for all workers in 2045. Thus, judged relative to payable benefits, the $16,417 received by the median-wage worker in 2045 would actually be an increase in benefits—$2,150 more than the $14,267 that the system can afford to pay in 2045 absent major reforms (in constant 2004 dollars).

A second relevant criterion is whether that $16,417 received by the median-wage worker in 2045 under progressive indexing constitutes an increase or decrease in purchasing power relative to today's benefits for a similarly placed worker. That worker in 2045 would receive a 14% increase in purchasing power as compared to a similar worker today—from $14,384 in 2005 to $16,417 in 2045 (expressed in 2004 constant dollars). In other words, median workers would be able to buy 14% more goods and services with their monthly checks from Social Security under progressive indexing in 2045 than they can buy with these checks today.

A third criterion is the impact of Social Security reform on replacement ratios—the percentage of pre-retirement earnings replaced by post-retirement benefits. Under the current schedule for Social Security, the replacement rate would be 36% for a median-wage worker retiring at age 65 in 2045; under progressive indexing, the replacement rate for that same worker would decline to 30%. However, the above replacement rates do not include any post-retirement income from private retirement plans like the 401(k) and IRA. A majority of median-wage workers already participate in such plans, and I would strongly support legislative measures to enhance participation rates for median-wage workers.

III. Increases in Payroll Taxes

Notwithstanding the above evaluations of the proposal for progressive indexing under alternative criteria, if Congress concludes that the reductions from scheduled benefits for median-wage workers are too large under the proposal, these can be softened by modifying the bend points and PIA factors utilized by the actuaries to implement the proposal. In that event, Congress could restore Social Security to solvency by adopting other benefit reforms (such as moving back the normal retirement age from 67 to 69 between 2055 and 2079), or by increasing revenue flow into the system. With regard to the latter approach, it may be helpful to calibrate the differential impact of various possible increases in payroll taxes on the system's solvency.

As you are aware, the payroll tax rate of 12.4% currently applies to all earnings up to $90,000 per year. Should Congress decide to close the whole long-term deficit of Social Security through payroll taxes, it would have to extend this 12.4% rate to all earnings (assuming minimal retirement benefits were paid in connection with these new payroll taxes). Thus, attaining solvency for Social Security in this manner would require one of the largest tax increases in American history for all workers with earnings above $90,000 per year.

Since such a huge extension of payroll taxes at 12.4% to all earnings does not appear to be politically viable, some commentators have suggested that the 12.4% rate be levied on all earnings up to $130,000 per year in today's dollars—which would automatically rise under current law to $150,000 per year by 2012. Yet even such a sharp jump in the earnings base subject to a 12.4% tax rate would close only one-fourth of the long-term deficit of Social Security. Moreover, this type of extension would be very unfair to those workers earning between $90,000 and $200,000 per year. Most of their earnings would be subjected to the 12.4% payroll tax, while most of the earnings of millionaires would escape this tax.

If Congress chose to raise payroll taxes as part of a reform package, a more workable structure would be a surcharge of 2.9% on all earnings above $90,000—loosely based on the model of the Medicare tax. This structure would more fairly spread the burden among all high-wage earners, and would have roughly the same solvency impact as applying a 12.4% tax rate to all earnings up to $130,000 per year in 2005. In both cases, the long-term deficit of Social Security would be cut by only one-fourth. Therefore, significant constraints on benefit growth would still be needed in order for the system to become solvent later this century.

IV. Types of Personal Accounts

Progressive indexing can stand alone as a strategy to move toward Social Security solvency, or it can be combined with various types of personal accounts. In this context, personal accounts can play two useful roles. First, they can increase the retirement income of workers, especially those who would experience slower growth in their Social Security benefits under progressive indexing. Second, they can provide a political "sweetener" to a legislative package otherwise containing benefit constraints and tax hikes.

Carve-out Accounts

Since progressive indexing would slow the growth of Social Security benefits for some workers, it could be combined with a personal retirement account (PRA) involving a voluntary allocation of a modest portion (such as 2% of earnings) of the 12.4% in payroll taxes. Any worker who made such an allocation to a PRA would have to accept lower traditional Social Security benefits since he or she would be paying in lower amounts to the traditional system and receiving the returns on his or her PRA in addition to traditional benefits. These lower traditional benefits should be calculated using an offset rate that is the same as the actual real rate of return on 30-year U.S. Treasury bonds, rather than an artificially selected rate such as a 3% real return. A PRA would have an excellent chance of providing a higher return than this actual real rate of return by investing consistently in a low-cost balanced account, comprised 60% of an equity index fund and 40% of a bond index fund, throughout the 30 to 35 years of someone's working life.

Some have expressed concern that carve-out PRAs would not improve the solvency of the Social Security system and would increase government borrowing. However, as calculated by the Social Security actuaries, a combination of progressive indexing and a carve-out PRA with an allocation of 2% of earnings (limited to $3,000 per year with the limit indexed to prices) would make Social Security solvent by the end of 2079. No government borrowing would be needed until 2030 to finance this combination, and such borrowing would be completed before 2079. Moreover, the government borrowing needed to finance this combination would be $2 trillion less than the government borrowing needed to finance the current schedule of Social Security benefits through 2079.

Add-on Accounts

For those who oppose carve-out PRAs, progressive indexing could be combined with various forms of add-on accounts in a legislative package. It bears emphasis that add-on accounts themselves would not make Social Security solvent and would increase the budget deficit. However, a combination of progressive indexing and modest expenditures for add-on accounts could be designed to substantially improve the solvency of Social Security. Instead of creating a new set of add-on accounts, Congress should enhance the existing structure of IRAs in order to promote more retirement savings in the most efficient manner.

One suggestion would be to transform the low-income tax credit for IRA contributions into a partially refundable tax credit. This would make the tax credit more effective for families with incomes below $40,000 per year, who often do not pay federal income taxes. Another suggestion would be to remove the income ceiling from the Roth IRA, which currently starts to phase out for families with incomes of more than $120,000 per year. Removing the income ceiling would be a political quid-pro-quo for high-wage earners with the slowest growth of Social Security benefits under progressive indexing. Yet another suggestion would be to allow all taxpayers to earmark a portion of any federal income tax refund for investment in an IRA. This would be a low-cost way to encourage retirement savings.

Opt-out Accounts

As mentioned above, if Congress chose to raise the payroll tax base, the fairest approach would be to impose a 2.9% surtax on all wages above $90,000 per year. Under this approach, what kind of retirement benefits should be associated with such a surtax? One possibility would be to dedicate the 1.45% of the surtax that would be paid by employers to improving Social Security solvency (worth about 0.25% of payroll), and allocate the 1.45% paid by the workers to a personal account invested in market securities. Since the allocation of this 1.45% would not divert existing payroll taxes from Social Security, the funding of these personal accounts would not involve incremental borrowing by the federal government. But such a personal account would effectively impose a mandatory IRA contribution on high-wage earners. A more flexible form of this approach would be to allocate 1.45% of earnings above $90,000 to an IRA, subject to an opt-out by the worker.

If this more flexible approach were attractive to Congress, it could also be applied to workers with earnings below $90,000 per year. For example, employers could be required to presumptively allocate to an IRA 1.45% of the annual earnings of all full-time workers on the job for at least one calendar year with annual earnings of at least $24,000. This allocation would be in addition to the payroll taxes now paid by such workers, but they could opt out of the presumptive allocation of this 1.45% to an IRA simply by notifying their employer. In practice, this flexible approach would harness the forces of human inertia and tax incentives to encourage retirement savings, while allowing any worker the choice of not participating in this type of retirement program.

Conclusion

Progressive indexing provides a fair and workable foundation for legislative efforts aimed at restoring solvency to the Social Security system. Many of the observations about progressive indexing can be resolved by careful legislative drafting, and the impact of progressive indexing on median-wage workers can be softened if Congress is prepared to adopt other benefit constraints or revenue raisers. Moreover, progressive indexing can be combined with various type of personal accounts that may be helpful in enacting a legislative package of Social Security reforms and encouraging retirement savings for American workers.

Thank you again for this opportunity to testify on Social Security reform. I recognize that this subject is politically challenging for any elected official and greatly respect your efforts. I would be glad to answer any questions you might have on progressive indexing or related points discussed in this testimony.

Nonpartisan Social Security Reform Plan

by Jeffrey Liebman, Maya MacGuineas, and Andrew Samwick

Overview

The three of us—former aides to President Clinton, Senator McCain, and President Bush—did an experiment to see if we could develop a reform plan that we could all support. The Liebman-MacGuineas-Samwick (LMS) plan demonstrates the types of compromises that can help policy makers from across the political spectrum agree on a Social Security reform plan. The plan achieves sustainable solvency through progressive changes to taxes and benefits, introduces mandatory personal accounts, and specifies important details that are often left unaddressed in other reform plans. The plan also illustrates that a compromise plan can contain sensible but politically unpopular options (such as raising retirement ages or mandating that account balances be converted to annuities upon retirement)—options that could realistically emerge from a bipartisan negotiating process, but which are rarely contained in reform proposals put out by Democrats or Republicans alone because of the political risk they present.

The LMS plan contains four key elements:

Benefit cuts (through progressive reductions in PIA factors and an increase in the retirement age).

New revenue (through a mandatory additional 1.5 percent contribution into personal retirement accounts and a gradual increase in the payroll tax cap to 90 percent of earnings).

Mandatory personal retirement accounts (equal to 3 percent of earnings, funded half by new contributions and half redirected from the Social Security Trust Funds, with full annuitization required upon retirement).

Other updates to the traditional system (minimum benefit for low-wage workers, increase in widow(er)s' benefits, decrease in spousal benefits, possible progressive matches for accounts).

The major compromises in the plan include:

(Report published December 2005, available at http://newamerica.net/Download_Docs/pdfs/Doc_File_2757_1.pdf; used with permission)

Revenue increases versus spending reductions—To fill the Social Security funding gap, roughly half the changes would come from benefit reductions and half from revenue increases. (Over the 75-year horizon, benefits cuts would equal 2.7 percent of payroll and revenue increases would equal 2.5 percent of payroll.)

Level of traditional benefits—In the long run, traditional benefits would be no smaller and no larger than the existing 12.4 percent payroll tax. Not allowing benefits to grow as promised would keep them from crowding out spending on other programs and minimize the need for distortionary tax increases and government borrowing. Not allowing them to fall below 12.4 percent would alleviate fears about starting down the slippery slope to total privatization. This level of benefit reductions is intermediate between price indexing and wage indexing. The benefit reductions are completely phased in by 2050 and benefits grow with real wages thereafter.

Level of benefits versus length of time of collecting benefits—Under the plan, the combination of traditional benefits and the money accumulated in accounts produces replacement rates (the ratio of retirement income to pre-retirement earnings) roughly equal to those that are currently promised. In addition, replacement rates from the traditional benefit alone are kept higher than they would otherwise be because benefits would be collected over a shorter period of time due to the increase in the age when participants become eligible for benefits.

Sources of PRA financing—Half of the revenue needed to fund the PRAs would come from mandatory worker contributions (an "add-on") and half would come from redirecting money from the Social Security Trust Funds (a "carve-out"). Rather than borrowing to cover the cost of the redirected funds, they would be paid for by raising the payroll tax cap and cutting benefits.

Storage for saving—While new money would be devoted to the Social Security system, on net, all of the new revenue would be stored in personal accounts rather than in government trust funds. Accounts wall off funds from the rest of government, thereby increasing the likelihood that they would contribute to national saving. Devoting the new revenues to accounts would also decrease their distortionary effects, as workers will be less likely to perceive their required contributions as a pure tax if they see those contributions being directed to an account that they own.

Size of the accounts—At three percent, personal accounts would be large enough to accumulate significant wealth for participants and to keep the administrative costs manageable but not so large as to overshadow traditional benefits.

Level of progressivity—Revenues and traditional benefits would be made more progressive but not so much as to undermine support for the universal social insurance system.

Details

I. Benefit Cuts

The LMS plan reduces scheduled benefits so that they can be covered by the current 12.4 percent payroll tax.[1] This represents a 35 percent reduction in aggregate spending relative to current benefit formulas. Because benefits for the disabled and young survivors are not reduced, the retirement benefit cut for a typical worker is larger—about 43 percent.[2] The benefit cuts are implemented by changing the primary insurance amount (PIA) formula and by increasing the full benefit age.

Changing the PIA Formula

The reductions in benefits via the PIA formula are done in such a way that benefits are reduced by a greater percentage for high earners than for low earners. The upper (15) and middle (32) PIA factors are gradually cut in half—to 7.5 and 16 percent, respectively. The lower PIA factor (90) is reduced by only a quarter, to 67.6 percent. The reduction in the top PIA factor is phased in for beneficiaries first becoming eligible for benefits between 2008 and 2045. The reductions in the other two PIA factors are phased in between 2013 and 2050. The speed at which the reductions are implemented is designed to align with the speed at which PRA balances accumulate so that total replacement rates (from the sum of traditional benefits and PRA annuities) remain roughly constant across cohorts.

Increasing the Retirement Age

Under current law, the age at which a worker can receive full retirement benefits is scheduled to rise from its current level of 66 to 67 between 2017 and 2022. The LMS plan would advance this transition by eleven years, starting the increase in 2006, and then would continue the increase in the full benefit age (FBA) until it reached 68 for those attaining age 62 in 2017. Absent a change in retirement date, an increase in the FBA represents a benefit reduction for beneficiaries.

The plan also includes an increase in the earliest eligibility age (EEA). Starting for people born in 1955, there would be an increase the EEA (which is currently 62) by 2 months per year until it reaches 65. When people delay receiving Social Security benefits, their remaining benefits are increased by an amount that is roughly actuarially fair. Therefore, an increase in the EEA has essentially no impact on Social Security's finances. However, it is likely to have positive labor market effects.

Raising the FBA and EEA reflects that with rising longevity and improved health at each age, an important part of reforming Social Security should be to pay benefits primarily at older ages, thereby encouraging people to work longer (in part by changing societal norms about when retirement should begin). We raise the EEA, even though it has no impact on Social Security's finances, because we want to maintain replacement rates in light of benefit cuts (particularly to protect individuals who might shortsightedly retire too early if given access to their Social Security benefits at too young an age).[3]

Protecting the Disabled and Child Beneficiaries from Benefit Cuts
Benefits for disabled workers and their dependents and for child beneficiaries would not be subject to the reductions in benefits from changing the PIA formula. These beneficiaries would continue to receive benefits under the current formula. For disabled beneficiaries who reach the full benefit age and are then converted to retired worker status, benefits would be paid as a weighted average of the benefits under the new formula and the old formula. Specifically, the benefits will equal the share of years the worker was not disabled times the new formula plus the share of years the worker was disabled times the old formula. Disabled workers will have access to their PRA annuities under the same terms as retired workers—i.e. they may choose to convert balances to an annuity and start receiving benefits at any age between 62 and 68.

II. New Revenue
There are two sources of new revenue in the plan: mandatory account contributions and an increase in the level of earnings subject to the payroll tax.

Mandatory Account Contributions
The personal retirement accounts (described in detail below) are financed half with mandatory new contributions from individuals and half with revenue diverted from the trust funds. The accounts are 3 percent of earnings, so the mandatory new contributions equal 1.5 percent of covered earnings.

Our plan would end the practice of using Social Security surpluses to fund general government operations. Thus, so long as Social Security surpluses exist, they would be directed to the personal retirement accounts and the required individual contributions would be less than 1.5 percent of payroll. For example, in 2008 the trust fund contribution rate would be 2.30 percent of payroll and the individual contribution rate would be 0.70 percent, in 2014 the trust fund contribution rate would be 1.94 percent of payroll and the individual rate would be 1.06 percent. Starting in 2018, the long run position is reached with 1.5 percent from the trust fund and 1.5 percent from individuals.

Raising the Taxable Maximum
A bit more than two-thirds of the 1.5 percent of payroll diverted from the trust fund is replaced by gradually restoring the percentage of earnings that is subject to the OASDI payroll tax to 90 percent (where it was in 1982) and maintaining it at that level thereafter. This increase in the taxable maximum would be phased in between 2008 and 2017. The new long run taxable maximum is equivalent to $171,600 at today's wage level.[4] The maximum level of earnings to be included in benefit calculations remains the maximum taxable earnings in current law—workers receive no incremental benefits from the increase in maximum taxable earnings.

III. Mandatory Personal Retirement Accounts

In order to keep total expected retirement benefits at levels comparable to those specified in current law, the LMS plan establishes personal retirement accounts equal to 3 percent of taxable payroll (using the current-law maximum as the cap).

The investment options for PRAs are designed to limit administrative costs and the risks to investors. PRAs would be invested with one of 15 private fund companies certified by the government to be eligible to receive PRA deposits. Each of these fund companies would be required to offer 5 broadly diversified investment options, patterned after the Federal Employee Thrift Savings Program. A central clearing house would handle transactions. Social Security actuaries estimate that administrative charges associated with PRAs would be approximately 30 basis points per year.

All payments from PRAs would be paid as annuities, which would initially be required to be fixed, inflation-indexed annuities provided by the Social Security Administration as part of a beneficiary's regular Social Security benefit. Full annuitization by age 68 is required, but beneficiaries can choose to spread annuitization between 62 and 68 if so desired. Married beneficiaries would be required to purchase joint and two-thirds survivor annuities. Annuities would be 10-year certain annuities to provide payouts to heirs of those who die soon after annuitization. The total balances in the accounts of the two spouses in a married couple would be split equally in the case of divorce.

Investment options are restricted and full annuitization is required because Social Security is meant to provide a basic level of retirement income support. For an average earner, the combination of the traditional benefit and PRA annuity will provide a replacement rate of about 35 percent. Retirement planners typically advise that retirees need an income level that is 70 to 80 percent of their pre-retirement earnings in order to maintain their standard of living. Thus, Social Security is designed with the expectation that the typical retiree will need to do additional saving (individually and/or through a pension plan at work) above and beyond Social Security. To the extent that retirees would like a different mix of investments or a different stream of payments in retirement, they can achieve that through their non-Social Security investments.

The progressivity in our plan comes on the revenue side from raising the taxable maximum and on the benefit side from reducing traditional benefits by a greater fraction for high earners than for low earners. But because the PRAs in our plan are equal to 3 percent of a worker's earnings, expected benefits are higher—relative to currently scheduled benefits—for high earners than for low earners. For example, as Table 1 shows, total benefits (including both traditional benefits and payments from a PRA annuity) for a 2-earner married couple are 96 percent of present law scheduled benefits for a scaled low-earner, 102 percent of present law benefits for a scaled medium earner, and 109 percent of present law benefits for a scaled high earner. In viewing these numbers it is important to remember that they show only the benefit side of the equation. They do not reflect the fact that high earners under the plan are paying a disproportionate share of the new revenues. However, all three of us support the use of progressive matches to augment the personal accounts of low-income workers as long as a funding mechanism for the matches is identified. Thus, we would support, for example, integrating a paid-for Saver's Credit with Social Security PRAs so that low-earners would have their PRA contributions matched by the government. We did not incorporate such a provision in our plan because changes to tax policy outside of Social Security are beyond the scope of our proposal.

IV. Other Updates to the Traditional Benefit System

Our proposal calls for making three other changes to update the Social Security system. These additional changes were not incorporated in the Actuaries' estimates of our plan because they have a relatively small impact of actuarial balance but would have added considerable complexity of the Actuaries' modeling task.

First, we would adopt the minimum benefit provision included in Model 2 of the President's Commission to Strengthen Social Security. This provision provides a minimum benefit for workers who work a large number of years at low-wages. Second, we would adopt the provision from the President's Commission to Strengthen Social Security that would guarantee a widow(er) 75 percent of the benefit the couple was receiving before the first spouse passed away. Poverty rates among widows are around 20 percent and this provision would concentrate extra resources on this high poverty population.

Third, we would reduce spousal benefits for those married to high earners. The current Social Security system provides higher spousal benefits for someone married to a high earner than for someone married to a low earner, implicitly placing more value on the work done in the home of people married to high earners than of people married to lower earners. We propose gradually moving to a cap on spousal benefits at 50 percent of the PIA of the average worker in the worker's cohort. This provision would help pay for the other two provisions.

Table 1
Benefits as Percent of Present Law Scheduled Benefits, 2056
(Assumes Expected Yield on Mixed Portfolio)

	Traditional Benefit Only	Traditional + PRA Two-Earner Couple, Married	Traditional + PRA Two-Earner Couple, Widowed	Traditional + PRA One-Earner Couple
Low Earner	62.6	96.3	107.5	85.3
Medium Earner	56.2	101.6	116.7	86.8
High Earner	54.2	109.0	127.3	91.2

Advantages of the LMS Plan

Sustainable solvency is achieved—The Social Security actuaries find that actuarial balance would improve by 2.14 percent of taxable payroll over the 75-year projection horizon. The current Social Security deficit is 1.92 percent of payroll. Therefore, the changes in the plan would lead to a 0.22 surplus. Trust fund balances in the last year of the actuaries' projection period are positive and increasing. (See http://www.ssa.gov/OACT/solvency/Liebman_20051117.pdf).

Fiscally responsible plan—The plan puts great emphasis on fiscal responsibility—borrowing less from general revenues than any other plan that has been scored by the Social Security actuaries in recent years. Table 3 compares the LMS plan with other recent Social Security reform plan. The first column compares general fund transfers to the OASDI Trust Funds. This is one measure of how much a plan relies upon unspecified resources from outside of Social Security to bring the system into balance. The LMS plan does not rely at all on general fund transfers, and instead uses changes to benefits and revenues to bring Social Security into balance. The second column shows the sum of all Social Security cash-flow deficits. In years in which Social Security benefits exceed revenues, the shortfall must be made up by the general funds of the government either through reductions in other government spending, increases in taxes, or issuing additional debt. Paying all currently scheduled benefits would require the rest of the government to come up with $6,372 billion in funds over the next 75 years. Under the LMS plan this number is reduced to $1,456 billion. None of the other 18 other plans scored by the Office of the Actuary in the past three years has lower cash-flow deficits than the LMS plan.

Many practical reforms are included—The plan includes a number of sensible policies including an increase in the retirement age to reflect growing life expectancies; mandatory rather than voluntary accounts (which greatly simplifies the system, particularly by eliminating the need for benefits offsets); and required annuitization of accounts balances to help ensure that participants do not spend down their savings too quickly.

Table 2
Contributions to 75-year Actuarial Balance

Policy (% of payroll)	Improvement in Actuarial Balance
Raise Taxable Maximum	1.00
Change in Benefit Formula	2.08
Increase in Full Benefit Age	0.62
Diversion of Trust Fund Revenue to PRAs	-1.56
Total	2.14

Table 3
Comparison with Other Plans

	General Fund Transfers (Present Value 2005 Dollars) (1)	Total Cash-Flow Deficits (Present Value 2005 Dollars) (2)
Scheduled Benefits	**6,372 billion**[a]	**6,372 billion**[a]
LMS Nonpartisan Plan	**0**	**1,456 billion**
Kolbe-Boyd	824 billion[a][b]	1,956 billion[b]
Shaw	4,817 billion[a][b]	1,906 billion[b]
Ryan-Sununu	8,920 billion[a][b]	9,891 billion[b]
Ball	0	1,972 billion[a][b]
Hagel	3,778 billion[b]	5,423 billion[b]
Pozen	1,994 billion[b]	3,778 billion[b]
Graham	3,696 billion[a][b]	4,109 billion[a][b]
Diamond-Orszag	0	2,424 billion[b]

Source: Plan memos from SSA Office of the Actuary.

a. Deficits continue beyond 75-year projection window. Numbers represent only 75-year deficits.

b. Numbers in actuaries' memo converted to 2005 dollars using 5 percent nominal interest rate.

Economically beneficial—The plan has two features that are highly likely to increase net national saving. First, all projected future Social Security surpluses and all net new revenues are invested in personal accounts rather than the Social Security trust funds. Historically, it appears that when the Social Security system has been in surplus, the expenditures on non-Social Security programs have increased or tax cuts have been implemented to absorb the funds. Certainly, that is the case now, with an explicit deficit reduction plan that ignores the distinction between Social Security and other revenues. Second, the plan does not rely on borrowing to fund the personal accounts. Borrowing to fund accounts will not in general raise national saving. The plan also raises revenue in a relatively non-distortionary way: the individual worker contributions are deposited directly into the worker's personal retirement account.

Good for future generations—By phasing in policy changes more quickly than most other plans, the LMS plan spreads the costs across more generations, thereby decreasing the burden any one generation must bear. Also, by prefunding the Social Security system in an economically meaningful way, future generations would expect to see higher real wages due to the increase in the capital stock. The prefunding of accounts also helps to preclude the need to increase the current 12.4 percent payroll by up to

6 percentage points, as would be the case if the system remained pay-as-you-go at currently projected replacement rates.

Balanced compromise—The plan represents a number of balanced compromises on issues of solvency, adequacy, and funding. These compromises show that while differences exist, there is a range of Social Security reform options that can receive support across the political spectrum. Key differences—over things like the relative amount of taxes and benefits and about the amount of choice people should have in making their investments—are along a continuum and can be resolved through compromise.

Notes

1. The payroll base for this calculation is the currently scheduled one, not the expanded one described below. Note also that these cuts to the traditional benefit are deeper than those required to bring the pay-as-you-go system into balance since revenue under the status quo includes both payroll tax revenue and revenue from the taxation of Social Security benefits.

2. These benefit reductions refer to *traditional* benefits only; they do not reflect the level of *total* benefits, which would be larger due to the combination of traditional benefits and the personal accounts.

3. We recognize that the choice of an EEA involves balancing the well-being of myopic individuals who claim benefits too soon (and are therefore helped by an increased EEA) against the well-being of individuals for whom it is optimal to retire before the EEA and who are liquidity constrained. 65 is the age at which benefits were first available in the first two decades of Social Security's existence, and recent research indicates that the typical 69 year old is at least as healthy as a 62 year old was in 1961—the year that men first became eligible for Social Security benefits. Therefore, we believe an increase in the EEA is likely to result in a net increase in well-being.

4. Our objective in raising the taxable maximum is to bring more revenue into the system in a way that reflects ability to pay. An alternative to raising the cap would be to tax all earnings above the cap at a lower rate—or to do some combination such as raising the cap (but not all the way to 90 percent of earnings) and then taxing earnings above the new cap at a lower rate. All three of us would be comfortable with any of these alternatives.

Jeffrey Liebman is Professor of Public Policy at Harvard University. From 1998 to 1999, he was Special Assistant to President Clinton for economic policy and coordinated the Clinton Administration's Social Security reform technical working group. Maya MacGuineas is Director of the Fiscal Policy Program at the New America Foundation. She was a Social Security adviser to Senator McCain during the 2000 presidential campaign. Andrew Samwick is Professor of Economics and Director of the Nelson A. Rockefeller Center for Public Policy at Dartmouth College. From 2003 to 2004, he was Chief Economist on the staff of President Bush's Council of Economic Advisers, where his responsibilities included Social Security.

AARP and Social Security: A Background Briefing

by AARP

Social Security is the most successful program in our country's history. People look upon it as a promise—without an expiration date—that our nation has made to America's workers, their families, and to our retirees.

History. The promise of a small measure of economic security at the end of one's working days came about during a time of deep and unanticipated economic downturn of historic proportions. Even many able-bodied workers could find no employment. As a result, some guaranteed replacement of at least a portion of income for those who had spent 30 or 40 years laboring seemed imperative. If we as a nation could not maintain the dignity and independence of our elder generation of lifelong workers, the very ideals of this country were at risk. And so, Social Security was born.

The program has been periodically re-tuned as the workforce and work skills have changed. Yet, its administrative expenses remain the lowest of any government program—less than 1%. While the program insures families against loss of their breadwinner throughout life, Social Security also has proven to help millions of older Americans maintain their standard of living in retirement.

Today. Social Security is financially strong now and in no danger of "going broke" anytime in the next couple of decades. However, it is true that the program is in need of long-term measures to keep it in fiscal balance so that it will be able to pay full benefits to every generation of Americans. The changes do not have to be drastic, as examples of solvency options will show. However, the longer we wait to adjust the system, the more difficult the adjustments. That is why it is advisable to act sooner rather than later.

One of four pillars. Social Security is only part of the overall retirement security structure. A secure retirement is supported by four pillars: 1) Social Security, 2) pension and savings, 3) continued earnings, and 4) adequate and affordable health insurance. In that context, the importance of Social Security today is evident as each of the other pillars faces mounting pressures.

(updated March 24, 2005; available at http://assets.aarp.org/www.aarp.org_/articles/presscenter/pdf/SocialSecurityBackgroundBriefing.pdf; used with permission)

Only half of working Americans have a pension plan available at their workplace, so millions of private sector workers have no regular payroll deduction mechanism to save for their future. Traditional defined-benefit pensions are disappearing. Many companies that do offer pensions are converting to defined-contribution plans [such as 401(k) plans], making workers absorb more risk. The defined-contribution plans are subject to early withdrawals, poor investment decisions, and the fact that most pensioners fail to annuitize their balance upon retirement. So even if a worker has contributed to a retirement savings plan, it is likely to provide for a much less adequate retirement income level than defined-benefit pensions.

Personal savings are at an all-time low according to Federal Reserve figures, and personal debt at an all-time high. Only a little over half of U.S. families own any tax-favored retirement account,[1] and the median value is $29,000. In contrast to previous generations who owned their homes free and clear by the time of retirement, many boomers may retire with substantial mortgages. Boomer median financial assets, excluding home equity, totaled $51,000 according to latest available figures.[2] Many report that they are planning to work in retirement. However, the job market for older workers is difficult for most without recent training and current skills, and age discrimination is still prevalent in the hiring process.

Rising health care costs also put strain on the goal of economic security. As health care expenses go up at almost double digits annually, insurers are reducing offerings, raising prices and shifting costs. Employers are cutting back on employee health benefits and retiree health benefits alike. So retirees are paying larger and larger portions of their post-work income for health care. Even with Medicare eligibility, millions of older Americans are spending a third or more of their retirement income for health care.

The average American today will need to work longer before retiring in order to educate the kids, possibly assist elderly parents, save adequately for retirement without supplemental defined benefits from a company pension to count on, and meet ever-rising out-of-pocket health care costs. Since other pillars are under so much pressure, the need to strengthen Social Security is all the more important.

Who participates in Social Security?

About 96% of all workers contribute to Social Security. Workers pay 6.2% of their earned income into Social Security, matched equally by 6.2 % from their employers. The highest wage earners do not pay in to Social Security on the portion of their salary over the "taxable maximum." This figure is adjusted annually by formula and is $90,000 in the year 2005.

Those who contribute for 40 quarters will earn retirement benefits. Today, approximately 47 million receive Social Security benefits. About 6% of beneficiaries are non-working married partners (mostly wives) whose payments are based on their spouses' earning record. Close to 19% of annual payments go to widows and widowers (and children) of deceased workers combined. Over 13% is paid to workers disabled during their work years. The remaining (less than 63%) goes to retired workers, beginning on a date of their choosing, but after age 62.

For the majority of Americans—that is, for *two-thirds* of current and future retirees, Social Security is, or will be, the largest part of their income in retirement.

Adequacy

The key measure of adequacy is the "Income Replacement Rate." Social Security is designed to favor the lower-wage worker, who might not have as much opportunity to save over a long worklife at the lower end of the wage scale. The Social Security

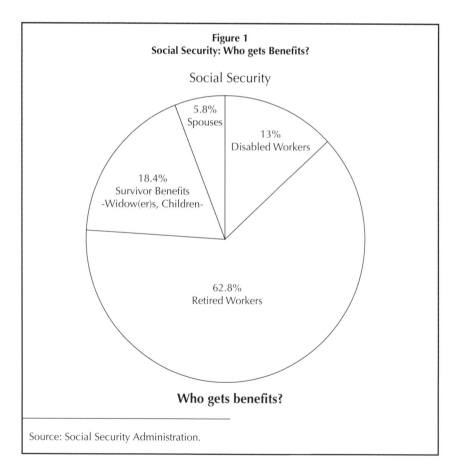

Figure 1
Social Security: Who gets Benefits?

Social Security

5.8%
Spouses

13%
Disabled Workers

18.4%
Survivor Benefits
-Widow(er)s, Children-

62.8%
Retired Workers

Who gets benefits?

Source: Social Security Administration.

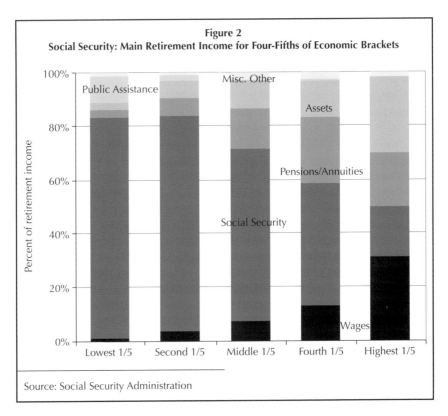

Figure 2
Social Security: Main Retirement Income for Four-Fifths of Economic Brackets

Source: Social Security Administration

benefit formula ensures lower-wage workers receive a higher wage replacement rate relative to their earnings so that their benefit might be more adequate.

Rate of Replacement:[3]

• 53.6% of low-wage workers' earnings replaced

• 39.9% of average-wage workers' earnings replaced

• 32.5% of high-wage workers' earnings replaced

• 24.8% of earnings replaced for those with consistent max-taxable-and-above wages.

Any changes to Social Security's formulas must recognize the goal of adequacy. Changes must ensure that, both by initial payment level and by cost-of-living adjustments, the adequacy of Social Security as a partial replacement for pre-retirement income is maintained.

Average Social Security Benefit, January 2005:

• Retired worker—$955

• Retired couple, both workers—$1,574

• Widow(er) with two children—$1,979

• Widow(er) of retired worker—$920

• Disabled Worker—$895.

Fairness

In an increasingly diverse nation where opportunities in the labor market have not been equally distributed in the past, another duty of those who would change the system is to promote fairness. African-American and Hispanic workers make up a disproportionate segment of the nation's low and moderate wage earners. At present, the Social Security benefit formula ensures some fairness in that all lower-wage workers receive a higher percentage replacement of salary in retirement relative to their lifetime earnings.

Life-expectancy *at birth* is still significantly lower for males of these groups. A shorter life span means a person contributes to Social Security without receiving as many years of retirement benefits. So the lower life-expectancy has sometimes been used to show lower-wage earners potentially contribute more than they draw out. However, life expectancy *at 65* is only a little over a year's difference and the gap is closing. A further balancing factor, in terms of distribution of funds, is that a higher percentage of low-wage workers draw disability benefits and a higher percentage of their families draw survivor benefits.

Women's equity issues. Women, too, are concentrated in low-wage work on average. Their median salary is $531 a week compared to $685 a week for men. In other words, women are paid about 78% of what men are paid, a figure which unfortunately tends to stand over a lifetime. For *one of every four* unmarried women over 75, their only source of income is their Social Security check. Since women tend to live longer, a Cost of Living Adjustment (COLA) calculated on the Consumer Price Index year after year is crucial to keep these lone former workers from falling into poverty as they age. Women (and men) who have been married to other workers get the higher of either benefits accruing (as spouses) from their partner's work record or their own work earnings, but not both.

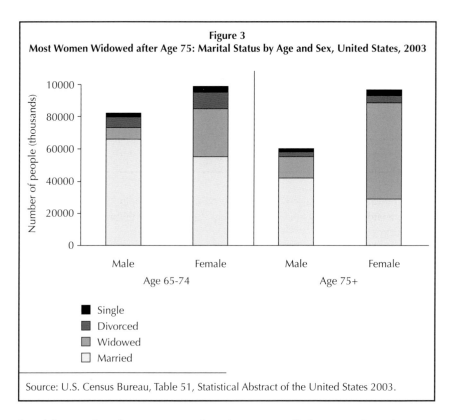

Figure 3
Most Women Widowed after Age 75: Marital Status by Age and Sex, United States, 2003

Source: U.S. Census Bureau, Table 51, Statistical Abstract of the United States 2003.

Social Security benefits are computed on the amount of salary earned, on the number of years workers pay in, and on age at the chosen time of retirement. The median earnings of full-time workers in 2002 were $38,884 for men and $29,680 for women—over $9,000 difference. Coupled with that, the median number of years of covered employment was 44 for men and 32 for women—12 years difference.[4] The disparity in work-years is due to the fact that many women stay out of the workforce to raise children and/or care for other family members for several years. These numbers—lower salaries combined with fewer years of work—typically result in much smaller Social Security checks for women every month the rest of their lives.

So, there are really three sets of Social Security reform issues. The first, less known and less reported, are the issues around the family structure and women in a world that now expects women both to work and to care for family—young and old. These *fairness* or equity issues arise because Social Security tracks one's link to the *paid* labor force without crediting caregiving years, which are nevertheless valuable to society. In fact *motherhood* is the single biggest risk factor for poverty in old age in the United States.[5]

Table 1 Poor and Near Poor, within 150% of Poverty, 2001		
Age	**Men**	**Women**
60-64	16%	20%
65-74	17%	24%
75+	20%	33%

Source: U.S. Census Bureau, Current Population Survey.

Issues of adequacy and solvency define the public debate today. Social Security solvency is a widely-shared goal, but approaches differ as to how best achieve that.

Solvency

Solvency is a major focus of the current reform discussion. According to the Social Security trustees, the system is out of long-range balance by about 1.92% of payroll.[6] The Congressional Budget Office (CBO) estimate is 1% of payroll. Either gap can be closed through the combination of a number of solvency options.

Since the Social Security system pays retirees, widows, orphans, and the disabled and their families each year out of the funds collected from current workers' payroll checks and some of the income taxes paid on benefits, it is sometimes referred to as a pay-as-you-go system.

Demographic changes including slower workforce growth and longer lives affect the projected annual Social Security balance sheet.

Recognizing well in advance the population bulge created when births were delayed by World War II (the phenomenon known as the baby boom), excess collections were legislated in the early '80s to create a surplus in the Social Security Trust Fund designed to meet the nation's obligations to boomers' retirement. For years, Social Security's income has exceeded its pay out, and the Trust Fund has grown, as intended.

Today's Trust Fund reserve is $1.7 trillion, and another $155 billion will be added in 2005. This surplus is invested in special U.S. Treasury bonds that currently generate almost $90 billion in interest at an average rate of 6% for the Trust Fund. These bonds are backed by the "full faith and credit of the United States." This means that the nation is fully obligated to honor them when they are redeemed.

Annual payments *into* the Trust Fund—payroll contributions and dedicated taxes—

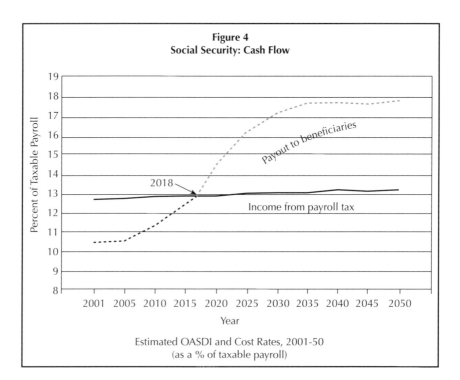

Figure 4
Social Security: Cash Flow

Estimated OASDI and Cost Rates, 2001-50
(as a % of taxable payroll)

are projected to *exceed* annual benefit payments until at least 2017. The CBO projects 2020. By then, the rising number of boomer retirees will have caused benefit payouts to rise. At that point, some of the interest that accrues each year will have to be combined with payroll taxes and income taxes to pay retirees.

The year payouts exceed income is a significant date for Social Security. It's important not because the program is in financial trouble at that point, but because the rest of the budget may be in trouble due to unsustainable fiscal policies. After more than 30 years of borrowing *from* Social Security, the U.S. Treasury will be called upon to transfer cash resources back to the Trust Fund. Right now the rest of government is borrowing more than $150 billion in revenue a year from Social Security, which the Congress is dedicating for various purposes at home and abroad.

In exchange for the borrowed funds, the Treasury promises future interest payments to the Trust Fund as well as return of principal. Right now that only requires the Treasury to pay the Trust fund in interest-earning bonds, not cash, whenever the interest is due. Yet, the Treasury will have to redeem those bonds later. It is estimated that beginning in 2017, Social Security will have to start calling upon the Treasury to make the interest payments in cash rather than bonds. That way, all Social Security benefits can be paid.

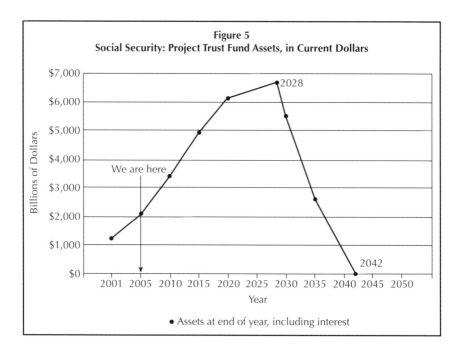

Figure 5
Social Security: Project Trust Fund Assets, in Current Dollars

• Assets at end of year, including interest

So 2017 (or 2020) is a problem not for Social Security but for the Congress. After those years, Congress must come up with the interest money the Treasury owes Social Security. Raising this money is a problem because the "unified budget" is already running large deficits—gross federal debt has increased by $1.7 *trillion* in the last four years with no sign of the trend abating. Our current fiscal policy therefore is the cause of the concern for the future of Social Security.

The situation changes again about 2027. Then, the annual payout will begin to exceed annual income plus interest earnings, and the bonds that the Trust Fund holds will need to start being redeemed. The Social Security actuaries conservatively project that the Trust Fund balance will be depleted by 2041. However, even after that date, Social Security will not be "bankrupt." *Annual collections from payroll taxes would be sufficient to pay over 74 % of promised benefits.*

The Congressional Budget Office (CBO) projects the Trust Fund will not be depleted until 2052, 11 years beyond the Social Security Administration projections. The difference is due to very small variations in economic assumptions, primarily interest rates. Differences illustrate the uncertainty of any attempt to project very far into the future.

The difference is significant because the CBO is using a very sophisticated new econometric model. Also, congressional leaders will rely on the CBO figures, not Ad-

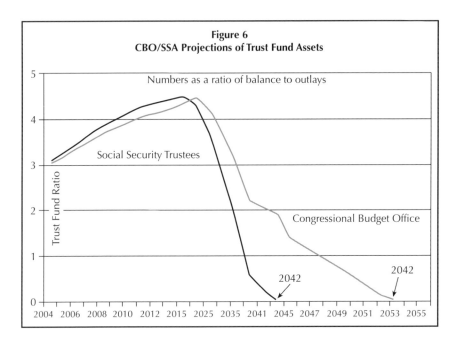

Figure 6
CBO/SSA Projections of Trust Fund Assets

Numbers as a ratio of balance to outlays

Social Security Trustees

Congressional Budget Office

Trust Fund Ratio

2042

2042

ministration figures, just as they did in the Medicare debate. Various economic and demographic assumptions plugged into the model result in a *broad range* of projected outlays and a narrower—but still significant—*range* of program income.

This serves to point out that there is not just one "solution" to Social Security's solvency. The CBO entry into the debate is also significant because the current long-term imbalance looks only half as big through the CBO lens. If the CBO projections are correct, more modest changes would be sufficient to guarantee current obligations and continuous Trust Fund solvency.

Social Security Solvency Options

There are many ways to adjust the Social Security program to achieve solvency. A number of the options presented here illustrate the range of possible changes that, taken in certain combinations, could be enacted to restore Social Security's long-term solvency. Each will be presented with: 1) current law, 2) estimated impact that passage of the measure would have on the projected Social Security shortfall after 2041 (using SSA figures as a baseline), and 3) brief acknowledgement of the arguments both for and against adopting the policy.

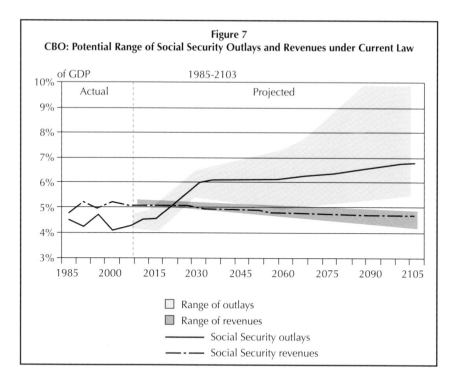

Figure 7
CBO: Potential Range of Social Security Outlays and Revenues under Current Law

Option 1. Raise Total Wage Base Taxed by Social Security to 90% of Nationwide Earnings

Under current law: About 85% of total wages nationwide are now taxed. The maximum wage subject to Social Security payments in 2005 is $90,000. (Higher salaries require no further payment into Social Security.) The proposed cap would be $140,000 phased in over 10 years.

Impact on projected shortfall: This measure would lower Social Security's projected shortfall by 43%.

Proponents point out that this would affect only a small number of workers (6%). Twenty years ago, Social Security received revenue from 90% of the total wage base paid in the U.S. However the growing gap between high and average salaries, and a slightly flawed calculation formula have dropped that figure to 85% today.

Opponents maintain that the new Social Security ceiling would be a "tax increase" for that 6% of people whose wages exceed the cap and for the businesses that employed them. So employers, especially, may object to added costs for their higher-paid employees.

Option 2. Include State and Local Government New Hires under Social Security beginning in 2005

Under current law: Approximately 95% of all jobs in the USA are now covered under Social Security. The largest exception is about 30% of state and local government workers.

Impact on projected shortfall: Lower by 9%.

Proponents point to the seamless career coverage workers would get from job to job instead of paying into a government pension system for a number of years and into Social Security for other years, thus failing to maximize retirement benefits. The disability coverage is quite a bit better under Social Security than in most state plans, and the payments for dependents and spouse in case of death much improved over state and local government pensions. In addition, few states and municipalities offer full cost-of-living adjustments, lack of which significantly reduces the value of their pensions over time. Others point out that many state and local government workers receive Social Security spousal benefits now as a result of marriage, and therefore it is only fair that they contribute. New federal employees, including Members of Congress, were brought under Social Security in 1983.

Opponents note that the positive impact on the Trust Fund for including the state and local workers diminishes over time as these new payees will eventually retire, and Social Security must meet that obligation. It is also politically unpopular since most state and local workers are opposed to the change, not realizing that for most, it would be a better and more secure retirement benefit, and provide superior insurance in the case of disability and dependent benefits, if needed.

Option 3. Raise the Social Security tax by ½ Percentage point (¼ Point each, Employer and Employee)

Under current law: The Social Security payroll tax equals 12.4% of wages. Half of this is paid by the employer, half by the employee on each salary up to $90,000. Those who are self-employed pay all 12.4.

Impact on projected shortfall: Adoption is estimated to lower Social Security's projected shortfall by 24%.

Proponents of this option point out that it is consistent with past policy: past payroll tax increases helped assure solvency. They emphasize that this option would only affect current workers, not retirees. Contribution rates would only change from 6.2 to 6.45 percent each.

Opponents fear it could have a negative impact on the creation of new jobs, and that it might reduce workers' personal savings outside of Social Security.

Option 4. Gradually Raise the Age at which One can Receive Full Benefits to 70 by 2083

Under current law: The age to collect full Social Security benefits is greater than 65 but less than 66 if a person is born between 1938 and 1943. The age is 66 if born between 1944 and 1954. The age is greater than 66 but less than 67 if born between 1955 and 1959. And for a person born in 1960 or later, the age for full benefits is 67. A person may collect *reduced* benefits anytime after age 62. Their reduction is pro-rated for the exact month their payment starts. Certain widow/widowers may collect reduced benefits at age 60.

Impact on projected shortfall: Lower by 38%.

Proponents refer to our longer projected life span, which at age 65 already has increased from 78 to 83. So increasing the number of working years in a now-longer lifetime makes sense, they say. In addition, longer work lives on the part of those already in the workforce would aid expected labor shortages.

Opponents calculate that this measure results in overall reduced benefits for *all* retirees. Extending work life has an unfair impact on those who do physical labor whose health and strength cannot endure. Coupled with this is the fact that these physical laborers are, in the main, lower-wage workers. For white collar workers, jobs for the same skill set may not exist that far into the future and career-changing later in life can be problematic, particularly for those who are *forced* to it. For every year the normal retirement age is increased, benefits are cut 7% for those retiring at the same age as before the change.

Option 5. Increase the Number of Work Years Calculated in Benefit Formulas from 35 to 38

Under current law: Social Security retirement benefits are based on a person's highest 35 contributing years. For each year less than 35, a zero is entered into the calculation.

Impact on projected shortfall: Lower by 16%.

Those who favor this policy option feel that it is logical: Since the Normal Retirement Age (NRA) has risen to 67, so the number of work years rises. It may encourage people to stay in the workforce longer. It's better than further increasing the Normal Retirement Age for all.

Those against show that such a measure equals a 3% reduction in benefits for new retirees. And it has the most impact on those with traditionally smaller wages and shorter work lives: women and low-wage workers.

Option 6. Index the Starting Benefit Level for Improvements in "Average Longevity" at 65

Under current law: With consistently growing life spans, increasing years of benefits are expected to be paid to retirees. To balance this, monthly payments could be slightly lower beginning in 2018, calculated on the basis of changes in longevity at age 65.

Impact on projected shortfall: Lower by 25%.

Proponents point out that, statistically, the actuarial total lifetime benefits would be kept equal. People will be given ample time to adjust to lower benefits expected in the future over today's retirees. This policy would act as an "automatic stabilizer" to protect the system from changes in average life spans.

Opponents show this would lower monthly benefits. Eventually, this measure lowers wage replacement rates that are so crucial to Social Security's adequacy.

Option 7. Reduce Benefits for New Retirees by 5%

Under current law: Benefits are scheduled to rise with real wages. This maintains a constant ratio to pre-retirement dollars.

Impact on projected shortfall: Lower by 26%.

Proponents show that this measure would preserve the wage-replacement "progressivity" of the benefit formula. Since the measure would not begin for 10 years and then would reduce initial benefits only 1% a year for 5 years, there would be ample time for the prospective retirement population to adjust plans to compensate for lower lifetime benefits.

Opponents point out that this measure hits low-wage earners with the least *non*-Social Security income the most. (Their total retirement income shrinks most.) It hurts the adequacy of benefits without regard to other income.

Option 8. Diversify 15% of Trust Fund Investments into a Total Market Index Fund

Under current law: Trust Fund may now be invested only in federal government-backed securities, which earn an average rate of return of 6%.

Impact on projected shortfall: Lower by 15%.

Proponents suggest that the stock market could give higher returns and that, if a portion of the Trust Fund *as a whole* were invested, the risk would be spread across the whole population and all generations. Administrative costs of this measure would be far less than for millions of personal accounts. Funds would be invested in a broad index fund (e.g., the Wilshire 5000), which invest in the entire market at very low expense.

Opponents are concerned that the U.S. Treasury, which now borrows heavily from the Social Security Trust Fund, would have to borrow more from other sources, especially foreign sources, increasing our poor economic position as a debtor nation.

Option 9. Use "Superlative" Index for Cost of Living Adjustments (COLA)
Under current law: Indexed to the Consumer Price Index (CPI) for wage earners.

Impact on projected shortfall: Lower by 14%.

Those who favor this measure maintain that the current CPI overstates price increases because people substitute products when prices increase (such as buying chicken instead of steak).

Those opposed reiterate that COLAs are *critical* to well-being of the longest-lived, especially single older women. They point out that the Bureau of Labor Statistics has already made technical calculation changes that have lowered the CPI by half a percent. A retiree with the average benefit amount of $955 per month in 2005 would loose 48 cents a month the first year, if the new index (the C-CPI-U) were just half a percent lower than the current CPI-W. The cumulative loss over 15 years would be more than $800.[7]

Option 10. Lower Benefits for Higher Wage Workers
Under Current Law: Benefits are designed to return a higher percent of pre-retirement wages to lower wage retirees than for those with higher lifetime wages.

Impact on projected shortfall: Lower by 11%.

Proponents argue that adjusting the formula further for those with higher earnings would save money without affecting lower wage workers. Higher wage workers have more opportunities to invest and save for their retirements. Further, the wages of higher paid workers have been increasing faster than those with lower paid jobs.

Opponents point out that this change lowers the "rate of return" for higher paid workers. They see a risk that many higher-income wage earners might no longer perceive Social Security to be a "good deal" for them, weakening support for the program overall among this influential community.

Criteria to Judge Options

The 10 options presented are not a comprehensive list but serve to give an idea of the range of the measures that might be adopted. Key questions in evaluating any package chosen from the options presented: Are future benefits adequate? Are costs and benefits fairly spread? Who bears what risk? Are benefits still "progressive"—that is, do benefits assist most those who have least? What is effect on public support, confidence, and understanding? Can people adjust easily to the change? How will the package or individual option affect rest of the U.S. budget?

Private Account Proposals

Although no specific, detailed solvency plan has been put forth by the Administration, most analysts assume President Bush is basing Administration proposals on "Plan 2" from the Social Security Commission's 2001 report. Key changes would include setting up a mechanism to allow workers under age 55 to transfer 4% of payroll to new individual private accounts.

The plan combines very aggressive cuts in guaranteed benefits with the creation of individual accounts designed to offset the impact of those cuts. One-third of payroll taxes (4% of 12.4%) would be diverted each year from the task of paying current retirees to funding investment accounts. Therefore, the Social Security Trust Fund's status would be made much worse. In fact the shortfall would be higher by 196%—that is, the shortfall is *quadrupled,* absent other changes.

Funded by Borrowing

Younger workers today would have to pay twice to finance this new plan. First, current benefits must continue to be paid even though there would be less revenue due to the diversion of payroll taxes into private accounts. So borrowing must take place to meet these obligations, requiring additional interest payments and potentially higher interest rates. Second then, the added debt must be paid off.

To compensate for the loss of Social Security revenue to private accounts, the federal government would have to borrow significant sums for the *next 50 years* in order to pay promised benefits. Proponents of this measure have not suggested another means of paying the estimated cost: $754 billion in the first 10 years, and $3.5 *trillion* in the following decade.

The massive borrowing by the federal government would permit individuals to invest in the stock market in the hope that the individual's investment returns will be greater than the interest cost and administrative expenses incurred. This is a form of *arbitrage,* borrowing money to invest in the hope that investment returns will exceed interest costs.

Private Accounts

The Administration has proposed a phased-in approach to establishing private accounts. The phase-in would reduce the amount of borrowing needed for the first 10 years. Beginning in 2011, workers then 54 or younger could elect to divert 4% of their Social Security contributions into one or more of five mutual funds. That year, $1000 would be the maximum contribution permitted with the annual limit increasing by $100 each year.

- Balances in worker's accounts could not be withdrawn, or borrowed against, before retirement.

- At retirement, each worker would be required to purchase (with account earnings) an annuity sufficient to bring the total annual benefit up to the poverty level.

- Any accrued balance larger than the cost of the annuity could be used for other purposes, including willed to heirs.

- The principle contributed to the private account over the years, and inflation plus a 3% imputed rate of return, would at retirement be *deducted from the guaranteed Social Security benefit*. This policy is referred to as a "clawback" to help fund solvency.

Proponents of this option believe that private accounts will earn higher returns for most individuals and promote an "ownership society."

Opponents point out that future guaranteed benefits would have to be cut deeply to finance these accounts, and that private accounts would shift risk onto the individual beneficiary, a risk not associated with Social Security now. A transition period would require heavy borrowing and additional interest obligations for taxpayers. Since small individual accounts would be expensive to administer, fees would reduce earning potential for the individual.

Solvency: Price Indexing

The Commission Plan 2 would achieve Social Security solvency solely by changing the way benefits are calculated. Workers' Social Security benefits would gradually become smaller over time by "price-indexing" initial benefit levels. Today, beginning benefit levels are calculated by indexing workers' wage histories to overall growth in wage levels. Retirees benefit from rising productivity during their worklife. Price-indexing would freeze the real value of earnings. This would result in about a 1.1% decrease in initial benefit level *per year* compounded for every year the policy is in effect. This could, in combination with the clawback just discussed, achieve solvency in the long run; however, it would do so *entirely by lowering guaranteed benefits* for future retirees.

5. *Women and Social Security: Important Issues for Financial Security of Older Americans,* presentation by Anna M. Rappaport, F.S.A, May 21, 2004, Mercer Human Resource Consulting.

6. 2005 Annual Report of the Board of Trustees of the Federal Old-Age and Survivors Insurance and Disability Insurance Trust Funds.

7. A reduction in the COLA has an impact every year, beyond the year of the reduction. Each succeeding year's benefit amount is calculated based upon the benefit amount of the prior year; thus, any COLA reduction is compounded annually into the future.

Saving Social Security (Part 2)

by Peter A. Diamond and Peter Orszag

Individual Accounts

The main lesson from our plan is that Social Security can be put on a solid financial footing for the long term without dramatically changing its current form. Instead, many recent reform plans would replace part of Social Security with individual accounts. Individual accounts, such as 401(k)s and Keoghs, already provide an extremely useful supplement to Social Security and can be improved (Munnell and Sunden, 2004; Gale and Orszag, 2003). In our view, however, individual accounts are not a desirable component of Social Security itself, especially in light of the trend in private pensions from defined benefit to defined contribution plans, which increases the correlation between the risks already being borne by workers and the risks in individual accounts.

By themselves, individual accounts do not reduce the actuarial deficit in Social Security. If financing such accounts includes diverting payroll tax revenue into individual accounts, then the immediate effect is to increase the deficit within Social Security. Individual accounts only improve the ability of Social Security to finance its traditional benefits if they are linked to reductions in traditional benefits (or increased revenues) in some way, either explicitly or implicitly. In that case, individual accounts can help reduce the projected deficit if they more than compensate for the diverted revenue. The interaction between diverted revenues and reduced benefits has two dimensions—a present value dimension and a cash-flow dimension.

To fix ideas, it is useful to consider an individual account plan that also reduces traditional benefits for accountholders so that traditional Social Security finances are unaffected in expected present value over the accountholder's lifetime. That is, a worker with an individual account is considered to owe a "debt" to the Social Security trust fund equal to the amounts diverted from the Social Security trust fund, plus the interest the trust fund would have earned on the diverted funds. Upon retirement, the debt is repaid by reducing the worker's traditional Social Security benefits. The result is no redistribution across cohorts in expectation as well as no impact on the infinite-horizon present-value of trust fund balances.[1]

(Originally published in *Journal of Economic Perspectives*, vol. 19, no. 2, Spring 2005, pp. 11-32; used with permission)

Note: This article is continued from Chapter 8, where the authors' plan for keeping Social Security is discussed. The second half of the article presented here discusses why the authors do not think Personal Accounts are a viable option.

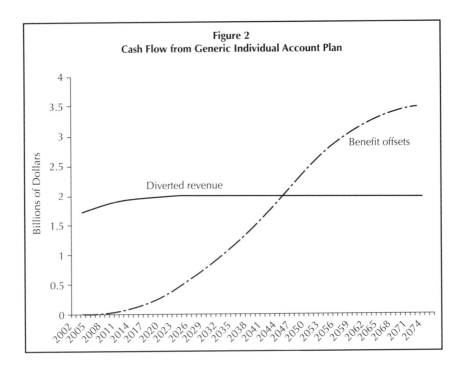

Figure 2
Cash Flow from Generic Individual Account Plan

Such accounts hold the Social Security trust fund harmless from the diversion of revenue over the lifetime of the average worker. But the timing of the cash flows out of Social Security is very different than that of the return flows. For each cohort, the flow of revenue into the individual accounts precedes by many years the offsetting reductions in traditional benefits. For example, Figure 2 shows the trust fund cash-flow effects of a plan with 2 percent of payroll diverted to individual accounts for those under age 55, with an offsetting reduction in traditional benefits upon retirement. The cash flow is negative over a period of more than 40 years.

If revenue were diverted into individual accounts, the reduced cash flow would drive the trust fund balance to exhaustion more than a decade sooner than currently projected, as shown in Figure 3. Such a diversion would require either some source of additional revenue to continue paying benefits or a reduction in concurrent benefits to offset the reduced revenue flow. Over an infinite horizon, the individual accounts have no effect on the trust fund in present value terms—the trust fund is eventually paid back in full for the diverted revenue. But the impact on the trust fund stays negative at each point in time since the trust fund has outstanding loans to individual workers.

Transition Financing
The challenge for plans with individual accounts financed out of the current payroll tax is how to restore solvency over the next 75 years given the adverse effects high-

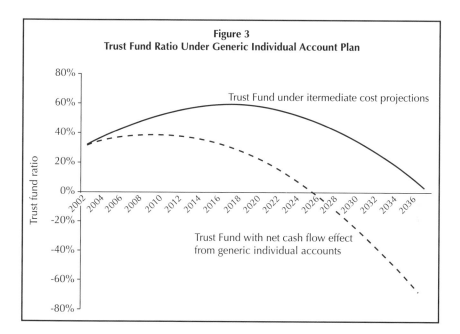

Figure 3
Trust Fund Ratio Under Generic Individual Account Plan

lighted in Figure 3. One possibility is to front-load benefit reductions significantly more than would be needed otherwise. That is, the benefit cuts in the near term would be larger, and the cuts further in the future smaller, than a pattern that restores actuarial balance without the accounts. The redistribution from older generations to younger ones inherent in such an approach may be politically difficult, however. Other approaches include raising the payroll tax or debt finance (which could result from relying on general revenues or allowing Social Security to borrow). Proposals differ in their mix of these approaches to deal with the additional financing problem triggered by the accounts.

To avoid debt financing and politically implausible benefit reductions, the payroll tax rate could be raised to finance individual accounts.[2] Politically, it may be easier to legislate an implicit tax linked to individual accounts than an explicit payroll tax increase of the same size (Gramlich, 1998), although it is difficult to know since strong backing is not currently in evidence for either approach. Our view is that the political system can provide adequate revenue increases without individual accounts and that given the shortcomings of accounts detailed below, it is worthwhile to seek a reform without them. Given a reluctance either to reduce benefits or raise taxes in time to address the financing problem highlighted above, some individual account proposals have simply assumed that the rest of the federal budget will transfer sufficient general revenue to Social Security to fill any remaining financing gap. Given the substantial deficits projected for the federal budget, any proposal for transfers that does not identify a specific funding source seems fiscally reckless. Many recent proposals are particularly problematic in this regard, since they rely on massive assumed general revenue transfers. (Some assert that the transfers will be financed by reduced government expenditures, but provide no specific mechanism for achieving the necessary reductions and thus lack credibility.) It seems most appropriate to think of such proposals as involving debt finance; to the extent of debt finance, the accounts are unlikely to raise national saving and may well reduce it.[3]

National Saving

One of several objectives in enacting Social Security reform is to raise national saving, which would increase future national income and thereby reduce the relative burden of paying future Social Security benefits. An argument often made for accumulating assets in individual accounts is that such an accumulation would represent a larger increase in national savings than would occur with the same funding channeled through the trust fund. This argument raises two questions. One is whether the argument itself is correct: whether the form in which the accumulation occurs has a substantial effect on the degree to which it increases national savings. The second question is the role that raising national saving should be given in designing Social Security policy.

Evaluating the effect of a reform plan on national saving involves the direct impact on saving from changes to benefits and revenue (assuming benefits and revenue affect only consumption), and the indirect impact of offsets to other saving within the private sector and the public sector. As with our plan, the nonaccount portion of a plan with accounts directly raises national saving by increasing revenue and/or reducing benefits compared to paying currently scheduled benefits. In contrast, individual account deposits do not directly raise national saving unless they are financed by additional front-loaded benefit reductions or revenue increases. Thus, identifying the source of the funds going into the accounts is critical for assessing the impact on national saving.

The indirect effects of reform plans on national saving are more difficult to assess. For example, individuals may increase or reduce their private saving in response to a reform. The similarity of individual accounts to private savings suggests more of a negative offset under a plan that includes such accounts.

Furthermore, if individual account balances were not required to be paid out as annuities after retirement, the result may also be less saving, since the assets in the accounts may be spent more rapidly on average than if they had been annuitized. Similarly, if preretirement access to individual accounts were allowed, saving may be reduced if some funds were consumed before retirement. Although we know of no evidence on the size of these effects, we speculate that the private-sector offset to individual accounts is plausibly larger than the same amount of funding under taken through the trust fund.

A central issue involves potential offsets within the federal budget. Indeed, those who favor individual accounts argue that policymakers seek to hit a deficit target defined solely in terms of the unified budget balance (that is, the budget including both the Social Security and non-Social Security components). If that were so, larger surpluses in the Social Security component of the budget would only trigger larger deficits in the non–Social Security component, with no net effect on the overall budget balance. Transfers to individual accounts would then increase the unified deficit and so national savings. Unfortunately, the underlying assumption about congressional behavior behind this view is not easily tested. The mere fact of deficits in the unified budget, for example, does not address the issue: The key question is whether the deficit outside Social Security is larger because of the increased Social Security surpluses, not whether the budget outside Social Security is in deficit or not.

Our interpretation of the relevant political economy is that increased Social Security surpluses (and reduced deficits) have had and will have a significant positive effect on national savings. The bottom line is that we see no reason to believe that the differential public-sector offset between a plan like ours and a plan with similar direct benefit and revenue changes that also contains individual accounts is likely to be substantial. This view is bolstered by the experience in Hungary, Poland and Sweden, where the deposits into individual accounts are treated as government revenue for budget reporting purposes. If Congress instructed the Congressional Budget Office to score deposits into individual accounts as loans rather than outlays, the effect would be that the deposits had little or no impact on the reported unified budget deficit. In addition, focus may shift back to the non–Social Security budget once Social Security is in deficit instead of surplus.

A distinct question is how much the opportunity to increase national savings should influence Social Security policy. On one hand, a wide consensus exists that current net national savings (less than 2 percent of national income in 2003) is too low. On the other hand, the federal government can increase national saving in many ways. Trading the quality of social insurance for additional savings, to the extent such a tradeoff does exist, does not seem attractive given the availability of other policy changes that can raise national savings. For example, repealing a permanent version of the 2001 and 2003 tax cuts would have a more substantial effect on the nation's fiscal imbalance than eliminating the actuarial deficit in Social Security (Auerbach, Gale and Orszag, 2004).

Rates of Return

Another argument made by some proponents of individual accounts is that the accounts would facilitate higher rates of return. This argument can be analyzed by breaking the difference between the expected rate of return on Social Security contributions and on stocks into two pieces: the expected return on Social Security contributions versus bonds, plus the expected return on bonds versus stocks (Diamond, 1999; Geanakoplos, Mitchell and Zeldes, 1998; Murphy and Welch, 1998).

The difference between the expected returns on Social Security contributions and bonds reflects the burden of the legacy debt discussed above: Social Security returns are now lower than the bond return precisely because they were higher in the past. The return on Social Security for some future generations could be raised to the bond return only by having other cohorts pay the legacy debt, which would further depress returns for the other cohorts. It is unfortunately all too common for this basic point to be obscured in analyses that simply contrast the rate of return on Social Security taxes with the rate of return on assets, which is equivalent to considering two steady-state outcomes (that is, the current system versus a system in which the legacy debt has already been fully paid off).[4] Such comparisons are sometimes followed, many pages later, with a comment or footnote about the transition cost implicit in moving from one steady state to the other and sometimes left without further explanation.

This approach provides little insight into the relevant tradeoffs. A more informative analysis would explore the implication of lower returns on taxes today (through increasing taxes or decreasing benefits) in order to have higher returns on taxes (some combination of lower taxes or higher benefits) in the future. This way of posing the question correctly focuses on the intergenerational redistributions inherent in paying off the legacy debt, rather than effectively assuming away that debt.

The second piece of the difference in returns reflects the expected return on bonds relative to stocks, which raises a broader question about how to assess the benefits of equity investments through individual accounts. The optimal portfolio for individuals fully financing their own retirement from accumulated assets is likely to include equities. For many workers, individual accounts would exist alongside investments outside Social Security. A worker who already invests in stocks and bonds outside of Social Security, perhaps through a 401(k) or IRA, will gain little or nothing from being able to invest a Social Security-linked individual retirement account in stocks, too. That is, the existing ability to adjust the overall portfolio makes the opportunity to trade bonds for stocks within Social Security of lesser value—and for some workers of no value at all. This opportunity to invest an individual account in stocks is presumably of more value to workers with little in the way of assets outside Social Security.

Furthermore, whatever the magnitude of the economic advantage of portfolio diversification, reporting the impact on a worker's lifetime utility requires at least some risk adjustment. The simplest way of doing a risk adjustment is to assume a bond rate of return on stocks, as the Congressional Budget Office has done, even though this understates the value of diversification to those with no outside assets. In the absence of a widely accepted normative calculation, this simple calculation seems more likely to be informative than the unadjusted expected value calculation that ignores the impact of portfolio risk on expected utility.[5]

The cost of financing the legacy debt and the simple risk adjustment explain the entire differential in expected rates of return between Social Security and stocks. To be sure, the simple risk adjustment is not adequate for some workers, and the legacy debt can be borne more by some generations than others. But the unadorned comparison of rates of return is fundamentally misleading and does not provide a justification for replacing part of Social Security with individual accounts.

A common rebuttal to a call to risk-adjust stock returns is that defined benefit systems are also subject to risk, as they are. But the relevant political risk for comparing alternative reform proposals is not that of the current (actuarially imbalanced) system, but rather that of a reformed system, such as the one we have proposed. It is true that even if the Social Security system achieved sustainable solvency, demographic and economic uncertainties would continue to imply a possible need to change future benefits or taxes. But plans that mix individual accounts with a large residual pay-as-you-go system would reduce this risk only marginally, while adding a substantial element of market risk. Furthermore, relying on general revenues from an unspecified source, as is commonly done in proposals for individual accounts, seems to us to result in far more political risk than is inherent in our plan.

Political Pressures and the Form of Retirement Income

Social Security's defined benefits are paid as joint-and-survivor real annuities. Thus, a worker and spouse are protected against the risks of outliving their assets or seeing them eroded by inflation during retirement. A system of individual accounts could mandate that account-holders purchase such annuities.[6] Mandatory annuitization, however, may be politically difficult to sustain over time. Indeed, one of the arguments put forth by some proponents of individual accounts is that the accounts can be bequeathed. With full annuitization, the pension dies with the annuitant; but in its absence, some individuals would likely make choices that are inconsistent with social insurance goals. Many individuals do not adequately appreciate the insurance value inherent in annuities, do not adequately value the importance of protecting a survivor and do not adequately recognize the importance of protection from inflation. In short, introducing the opportunity to avoid annuitization would undercut one of the basic principles of Social Security—to provide benefits that are protected against inflation and last as long as the beneficiary is alive. It is therefore noteworthy that the Bush administration's proposal from early 2005, like those of the President's Commission from 2001, required only partial annuitization, not full annuitization.

Another major issue involves whether workers would have preretirement access to account balances. Although many individual account plans do not allow workers any access before retirement, earlier access to the funds in individual accounts could be legislated, either at the time of their enactment or later, just as many workers today may borrow from their 401(k) accounts and penalty-free preretirement withdrawals from Individual Retirement Accounts have been expanded over time. Indeed, because of their similarity to 401(k) and other existing accounts, the political pressure to allow preretirement withdrawals from individual accounts is likely to be much greater than the pressure to allow preretirement withdrawals by reducing Social Security defined benefits. If earlier access were allowed, it would undercut another basic principle of Social Security—to preserve retirement funds until retirement.

Third, the pattern of benefits from individual accounts would likely differ from that under Social Security both within and across generations. For example, whereas the trust fund can be used to spread the risks associated with fluctuations in financial market returns across many generations, individual workers would bear these risks in a system of individual accounts. The inevitable variation in returns on portfolios means that some cohorts of workers will retire at a time when financial markets are depressed and asset values far less than they anticipated (Burtless,2001). Although traditional Social Security benefits must eventually adjust to the rates of return earned by assets in the trust fund, that adaptation can be spread out over time.

Fourth, the organization and regulation of individual accounts can affect both the quality of investment decisions and the administrative costs. Many existing investors are insufficiently diversified and trade excessively. While rules about individual account investments might prevent such behavior, without such restrictions, adding more inexperienced investors will add to the extent of this problem, and attempts to educate such workers would add greatly to administrative costs. Currently, the average charge on equity-based mutual funds is over 1 percent of assets per year. While a less costly individual account system can be designed, the question is not what might be accomplished by a good design, but rather what is likely to emerge from the political process. Individual Social Security accounts of the size generally discussed in U.S. reform proposals are small. For example, 2 percent of earnings for a worker with median Social Security earnings of about $25,000 would lead to an annual contribution in an individual account of just $500, which suggests that fixed costs per account may be substantial. In considering the impact of such annual charges, it is worth remembering that over a 40-year career, deposits are in accounts on average roughly 20 years, so the total percentage loss in accumulation by retirement is roughly 20 times the annual charges (Diamond, 1999, 2000).

More generally, any radical change in Social Security's structure would reopen largely settled questions about the broad approach through which the political process will meet a range of social insurance goals (Heclo, 1998). In short, drastic changes in Social Security would alter the political environment from one of basic agreement to one of substantial flux and uncertainty, which should concern anyone who benefits from the current structure or who is concerned about those who rely on the current structure. Indeed, the variety of rules proposed across the various individual accounts plans offered to date shows how it is hard to predict what will emerge from such proposals if and when they are enacted, much less over time as political forces evolve.

Feldstein-Samwick Proposals and Analyses

Far more individual account plans exist than we have room to discuss here. As one example, we consider the plan most recently put forth by Feldstein and Samwick (2002). Their goal is to provide expected benefits at least equal to those under current law while achieving sustainable solvency: "This paper presents several alternative social security reform options in which the projected level of benefits for every future cohort of retirees is as high as or higher than the benefits projected in current law. These future benefits can be achieved without any increase in the payroll tax or in other tax rates." We emphasize two aspects of the Feldstein-Samwick proposals: the funding mechanisms to address the combination of the existing imbalance and the financing problems caused by individual accounts, and the implicit normative analysis.

The basic Feldstein and Samwick (2002) plan diverts a matching contribution of 1.5 percent of payroll from existing payroll taxes for workers who also make a voluntary contribution of 1.5 percent of payroll to individual accounts. As we noted above (in footnote 10), the labor supply effects of such an induced voluntary contribution are similar to a 1.5 percent payroll tax increase. The benefit calculation in the plan includes the annuities financed by the voluntary portion as well as those financed by the diverted revenue.

In the Feldstein and Samwick (2002) calculations, each dollar flowing into the individual accounts is credited with a 5.5 percent real annual return, rather than the 3.0 percent real Treasury interest rate assumed by the Social Security trustees. At retirement, traditional benefits are reduced for each year of participation in the individual accounts. Since Feldstein and Samwick examine whether the expected variable annuity from individual accounts plus reduced traditional benefits are sufficient to match projected benefits under current law for each cohort, implicit in the analysis is a 100 percent "clawback" for as long as needed—that is, the calculations imply a reduction of $1 in expenditures from the trust fund for each $1 in expected benefits financed by the accounts. The plan is deemed to accomplish its goal as long as the sum of expected benefits exceeds that in current law.

Feldstein and Samwick (2002) do not adjust the account returns for risk; expected benefits, not risk-adjusted benefits, are maintained. Therefore, since the accounts are assumed to be earning 5.5 percent per year, whereas the diverted revenue costs Social Security only 3 percent per year, they effectively use the equity premium to meet their goal of financing current-law benefits. As we discussed above, a failure to risk adjust benefits for workers is an inaccurate guide to expected utilities.

Under the Feldstein and Samwick (2002) plan, payroll taxes are diverted from existing Social Security right away, while the benefit reductions occur at retirement, which leads to a significant cash-flow problem as in our example above. To cover the net cash shortfall, their basic plan transfers 1 percent of the aggregate balances in individual accounts from the rest of the budget to the Social Security trust fund. This general revenue transfer is defended on the grounds that the reform plan will raise national savings, which in turn will raise GDP and corporate profits, and so will raise corporate tax revenues.[7] That is, the plan transfers the extra corporate tax revenue that the authors believe will be associated with an increased capital stock.

We are skeptical of such "dynamic scoring," especially since it is not clear that national saving would be any higher under their plan than under alternative plans that restore actuarial balance without accounts. For policy comparisons, the same type of scoring should be done for all plans. Furthermore, the scale of the assumed transfers is noteworthy. Over 75 years, the net present value of these proposed transfers amounts to $2.4 trillion, a substantial share of the $4 trillion actuarial deficit over the same period. Another perspective on the same point is that the assumed increase in corporate taxes amounts to about 1 percent of projected GDP in 2075. Yet corporate income tax revenue in 2004 amounted to 1.6 percent of GDP, and the Congressional Budget Office projects that it will reach 1.8 percent of GDP in 2015. We are highly skeptical that either the individual account portion of the Feldstein-Samwick plan or the entire plan would lead to an increase in corporate tax revenue relative to GDP of more than half its current level.

The Feldstein and Samwick (2002) conclusion that they can raise benefits without raising taxes thus involves three critical steps. First, they undertake no risk adjustment for the effect of stock yields on benefits. Second, they ignore how induced contributions to individual accounts will function like a tax. And third, they assume a form of dynamic scoring related to higher national saving and higher corporate taxes that is implausible.

Conclusion

Social Security reform is controversial, as it should be. After all, Social Security plays a critical role in the lives of millions of Americans and in the federal budget. Moreover, reform will involve pain for some voters. Reforms to such an important program should generate political interest and debate. Yet, our plan demonstrates that Social Security can be mended without resorting to the most controversial and problematic elements like individual accounts, without accounting gimmicks, and without simply assuming the availability of funds from the rest of the budget that are not likely to be there. Moreover, rather than replacing part of Social Security with individual accounts, existing tax-preferred retirement accounts could be reformed and improved.

Notes

1.   This approach is modeled on a design put forth by the General Accounting Office (1990) in response to a request from Representative Porter and used by the Commission to Strengthen Social Security. It is also the approach proposed by the Bush administration in early 2005. We ignore the complications arising from workers who die before starting retirement benefits. The Commission proposed a system that would have subsidized the individual accounts by charging an interest rate on the amounts diverted from the trust fund) that is lower than the return the trust fund earns on its reserves. Thus, these proposals would worsen Social Security's financial status even on an infinite horizon basis. We see no reason why such a subsidy is warranted. For a further analysis of the Commission proposals, see Diamond and Orszag (2002).

The authors thank Henry Aaron, Alan Auerbach, Jeffrey Brown, Robert Cumby, William Gale, Stephen Goss, Edward Gramlich, Virginia Reno, Alicia Munnell, Peggy Musgrave, Richard Musgrave, Bernard Saffran, David Wilcox and the editors for comments and helpful discussions.

Peter A. Diamond is Institute Professor, Massachusetts Institute of Technology, Cambridge, Massachusetts. Peter R. Orszag is the Joseph A. Pechman Senior Fellow in Economic Studies, The Brookings Institution, Washington, D.C

2. Another mechanism for generating additional funds is by a matching program encouraging voluntary contributions (Feldstein and Samwick, 2002; Commission to Strengthen Social Security, 2001). Such proposals use existing tax revenues for the matching funds. Analytically, it is helpful to use a mandatory tax increase as a baseline for comparison with a matching program of the same total size. Surprisingly, to a rough approximation, a tax increase that is half the size, but available only if matched, is equivalent to the full tax in terms of its labor market effects. To be sure, the two approaches are not identical. But for the workers who do make the matching contribution, the impact on present and future consumption from an additional dollar of earnings is the same whether the program has mandated savings or a matching plan of the same aggregate size. A difference arises only for those not taking up the match, who will perceive a tax of half the size, but not an offsetting benefit increase.

3. Although debt-financed deposits do not contribute to national savings, some have argued that converting the debt implicit in the current actuarial imbalance into explicit debt is of little consequence. Especially given the projected actuarial imbalance, such a conversion does have meaning in our view: implicit debt differs from explicit debt. For example, no one has proposed renegotiating the public debt, but proposals that would decrease the implicit debt through future benefit reductions are common. Purchasers of U.S. Treasury debt, aware of this distinction, are likely to require an interest rate increase from such a conversion of implicit to explicit debt. Moreover, the level of explicit debt being regularly rolled over affects the degree of exposure to movements in bond demand, for example, from the willingness of foreign governments to purchase U.S. bonds.

4. Although the presence of taxation of capital income must be taken into account in a comprehensive analysis of the welfare implications of different reform plans, merely comparing the marginal product of capital with the implicit rate of return on taxes in a pay-as-you-go system is insufficient for reaching a normative conclusion. Even asymptotically, the social welfare optimum in an optimal taxation overlapping generations model can have a higher marginal product of capital than the growth of wages (Diamond, 1973; Erosa and Gervais, 2002). These models have no technical progress. The growth of wages from technical progress introduces an additional basis for possible deviation between these two rates in an optimum.

5. A similar concern arises with regard to how to report the impact, if any, of diversification on Social Security's finances. For example, some proposals create individual accounts but then share some of the return on stocks with the traditional Social Security system, through a so-called "clawback" mechanism. Under this mechanism, withdrawals from individual accounts upon retirement trigger reductions in Social Security benefits or other transfers back to Social Security. With such a clawback, realized returns affect not only the individual investor, but also the financial position of Social Security. Failing to risk-adjust the returns generates a political free lunch; that is, a policy of borrowing at the Treasury rate in order to invest in stocks (through individual accounts) becomes unduly attractive, even though the aggregate economic effects are small.

6. Despite the plethora of individual account proposals over the past few years, many of the details associated with how a system of individual accounts might operate in practice have not yet been resolved. A recent panel formed by the National Academy of Social Insurance (2005) has examined the practical issues associated with the pay-out stage from a system of individual accounts. The panel includes Peter Orszag.

7. The 1 percent factor is derived by Feldstein and Samwick (2002) as 80 percent (the fraction of incremental savings in corporate capital) multiplied by a 29 percent corporate tax rate multiplied by an 8.5 percent marginal return on capital, divided by half. They offer a rationale for the final division (by half): that the payroll diversion would not increase national saving, whereas all of the voluntary contribution would—or at least the deviations from these assumptions are roughly balanced.

References

Auerbach, Alan J., William G. Gale and Peter R. Orszag. 2004. "Sources of the Long-Term Fiscal Gap." Tax Notes. May 24, 103:8, pp. 1049-059.

Burtless, Gary. 2001. "Testimony Before the Subcommittee on Social Security of the House Committee on Ways and Means, Hearing on Social Security and Pension Reform: Lessons From Other Countries." July 31.

Diamond, Peter A. 1973. "Taxation and Public Production in a Growth Setting," in Models of Economic Growth. J. A. Mirrlees and N. H. Stern, eds. London: MacMillan, pp. 215-35.

Diamond, Peter A., ed. 1999. Issues in Privatizing Social Security, Report of an Expert Panel of the National Academy of Social Insurance. Cambridge: MIT Press.

Diamond, Peter A. 2000. "Administrative Costs and Equilibrium Charges with Individual Accounts," in Administrative Costs and Social Security Privatization. John Shoven, ed. Chicago: University of Chicago Press, chapter 4.

Diamond, Peter A. and Peter R. Orszag. 2002. "An Assessment of the Proposals of the President's Commission to Strengthen Social Security." Contributions to Economic Analysis and Policy. 1:1, Article 10.

Diamond, Peter A. and Peter R. Orszag. 2004. Saving Social Security: A Balanced Approach. Washington: Brookings Institution Press.

Elo, Irma and Kirsten P. Smith. 2003. "Trends in Educational Differentials in Mortality in the United States." Presented at the Annual Meeting of the Population Association of America, May. Erosa, Andres and Martin Gervais. 2002. "Optimal Taxation in Life-Cycle Economies." Journal of Economic Theory. 105:2, pp. 338-69.

Favreault, Melissa M., Frank J. Sammartino and C. Eugene Steuerle. 2002. "Social Security Benefits for Spouses and Survivors: Options for Change," in Social Security and the Family. Melissa M. Favreault, Frank J. Sammartino and C. Eugene Steuerle, eds. Washington: Urban Institute Press, pp. 177-228.

Feldstein, Martin and Andrew Samwick. 2002. "Potential Paths of Social Security Reform," in Tax Policy and the Economy 2002, Volume 16. James Poterba, ed. Cambridge: MIT Press, pp. 181-224; Also available as NBER Working Paper No. 8592 2001.

Gale, William G. and Peter R. Orszag. 2003. "Private Pensions: Issues and Options," in Agenda for the Nation. Henry J. Aaron, James M. Lindsay and Pietro S. Nivola, eds. Washington: Brookings Institution Press, pp. 183-216.

Geanakoplos, John, Olivia S. Mitchell and Stephen P. Zeldes. 1998. "Would a Privatized Social Security Really Pay a Higher Rate of Return?" in Framing the Social Security Debate. R. Douglas Arnold, Michael J. Graetz and Alicia H. Munnell, eds. Washington: National Academy of Social Insurance, pp. 137-57.

General Accounting Office. 1990. "Social Security: Analysis of a Proposal to Privatize Trust Fund Reserves." GAO/HRD-91-22, December 12.

Gramlich, Edward. 1998. Is It Time to Reform Social Security? Ann Arbor: University of Michigan Press.

Heclo, Hugh. 1998. "A Political Science Perspective on Social Security Reform," in Framing the Social Security Debate. R. Douglas Arnold, Michael J. Graetz and Alicia H. Munnell, eds. Washington: National Academy of Social Insurance, pp. 65-93.

Holden, Karen and Cathleen Zick. 1998. "Insuring against the Consequences of Widowhood in a Reformed Social Security System," in Framing the Social Security Debate: Values, Politics, and Economics. R. Douglas Arnold, Michael J. Graetz and Alicia H. Munnell, eds. Washington: National Academy of Social Insurance, pp. 157-81.

Leimer, Dean R. 1994. "Cohort Specific Measures of Lifetime New Social Security Transfers." Social Security Administration, Office of Research and Statistics Working Paper No. 59, February.

Light, Paul C. 1985. Artful Work: The Politics of Social Security Reform. New York: Random House. Martin, Teran and Paul S. Davies. 2003-2004. "Changes in the Demographic and Economic Characteristics of SSI and DI Beneficiaries between 1984 and 1999." Social Security Bulletin. 65:2, pp. 1-13.

Munnell, Alicia. 2003. "The Declining Role of Social Security." Boston College Center for Retirement Research. Just the Facts #6. February. Munnell, Alicia and Annika Sunden. 2004. Coming up Short: the Challenge of 401(k) Plans. Washington: Brookings Institution Press.

Murphy, Kevin and Finis Welch. 1998. "Perspectives on the Social Security Crisis and Proposed Solutions." American Economic Review. May, 88:2, pp. 142-50.

National Academy of Social Insurance. 2005. Uncharted Waters: Paying Benefits from Individual Accounts in Federal Retirement Policy. January; Available at http://www.nasi.org.

President's Commission to Strengthen Social Security. 2001. Strengthening Social Security and Creating Personal Wealth for All Americans: Final Report of the President's Commission to Strengthen Social Security. December 21.

Sandell, Steven H., Howard M. Iams and Daniel Fanaras. 1999. "The Distributional Effects of Changing the Averaging Period and Minimum Benefit Provisions." Social Security Bulletin. 62:2, pp. 4-13

Myths and Realities about Social Security and Privatization

by the National Committee to Preserve Social Security and Medicare

Myths and Realities about Social Security and Privatization

For 70 years the Social Security program has been protecting Americans against the loss of income due to retirement, death or disability. Over 154 million workers and their families are covered by their contributions to Social Security, and nearly 48 million Americans currently receive Social Security benefits.

Social Security is an enormously successful program which is essential to the retirement security of the vast majority of Americans. Social Security is the single largest source of retirement income. Two-thirds of Social Security beneficiaries receive over half their income from Social Security. For nearly 20 percent of retirees, Social Security is their only source of income. Without Social Security, nearly half of the elderly would fall into poverty. Social Security provides a sound, basic income that lasts as long as you live.

Despite Social Security's continuing successes, the program is under attack by those who would like to privatize it. President Bush has said that he wishes to divert money away from Social Security into private investment accounts. Young workers are intrigued by the idea of diverting their payroll taxes into Wall Street accounts. Proponents of privatization promise ownership of accounts and big investment returns.

They argue that Social Security is in a deep and immediate financial crisis that cannot be resolved without dismantling Social Security and converting it into a system of market-based individual investment. To support their arguments, proponents of privatization have used misleading arguments about the nature of Social Security, the crisis facing it, and the value of converting Social Security to private investment accounts. Here are some of the myths and realties surrounding the Social Security debate.

Myths and Realities

Myth 1: Privatization is a plan to save Social Security.

Reality: Privatization isn't a plan to save Social Security. It is a plan to dismantle Social Security. Private accounts do nothing to address Social Security solvency. In fact, because private accounts are financed by taking money out of Social Security, privatization actually increases Social Security's funding gap and moves forward the date

---

{First part on Social Security myths available at http://www.ncpssm.org/news/archive/myths; 2006; second part on women's issues available at http://www.ncpssm.org/news/archive/womenSSQA, 2004; used with permission)

of its insolvency from 2040 to 2030. The plan proposed by President Bush, which would divert two-thirds of the current employee-paid Social Security tax into private accounts, would cause an almost immediate cash-flow problem for Social Security.

Myth 2: Returns from private accounts will make up for the cuts in Social Security benefits.

Reality: Privatization results in huge cuts in Social Security benefits with no guarantee that private investment can replace lost benefits. The privatization plan favored by President Bush, known as the "price-indexing" plan, would reduce guaranteed Social Security benefits over time by nearly 50 percent, *even for those people who do not choose a private account.* For those who opt for a private account, benefits would be reduced even further. Under the President's plan, an individual's already-reduced Social Security benefit would be cut by one dollar for every dollar that he or she has saved in the private account up to a limit specified in law. The Center on Budget and Policy Priorities has calculated that an average-earning individual, who chooses to keep his or her private account assets in a safe investment, earning the same return as U. S. Treasury Securities, will find that his or her Social Security benefit has been reduced to nearly zero. As a consequence, that individual will have almost none of the special protections afforded by traditional benefits. Moreover, his or her total income, consisting almost entirely of proceeds from the private account, would be 50 percent below currently-scheduled Social Security benefits.

Myth 3: Private account assets can be passed along to one's heirs.

Reality: Privatization leaves little to be passed on to one's heirs. The President's plan would force account holders, upon retirement, to use the assets in their private accounts to purchase an annuity sufficient to raise their total remaining Social Security benefits and monthly annuity payments to a poverty level income. The remaining assets in the account could then be used during retirement to make up for the plan's huge cuts in Social Security benefits. Only the excess after required annuitization and after expenses of retirement would be available to pass on to one's heirs. This is likely to amount to very little.

Myth 4: Private accounts are voluntary.

Reality: Private accounts may be voluntary, but the cuts are not. Even for those people who choose not to participate in a private account, Social Security benefits would be cut nearly in half. Under the plan favored by the President, known as the "price-indexing" plan, cuts in benefits would be considerably larger than necessary to solve Social Security's financing problem. Those cuts would effectively transfer money from those who opt out of accounts to those who opt in, forcing workers who decide against exposing themselves to the risks of Wall Street to subsidize those who are more willing to gamble with their retirement.

Myth 5: Privatization will exempt retirees and near retirees.

Reality: Retirees and near retirees should not count on being exempt. Because privatization diverts two-thirds of the employee-paid Social Security tax away from Social Security and into private accounts, Social Security's financial status is worsened and benefits for every retiree are threatened. In order to continue to pay benefits to retirees, privatization plans must borrow trillions of dollars over several decades from the general fund of the Treasury, causing an already huge federal deficit to balloon. This will increase the debt burden on all Americans, forcing policy makers to consider cuts in all federal programs, including Social Security.

Myth 6: Younger workers will receive a higher rate of return under a privatized system.

Reality: Younger workers will receive a lower rate of return under privatization than they will under Social Security. That is because younger workers will have to pay twice—once to fund the benefits of current retirees under Social Security's pay-as-you go system and a second time to fund their own individual accounts. The Congressional Budget Office concluded in a recent study that the costs of the transition to a privatized, prefunded system would reduce the rate of return on today's young people, the transitional generation, to a level *lower* than the rate of return on Social Security.

Myth 7: Private accounts will cost only about $750 billion in the first 10 years.

Reality: Private accounts will increase the national debt by nearly $5 trillion in the first 20 years after full implementation, and costs will continue to grow thereafter. The 10-year costs of the President's private accounts are misleading because those accounts are not fully phased in until 2011. According to the Center on Budget and Policy Priorities, private accounts will increase the national debt by nearly $5 trillion in the first 20 years after full implementation. In about 50 years, costs will reach nearly 30 percent of GDP and will remain at that level for the full 75-year projection period.

Myth 8: The cost of fixing Social Security is over $11 trillion.

Reality: According to the Social Security actuaries, the 75-year cost of fixing Social Security is estimated to be $4.6 trillion (in present value). Some proponents of privatization set the cost of financing Social Security at $13.4 trillion. However, this figure is the liability of the system into infinity. It includes the costs of not just the baby boom generation, but everyone alive today and people not yet born.

The Realities about Social Security's Solvency

Social Security is a successful program that will be able to pay benefits for decades to come. This year Social Security has an accumulated surplus of over $1.9 trillion. By 2015, that surplus will be over $3.9 trillion or more than four times the amount needed to pay benefits in that year. While payments from Social Security will begin to exceed Social Security tax revenues in about 2017, Social Security will have sufficient reserves to pay benefits until 2040. Even after 2040, Social Security will have enough money to pay nearly 74 percent of the benefits owed, according to the Social Security actuaries.

The Congressional Budget Office has concluded that Social Security will be solvent even longer, through 2052, and will be able to pay nearly 80 percent of benefits thereafter. Moreover, Social Security money is held in the safest investment available—U.S. government securities. Those securities are legal obligations of the U.S. to pay principal and interest to the holder of the bonds. The securities have the same status as U.S. government bonds held by any other investor, including individual Americans and pension funds, and the Social Security Trust Fund has a legal obligation to pay full benefits as long as it has the funds to do so.

Conclusion

Many myths and misconceptions have contributed to the belief that Social Security is in imminent danger and that Social Security privatization is the answer. Nothing could be further from the truth. The reality is that Social Security will continue to provide millions of retirees a sound, stable retirement. It may require some modest adjustments over a period of time, but it does not face an insurmountable crisis requiring major structural changes. Privatization, on the other hand, will unravel Social Security's important insurance protections, force huge cuts in benefits, increase risks to retirees, and cost trillions of dollars. Social Security has been providing Americans a secure retirement for nearly three quarters of a century. With sensible action it can continue to provide that security for decades to come.

Questions and Answers on Women and Social Security Privatization

Why is Social Security so Important to Women?
The answer is simple. Women live longer than men. On average, women today who reach 65 outlive men by 4 years. That is, women can expect to live to age 85, while men are likely to live to age 81. We just have to look around us for evidence of women's longevity. Nursing homes are predominately filled with women. In fact, among people 85 years and over, over 70% are women. For most women, Social Security is their bedrock.

What are the Protections that Social Security offers Women?

Social Security has two protections that are particularly important to women. First, Social Security has a benefit that lasts as long as you live. Second, it has a cost-of-living adjustment to protect against increases in the prices of the things you buy. If your income does not keep up with prices, you will become poorer and poorer with each passing year. Women can count on these two features of Social Security to protect them, regardless of their longevity.

Don't Women Have Pensions and Other Savings to Protect Them?

No. Women are less likely to have an employer pension than are men. According to the Institute for Women's Policy Research, only 38% of women today participate in an employer pension plan compared to 51% of men. Moreover, when a woman does have a pension, it is likely to be smaller than a man's. Among today's retirees, the average private pension benefit for women is less than half the amount it is for men.

Why are Women Less Likely to Have a Pension and Other Savings?

Women who are employed full-time earn 25% less than men. In addition, women are more likely to have low-wage part-time jobs or to take time out of the workforce to care for their children. The typical woman is in the workforce for 32 years, compared to 44 years for men. This shorter work history combined with lower wages means that the lifetime earnings for women are on average lower than for men.

Does the Reduced Pension Income Mean that Women are More Reliant on Social Security than Men are?

Yes. Nearly two-thirds of all Social Security retirees are reliant on their Social Security benefits for most of their income. This includes both men and women. The statistics do not tell us how many women rely on Social Security for most of their income, but we can guess from what we know about the lack of pension income and other savings for women that women are more reliant on Social Security than are men.

Would Privatizing Social Security Hurt Women?

Yes. Privatizing Social Security would replace traditional Social Security benefits with individual investment accounts. Under most privatization plans, only a minimal Social Security benefit would remain. The size of the individual's retirement nest egg would depend on the success of his or her investments. The two longevity protections of Social Security—the cost-of-living adjustment and the guarantee that your retirement income will last as long as you do—would nearly disappear.

Could you Outlive your Retirement Assets under Privatization?

Yes. Under privatization, each individual is responsible for deciding how to parcel out funds from the individual account over his or her own lifetime. If the individual makes a bad guess about longevity, his or her money may run out. Likewise, if the individual has unforeseen expenses or if the prices of everyday purchases rise faster than expected, his or her assets may be depleted.

Could you Purchase an Annuity to Avoid the Risk of Outliving your Assets?
Yes, but it would reduce your nest egg. You could use the money in your account to purchase an annuity. Then, the company from which you purchase the annuity, such as an insurance company, would bear the risk of how long you might live. The insurer would be willing to bear this risk because it employs actuaries, who know a lot about life expectancy. Moreover, the insurer would reduce its risk by including you in a pool of all the people it insures. However, the company would charge you a fee for taking the risk, and you would then have less money in retirement.

What About Being Able to Inherit Your Husband's Account? Wouldn't That Help You?
Maybe. You could inherit whatever funds your husband had not used before he died. However, his fund might have been depleted for many reasons, including an inaccurate guess about his own longevity; increased family expenses; or the cost of his last illness. There is no guarantee that your husband's account would have any assets remaining to pass to you.

The National Committee is a nonprofit, nonpartisan organization that acts in the interests of its membership through advocacy, education, services, grassroots efforts and the leadership of the board of directors and professional staff. The work of the National Committee is directed toward developing a secure retirement for all Americans.

Why the President's Social Security Proposals Could Ultimately Lead to the Unraveling of Social Security

by Jason Furman, Robert Greenstein, and Gene Sperling

Summary

President Bush has now endorsed a combination of "progressive price indexing," a change in the Social Security benefit structure proposed by investment executive Robert Pozen, and private accounts carved out of Social Security. This combination spells danger for the future of the Social Security system.

Proponents of progressive price indexing present it as a way to protect low-income workers from Social Security benefit cuts and to moderate the effects on middle-income workers, while reducing benefits most for high-income workers. Careful examination suggests, however, that the combination of progressive price indexing and the private accounts that President Bush has proposed would pose serious risks to all workers, because such a package could put Social Security on a path likely to weaken support greatly for Social Security over time.

To be sure, making the Social Security benefit structure somewhat more progressive is desirable, although doing so creates some political risk for the program. But when progressive price indexing is coupled with the President's private accounts, the political risk escalates sharply, because middle-income as well as more affluent workers would eventually get *only a tiny Social Security check—or no check at all*—despite having paid considerable payroll taxes into the Social Security system.

- **Progressive price indexing** represents a large benefit cut. While the deepest benefit reductions would fall on those with earnings at or above the Social Security payroll tax cap (now $90,000 a year), workers who earn much less than that would face very substantial benefit reductions as well.

  - A medium earner (one who earns $36,600 today) retiring in 2055 would face a 21 percent reduction in his or her Social Security benefits (relative to the current benefit structure).

  - A worker who earns 60 percent above the average wage—about $59,000 today—and retires in 2055 would face a 31 percent benefit cut.[1] (These figures

(report published May 2, 2005, by the Center on Budget and Policy Priorities; available at http://www.cbpp.org/5-2-05socsec2.htm; used with permission) are based on the Social Security actuaries' analysis of the progressive price indexing proposal.)

- For those retiring in subsequent years, the benefit reductions would be significantly larger.

The benefit cuts would be this large because progressive price indexing is designed to reduce benefits enough to close 70 percent of Social Security's 75-year funding gap by itself. Plans that include progressive price indexing thus rely heavily on benefit reductions to restore Social Security solvency, rather than on a balanced mix of benefit reductions and revenue increases as was done in 1983.

- **Under the private accounts that the President has proposed,** the cost of the accounts would be offset by reducing the Social Security benefits of those electing the accounts. For every dollar in payroll taxes that a worker diverted from Social Security to an account, the worker's Social Security benefits would be cut a dollar

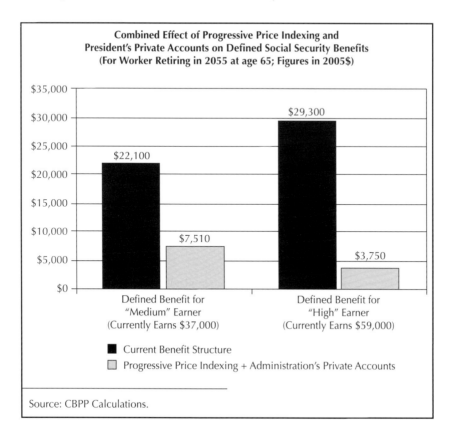

Combined Effect of Progressive Price Indexing and President's Private Accounts on Defined Social Security Benefits (For Worker Retiring in 2055 at age 65; Figures in 2005$)

Source: CBPP Calculations.

plus an interest charge equal to three percent above inflation. Thus, under the proposal to combine progressive price indexing with private accounts, Social Security benefits would be lowered twice—once due to the indexing changes, and a second time to pay for the private accounts.

• The result would be that *millions of middle-income workers would receive little or no Social Security benefits in retirement.* They would largely be left with only their private account.

• For a medium earner who retired in 2055, the defined Social Security benefit would be reduced by 66 percent—from $22,100 a year to $7,510 (in 2005 dollars).

• For a worker who earns 60 percent above the average wage (about $59,000 today), the reduction in Social Security benefits would be 87 percent—from $29,300 a year to $3,750 (in 2005 dollars), or a reduction of more than $25,000 a year. (See graph above and Table 1.)

• As noted, the reductions in Social Security benefits would grow still deeper in subsequent years. For a worker earning 60 percent above the average wage who retired in 2075, the reduction in defined Social Security benefits would be 97 percent. (See Table 2.)

• Furthermore, *these figures reflect Social Security benefits before Medicare premiums are subtracted.* Medicare premiums are collected by being deducted from Social Security checks. Since Medicare premiums grow at the rate of health care costs, which is faster than either prices or wages, they will consume a steadily increasing share of Social Security benefits over time.

• For many middle-income workers, Medicare premiums would consume *most or all* of the very small monthly Social Security benefit that would remain under the combination of progressive price indexing and the President's private accounts. Social Security checks for millions of ordinary American workers would be close to or at zero.

If this occurred, the stage would be set for advocacy campaigns to be mounted calling for private accounts to be expanded and to replace much or all of what remained of Social Security. After all, workers would appear to have placed 8.4 percent of their wages in Social Security but to be receiving little or nothing in return. The miniscule Social Security benefits that many workers would receive under the combination of progressive indexing and private accounts would almost surely be seized upon by some on the political right to argue that Social Security had become a terrible deal for American workers and that workers would benefit greatly from converting much or all of what remained of Social Security to private accounts.

Stated another way, the combination of progressive price indexing and carve-out private accounts would likely lead millions of Americans to undervalue Social Security (and to overvalue their private accounts). Their private account might lose money for them; for many workers, the accounts might earn less than the amount that their Social Security benefits would be reduced to offset the cost of the accounts. But people nevertheless could *appear* to be getting more for the four percent of their wages placed in their accounts than for the 8.4 percent that went to Social Security, especially if they never became disabled and did not need Social Security disability benefits.

Progressive price indexing presents one other serious problem, as well: it is unsound economics. It cuts Social Security benefits (relative to the current benefit structure) by the degree to which wages outpace inflation. As a result, *the more that real wages grow, the deeper the reduction in Social Security benefits would be*. If the economy performed *better* in future decades than is currently forecast, the Social Security benefit cuts would be *larger* even though the stronger economic growth would cause the Social Security shortfall to become *smaller*. The Congressional Research Service recently took note of this serious design flaw in the proposal in an analysis of progressive price indexing, in which CRS stated: "Thus, somewhat paradoxically, if real wages rise *faster* than projected, price indexing [either full price-indexing or progressive price-indexing] would result in *deeper* benefit cuts, even as Social Security's unfunded 75 liability would be shrinking."[2] For each dollar such workers divert to new private accounts, their Social Security benefits would be cut one dollar plus an interest charge equal to three percent above inflation.

The President's Proposal: Progressive Price Indexing and Carve-out Private Accounts

The private accounts that President Bush has proposed would be financed by additional benefit reductions in Social Security for those who elect the private accounts. For each dollar in payroll taxes that workers directed to private accounts, their Social Security benefits would be cut by a dollar plus an interest charge equal to 3 percent above inflation. If progressive price indexing is included in a Social Security plan alongside private accounts of this nature, Social Security benefits thus will be cut twice for workers who elect the accounts, other than people in the bottom 30 percent of the wage distribution (who would not be affected by progressive price indexing).

The combined effect of these two benefit reductions would be dramatic, and not just for high-income workers. Tables 1 and 2 show the level of Social Security benefits under: 1) the current benefit structure; 2) progressive price indexing; and 3) progressive price indexing combined with private accounts structured as President Bush has proposed.

Table 1 shows the effects on workers who are 15 years old today and retire at age 65 in 2055. As the table shows, with progressive price indexing and the President's

Table 1
Annual Social Security Benefit For Workers Retiring in 2055
(Benefits in 2005 dollars, does not include the value of private accounts)

	Current-law Formula	With Progressive Price Indexing	With Progressive Price Indexing and Benefit Offsets for 4% Accounts	Percentage Change
Low earner (earnings of $16,470 today)	$13,413	$13,413	$8,906	-34%
Medium earner (earnings of $36,600)	22,097	17,545	7,513	-66%
High earner (earnings of $58,560)	29,296	20,214	3,750	-87%
Maximum earner (earnings of $90,000)	35,751	22,666	2,717	-92%

Source: Calculations based on Social Security Administration, Office of the Chief Actuary, "Estimated Financial Effects of a Comprehensive Social Security Reform Proposal Including Progressive Price Indexing- INFORMATION," February 10, 2005; and "Preliminary Estimated Financial Effects of a Proposal to Phase In Personal Accounts- INFORMATION," February 3, 2005. Note that the 4% accounts are assumed to have a maximum contribution of $1,000 in 2009, growing by $100 per year plus wage inflation, along the lines proposed by the President.

private accounts, Social Security's defined benefit would drop dramatically for everyone except low earners.

• By 2055, Social Security defined benefits for medium earners—those roughly in the middle of earnings scale—would drop 66 percent, or two thirds, compared to the current benefit structure. (A medium earner in 2005 makes $36,600.) Instead of receiving a Social Security benefit of $1,844 a month in today's dollars (or $22,709 a year), the worker's benefit would be $626. The worker also would have a private account that would be subject to market risk.

• In addition, the group whom the Social Security actuaries label "high earners"—workers whose average earnings are 60 percent above those of the medium earner, or $59,000 today—would face a Social Security defined benefit cut of 87 percent in 2055. Instead of a monthly Social Security benefit of $2,441 in today's dollars, their benefit would be $311.

After Medicare Premiums Are Subtracted, Many Retirees Would Receive No Social Security Benefit at All

Moreover, many of these individuals would receive no Social Security check at all. Medicare premiums are collected by being subtracted from Social Security benefits; the Social Security checks sent out each month equal a beneficiary's Social Security benefit *minus* his or her Medicare premiums. Medicare premiums rise at the same rate as health care costs, which is to say, considerably faster than wages or the general inflation rate. As a result, with each passing year, Medicare premiums consume a larger proportion of Social Security benefits.

- The figures just cited—that by 2055, the combination of progressive price indexing and the Administration's private accounts would eliminate 66 percent of the Social Security benefit for median earners, and 87 percent for so-called "high" earners—reflect the Social Security benefits that would remain before Medicare premiums are taken into account.

- It is from these greatly reduced benefit amounts that the premiums for Medicare physicians' coverage (Medicare Part B) and the prescription drug

---

Table 2
Annual Social Security Benefit For Workers Retiring in 2075
(Benefits in 2005 dollars, does not include the value of private accounts)

	Current-law Formula	With Progressive Price Indexing	With Progressive Price Indexing and Benefit Offsets for 4% Accounts	Percentage Change
Low earner (earnings of $16,470 today)	$16,599	$16,599	$11,022	-34%
Medium earner (earnings of $36,600)	27,344	19,715	7,301	-73%
High earner (earnings of $58,560)	36,254	21,100	1,233	-97%
Maximum earner (earnings of $90,000)	44,236	22,428	0	-100%

Source: Calculations based on Social Security Administration, Office of the Chief Actuary, "Estimated Financial Effects of a Comprehensive Social Security Reform Proposal Including Progressive Price Indexing- INFORMATION," February 10, 2005; and "Preliminary Estimated Financial Effects of a Proposal to Phase In Personal Accounts- INFORMATION," February 3, 2005. Note that the 4% accounts are assumed to have a maximum contribution of $1,000 in 2009, growing by $100 per year plus wage inflation, along the lines proposed by the President.

---

benefit (Medicare Part D) would be subtracted. The Social Security check that beneficiaries received would be what was left. For millions of workers, the amount of the monthly Social Security check would be at or near zero.

The crunch would become even more severe after 2055. By 2075, as Table 2 shows, the combined effect of progressive price indexing and the President's private accounts would be to reduce Social Security defined benefits by 73 percent for medium earners and 97 percent for the so-called "high earners," even before Medicare premiums are taken into account.

In other words, this approach ultimately would decimate traditional Social Security benefits for most workers. As a result, it would raise serious questions about whether the Social Security system would remain politically viable. With private accounts being financed through reductions in Social Security benefits rather than in the private-account balances, this approach would make it appear as though most

---

Are Private Account Plans Designed to Devalue Social Security?*

Social Security is a compact among all Americans designed to ensure a modicum of economic dignity no matter what life may bring. Much of the value of Social Security lies in its role as insurance against the threat to economic dignity that can come through disability, the early death of a provider, poverty, or living to a very old age and exhausting one's savings. One-third of Social Security benefits now go to survivors or workers who have become disabled and their dependents.

Advocates of replacing part of Social Security with private accounts often paint a distorted picture of Social Security's value by describing it only in terms of its "return on investment." No one would think it made sense to tell parents who had purchased auto and fire insurance that they had been terrible investors and had robbed their children of their inheritance because, with no accidents or fires, they had a negative return on their insurance premiums. That would be a distorted frame for assessing the value of insurance; you hope you never need it, but insurance can make all the difference for a family if life takes a difficult and unexpected turn.

Many private-accounts plans are designed in such a way that Social Security recipients would be likely to undervalue the benefits of Social Security and to overvalue their private account. Most "carve-out" private-account plans, such as the plan the President has outlined, are designed in a way that is likely to lead people to think the accounts are a better deal than they are, because the plans obscure the fact that the accounts have a large cost that must be incurred. The White House purposely designed its proposal so that the "offset" (i.e., the reduction in benefits needed to pay for the accounts) would not be taken out of the accounts themselves, but out of Social Security checks instead. A more transparent design,

workers were contributing 8.4 percent of their wages to Social Security and getting little or nothing back. Workers would appear to be getting much more back for the four percent of wages they placed in their private accounts.

The difference would reflect, in part, the fact that the costs of the private accounts were being recouped through reductions in Social Security benefits rather than in the account balances. The reductions *could* be made directly in the account balances, but most private-account proponents do not favor that, because the accounts would then appear less attractive. The difference between Social Security pay-outs and pay-outs from private accounts also would reflect the fact that a portion of Social Security payroll taxes go for disability and survivors insurance, for raising the benefits of retirees who have worked at low wages, and, most importantly, to cover the "legacy debt" that Social Security inherited as a result of the decision made when the program started 65 years ago to cover people who were retiring at that time and had paid little or nothing into the system

---

under which the Social Security Trust Fund would be paid back directly from the account balances, rather than by cutting Social Security benefits, would make the accounts look much more modest to beneficiaries and traditional Social Security benefits look more robust.

Moreover, most private-account proposals would make Social Security appear to be a worse deal relative to private accounts than would be the case, for another reason as well. A substantial share of the payroll taxes dedicated to Social Security are used to finance the cost of survivors and disability benefits and of raising benefits for those who worked for low wages throughout their careers. Any structure that encourages beneficiaries to compare the monthly check they receive from private accounts to the monthly retirement check that Social Security provides thus is likely to lead to serious misunderstanding by workers and beneficiaries of the relative value of the two systems.

The architecture of plans designed to integrate private accounts into the Social Security system, whether by intent or effect, consequently would create a distorted picture of Social Security that ultimately could lead many people to favor measures allowing them to withdraw from Social Security to a greater degree. These plans thus run the risk of starting the nation down a slippery slope toward a greater weakening of Social Security and its vital social insurance functions.

Social Security has been the crown jewel of U.S. social programs for decades, in no small part because it is a compact not only across the generations but also among all working Americans—the healthy and the middle class as well as those who work for low wages and those who suffer from disabilities. Unraveling this compact would make ours a very different, and less humane, society.

---

* This box is drawn from an April 1, 2005 Memorandum ("Open Letter to Progressive Policymakers") written by Gene Sperling and issued by the Center for American Progress.

because Social Security wasn't yet in existence during most of their work careers. (See the box on below for a further discussion of these issues.)

It is unlikely that a system under which Social Security appeared to be such an abysmal deal when compared to private accounts would be politically sustainable over time.

Notes

1.   For further analyses of progressive price indexing, see Jason Furman, "An Analysis of Using "Progressive Price Indexing" to Set Social Security Benefits," Center on Budget and Policy Priorities, March 21, 2005.

2.   "Progressive Price Indexing" of Social Security Benefits, Congressional Research Service, April 22, 2005.

Gene Sperling is a Senior Fellow at the Center for American Progress. Jason Furman is a non-resident Senior Fellow, and Robert Greenstein is Executive Director, of the Center on Budget and Policy Priorities

Universalism Without the Targeting: Privatizing the Old-Age Welfare State

by Pamela Herd

Abstract

Decades of conservative attempts to scale back Social Security and Medicare, by limiting the program's universality through means testing and drastic benefit cuts, have failed. Thus, after numerous unsuccessful attempts at dismantling the U.S.'s universal old-age welfare state, or even meaningfully restraining its growth, conservative critics have developed a new approach. They are wrapping promarket "privatization" policy proposals in the popular universal framework of Social Security and Medicare. What is fundamentally different about privatization is that it embraces (or at least acquiesces to) key aspects of universalism, including broad-based eligibility and benefits that "maintain accustomed standards of living," which leave universal programs with rock-hard public support. Proponents argue privatization will "save" these programs. What distinguishes this approach from past retrenchment efforts is that promarket privatization policies, while supporting key universal tenets, will retrench Social Security's and Medicare's redistributive facets. Instead of limiting the most popular features of universalism, privatization proposals limit the redistributive elements of our large social insurance programs.

Social Security and Medicare are the United States' most popular social welfare policies. Despite decades of conservative attempts to scale them back, our universal old-age welfare state remains the bedrock of American social policy. Attempts to limit the programs' universality through means testing and drastic benefit cuts have failed. Moreover, Social Security and Medicare have almost exclusively expanded their breadth and depth since their inceptions.

Thus, after numerous unsuccessful attempts at dismantling the U.S.'s universal old-age welfare state, or even meaningfully restraining its growth, conservative critics have developed a new approach. They are wrapping promarket "privatization" policy proposals in the popular universal framework of Social Security and Medicare. As President Bush argues, he wants to institute individual accounts to save Social Security. What is fundamentally different about privatization as a reform goal is that it embraces (or at least acquiesces to) key aspects of universalism, including broad-based eligibility and benefits that "maintain accustomed

(originally published in *The Gerontologist,* vol. 45, no. 3, June 2005, pp. 292-298; Copyright © The Gerontological Society of America; adapted by permission of the publisher)

will maintain the aspects of universalism that keep programs popular—broad-based eligibility and generous benefits.

The Growing Popularity of Privatization

Unlike past retrenchment efforts, the idea of privatization is gaining traction among the public. Support for privatizing Social Security varies from 50% to 70% depending on the question wording, though the support is far greater among younger than older Americans. Contrastingly, public support for past retrenchment efforts is far weaker. The percentage of individuals approving means testing Social Security benefits comes in at about 40%, while reducing benefits comes in at 35% (Public Agenda, 2004). Even in the most recent polls where support for President Bush's partial privatization plan has fallen, the majority of Americans (56%) support diverting a portion of their payroll tax into an individual account, whereas support for means testing benefit cuts is much lower (Social Polling Report, 2005).

Support for privatizing Medicare is even more striking. To fix Medicare's fiscal problems, almost 8 in 10 Americans support allowing seniors to choose among many private health plans with a fixed monetary contribution from the government (Employee Benefit Research Institute [EBRI], 2001). Comparatively, 54% support increasing Medicare premiums for those with incomes above $50,000, while 27% favor increasing the age of eligibility (EBRI).

The following two sections, which explore Social Security and Medicare separately, answer these two questions. First, why is privatization more popular than past reform or retrenchment efforts? Specifically, how is this reform agenda being sold? Second, how does this reform agenda line up with the conservative agenda and what are the impacts of this on the redistributive elements of Social Security and Medicare?

Social Security

Most Social Security privatization proposals entail shifting about 2%- 4% of the 12.4% payroll tax (split between employers and employees) into individual accounts that Americans would invest in the stock market. That 2%- 4% would now be a contribution to an individual account. The key reason for the popularity of these reform proposals, compared to past reform approaches, is that they do not undermine the principles of universalism that have kept the program popular. These reforms promise the maintenance of relatively generous benefits and universal eligibility. In fact, proponents argue that privatizing Social Security will "save" it from bankruptcy and limit the need for large benefit cuts to fix its fiscal problems (President's Commission to Strengthen Social Security, 2001).

While I will examine these claims momentarily, what is critical to point out is that a major reason why privatization has been a relatively popular reform idea is because politicians and policy advocates no longer talk about eliminating or downsizing the program. Instead, privatization is framed as a way to save Social Security. Yet, this is a reform that can still meet a common conservative principle: limited government intervention. Specifically, privatization would give individuals more control over their payroll taxes, and the government would have a lesser ability to redistribute. Privatizations falls in line with past retrenchment efforts, means testing and benefit cuts, because it shifts individual contributions back toward individuals who would bear the risks and rewards of controlling these resources.

Part of the public support for privatization is because proponents argue it will help save a bankrupt social policy. But is it really bankrupt? Many have shown how the "crisis" is severely overstated (Quadagno, 1996). The Social Security trustees estimate that the program's 75-year shortfall could be fixed by a 1.9% increase in payroll tax (shared between employers and employees), which hasn't been raised since 1983, while the Congressional Budget Office (CBO, 2004a) estimates a 1% increase. Another way to lend some proportion to the issue is that while President Bush has specifically argued Social Security is financially unsustainable in its current form, the money spent on the recent tax cut would have completely offset the 75-year shortfall. Finally, the projections that show a deficit are based on all kinds of assumptions about fertility, mortality, immigration, and the economy. For those in their 20s, the analogous forecast is predicting what their children, who are not born yet, will be doing in retirement. (Herd & Kingson, 2005)

Further, would privatization "save" Social Security? The argument to prefund the system is theoretically appealing. There would be no fiscal problem if each individual was funding their own retirement. But when theory hits the ground, the possibility that creating individual accounts will financially save Social Security is not even a remote certainty (Diamond & Orszag, 2002). First and foremost it would cost around 2 trillion dollars to switch the system over. Current beneficiaries need their benefits as future individual account holders shift their payroll taxes towards those accounts. Thus, there is a need for additional revenue.

And though proponents argue privatization would increase peoples' benefit, this claim is questionable. The privatization proposal that came from the President's Commission to Strengthen Social Security made benefit comparisons between the current and proposed system based on current projected benefit levels reduced by 30% to account for the shortfall (Diamond & Orszag, 2002). Then, using this baseline, they claimed privatization would increase Social Security benefits when, in fact, benefits would be substantially reduced to address the shortfall. Aside from the shortfall issue, administrative costs and the ability of individuals to invest wisely call into question whether individual accounts can produce the strong return proponents of privatization hope for (CBO, 2004a).

How Privatizing Undermines Redistribution

The effort to privatize Social Security has its roots in neoliberalism, which argues against most government intervention. The basic theory is that income is best left in the hands of individuals, as opposed to the government. The notion of redistribution, shifting resources from wealthier to poorer Americans, runs contrary to this sentiment. And this is precisely why opponents of government intervention dislike Social Security. While it is questionable that privatizing Social Security will "save" it, there is little doubt it will have a significant and negative impact on the program's progressiveness. So how does creating individual accounts, or privatizing Social Security, undermine the program's progressiveness? Privatization limits the program's ability to redistribute.

While Social Security's universal structure has engendered wide public support among middle class Americans, it has also been enormously successful at protecting some of the poorest Americans. In 1970, before the largest expansion of Social Security benefits with the automatic cost of living increases, about 1 in 4 elderly persons lived below the poverty line. In 2003, just 1 in 10 elderly persons lived below the poverty line (Census Bureau, 2004). Comparatively, the poverty rate for children rose and remained stagnant for working-age adults.

Social Security protects poor Americans because, as Theda Skocpol (1991) argues, it "targets within universalism." Poor Americans benefit from the redistributive benefit formula. Simply, low-income workers have a higher percentage of their lifetime earnings replaced by their benefits than do high-income workers. It is these beneficiaries who are most vulnerable to poverty. Not including Social Security benefits in individuals' incomes raises the poverty rate from 10% to almost 50% (Porter, Larin, & Primus, 1999).

Targeting, however, is done under the cover of universalism. Unlike means tested programs, like the eliminated Aid to Families with Dependent Children (AFDC), which are constantly retrenched because they lack broad support, universal programs like Social Security maintain popular support because everyone contributes to and benefits from the program.

The shift toward individual accounts would restrain Social Security's ability to redistribute resources. The high-income replacement rates that low-income workers receive may be threatened by privatization. Quite simply, the more payroll taxes are diverted to individual accounts, the less the government will be able to redistribute those resources. Of course, women, Blacks, and Hispanics would be particularly hard hit given their relatively low earnings. Compared to the White man's dollar, women still earn just 70 cents, Black women earn just 63 cents, Hispanic women earn 53 cents, and Black and Hispanic men earn 60 cents (National Committee on Pay Equity, 2004).

One of the most enlightening studies of privatization was done in the county of Galveston, Texas (Wilson, 1999). On January 1, 1982, the county opted out of Social Security and developed a privatized system. The study found that those with higher earnings had higher benefits under this plan than they would have under the Social Security system. Contrastingly, low earners had lower benefits under the plan than they would have under Social Security. Their initial benefit was about 4% lower. But because Social Security institutes cost of living increases to offset inflation, the difference grows over time. So after 15 years, their benefit would be 63% of what it would have been under Social Security. More moderate earners would have a higher initial benefit, but after 15 years their benefit would be 91% of their original benefit and after 20 years it would be just 78%. Contrastingly, the highest earners would have an initial benefit 177% of their Social Security benefit. After 20 years it would be equivalent to what their Social Security would have been. Overall, they would have obtained a substantial gain through a private contribution system.

There are numerous reasons other than restricting redistribution as to why disadvantaged groups do not fare well. There is concern about peoples' ability to make good investment decisions (Williamson & Rix, 1999). Others point out the relatively high administrative costs for small accounts (CBO, 2004b). Women, who live 7 years longer than men on average, will not gain as much from individual benefits more directly linked with overall contributions; Social Security does not penalize women for their longer life spans (Williamson & Rix). And of course the smaller one's income in retirement the less able one is to absorb large changes in income that would likely occur if it was heavily tied to the stock market (Herd & Kingson, 2005).

A final salient concern is how those benefiting from the insurance portion of the program, particularly disabled workers and survivors, would fare given money would be shifted out of the insurance portion of the program and into private accounts. The basic insurance benefit would thus be around one third lower for survivors and disabled beneficiaries (Diamond & Orszag, 2002). Survivors, however, could inherit whatever savings had built up in the deceased worker's account, which would be highly dependent on the age he or she died at. The size of disabled workers' accounts would be highly dependent on the age at which they became disabled. Generally, the individual account, particularly for disabled workers, would not have accrued enough value, leading to lower benefits overall than under the current system.

Medicare

Currently, older Medicare beneficiaries pay the same premiums, deductibles, and co-payments to their primary health insurance provider: the federal government. A small percentage of beneficiaries are covered by HMOs. But regardless of whether beneficiaries participate in fee-for-service or an HMO, individuals are guaranteed a set of covered services (benefits) regardless of cost. It is a defined benefit. Moreover, all those individuals are placed in the same "pool" to determine the cost of premiums. The most common privatization proposal for Medicare would basically entail providing older Americans with a voucher with which they would buy their health insurance coverage from a host of private insurance providers, who would offer an array of different plans with varying copayments and services, in addition to traditional Medicare. In essence, the system would shift toward a defined contribution approach, where a contribution, as opposed to a certain level of benefits, is guaranteed. Unlike in the current system (a defined benefit) where the government contributes more toward sicker and generally poorer beneficiaries, everyone would receive the exact same monetary voucher benefit (a defined contribution). How this amount is determined will depend upon policy details. A pure defined contribution would pay, for example, $500 toward a premium. Another variation, however, premium support, would set the amount at a percentage, say 90%, of the average premium amount. Another key difference is that older Americans would no longer be in the same insurance pool. The result is that premiums and benefits would vary widely.

The reason privatizing Medicare is a more popular reform than limiting eligibility through significant means testing or raising the program's eligibility age is because, similar to privatizing Social Security, privatizing Medicare is being sold as the way to save this universal program. Some privatization proponents argue it would protect Medicare from fiscal ruin and improve its benefits without requiring increases to the eligibility age, benefit cuts, or significant means testing (Bush, 2004). Other proponents, however, are more pragmatic and acknowledge benefits cuts will be necessary (Pauly, 2004). While I will examine these claims momentarily, it is critical to note that privatization is being sold in such a way that does not challenge the basic aspects of universalism that make Medicare popular. Everyone contributes and everyone would continue benefiting; the size of the beneficiary pool would not be decreased due to an increased age of eligibility or significant means testing. What would change is the extent to which Medicare subsidizes the sickest, and generally the poorest, beneficiaries.

Much like the claims made by proponents of privatizing Social Security, there is no evidence that privatizing Medicare will improve its fiscal problems. Medicare's dilemma is far more serious than Social Security's. Currently, Medicare comprises 2.7% of gross domestic product (GDP). By 2030 it will comprise 7% of GDP (MedPAC, 2004). But what is often ignored is that Medicare's fiscal problems are rooted in the larger problems of the U.S. health care system. Overall, health care spending is expected to rise from 15.3% of GDP to 25% of GDP from 2004 to 2030 (MedPAC). The only country in the industrialized world without the government as the primary health insurer for its citizens and residents is also consistently the most expensive system in the world.

Proposals to privatize would severely limit the government's role as the primary health insurer to all older Americans and expand the private sector's role. But Medicare has been far more effective at controlling health care costs than the private sector has been (Boccuti & Moon, 2003). From 1972 to 2002, average annual cost increases have been 9.6% in Medicare compared to 11.1% in the private sector. There are two reasons for the government's success at holding prices down. First, the large pool of beneficiaries (almost all older Americans) makes it easy to negotiate low prices with health care providers and suppliers. Second, it has much lower administrative costs: 3% compared to the private sector's 12.8% (Davis, 2004).

The goal of privatizing Medicare is to reduce the government's current role as the primary health insurer for almost older Americans. Proponents argue that older Americans should be able to "decide what kind of health plans they want, the kinds of benefits packages they want, the medical treatments and procedures they want, and the premiums, co-payments, deductibles, and coinsurance they are willing to pay"

(Lemieux, 2003; Moffit, 2004). More choice will lead to more competition and further reduce prices. Ultimately, proponents argue that the increased competition that results from privatizing Medicare is a way to "save" and improve Medicare without resorting to benefit cuts or tax increases.

But there is no evidence that increased competition will reduce costs (Moon & Herd, 2002; Rice & Desmond, 2002). First, the larger number of companies, and consequently different health plans, involved will increase administrative costs. Second, for competition to reduce costs, elderly people would have to switch plans on an almost yearly basis, but there is significant evidence that older adults will not switch plans (Buchmueller, 2000). Third, it will be very difficult for seniors to sort out which plans will give them the most for their money. It is difficult to compare plan benefits and costs because plans vary so widely within and between health insurance companies.

How Privatization Will Undermine Redistribution Within Medicare

How does Medicare redistribute? The redistributive nature of Medicare is less obvious than Social Security's. But the key progressive feature of Medicare is that, regardless of how sick or poor, individuals are guaranteed access to the same basic coverage at the same costs as wealthier and healthier individuals. This is most certainly not the case for younger Americans who may not be able to access health insurance or often have to pay considerably more for it depending on their employment status, health status, and where they live.

The key to understanding Medicare's success is understanding what older people's health insurance dilemmas were before Medicare. Before Medicare was enacted in 1965 about three quarters of older Americans had inadequate health insurance coverage, and half had no coverage whatsoever (Century Foundation, 2001). Wealthier older Americans were the only ones able to afford health insurance. Moreover, buying health insurance as individuals in the market left them with few protections. The sickest older Americans could be charged exorbitant premiums making the coverage unaffordable. Now all older Americans are guaranteed affordable health insurance. Their Medicare premiums are not effected by how sick they are or where they live. And most polls show approval ratings for the program at almost 90% among the elderly people who rely on it (Public Agenda, 2004).

Again, the long-term goal of privatization supporters is to dramatically reduce the role of Medicare fee-for-service or rather limit the government's current role as the primary health insurance provider for older Americans. Though the government does contract out Medicare's administrative responsibility to private companies, ultimately the government determines what services beneficiaries receive and how much they have to pay. Under a defined contribution approach, the government plan—Medicare fee-for-service—would just be one of hundreds of primary health insurance plans with varying premiums and services covered.

The problem for poorer and sicker beneficiaries is that these changes are likely to increase their health care costs. Multiple insurance pools make it much harder to spread and redistribute the costs of health care from the sickest and poorest beneficiaries to the healthiest and wealthiest. In the current system, everyone is in the same insurance pool so costs are spread evenly; the more pools, the harder to evenly spread costs. The problem is that HMOs are skilled at attracting the healthiest individuals who bring the highest profits. Studies show that sicker individuals end up concentrated in certain plans when people have multiple options. With a defined contribution approach, the sickest and most expensive beneficiaries would be concentrated in fee-for-service Medicare. Sick and expensive beneficiaries concentrated in one plan drives up costs, leaving these vulnerable beneficiaries with extraordinarily high premiums, deductibles, and copayments (Moon & Herd, 2002; Rice & Desmond, 2002).

Unlike with Social Security, partial privatization of Medicare has already begun. And these experiments demonstrate the problems with privatization for sicker and poorer Americans. The main example is the participation of HMOs in Medicare. Millions of older Americans have participated in an HMO as opposed to traditional Medicare fee-for-service. Beneficiary premiums remained the same, but for years those elders in HMOs, who are the healthiest and wealthiest, received better benefits than the average participant in Medicare fee-for-service. The government was overpaying the HMOs. But as soon as the reimbursements were corrected, HMOs began dropping Medicare coverage. In 1998, 17% of beneficiaries participated in an HMO; by 2004 that had fallen to 11% (Kaiser Family Foundation, 2004a). In 2002, Congress significantly increased reimbursements to HMOs to further encourage their participation. Currently, the government pays an extra $552 per enrollee in Medicare HMOs as compared to fee-for-service, even though the sickest and poorest beneficiaries are in Medicare fee-for-service (Cooper, Nicholas, & Biles, 2004).

The second piece of privatization in Medicare is the new prescription drug bill, whereby private insurers, as opposed to the government, will provide coverage (Kaiser Family Foundation, 2004b). The benefit premium will vary depending on where beneficiaries live and what kind of plan they choose. Beneficiaries already in HMOs will simply receive their coverage through them. Beneficiaries who want to remain in Medicare fee-for-service (who are sicker and poorer beneficiaries) will have to buy an additional policy from a private insurer, which is on top of whatever Medigap coverage they currently have. There is concern that Medicare fee-for-service participants will have to pay more for less coverage due to the stand-alone nature of the coverage. The overall incentive is to push more individuals into HMOs and away from fee-for-service Medicare.

Conclusion

Neither privatizing Social Security nor privatizing Medicare explicitly threatens two basic universal principles that keep these programs popular: broad-based eligibility and relatively generous benefits for the middle class. While additional policy changes to deal with these programs' fiscal problems could threaten either of these principles, proponents argue that privatization will help offset the impact of any benefit cuts.

This is likely a key explanation as to why these reforms have received far more public support than past attempts at retrenching Social Security and Medicare. Instead of attacking Social Security and Medicare as draining and wasteful programs that should be limited, proponents argue privatization will "save" these programs.

What privatization does clearly limit is the redistribution that occurs within these programs. The magnitude of the impact on redistribution, however, will depend on policy details. A few recent proposals for Medicare and Social Security have tried to limit the impact of reform on poor beneficiaries (see Pauly, 2004). That said, the basic premise of these proposals is to more tightly link individual contributions with individual benefits, which reduces the potential for redistribution. Given Social Security's and Medicare's success at securing the incomes and protecting the health of elderly Americans, we need to pay close attention to the ramifications of privatization on the beneficiaries who need these programs the most.

References

Boccuti, C., & Moon, M., (2003). Comparing Medicare and private insurers. *Health Affairs, 22,* 230-237.

Buchmueller, T. C., (2000) The health plan choice of retirees under managed competition. *Health Services Research, 35,*. 949-957.

Bush, G. W., (2004). *Framework to modernize and improve Medicare fact sheet.* Retrieved September 15, 2004, from http://www.whitehouse.gov/news/releases/2003/03/20030304-1.html.

Census Bureau. (2004). *Income, poverty, and health insurance coverage in the United States: 2003.* Retrieved September 10, 2004, from http://www.census.gov/prod/2004pubs/p60-226.pdf.

Century Foundation. (2001). *Medicare reform.* Retrieved September 10, 2004, from http://www.medicarewatch.org.

Congressional Budget Office. (2004a). *The outlook for Social Security.* Retrieved January 15, 2005, from http://www.cbo.gov/showdoc.cfm?index=5530&sequence=0.

Congressional Budget Office. (2004b). *Administrative costs of private accounts in Social Security.* Retrieved January 15, 2005, from http://www.cbo.gov/showdoc.cfm?index=5277&sequence=0.

Cooper, N., Nicholas, L., & Biles, B., (2004). *The cost of privatization.* New York: Commonwealth Fund.

Davis, K., (2004). Making health care affordable for all Americans. Testimony before the Senate Committee on Health, Education, Labor, and Pensions, January 28, 2004. Retrieved January 15, 2005, from http://www.cmwf.org/usr_doc/davis_senatehelptestimony_714.pdf.

Derthick, M., (1979). *Policymaking for Social Security.* Washington, DC: Brookings Institution.

Diamond, P., & Orszag, P., (2002). *Reducing benefits and subsidizing individual accounts.* New York: The Century Fund.

Employee Benefit Research Institute (EBRI). (2001). *Medicare awareness, satisfaction, confidence, and reform.* Retrieved September 10, 2004, from http://www.ebri.org/facts/0701fact.pdf.

Ferrara, P., (1998). *The next step for Medicare reform.* Policy analysis no. 305. Washington, DC: CATO Institute.

Herd, P., & Kingson, E., (2005). Selling Social Security. In R. Hudson (Ed.), *The future of age-based public policy* (pp. 183–204). Baltimore, MD: Johns Hopkins University Press.

Kaiser Family Foundation. (2004a). *Medicare fact sheet: Medicare Advantage, March 2004*. Retrieved January 15, 2005, from http://www.kff.org.

Kaiser Family Foundation. (2004b). *Summaries of the Medicare Modernization Act of 2003*. New York: Author.

Kingson, E., (1994). Testing the boundaries of universality. *The Gerontologist, 34,* 736-742.

Korpi, W., (1983). *The Democratic class struggle*. London: Routledge.

Korpi, W., & Palme, J., (1998). The paradox of redistribution and strategies of equality. *American Sociological Review, 63,* 661-687.

Lemieux, J., (2003). *Explaining premium support*. Retrieved September 1, 2004, from http://www.centrists.org.

MedPac. (2004). *A data book: Health care spending and the Medicare program*. Medicare Payment Advisory Commission. Retrieved September 1, 2004, from http://www.medpac.gov/publications/congressional_reports/Jun04DataBookSec6.pdf.

Moffit, R., (2004). What federal workers are doing today that you can't. Webmemo #604. Washington, DC: The Heritage Foundation.

Moon, M., & Herd, P., (2002). *A place at the table*. New York: The Century Foundation.

National Committee on Pay Equity. (2004). *Fact sheet on gender pay gap*. Retrieved September 3, 2004, from http://www.pay-equity.org/info.html.

Pauly, M., (2004). Means testing in Medicare. *Health Affairs, web exclusive, W4* (549).

Porter, K., Larin, K., & Primus, W., (1999). *Social security and poverty among the elderly*. Washington, DC: Center on Budget and Policy Priorities.

President's Commission to Strengthen Social Security. (2001). *Strengthening Social Security and creating personal wealth for all Americans*. Retrieved September 4, 2004, from http://www.css.gov.

Public Agenda. (2004). *Opinion polling on Medicare*. Retrieved Month, day, year, from http://www.publicagenda.org/issues/major_proposals_detail.cfm?issue_type=ss&list=1.

Quadagno, J., (1996). Social Security and the myth of the entitlement crisis. *The Gerontologist, 36,* 391-399.

Rice, T., & Desmond, K., (2002). *An analysis of reforming Medicare through a premium support plan*. New York: Henry J. Kaiser Foundation.

Rice, T., Desmond, K., & Gabel, J., (1990). The Medicare Catastrophic Coverage Act. *Health Affairs, 9,* 75-87.

Skocpol, T., (1991). Targeting within universalism. In C. Jencks & P. E. Peterson (Eds.), *The urban underclass,* (pp. 411–436). Washington, DC: The Brookings Institution.

Polling Report. (2005). Title of report. Retrieved April 3, 2005, from http://www.pollingreport.com.

Williamson, J., & Rix, S., (1999). Social Security reform: Implications for women. Boston College, Boston, MA. Retrieved September 1, 2004, from http://www.bc.edu/centers/crr/papers/wp_1999-07.pdf.

Wilson, T., (1999). Opting out: The Galveston plan and Social Security. PRC WP 99-22, Wharton School, University of Pennsylvania, Philadelphia.

Point/Counterpoint: Would Private Accounts Improve Social Security?

by Jeffrey R. Brown and Kenneth S. Apfel

Would Private Accounts Improve Social Security?

This feature is on the proposal by the Bush administration to establish personal accounts for Social Security. Supporting this idea is Jeffrey R. Brown, associate professor of finance at the University of Illinois at Urbana-Champaign, who served on the staff of the President's Commission to Strengthen Social Security (2001) and was recently nominated by President Bush to serve on the Social Security Advisory Board. Taking the other side is Kenneth S. Apfel, Sid Richardson chair, Lyndon B. Johnson School of Public Affairs, University of Texas at Austin, who served as commissioner of Social Security from 1997 to 2001.

Affirmative: Private Accounts Would Improve Social Security
Jeffrey R. Brown

During 2005, we witnessed the debate about the future of Social Security rise to the very top of the domestic political agenda in the U.S., and then fall from prominence without any meaningful legislative changes to ensure its long-term health. While opponents of reforming the system won a temporary political battle, one simple reality remains: Social Security must change if it is to be made financially secure.

Social Security is often heralded as one of the great successes of 20th-century policymaking, and for good reason: The program has met President Roosevelt's vision of providing "some measure of protection to the average citizen and to his family . . . against poverty-stricken old age." Unfortunately, the basic financial structure of Social Security, designed during the depths of the Great Depression, is not well equipped to handle the substantial demographic changes that are under way in the United States. Social Security simply cannot afford to pay currently scheduled benefits in the coming decades without imposing an ever-larger tax burden on younger workers. In the face of this reality, "doing nothing" is simply not a viable policy option.

This article begins by briefly reviewing the structural reasons that the Social Security system is in long-run financial distress. It then discusses why the system can only be restored to secure financial footing by making politically difficult reductions in

(Originally published in the *Journal of Policy Analysis and Management,* vol. 25, iss. 3, Summer 2006, pp. 679-690; used with permission)

scheduled benefits or increases in taxes. The remainder of the article focuses on why personal retirement accounts ought to be part of any reformed system, even though the first-order effect of establishing such accounts is to neither hurt nor help the long-run finances of Social Security.

To understand the fiscal challenge, one must first understand that Social Security is not a savings program. Rather, it is an income transfer system that taxes today's workers to pay benefits for today's retirees and other beneficiaries. Economists call such a financial structure a "pay-as-you-go" system. This is in sharp contrast to the pre-funded nature of most private-sector pension plans, in which the money contributed to a worker's pension is invested in real financial assets (for example, stocks or bonds) that are then used to pay benefits when the worker retires. The primary economic disadvantage of a "pay-as-you-go" system relative to a pre-funded system is that it reduces national saving, reduces economic growth, and therefore shrinks the future size of the economic pie (Feldstein, 1974).

Despite its disadvantages, a pay-as-you-go system can still function reasonably well when there is a large number of workers paying taxes to support each beneficiary. Back in 1950, for example, there were sixteen workers paying taxes to support each Social Security beneficiary, and thus a payroll tax rate of only 3 percent was sufficient to support the program. As the Social Security system has expanded and matured, however, the ratio of workers to retirees has fallen substantially. Today there are only 3.3 workers to support each beneficiary, and the combined payroll tax rate has risen to 12.4 percent of income on the first $94,200 in earnings. As a result of population aging, this ratio will fall to just 2 within a generation, and unless the benefit formula is changed, taxes will need to rise substantially to keep the system in balance.

The current 12.4 percent tax rate, combined with a small amount of revenue obtained from income taxation of Social Security benefits, raised approximately $487 billion in 2004.[1] Total Social Security expenditures in that year were $421 billion, leaving Social Security with a cash surplus of approximately $66 billion. According to official projections by the Social Security Administration, however, these surpluses will be short-lived, dwindling to zero around the year 2017. For approximately 25 years after the start of these growing deficits, the Social Security Administration will have the legal ability to continue to pay full scheduled benefits to retirees, thanks to the balances held in the Social Security trust funds, which are projected to be exhausted in 2042. However, the economic burden of redeeming the government bonds held in the trust funds is real. Just three decades from now, when today's 37-year-old workers reach their normal retirement age, the cash flow deficits facing Social Security will reach $325 billion (in 2004 dollars), requiring that the federal treasury find that much money to redeem those bonds. For perspective, $325 billion is more than we spent in 2005 on discretionary spending through *all* of the following government agencies *combined:* Education, Energy, Homeland Security, Housing and Urban Development, Interior, Justice, Labor, Transportation, the Environmental Protection Agency, and the National Science Foundation (OMB, 2006). These deficits will continue to grow substantially in the decades beyond. Once the trust funds run dry in 2042, Social Security will only have enough income to pay approximately 70 percent of the benefits that have been promised.

Imagine asking the question, "How much money would our nation need to set aside today so that, if we invest it in government bonds, we would have enough money to cover all future Social Security deficits without raising taxes or cutting benefits?" In technical terms, this is a measure of the "net present value" of Social Security's unfunded obligations. The answer, according to the 2005 Social Security Trustee's Report, is $11 *trillion*, of which $4 trillion is the shortfall just over the next 75 years. For perspective, this unfunded obligation is roughly 2.4 times larger than the $4.6 trillion in "national debt" (that is, debt held by the public). It is also nearly 90 percent of the gross domestic product (GDP) of the United States in the year 2005.

Despite the wishful thinking of politicians on both sides of the aisle, this problem will not go away on its own. Nor can it be solved simply by investing Social Security funds in the stock market. Most economists understand that only two options exist for filling this large fiscal hole: raise taxes or reduce the rate at which benefits grow.

Raise taxes. If we raise taxes from the current 12.4 percent rate to pay for the benefits scheduled under current law, before today's college seniors retire this tax rate would need to rise to 17 percent to keep the system's cash flows in annual balance. In the decades to follow, tax rates would rise even farther. These increases are on top of the substantial tax increases required to fund rising Medicare expenditures, not to mention all other government programs. This approach is very costly: A 2004 study by Edward Prescott, the 2004 Nobel Laureate in economics, indicates that higher tax rates slow economic growth.

Reduce benefit growth. An alternative is to reduce the rate at which Social Security benefits grow in the future. Under current law, when today's college seniors retire, they will receive benefits that are approximately 50 percent greater than what today's retirees receive, even after adjusting for inflation. For perspective, if we simply slow the growth rate of benefits so that future retirees receive the same inflation-adjusted benefit as today's retirees, Social Security would be able to live permanently within its means without raising payroll taxes. Indeed, the cost savings would be large enough that we could boost benefits to low-wage workers and widows by more than the rate of inflation, thus increasing progressivity while permanently fixing Social Security's finances. Importantly, we can do this while keeping our promise to today's retirees and those nearing retirement—they would not see their benefits reduced by a single penny.

The only alternative to continually raising taxes or cutting benefits as needed to keep Social Security in annual fiscal balance over the long run is for our nation to save more today. Just as a family who wishes to finance their children's future college education can save more today in order to reduce the future financial burden on their children, so too can our nation reduce the burden on future generations by reducing current consumption.

In theory, we can partially pre-fund Social Security by running cash surpluses and saving them for the future in the Social Security trust funds. Indeed, as of the end of 2004, the Social Security trust funds held nearly $1.7 trillion in government bonds. From an economic perspective, however, it is unlikely that our nation has actually saved this $1.7 trillion. For most of the past two decades, these surpluses have been used to offset deficit spending elsewhere in the federal budget. To the extent that Social Security surpluses make it easier for Congress and the president to run larger deficits in the rest of the budget, the contribution of these surpluses to national saving is reduced.

This is where Personal Retirement Accounts (PRAs) come in. Personal accounts, by themselves, do virtually nothing to eliminate the present value of the funding shortfalls facing Social Security. Nor, as some opponents of PRAs have misleadingly suggested, do PRAs make the funding problem worse. If establishing PRAs has so little effect on the present value of the funding shortfalls, then what good are they? By moving to a mixed system that includes both personal accounts and traditional Social Security defined benefits, we have the opportunity to improve the system in four ways:

1. PRAs provide a tool to potentially increase national saving. Suppose that we increase taxes or reduce scheduled benefits in order to run larger surpluses in the coming decades—how do we ensure that this money is actually saved, given that the government has shown again and again that it cannot reliably save money for the future? By investing part of the payroll tax revenue in personal retirement accounts instead of the trust funds. PRAs put the control of contributions into the hands of individuals, not the government, making it much more difficult for politicians to use these funds to mask increased spending on other programs. PRAs offer the opportunity to safeguard savings and partially pre-fund future benefits.

2. Pre-funding Social Security through PRAs, when combined with other changes to the system to reduce expenditure growth, can benefit the economy. If we fund the transition to personal accounts from new revenue or decreased government spending, we can increase national saving and boost economic growth. This increase is on top of the substantial increase in national savings that comes from slowing benefit growth. A study by the nonpartisan Congressional Budget Office estimates that changing the way initial benefits are calculated so that they rise with prices rather than wages, combined with personal accounts similar to those proposed by President Bush, would increase national wealth over the next 75 years by 10 percent to 12 percent more than under the current Social Security system. In short, if we reduce consumption today and save for the future by pre-funding PRAs, we can make our children and grandchildren substantially better off.

3. By providing a clearer link between individuals' Social Security contributions and

the benefits they will receive, personal accounts may improve labor supply incentives. Under the current system, individuals have a difficult time determining to what extent additional payroll taxes lead to additional benefits. Because of this, many workers view the payroll tax as a pure tax, which discourages work. Allowing workers to see that their additional efforts lead directly to larger account balances may improve work incentives and thus help grow the economy.

4. Allowing workers to build a financial nest egg represents an unparalleled opportunity to extend the benefits of asset ownership to millions of American families who currently lack this opportunity. Nearly half of American families do not have a single dollar invested in stocks or mutual funds. What better way is there to extend to every American family the same benefits that most higher-income families enjoy—the opportunity to build a retirement nest egg through low-cost, diversified investments in real financial assets?

Individuals could choose from a limited number of well-diversified investment options that would be selected by an independent advisory board. Those who want to reduce risk could invest in safe assets like bonds. Those who wish to take on more risk in search of higher expected returns could invest in stocks. The nonpartisan Social Security Office of the Chief Actuary has determined that the federal government could centrally administer such a system with annual costs of only 0.3 percent of account balances, on a par with low-cost providers. These accounts would come with enforceable property rights, one of which is to pass the financial assets to one's spouse and children as inheritance.

The sooner we act to address the significant financial problems facing Social Security, the more options we have available to us. Failing to act simply passes a growing problem on to future generations. The time to act is now. While the establishment of personal retirement accounts is not the solution to Social Security's long-term financial problems, the accounts can improve our ability to save for the future, provide incentives for labor force participation, and extend opportunities for asset ownership to the millions of Americans who now lack it.

Note

1. Except where otherwise noted, all statistics relating to the financial status of the Social Security system come from The 2005 Annual Report of the Board of Trustees of the Federal Old-Age and Survivors Insurance and Disability Insurance Trust Funds.

References

Feldstein, M. (1974). Social Security, induced retirement, and aggregate capital accumulation. Journal of Political Economy, 82(5), 905–926.

Office of Management and Budget. (2006). Analytical perspectives, budget of the United States government, fiscal year 2006. Washington, DC: Author.

Negative: Private Accounts Would Not Improve Social Security

Kenneth S. Apfel

Professor Brown and I agree that changes must be made to Social Security, and the sooner we make them, the better. We disagree, however, on the magnitude of the changes to be made, the reliance on benefit changes to restore solvency, and the implications of replacing some of Social Security's benefit protections with private accounts.

Are Major Structural Changes Required?

Our growing aging population will clearly create real pressures on Social Security financing. It is prudent to take action to stabilize the system over the long term. While Professor Brown and I are in agreement that changes are needed, he also argues that Social Security's basic financial structure is not well equipped to handle the demographic changes now under way in the United States. I argue that the structure of the system is not only well designed for the future, but that Social Security's basic design can and should play a centrally important role in assuring the economic security of future generations.

The Social Security financing shortfall is certainly manageable without major structural changes. While the system does face a long-term deficit, it is now generating very large surpluses—about $150 billion this year, including trust fund interest. It's been running surpluses for the past two decades and will likely stay in surplus for many years into the future. Social Security revenues can pay about 70% to 80% of today's benefit commitments even a half-century from now (Board of Trustees of the Old-Age and Survivors Insurance and Disability Insurance Trust Funds, 2005; CBO, 2005).

The Social Security deficit over the next 75 years translates into about half of a percent of GDP. Even if one uses an even longer time frame, the shortfall is still only a little over one percent of GDP. Social Security revenues now amount to about five percent of GDP—that's the price that we as a society have been paying to provide basic economic security for millions of elderly and disabled Americans. Is six percent of GDP too much to pay for basic economic security? Will six percent greatly weaken the economy? I think not.

It's hard to comprehend shortfall estimates measured in the trillions of dollars. To put these dollars in context, the tax cuts enacted over the past five years are three times the size of the Social Security shortfall (Kogan & Greenstein, 2005). Simply repealing a modest share of the tax cuts would be the equivalent of resolving a significant part of the Social Security shortfall.

We may chose to significantly restructure the Social Security system, but it is but one choice we have among many. It's just not the case that the demographic challenge we face compels us to significantly change the core structure of Social Security.

Social Security has been a major success story of the 20th century, and future generations will also need its protections. Younger Americans will increasingly rely on individual savings for retirement security, as Social Security payments decline and pensions shift away from defined benefit payments (Munnell, 2004). Given the continued shift of retirement risks away from employers and toward individuals, the importance of that basic monthly inflation-protected Social Security benefit—something that can be counted on over a lifetime—becomes even more important for future generations.

Should Changes Be Made Primarily to Benefits?

Professor Brown and I agree that the only way to resolve the shortfall is through tax or benefit changes, but he argues that the better approach would be benefit changes. He argues for slowing the growth rate of benefits so that most future retirees would get about the same inflation-adjusted benefits as today's retirees.

If this approach had been put in place a generation ago, the benefits for today's retirees would be about 20% lower than current levels. Social Security currently replaces about 40 percent of pre-retirement earnings. Financial planners indicate that an adequate income in retirement requires post-retirement income to replace about 70 to 80 percent of pre-retirement income. If we moved to such a scheme, Social Security's "replacement rate" would be cut by a third to a half for most people over time (Furman, 2005). The foundation of support that Social Security now provides would be seriously eroded.

The president proposed benefit cuts of this magnitude by "price indexing" future benefits. Even if one supported restoring solvency entirely through reductions in benefits, price indexing is a poorly designed way to do so, because it fails to keep revenues and expenditures in balance as economic conditions change in the future. The Congressional Research Service recently concluded that, "paradoxically, if real wages rise faster than projected, price indexing would result in deeper benefit cuts, even as Social Security's unfunded 75 year liability would be shrinking" (CRS, 2005). In other words, the smaller the long-term shortfall, the larger the benefit cuts. That makes no sense. Americans appear very reluctant to support major changes in benefits. Rather than relying mainly on benefit cuts, most Americans seem to prefer relying on tax increases or a mix of tax and spending changes to restore solvency (Blinder & Krueger, 2004). I certainly agree.

Would Private Accounts Improve Social Security?

Replacing part of Social Security with private accounts shifts too much retirement risk to individuals. Market investments can lead to high returns over time, but what goes up also comes down, and trying to retire in a time of down market conditions can be risky. Private accounts add other risks as well: the risk that the cost of annuities will be very expensive if interest rates are low at the time of retirement, and the risk that annuities will decline in value over time if inflation is high after retirement.

Studies have shown major variations in retirement income based simply on timing (Burtless, 2003; Munnell, Saas, & Soto, 2005).

The president has proposed that private accounts be "offset" through added cuts in future Social Security benefit commitments. Under the proposal, for every dollar in payroll taxes diverted from Social Security, the worker's future Social Security benefit would be cut by an equal amount, plus an interest charge equal to 3% above inflation. Under this proposal, some workers may do better than current law if they can beat the 3% above inflation cut. Some workers will do worse.

Some economists predict that about one-third to two-thirds of workers may end up losers under such plans (Shiller, 2005). No one knows for sure. In the case of the death of the worker, the private account would be passed on to heirs, but so would the future Social Security benefit cuts; it is therefore unclear which spouses or family members will be losers. It is also hard to envision how disability beneficiaries will not be negatively affected by private accounts.

Combining private accounts and offsets with "price indexing" would lead to even more drastic results. An average worker would see the defined Social Security benefit cut by two-thirds. For workers earning about $60,000 today, the Social Security benefit would be virtually eliminated. After paying a lifetime of payroll taxes for Social Security, millions of persons would receive little or no Social Security benefits (Furman, 2005). The long-term sustainability of the Social Security retirement system and the economic security of millions would be at risk if such an approach was adopted.

Let's put all this "added risk" in context. During my years as commissioner, I met the head of Chile's system during an economic downturn. At the time, he was publicly urging older workers to delay retiring until economic conditions improved so workers would not receive inadequate retirement benefits. This senior government official was urging older people to keep working until the markets came back.

Do markets bounce back quickly? Sometimes they do. And sometimes it takes many, many years for markets to come back. The problem, of course, is that we can't predict future market conditions. Future Social Security Commissioners ought not to be urging America's older workers to "just keep working until the markets come back." Social Security ought to represent a foundation of support over a lifetime that can be counted in retirement, no matter what happens to the markets.

Would Establishing Private Accounts Be Good For The Economy?

Professor Brown argues that private accounts can be beneficial to the economy. Even if individuals are put at more risk with private accounts, is it still worth the risk because of the overall economic effects? Would moving to a system of private accounts increase savings, jobs, and growth?

The answers to these questions are highly debated. Many noted economists question whether shifting to private accounts would increase savings and growth or change labor incentives (Diamond & Orszag, 2004; Orszag & Stiglitz, 1999), and whether

Social Security has a major impact on labor force or economic growth (Krueger & Meyer, 2002; Galbraith, 2005).

Would faster accumulation of retirement assets produce higher savings? If added private savings are offset by increased government borrowing, then private accounts would lead to no increase in national savings. In addition, because savers tend to offset faster accumulation of assets in pension accounts with lower savings in non-pension accounts (Bosworth & Burtless, 2004), financing private accounts through government borrowing could actually reduce national savings.

Private account plans finance the "transition" by borrowing. The president's plan dramatically increases the national debt over the next half century—a 50% increase in debt. Added interest payments a half century from now would amount to the equivalent of $133 billion a year, more than the government now spends on education, veterans health, science, conservation, pollution control, and job training programs combined (Horney & Kogan, 2005). This level of added government borrowing is a source of major concern to many fiscal policy experts.

Promising higher growth from private accounts is also highly speculative. The Congressional Budget Office shows tiny growth differentials when comparing plans that create private accounts versus plans that make changes through traditional tax and benefit changes. Even these miniscule differences appear to be due to the severity of the benefit reductions, not the creation of private accounts (CBO, 2004).

If we really want to increase savings, we ought to do it the old-fashioned way—by reducing consumption. If added retirement savings for low and moderate income workers is desired—and it should be—it should not come at the expense of Social Security. Instead, we should make changes in our retirement savings system and then pay for the changes so that added government borrowing does not undo the benefits of expanded private savings.

What Should We Do?

First, rather than establishing private accounts that do nothing to strengthen Social Security's financing, the first order of business should be Social Security solvency. Setting a goal of 75-year solvency may be too modest a goal, but let's not set an overly ambitious goal of "permanent solvency" by trying to solve a potential problem that may exist a century from now. Frankly, who knows what our fertility rates or our economic growth rates will be in the year 2100? If we find that we need to make further changes a half century from now, so be it.

Second, more revenue over the long term for Social Security will be needed, not less, and most of the long-term solution should come from revenues. Payroll tax rates could be increased over time by a point or so and the income ceiling on payroll taxes significantly increased. If we want increased returns, some new revenues should be invested, not only in government bonds but also in equities. A first step would be to use some of the added revenues to purchase GNMA mortgage-backed securities, which receive higher returns than bonds. Taking this step ameliorates benefit cuts and tax increases and would help put an end to the argument that the trust funds are worthless IOUs or that they do not have a beneficial effect on national savings (Munnell, 2005; Hungerford, 2006).

Third, future Social Security benefit growth will have to be modestly slowed, particularly for middle- to higher-wage earners, but not even close to the level of cuts envisioned by "price indexing." In addition, we may need to see further modest increases in the retirement age for full benefits, but only if we can develop ways to liberalize our disability system for older workers. People with higher earnings are, on average, living longer lives than lower-income workers, so higher-income workers are receiving an increasingly higher share of benefits over their lifetimes. In effect, the Social Security benefit structure over time is becoming less progressive. Future changes need to make the system more progressive.

The objectives of these tax and benefit changes are threefold: restoring solvency for decades into the future without massive added government borrowing, retaining the current Social Security structure to assure a continued foundation of support for all Americans, and softening the solvency burden on low- and middle-income workers.

To summarize, a major restructuring of Social Security is unnecessary, given the manageable size of the long-term problem. A sizeable cut in benefits puts future generations at risk, and the creation of private accounts greatly adds to that risk, possibly destabilizing the system. Let's keep the word "secure" in Social Security for current and future generations.

References

Blinder, A. S., & Krueger, A. B. (2004). What does the public know about economic policy and how does it know it? (CEPS Working Paper No. 99), May. Retrieved December 6, 2005, from http://www.princeton.edu/~ceps/workingpapers/99blinderkrueger.pdf.

Board of Trustees of the Old-Age and Survivors Insurance and Disability Insurance Trust Funds. (2005). Annual report. Retrieved December 7, 2004, from http://www.socialsecurity.gov/OACT/TR/TR05/.

Bosworth, B., & Burtless, G. (2004). Supply side consequences of Social Security reform: Impacts on saving and employment. Center for Retirement Research at Boston College (CRR WP 2004-01), January. Retrieved December 5, 2005, from http://www.bc.edu/centers/crr/papers/wp_2004-01.pdf.

Burtless, Gary. (2003). What do we know about the risk of individual account pensions? Evidence from industrial countries. American Economic Review, Papers and Proceedings 93(2), 354–359.

Congressional Budget Office. (2004). Long-term analysis of Plan 2 of the President's Commission to Strengthen Social Security. Congressional Budget Office, July 21. Retrieved from http://www.cbo.gov/showdoc.cfm?index=5666. (7 December 2005).

Congressional Budget Office. (2005). Updated long-term projections for Social Security. March. Retrieved December 7, 2005, from http://www.cbo.gov/showdoc.cfm?index=6064& sequence=0.

Congressional Research Service. (2005). "Progressive price indexing" of Social Security benefits. Patrick Purcell. April 22. Retrieved December 6, 2005, from http://www.tcf.org/Publications/Retirement-Security/CRS_Price_Indexing_04-22-05.pdf).

Diamond, P. A., & Orszag, P. R. (2004). Saving Social Security: A balanced approach. Washington, DC: Brookings Institution Press.

Furman, J. (2005). An analysis of using "progressive price indexing" to set Social Security benefits. Center on Budget and Policy Priorities, May 2. Retrieved October 5, 2005, from http://cbpp.org/3-21-05socsec.htm.

Galbraith, J. (2005). Dazzle them with demographics. Texas Observer, August 13. Retrieved December 7, 2005, from http://www.texasobserver.org/showArticle.asp?ArticleID=1731.

Horney, K., & Kogan, R. (2005). Private accounts would substantially increase federal debt and interest payments. Center on Budget and Policy Priorities, August 2. Retrieved December 5, 2005, from http://www.cbpp.org/7-27-05socsec.pdf.

Hungerford, T. (2006). The effects of investing the Social Security trust funds in GNMA mortgage-backed securities. AARP Issue Brief 206-02. Retrieved January 31, 2006, from http://www.aarp.org/research/socialsecurity/reform/2006_01_ss_gnma.html.

Kogan, R., & Greenstein, R. (2005). President portrays Social Security shortfall as enormous, but his tax cuts and drug benefit will cost at least five times as much. Center on Budget and Policy Priorities, February 11. Retrieved November 11, 2005, from http://www.cbpp.org/1-4-05socsec.htm.

Krueger, A. B., & Meyer, B. D. (2002). Labor supply effects of social insurance. National Bureau of Economic Research (Paper 9014), February. Retrieved December 2005, from http://www.northwestern.edu/ipr/publications/papers/2002/WP-02-05.pdf.

Munnell, A. (2004). Retirement blues. Boston College Magazine, Spring. Retrieved December 7, 2005, from http://www.bc.edu/publications/bcm/spring_2004/ft_retirement.html.

Munnell, A. (2005). Are the Social Security trust funds meaningful? Center for Retirement Research at Boston College, May (30). Retrieved December 5, 2005, from http://www.bc.edu/centers/crr/issues/ib_30.pdf>.

Munnell, A. H., Sass, S. A., & Soto, M. (2005). Yikes! How to think about risk? Center for Retirement Research at Boston College, January (27), 2. Retrieved October 4, 2005, from www.bc.edu/centers/crr/issues/ib_27.pdf.

Orszag, P. R., & Stiglitz, J. E. (1999, September). Rethinking pension reform: Ten myths about Social Security systems. Presented at the World Bank Conference, "New Ideas About Old Age Security." Retrieved December 6, 2005, from http://www2.gsb.columbia.edu/faculty/ jstiglitz/download/2001_Rethinking_Pension_Reform_Ten_Myths.pdf.

Shiller, R. (2005). The life-cycle personal accounts proposal for Social Security: An evaluation. March. Retrieved December 3, 2005, from http://irrationalexuberance.com/ShillerSocSec.doc.

Response to Kenneth S. Apfel

Jeffrey R. Brown

In my opinion, the fact that Ken and I fully agree that Social Security's current fiscal path is unsustainable, and that reform is essential, is the most notable aspect of this exchange. Among amicable academics, such agreement may not seem particularly surprising. Indeed, if Professor Apfel and I were jointly given legislative power for one day, I believe we could develop an intellectually honest and economically responsible compromise plan that both of us could live with, if not love.

Unfortunately, such a bipartisan willingness to engage on this issue was missing in the 2005 national debate. When President Bush placed Social Security reform on the national agenda—making specific proposals to shift to "progressive price indexing" and create personal accounts—the leadership of the Democratic Party failed to offer a single alternative proposal. While this "do nothing" strategy handed the Democrats a short-term political victory, it has left a serious fiscal problem for future generations that will only grow worse with time.

I wish to respond to two specific issues raised by Professor Apfel:

1. *The need for structural change:* Professor Apfel's preferred solution of relying primarily on higher payroll taxes can be implemented in one of two ways. First, taxes can be raised on a pay-as-you-go basis. According to the Social Security actuaries, such an approach would require tax revenue nearing 20 percent of covered payroll by the year 2080. This tax burden would be on top of the income tax and the high Medicare payroll taxes. It is difficult to argue that such an approach will not serve as a drag on economic growth. A second approach would be to raise tax rates immediately, in the hope of pre-funding future benefits. The problem is that without a structural change to Social Security, such as replacing the trust funds with personal accounts, the likely outcome of the unified budget process is that those additional tax dollars will not be saved, but rather will be used to finance larger non-Social Security deficits.

2. *The role of risk:* While allowing individuals to invest part of their accounts in equity markets does expose one to financial market risk, it also provides access to higher expected portfolio returns as compensation for bearing that risk. The fact that people have different tolerances for risk is precisely why we ought to allow the individuals to choose (within limits) the portfolio that best matches their preferences. The current system forces everyone into a one-size-fits-all portfolio of underfunded future benefit promises. That approach does not strike me as "secure."

It is an economic reality that Social Security is in need of reform. It is a political reality that the reform of such an important program will require bipartisan support. We need even more voices, like those of Ken Apfel, forwarding constructive ideas in order to move ahead. It is my sincere hope that, through continued bipartisan dialogue, our elected leaders will ultimately choose to take the responsible course of action and act soon to reform Social Security.

Response To Jeffrey R. Brown
Kenneth S. Apfel

It should be clear from this Point/Counterpoint that changes should be made to strengthen Social Security, but there are very real differences on both the magnitude and the overall direction of these changes. Last year, Democrats correctly argued that progress will not take place on this issue until there is agreement to drop consideration of replacing part of Social Security with private accounts. Professor Brown and I could likely agree to a plan to restore long-term solvency if private accounts aren't part of the equation.

Absent private accounts, there are still very tough choices to be made. Professor Brown's preferred solution would reduce future benefit commitments and place too much risk on most Americans for basic economic security. It is certainly the case that people have different risk tolerances. The place to handle risk, however, should be our retirement savings system, not the basic foundation of support provided by Social Security.

Professor Brown and I both strongly support candid discussion and bipartisanship on Social Security. Jeff has been an important voice urging solid analysis and open discussion on the issue. That's the only way we'll ever make any real progress.

President Clinton reached out openly to both parties on this issue. Changes should not be adopted, as was attempted last year, by trying to assemble a majority of Republicans, coupled with the hope of picking up a tiny fraction of members from the Democratic side of the aisle. Any changes to Social Security must receive broad-based support. Any other approach creates an unstable reform—sowing the seeds for future discord—when a long-term resolution on this issue is what the nation really wants and needs.

Will we resolve this issue over time? Of course we will. Americans want and need a strong Social Security system. When we finally do resolve the issue, I expect that Americans will have access to expanded retirement savings mechanisms as well as a solid but somewhat more modest Social Security system—one that provides a foundation of support for individuals and their families that can be counted on over a lifetime in the case of old age, death, and disability. That basic framework should sound familiar to the reader, because President Roosevelt articulated that vision generations ago—a vision that still has relevance not only for today's retirees, but also for future generations.

Conference Contributors

Kenneth S. Apfel
Sid Richardson Chair in Public Affairs; former U.S. Social Security Commissioner

Kenneth S. Apfel joined the faculty of the LBJ School of Public Affairs at the University of Texas at Austin in January 2001. His major teaching and research interests are in the areas of social policy and public leadership and management, with a particular focus on aging, health care and retirement issues.

Prior to his academic appointment, Apfel served as Commissioner of the Social Security Administration (SSA) from 1997 until his term ended in January 2001. He was the first Senate-confirmed Commissioner of Social Security after SSA became an independent agency and the Cabinet-level position was authorized by Congress. During his tenure as Commissioner, Apfel was deeply involved in efforts to strengthen the long term solvency of Social Security. He significantly strengthened the policy, planning and public education activities at the Social Security Administration. He also played a leadership role in efforts to strengthen childhood disability programs, to expand retirement planning activities and to enable persons with disabilities to return to work. In addition, he served from 1997 to 1999 as a member of the President's Management Council.

Before becoming Social Security Commissioner, Apfel worked in the Office of Management and Budget (OMB) in the Executive Office of the President, where he served from 1995 to 1997 as the Associate Director for Human Resource Programs. Prior to that appointment he served from 1993 to 1995 as Assistant Secretary for Management and Budget at the U.S. Department of Health and Human Services. From 1983 to 1993, Apfel worked for Senator Bill Bradley, as Bradley's Legislative Director and his chief staff person for federal social and budget policy, with a particular focus on the Social Security, Medicare, Medicaid, and welfare programs under the jurisdiction of the Senate Finance Committee. Between 1980 and 1982, Apfel was committee staff for human resource programs for the U.S. Senate Budget Committee. From 1978 to 1980, he held a Presidential Management Internship at the U.S. Department of Labor. He was a college administrator from 1973 to 1976 at Newbury College in Massachusetts.

Apfel received his bachelor's degree from the University of Massachusetts, Amherst, in 1970; a Master's degree in rehabilitation counseling from Northeastern University in 1973; and a Master's degree in public affairs from the LBJ School of Public Affairs in 1978. He is a Principal of the Council for Excellence in Government and an elected Fellow of the National Academy of Public Administration and the National Academy of Social Insurance.

Stuart M. Butler
Vice-President for Domestic and Economic Policy Studies, The Heritage Foundation

Stuart M. Butler is Vice-President for Domestic and Economic Policy Studies at The Heritage Foundation in Washington, D.C. He plans and oversees the Foundation's research and publications on all domestic issues. He has been with Heritage since 1979 and is an expert on health, welfare, and Social Security policy. He is also an Adjunct Professor at Georgetown University Graduate School and in 2002 he was a Fellow at Harvard University's Institute of Politics.

Butler has played a prominent role in the debate over Medicare, health care for working Americans, and Social Security reform, arguing for solutions based on individual choice and market competition. He has written extensively on these issues and has testified frequently before Congress on a broad range of issues.

Butler was born in Shrewsbury, England. He emigrated to the United States in 1975 and became an American citizen in 1995. He was educated at St. Andrews University in Scotland, where he received a Bachelor of Science degree in physics and mathematics in 1968, a master's degree in economics and history in 1971, and a Ph.D. in American economic history in 1978. He is married with two daughters, and resides in Washington, D.C.

Betty Sue Flowers, Ph.D.
Director, LBJ Library and Museum

Betty Sue Flowers, appointed Director of the Lyndon Baines Johnson Library in 2002, was Kelleher Professor of English and member of the Distinguished Teachers Academy at the University of Texas at Austin. She is also a poet, editor, and business consultant, with publications ranging from poetry therapy to the economic myth, including four television tie-in books in collaboration with Bill Moyers, among them, *Joseph Campbell and the Power of Myth*. She hosted "Conversations with Betty Sue Flowers" on the Austin PBS-affiliate, KLRU, and has served as a moderator for executive seminars at the Aspen Institute for Humanistic Studies, consultant for NASA, member of the Envisioning Network for General Motors, Visiting Advisor to the Secretary of the Navy, and editor of Global Scenarios for Shell International in London and the World Business Council in Geneva (on global sustainable development and, most recently, on the future of biotechnology).

Pamela Herd, Ph.D.
Assistant Professor, LBJ School of Public Affairs

Pamela Herd joined the LBJ School of Public Affairs in the fall of 2004 as an assistant professor. Before that she was a Robert Wood Johnson Scholar in Health and Health Policy at the University of Michigan, Ann Arbor. She received her Ph.D. in Sociology at Syracuse University in the Maxwell School of Citizenship and Public Affairs in 2002. She received dissertation awards from Syracuse University and the National

Academy for Social Insurance. Her research interests are old age policy, health, and inequality. She is currently working on a book with Madonna Harrington Meyer entitled *Retrenching Welfare, Entrenching Inequality: Gender, Race and Old Age in the U.S.* to be published as a part of the American Sociological Association's Rose Series in Sociology.

Dalmer D. Hoskins, Ph.D.
Secretary General, International Social Security Association
Dalmer Hoskins was elected in May 1990 to the position of Secretary General of the International Social Security Association (ISSA) headquartered in Geneva, Switzerland. He has also been appointed by the United Nations Secretary General to the board of the UN International Institute on Ageing and has been elected to the board of HelpAge International. Hoskins has spent most of his professional career working on international social security questions, beginning in the Social Security Administration's Office of Research and Statistics and subsequently moving to the ISSA Headquarters, where he became Director of the Research and Documentation Program. Between 1983 and 1990, he returned to the Social Security Administration, where he served as Special Assistant to the two Public Trustees and Director of the Office of Policy Development. A member of the National Academy of Social Insurance since 1989, Hoskins did both his master's and doctoral studies in political science at the University of Michigan, with additional studies in Tokyo, Paris, and Geneva.

Barbara B. Kennelly
President/Chief Executive Officer, National Committee to Preserve Social Security and Medicare
Barbara B. Kennelly became President and Chief Executive Officer of the National Committee to Preserve Social Security and Medicare in April 2002 after a distinguished 23-year career in elected public office. She was appointed to the Policy Committee for the 2005 White House Conference on Aging. The Congresswoman served 17 years in the United States House of Representatives representing the First District of Connecticut, which includes Hartford and surrounding towns. Mrs. Kennelly won her congressional seat in a special election in January 1982. In 1996, she was elected to her eighth full term with over 74 percent of the vote, but did not run for reelection.

After serving in Congress, Mrs. Kennelly was appointed to the position of Counselor to the Commissioner at the Social Security Administration (SSA). As Counselor, Mrs. Kennelly worked closely with the Commissioner of Social Security Kenneth S. Apfel and members of Congress to inform and educate the American people on the choices they face to ensure the future solvency of Social Security. Upon leaving SSA, Mrs. Kennelly joined the law firm of Baker & Hostetler LLP, where she was a lobbyist within the federal policy practice group.

A life-long resident of Hartford, Congresswoman Kennelly received a B.A. in Economics from Trinity College, Washington, D.C. She earned a certificate from the Harvard Business School on completion of the Harvard-Radcliffe Program in Business Administration and a Master's Degree in Government from Trinity College, Hartford.

Prior to her election to Congress, Mrs. Kennelly was Secretary of the State of Connecticut and a member of the Hartford Court of Common Council. Her late husband, James, was Speaker of the Connecticut State House. Mrs. Kennelly has three daughters and a son, and nine grandchildren. Among her many civic involvements, Mrs. Kennelly serves as Vice Chair of the Advisory Board of the Thomas J. Dodd Research Center, University of Connecticut. Mrs. Kennelly also serves on the Board of Directors of the United States Association of Former Members of Congress; the International Foundation for Election Systems; the Board of Electors, Wadsworth Athenaeum Museum of Art, Hartford, Connecticut; and the Advisory Boards of *BNA's Medicare Report* and the Washington Center.

Lindsay J. Littlefield
Research Assistant, LBJ School of Public Affairs
Lindsay J. Littlefield graduated *summa cum laude* and with honors in political science from Wake Forest University in 2003. While attending Wake Forest, Lindsay majored in political science and communication and earned a minor in Women's and Gender Studies. She was named a 2002 Harry S. Truman Scholar from Minnesota. Upon graduation, Lindsay served as the AmeriCorps Volunteer Assistant at Austin Habitat for Humanity. In 2004, she entered the Lyndon B. Johnson School of Public Affairs at the University of Texas at Austin. While attending the LBJ School, she interned at Texans Care For Children and National Conference of State Legislatures. She also acted as research assistant for two professors at the LBJ School. Lindsay will graduate with her masters in public affairs in May 2006.

Maya C. MacGuineas
President, Committee for a Responsible Federal Budget, and Director of the Fiscal Policy Program at the New America Foundation
Maya MacGuineas is the President of the Committee for a Responsible Federal Budget and Director of the Fiscal Policy Program at the New America Foundation. Her areas of expertise include the budget, entitlements, and tax policy. Her work has been published in a variety of outlets including *The Atlantic Monthly, The Washington Post, The Financial Times, The Los Angeles Times, The San Francisco Chronicle, The Chicago Tribune,* and *The Washington Monthly*. She has testified multiple times before Congress, and her media appearances include The News Hour with Jim Lehrer, Washington Journal, Voice of America's Economic Forum, International Herald Tribune television, Reuters television and National Public Radio. She has been selected to participate in The Next Generations Leaders Conference on the future of biotechnol-

ogy, The American-German Leaders Conference in Germany, and the CSIS Young Turks Program in Taiwan.

Before coming to New America, MacGuineas worked as a Social Security adviser to the McCain presidential campaign. Prior to that, she worked at the Brookings Institution, the Concord Coalition, and on Wall Street. She received her Master in Public Policy from the John F. Kennedy School of Government at Harvard University and serves on the boards of a number of national, nonpartisan organizations.

Peter R. Orszag
Joseph A. Pechman Senior Fellow in Economic Studies, The Brookings Institution
Peter R. Orszag is the Joseph A. Pechman Senior Fellow in Economic Studies at The Brookings Institution; Co-Director of the Tax Policy Center, a joint venture of the Urban Institute and Brookings Institution; Director of the Retirement Security Project; and Research Professor at Georgetown University. He previously served as Special Assistant to the President for Economic Policy, and as Senior Economist and Senior Adviser on the Council of Economic Advisers, during the Clinton Administration. His current areas of research include pensions, budget and tax policy, Social Security, higher education, and homeland security.

Dr. Orszag graduated *summa cum laude* in economics from Princeton University, and obtained a M.Sc. and a Ph.D. in economics from the London School of Economics, which he attended as a Marshall Scholar. He is the co-editor of *American Economic Policy in the 1990s* (MIT Press: 2002), co-author of *Protecting the American Homeland: A Preliminary Analysis* (Brookings Institution Press: 2002), and co-author of *Saving Social Security: A Balanced Approach* (Brookings Institution Press: 2004). He has also been an author on a number of other publications.

Dr. Orszag has testified on numerous occasions before Congress and is a regular commentator on economic policy in the national press.

John Rother
Director of Policy and Strategy, AARP
As Director of Policy and Strategy for AARP, John Rother guides formation of the federal and state public policies of the Association, sets international initiatives, and focuses AARP's overall strategic direction. He is an authority on Medicare, managed care, long-term care, Social Security, pensions, and the challenges facing the boomer generation. Mr. Rother leads the development of the Association's public policy goals and advocacy strategies. He also directs a very active public policy research program. The AARP Public Policy Institute publishes original and collected research to build a strong foundation for the priorities and positions of AARP.

In addition, Mr. Rother provides direction to AARP's global aging program, which strives to facilitate international understanding and dialogue around the global aging agenda. AARP was one of the first organizations to recognize growing aging populations as a worldwide phenomenon that truly requires global cooperation.

Before serving as Policy Director, Mr. Rother was the Legislative Director of AARP. There, he crafted advocacy efforts that are helping to reduce age discrimination in the workplace, expand Medicare to include prescription drug coverage, and improve the quality and safety of health care. He played an important role in the advocacy efforts that tackled national health care reform.

Prior to coming to AARP, Mr. Rother served eight years with the U.S. Senate: first, as Special Counsel for Labor and Health to Senator Jacob Javits (R-NY), then as Staff Director and Chief Counsel for the investigative Special Committee on Aging under its Chairman, Senator John Heinz (R-PA), where he participated directly in the strengthening of Social Security through major reform. While the news media immediately consults with Mr. Rother on hot legislative topics affecting Medicare, prescription drugs and Social Security, he also provides insight on issues relating to boomers and intergenerational concerns. He is frequently quoted in publications such as *The Wall Street Journal, The New York Times, The Washington Post, The National Journal, Congressional Quarterly, Time* and *Newsweek*. He often appears on CNN, CNBC, the MacNeil-Lehrer News Hour and the nightly news programs of ABC, CBS and NBC.

Mr. Rother participates in 70 to 90 speaking engagements and panel discussions each year. He regularly keynotes at conferences and testifies at congressional briefings, always with an underlying concern that one generation never be pitted against another in national policymaking. Some of his recent audiences include members of the National Institutes of Health, the California Medical Association, the American Journal of Health Promotion, an administerial meeting of the European Union, and the Institute of Medicine. He has presented on a wide variety of topics, including "The Impact of Technology on Long-term Care," "Community Service and the Potential of Older People," and "Demographic Change and the Labor Market" and is a champion of "Independent Living" for elders. He lectures annually at Harvard University on health policy development.

John Rother serves on several boards and commissions, including Generations United, the National Health Care Quality Forum, the American Board of Internal Medicine Foundation, National Academy on Aging, and Civic Ventures. Throughout 1996, Mr. Rother was on a sabbatical assignment, enriched by working from diverse locations across America, to study the consumer implications of the managed care revolution and the economic challenges facing the boomer generation. John Rother graduated with honors from Oberlin College and the University of Pennsylvania Law School.

Thomas R. Saving, Ph.D.
Director, Private Enterprise Research Center, Texas A&M University
Dr. Thomas R. Saving is the Director of the Private Enterprise Research Center at Texas A&M University. A University Distinguished Professor of Economics at Texas

A&M, he also holds the Jeff Montgomery Professorship in Economics. Dr. Saving received his Ph.D. from the University of Chicago and served on the faculty at the University of Washington at Seattle and Michigan State University before moving to Texas A&M University in 1968. Dr. Saving's research has covered the areas of antitrust economics, monetary economics, and health economics. He has served as a referee or as a member of the editorial board of the major United States economics journals, and he is currently co-editor of *Economic Inquiry*. His current research emphasis is on the benefit of markets in solving the pressing issues in health care and Social Security. He is the co-editor of *Medicare Reform: Issues and Answers,* University of Chicago Press, 1999, and the co-author of *The Economics of Medicare Reform,* W.E. Upjohn Institute, 2000. In addition, he has many articles in professional journals and two influential books on monetary theory. Dr. Saving has been elected to the post of President of the Western Economics Association, the Southern Economics Association and the Association of Private Enterprise Education. In 2000, President Clinton appointed Dr. Saving as a Public Trustee of the Social Security and Medicare Trust Funds. On May 2, 2001, President Bush named Dr. Saving to the bipartisan President's Commission to Strengthen Social Security.

Taylor Willingham
Director, Texas Forums

Taylor Willingham is the project coordinator for Texas Forums, a member of the LBJ Family of Organizations. She is research associate for the Kettering Foundation and a former board member for the National Issues Forums Institute. Current projects include a national dialogue to determine how Americans view Russia in partnership with colleagues in Russia, and an online community collaborative research project involving organizations that promote deliberation. She also teaches distance education courses for two graduate library schools: University of Illinois at Urbana-Champaign and San Jose State University.

Taylor has moderated over 200 public forums in person and online, and has trained over 1,000 moderators across the United States as well as citizens from countries such as Croatia, Tajikistan, Russia, and Colombia. At the invitation of the State Department, she conducted introductory workshops on the role of libraries in emerging democracies in Vologda and Petrozavodsk and helped librarians from Lithuania, Russia, Latvia, and Kyrgystan develop a public forum framework for a discussion about youth.